BLITZKRIEG NO LONGER

The German Wehrmacht in Battle, 1943

Samuel W. Mitcham, Jr.

STACKPOLE
BOOKS

Published by
STACKPOLE BOOKS
5067 Ritter Road
Mechanicsburg, PA 17055
www.stackpolebooks.com

Printed in the United States of America

10 9 8 7 6 5 4 3 2 1

Library of Congress Cataloging-in-Publication Data

Mitcham, Samuel W.
  Blitzkrieg no longer : the German Wehrmacht in battle, 1943 / Samuel W. Mitcham, Jr.
      p. cm.
  Includes bibliographical references and index.
  ISBN 978-0-8117-0533-2
  1. Germany—Armed Forces—History—World War, 1939–1945. 2. World War,
1939–1945—Germany. 3. World War, 1939–1945—Campaigns—Europe. I. Title.
  D757.M56 2010
  940.54'21—dc22
                              2009027630

TABLE OF CONTENTS

INTRODUCTION

The purpose of this book is to write the military history of Nazi Germany and its war effort in 1943. Other aspects of the Third Reich will be touched upon as well, including German diplomacy, geopolitics, the attitudes of German civilians, their morale and adjustments to life under the constant threat of aerial attacks, and the war economy, but the focus is on pure military history.

Since 1960, there has arisen in the Western world what might be termed "social military historians." They deal with war from a sociological—or in some cases pseudo-sociological—point of view, without discussing battles and campaigns, which are dismissed with a wave of the hand, if they are mentioned at all. I believe that war has its sociological and philosophical elements, but it also involves strategy, operations, and tactics, as well as logistics, training, the inclination of a people to wage war, and the warrior himself, be he general or private. In other words, this book will follow a more "nuts and bolts" approach, in which strategy, battles, and campaigns are emphasized, rather than sociological motivations.

I would like to thank all those who helped in the researching, writing, and production of this book, especially my wife, Donna. I also wish to thank Professor Melinda Mathews of the Interlibrary Loan Department of the University of Louisiana at Monroe for all of her assistance. Thanks also go to the archivists and other employees at the National Archives in Washington, DC, the Bundesarchiv, the War College, the Center of Military History, and the Imperial War Museum, as well as the late Friedrich von Stauffenberg and anyone else who shared information, advice, photographs, or memoirs with me. Finally, thanks go to my editors, Chris Evans and David Reisch. I alone assume responsibility for any mistakes.

CHAPTER 1

Nazi Germany and the *Wehrmacht*, 1933–42

When Adolf Hitler came to power on January 30, 1933, the German *Reichswehr* (armed forces) had two branches: the *Reichsheer* (army) and the *Reichsmarine* (navy). According to the Treaty of Versailles, which ended World War I, the army was limited to 100,000 men (4,000 of whom could be officers), while the navy was limited to 15,000 officers and men. The *Reichswehr* was denied all four of the innovative weapons of World War I—tanks, airplanes, poisonous gas, and submarines.

Hitler began his secret military expansion almost as soon as he achieved power. On March 9, 1935, he announced the existence of the *Luftwaffe*, which his cronies, Hermann Goering and Erhard Milch, had been building for some time. The reaction of Germany's potential enemies—primarily Great Britain and France—was so tepid as to be almost nonexistent, and this encouraged Hitler, who renounced the Treaty of Versailles (which the Germans called the Versailles *Diktat*) a week later. He was now free to pursue his military build-up in even greater earnest.

Because he and his Nazi paladins considered themselves revolutionaries, he also tended to embrace revolutionary military concepts, such as terror bombing and the *blitzkrieg*. The same day Hitler renounced the Treaty of Versailles, the German Army activated the first three panzer divisions.

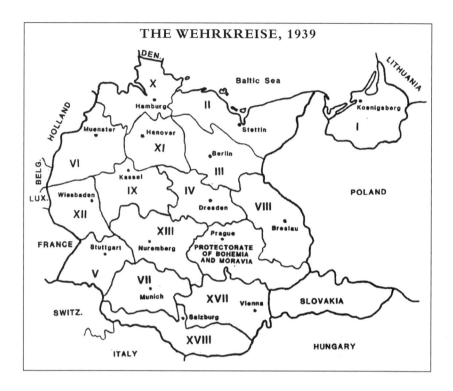

The military entity Hitler used to expand, recruit, and train his armies was the *Wehrkreis*—the German military district, which had served the Second Reich well. (Its counterpart in the *Luftwaffe* was the *Luftgau*, or air district.) By August 26, 1939, when the Home (or Replacement) Army was created to control the *Wehrkreise* (also spelled *Wehrkreisen*), four "waves" of divisions had been created; Hitler used these to conquer Poland. Thirty-one more waves would be formed and sent into action by January 1945, along with several divisions which did not belong to specific waves. By 1943, there were eighteen *Wehrkreise* forming and/or training German divisions: I, II, III, IV, V, VI, VII, VIII, IX, X, XI, XII, XIII, XVII, XVIII, and XX, as well as Bohemia and Moravia in what had been Czechoslovakia, and *Wehrkreise General Gouvernement* in what had been Poland. The table on the next page and the map above show the *Wehrkreise* and their territorial responsibilities.

In early 1938, it was discovered that Field Marshal Werner von Blomberg, the defense minister, had married a prostitute. He was forced to retire in disgrace. Heinrich Himmler and his deputy, Reinhard Heydrich, chose this moment to bring trumped-up charges of homo-

THE WEHRKREISE AND THEIR TERRITORIAL RESPONSIBILITIES

Wehrkreis	Headquarters	Territorial Extent
I	Koenigsberg	East Prussia; extended in 1939 to include Memel and portions of northern Poland
II	Stettin	Mecklenburg and Pomerania
III	Berlin	Altmark, Neumark, and Brandenburg
IV	Dresden	Saxony and part of Thuringia; later annexed part of northern Bohemia
V	Stuttgart	Wuerttemberg and part of Baden; extended in 1940 to include Alsace
VI	Munster	Westphalia and Rhineland; later extended into eastern Belgium
VII	Munich	Southern Bavaria
VIII	Breslau	Silesia and Sudetenland; later parts of Moravia and southwestern Poland
IX	Kassel	Hessen and part of Thuringia
X	Hamburg	Schleswig-Holstein and northern Hanover; extended in 1940 to include part of Danish Slesvig
XI	Hanover	Braunschweig (Brunswick), Anhalt, and most of Hanover
XII	Wiesbaden	Eifel, the Palatinate, and the Saar; part of Hesse; extended after the fall of France to include Lorraine, including the Nancy area
XIII	Nuremberg	Northern Bavaria; extended in 1938 to include part of western Bohemia
XIV	Berlin	No territorial responsibilities; ceased to exist as a Wehrkreis in 1939; later became Headquarters, XIV Panzer Corps
XV	Berlin	No territorial responsibilities; ceased to exist as a Wehrkreis in 1939; later became Headquarters, 3rd Panzer Army
XVI	Berlin	No territorial responsibilities; ceased to exist as a Wehrkreis in 1939; later became Headquarters, 4th Panzer Army
XVII	Vienna	Northern Austria; extended in 1939 to include the southern districts of Czechoslovakia

THE WEHRKREISE AND THEIR
TERRITORIAL RESPONSIBILITIES

Wehrkreis	Headquarters	Territorial Extent
XVIII	Salzburg	Southern Austria; extended in 1941 to include the northern parts of Slovenia
XX	Danzig	The former Danzig Free State, the Polish Corridor, and the western part of East Prussia
General Gouvernement	Warsaw	Created in 1943 and included central and most of southern Poland
Bohemia	Prague	Most of what was formerly Czechoslovakia; created in late 1942 and Moravia

Note: The territorial adjustments made by Reichsfuehrer-SS Himmler in late 1944 are not included in this table; they were relatively minor in any event.

sexuality against the non-Nazi commander in chief of the army, Col. Gen. Baron Werner von Fritsch. Although later exonerated, Fritsch was also forced to resign.[1] Hitler took advantage of this situation to end the corporate independence of the army, place it solidly under Nazi control, and simultaneously set up Germany's command structure for the next war. On February 4, 1938, he named himself Supreme Commander of the Armed Forces (*Wehrmacht*). His new chief executive officer would be Gen. of Artillery (later Field Marshal) Wilhelm Keitel, who held the title of commander in chief of the High Command of the Armed Forces (*Oberkommando der Wehrmacht*, or OKW). Keitel was a nonentity and became a notorious yes-man for Adolf Hitler.[2] The real brain at OKW was its chief of operations, Maj. Gen. (later Col. Gen.) Alfred Jodl.[3]

Under OKW in the German organizational structure were the High Command of the Army (*Obercommando des Heeres*, or OKH), the High Command of the Navy (*Oberkommando der Kriegsmarine*, or OKM), and the High Command of the *Luftwaffe* (*Oberkommando der Luftwaffe*, or OKL). This, of course, was the formal chain of command, which was largely theoretical. In practice, the navy and air force went their own way, and their commanders, Grand Adm. Erich Raeder and *Reichsmarschall* Hermann Goering, tolerated no interference from Keitel or OKW. This was a policy OKH could not adopt.

To gain effective control of the high command of the army, Hitler made an unsavory deal with Gen. of Artillery Walter von Brauchitsch.

The Nazi Party paid his estranged wife a large lump sum of money; in exchange, she granted Brauchitsch a quiet divorce, leaving him free to marry his sexy pro-Nazi mistress. As his part of this bargain with the devil, Brauchitsch had to agree to accept the new organizational structure, placing OKH under OKW (i.e., under Hitler). Brauchitsch also had to agree to purge the High Command of his anti-Nazi or non-Nazi elements by forcing the officers Hitler did not like into retirement or transferring them out of Berlin. Brauchitsch accepted the deal and assumed command of OKH on February 4, 1938, the same day he was promoted to colonel general.[4]

The first to go was Lt. Gen. Victor Schwelder, the chief of the powerful Army Personnel Office (*Heerespersonalamt*, or HPA), who had consistently rejected Nazi attempts to obtain the best appointments for NSDAP sympathizers. He was transferred to Dresden, where he assumed command of *Wehrkreis IV.*[5] Schwelder was succeeded by Col. Bodewin Keitel, the brother of Wilhelm.[6] Both of Schwelder's deputies, Col. Adolf Kuntzen and Col. Hans Behlendorff, were also transferred.[7] Future Field Marshals Ritter Wilhelm von Leeb and Ewald von Kleist were forced into retirement, along with dozens of lesser lights. All were succeeded by Nazis or officers favorably inclined toward National Socialism. Among those arbitrarily sacked was Oswald Lutz, the chief of the Panzer Branch and the first general of panzer troops, who heard about his dismissal on the public radio. He was replaced by his deputy, Heinz Guderian, who did not utter a word of protest on behalf of his longtime defender and mentor and who seems to have been delighted to assume his vacant chair.[8] Only Gen. of Artillery Ludwig Beck and Gen. of Mountain Troops Wilhelm Adam registered significant objections to the Brauchitsch purge. Both were retired before the year ended.[9]

With the army firmly under his control, Hitler had removed the last force which had the physical power to overthrow him and end his dictatorship. Now free of all restraints, he pursued his policy of *Lebensraum*, acquiring "living space" for the German people in the east. In Europe, of course, this could be accomplished only by resorting to war, which Hitler ignited on September 1, 1939, when he invaded Poland. Only his former economics minister, Hjalmar Horace Greeley Schacht, raised strenuous objections. He called upon Brauchitsch to meet with him to discuss the illegality of Hitler's actions, but the commander in chief of the army replied that Schacht would be arrested if he even set foot on army property. Not surprisingly, Schacht ended the war in a concentration camp.

For Hitler and Nazi Germany, there followed an almost unbroken string of victories: Poland (1939); Denmark, Norway, Luxembourg, the Netherlands, Belgium, and France (1940); Yugoslavia, Greece, Crete, and much of North Africa (1941). For a time, only Great Britain's Royal Navy and Royal Air Force denied Germany the complete mastery of Europe—and even that was a near thing. Then, on June 22, 1941, Hitler made a fatal mistake: he invaded the Soviet Union.

Even in Russia, there were impressive victories in the beginning. Striking with three army groups—3.2 million men—the German Army mauled the 4.7 million Soviet defenders of European Russia. Simultaneously, the *Luftwaffe* virtually annihilated the Red Air Force in the frontier zone, destroying 4,017 enemy aircraft in the first week of Operation Barbarossa, as the campaign was code-named. Over that same period, the German Air Force lost 150 aircraft destroyed or heavily damaged, a ratio of twenty-seven to one.[10]

Unfortunately for the Germans, the *Luftwaffe* had been designed primarily to be "flying artillery" for the army. Its bombers lacked the range to disrupt rail traffic east of the Dnieper River. Because Germany lacked a strategic air force, Soviet engineers were able to dismantle much of their military-industrial complex and move it to the east, where it was reassembled in the Urals or beyond. In all, 1,300 industrial complexes and smaller factories were removed from the path of the German *Wehrmacht* before they could be overrun or destroyed. These moves, which required 6.5 million railroad cars, dislocated Soviet industry but did not destroy it. When the German Army failed to decisively defeat the Soviet Union in 1941, the Russian armaments industry began to recover with remarkable speed.

Hitler's vanguards pushed to within sight of the Kremlin but were unable to capture Moscow. On December 6, 1941, Stalin unleashed his first winter offensive, attacking with 100 full-strength divisions along a 500-mile front. The next day, the Japanese attacked the American naval base at Pearl Harbor, Hawaii. On December 11, Hitler joined his ally and declared war on the United States. It was one of the major turning points of the war.

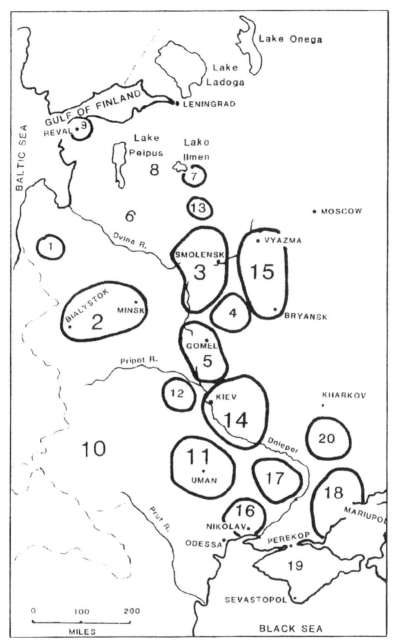

The Battles of Encirclement on the Eastern Front, 1941

1. *Rossizny*	**6.** *Divina*	**11.** *Uman*	**16.** *Nikolav*
2. *Bialystok-Minsk*	**7.** *Staraya Russa*	**12.** *Zhitomir*	**17.** *Dnieper Bend*
3. *Smolensk*	**8.** *Luga*	**13.** *Valdai Hills*	**18.** *Mariupol (Sea of Azov)*
4. *Roslavl*	**9.** *Reval*	**14.** *Kiev*	**19.** *Crimea*
5. *Gomel*	**10.** *Galacia*	**15.** *Vyazma-Bryansk*	**20.** *The Donetz*

As the crisis deepened, Hitler sacked Field Marshal Brauchitsch on December 19 and installed himself as commander in chief of the army. Henceforth, the Russian Front would be the provenance of OKH and the chief of the General Staff, Col. Gen. Franz Halder.[11] The other sectors (including the Far North sector of the Eastern Front, which was in Lapland) were considered OKW theaters. The table below shows the Order of Battle of the German Army in January 1943.

ORDER OF BATTLE, GERMAN ARMY, JANUARY 1943

OKH Forces

Commander in Chief of the Army: Adolf Hitler
  Chief of the General Staff: Col. Gen. Franz Halder

Army Group North: Field Marshal Georg von Kuechler
  18th Army: Col. Gen. Georg Lindemann
  16th Army: Col. Gen. Ernst Busch[a]

Army Group Center: Field Marshal Guenther von Kluge
  9th Army: Col. Gen. Walter Model
  3rd Panzer Army: Col. Gen. Hans-Georg Reinhardt
  4th Army: Col. Gen. Gotthard Heinrici
  2nd Panzer Army: Col. Gen. Rudolf Schmidt

Army Group B: Field Marshal Baron Maximilian von Weichs
  2nd Army: Gen. of Infantry Hans von Salmuth[b]
  2nd Hungarian Army: Gen. Gusztav Jany
  8th Italian Army: Gen. Italo Gariboldi
  Army Detachment Fretter-Pico[c]: Gen. of Artillery Maximilian Fretter-Pico

Army Group Don: Field Marshal Erich von Manstein
  Army Detachment Hollidt: Gen. of Infantry Karl Adolf Hollidt
  6th Army[d]: Col. Gen. Friedrich Paulus[e]
  Army Group Hoth: Col. Gen. Hermann Hoth
    4th Panzer Army: Gen. of Panzer Troops Erhard Raus
    4th Romanian Army: Gen. Constantin Constantnescu[f]

Army Group A: Col. Gen. Ewald von Kleist[a]
  1st Panzer Army: Gen. of Cavalry Eberhard von Mackensen
  17th Army: Colonel Gen. Richard Ruoff

ORDER OF BATTLE, GERMAN ARMY, JANUARY 1943

OKW Theaters

20th Mountain Army[g]: Col. Gen. Eduard Dietl

Army of Norway: Col. Gen. Nikolaus von Falkenhorst

OB West: Field Marshal Gerd von Rundstedt
  Military Commander Netherlands: Gen. of Fliers Friedrich Christiansen
  15th Army: Gen. of Panzer Troops Heinrich von Vietinghoff
  7th Army: Col. Gen. Friedrich Dollmann
  1st Army: Col. Gen. Johannes Blaskowitz
  Army Detachment Felber[h]: Gen. of Infantry Hans Felber

OB South: *Luftwaffe* Field Marshal Albert Kesselring
  1st Italian-German Panzer Army[i]: Field Marshal Erwin Rommel

Army Group E[j]: *Luftwaffe* Col. Gen. Alexander Loehr

Replacement Army: Col. Gen. Friedrich Fromm

Notes:
  a. Promoted to field marshal, February 1, 1943.
  b. Relieved of command, February 4, 1943, and replaced by Gen. of Infantry Walter Weiss, who was promoted to colonel general, effective February 1, 1943.
  c. Reverted back to XXX Corps, February 3, 1943.
  d. Destroyed in Stalingrad, January 31–February 2, 1943.
  e. Promoted to field marshal, January 31, 1943, and surrendered the same day.
  f. Relieved of command, February 10, 1943, and replaced by Gen. Constantin Sanatescu.
  g. Controlled forces in Lapland (northern Norway, northern Finland, northern Russia).
  h. Upgraded to 19th Army on August 26, 1943.
  i. Divided and upgraded to Army Group Afrika, February 22, 1943.
  j. Created on January 1, 1943, from Headquarters, 12th Army, to control German, Italian, Croatian, and Bulgarian forces in Serbia, Croatia, and Crete.

Although Hitler ordered his divisions to "hold at all costs" and not to take one step to the rear, they were in fact pushed back 100 to 200 miles on the central sector. Stalin, however, was not able to destroy the *Wehrmacht*, although he did severely damage it. As early as December 19, 1941, for example, the 2nd Panzer Army was down to a strength of 70 operational tanks (called "runners"), with 168 in the repair shops. It had 970 tanks when the campaign began in June. By New Year's Day, the *Wehrmacht* had lost 173,722 killed, 621,308 wounded, and 35,873 missing. According to Franz Halder, losses in Russia equaled 25.96 percent of the 3.2 million men engaged.[12] From November 30, 1941, to April 1,

1942, the German Army lost 2,800 to 3,500 casualties a day. In temperatures as low as forty-nine degrees Fahrenheit below zero, tens of thousands of German soldiers suffered severe frostbite, many of when
required one or more amputations and were thus permanent losses.

In early April 1942, the *rasputitsa*—the spring thaw—set in. During
the winter, the ground, which had been saturated by the fall rains, had
frozen to a depth of eight feet or more, and several feet of ice and snow
had accumulated on the top of that. Now it began to melt from the top
downward, creating a progressively deepening layer of water and mud on
top of frozen ground. The water could not go anywhere until the lowest
layer of frozen soil had completely thawed, a process that usually took
five or six weeks. During the worst three weeks of the *rasputitsa*, the mud
was too deep for movement by motorized vehicles or even by horse-
drawn vehicles, other than two-wheeled *panje* (peasant) wagons, which
had high wheels and low weight. By mid-April, operations were virtually at a standstill throughout the combat zone. Stalin's first winter offensive was over.

————————

The German Army of 1942 was a far cry from the one that had crossed
into the Soviet Union so confidently in June 1941. Its losses in men and
equipment had been tremendous, and its civilian-oriented industry was
insufficient to replace its losses. It had lost more than 2,000 panzers and
assault guns since Barbarossa began, but less than a third of these had
been replaced. Almost 75,000 trucks and motorized vehicles had been
lost, but only 7,500 had been replaced. The deficit was so great that
Halder almost completely demotorized the standard infantry divisions.
Only the ambulance companies remained fully motorized in the
"marching infantry" divisions. More than 179,000 horses had died, but
only 20,000 could be replaced. The *Wehrmacht* had lost nearly 7,000
artillery pieces on the Eastern Front, and only a fraction of them could
be replaced.

In terms of men, virtually the entire class of 1922 had been drafted,
and the armies on the Eastern Front had received 1.1 million replacements since June 22, 1941, but were still short 625,000 men as of May 1,
1942. As of July 1, 1942, the German Army had 2.847 million men in
the East, as compared to 3.206 million on June 22, 1941.[13] The shortages

were especially serious in the infantry, where the typical regiment was at less than 50 percent of its June 21, 1941, strength. In the spring of 1942, therefore, Hitler could hope to launch a major offensive in only one sector, and he chose to attack in the south.

Halder proposed disbanding eleven divisions to bring the others up to strength, but Hitler refused to do so, on the grounds that such a move would have a detrimental effect on Axis morale and would encourage the enemy. The flaw in this reasoning was that the understrength divisions were now completely out of balance. They had full-strength or nearly full-strength staffs, headquarters, support units, and service units, but the infantry regiments—which naturally had suffered the majority of the casualties—had very few riflemen left. After the failure of Stalin's winter offensive of 1941–42, the strength of the average German infantry company was reduced from 180 to 80. The combat value of the typical German infantry company, however, did not decline by a corresponding percentage because of the more effective organizational structures of the smaller companies and because the numbers of automatic weapons and machine guns in the smaller units were greatly increased.

Many of the veteran divisions were reorganized and were reduced from nine to six infantry battalions each. By July 1942, there were twenty-nine more divisions on the Eastern Front than in June 1941, but the German strength in Russia had fallen by 359,000 men.[14] As a result, the German divisions earmarked for Hitler's summer offensive of 1942 could be brought up to strength in terms of manpower only by reducing the divisions of Army Groups North and Center to 50 percent or less of their authorized establishment and reducing the training time for the replacements sent to these army groups from six to two months. The panzer divisions of Army Group South were brought up to a strength of three tank battalions each, but the panzer divisions of the other army groups were cut to a strength of only one or two tank battalions. Even so, the spearhead divisions of Army Group South would attack with only 85 percent of their authorized vehicle strength and only 80 percent of their authorized tank strength.[15] The artillery battalions of Army Group South could only be brought up to strength via similar measures; the artillery batteries of Army Groups North and Center had to be reduced from four to three guns, and many of these were obsolete or captured pieces. In short, the number of divisions in the German *Wehrmacht* was

now a misleading statistic because the combat power of many of them—
and eventually almost all of them—no longer warranted the term. In
addition, the divisions created after the spring of 1942 would be much
weaker than divisions formed previously.[16]

To make matters worse, as historian Alan S. Milward wrote, "The
whole mechanism of distributing arms at the front was faulty." Newly
formed divisions got 90 percent of all the newly manufactured (and best)
weapons and equipment; the veteran divisions received 10 percent.[17]
Naturally, the new divisions suffered heavier losses in their first battle
than the experienced units, resulting in an unnecessarily high loss of
new weapons and equipment, while the veteran infantry regiments
struggled with worn-out and outmoded guns, equipment, and vehicles.

One potential source of manpower shunned by Hitler and the Nazis
was the Eastern volunteer. Some enterprising German generals were
recruiting and forming ad hoc Eastern battalions as early as the summer
of 1941. By the spring of 1942, German forces had "absorbed" an estimated 700,000 former Red Army soldiers into their ranks, including
4,000 officers. Ultimately, more than a million Eastern volunteers (many
of them former Soviet soldiers) joined the German Army, mostly as
"Hiwis" (*Hilfsfreiwillige*, or auxiliary volunteers).[18] Hitler disapproved of
recruiting these "racially inferior" volunteers and, on February 10, 1942,
issued an order forbidding further recruitment. This order was not
strictly observed in some places while other commands ignored it altogether. By the summer of 1942, Soviet POWs and volunteers made up
15 percent of the personnel of some divisions. Many were used only as
auxiliaries at first (cooks, mess hall helpers, drivers, stretcher bearers, and
the like), but as time went on, more and more were employed as combat
troops, and many of them performed superbly. Because of this fact,
which flew in the face of his racist theories, Hitler issued another order
in June 1942 stating that no further units of this type were to be formed
after August 1.[19] Again his order was largely ignored, especially by Col.
Gen. Ewald von Kleist, the Prussian ex-cavalryman who now commanded the 1st Panzer Army and continued to form large numbers of
Cossack cavalry battalions and use them most effectively.

Despite the continued "illegal" recruitment of Hiwis, the Axis forces
in the East had a strength of only 3,010,370 men as of September 20,
1942. They were opposed by 4,255,840 Soviet troops, even after the Red

Army suffered appalling losses in 1941 and 1942. In addition, the Russians would receive 1,400,000 men from its recruiting class of 1925—three times the number Germany would receive. Quantitatively, the odds against the *Wehrmacht* on the Eastern Front were already growing long.[20] Morale in the *Wehrmacht*, however, remained quite high. Having held off the Soviet threat in the winter, the Germans felt that they had shown that they could defeat the enemy at his best.

THE ODDS ON THE EASTERN FRONT, SEPTEMBER 20, 1942

Unit	Axis Forces	Soviet Forces
Army Group North	708,400	1,001,610
Army Group Center	1,012,070	1,356,340
Army Group B[a]	818,250	1,379,300
Army Group A[a]	266,350	518,590
TOTALS	**3,013,370[b]**	**4,255,840**

Notes:
    a. Formed when Army Group South was divided on July 7, 1943.
    b. Ration strength only. Ration strength was an estimated 250,000 men higher than actual combat strength.
Source: Ziemke, *Stalingrad to Berlin*, 34–35.

On the other side of the line, Stalin was much less hesitant than Hitler to convert to a total war economy. During the first half of 1942, Soviet industry turned out more than 53,000 pieces of artillery, compared with 30,000 in the last six months of 1941. Airplane output remained steady at 8,300, but tank production increased to 11,200 during the first half of 1942—almost four times the German output of 3,000 over the same period. By the spring of 1942, Stalin had 5.6 million men in his armed forces and could field 348 rifle or cavalry divisions, 239 rifle or independent tank brigades, and 329 independent regiments (excluding 10 armies in Stavka reserve). By the time the spring offensive began, he had 6,000 tanks, 55,600 guns, and about 3,000 modern combat aircraft. Hitler, on the other hand, had 3.9 million men in the ground forces, of which 2.6 million were on the Eastern Front, 212,000 in occupied Russia, 150,000 in Finland, and 1.3 million in the Replacement Army in occupied Europe or North Africa. These figures exclude allied forces, which were listed as follows: Finnish, 300,000; Romanian, 330,000; Hungarian, 70,000; Italian, 68,000; Slovakian,

28,000; and Spanish volunteers, 14,000.[21] Most of the allied formations, however, were of limited value at best, except the Finns and Spaniards.

Meanwhile, the *Luftwaffe* was also having serious problems. First, it had lost its numerical parity. From July to December 1941 alone, Russian factories turned out 5,173 fighters, British factories produced 4,408 fighters, and the Americans manufactured even more, but German factories could produce only 1,619 fighters for the *Luftwaffe*.[22] Second, it had lost its technical advantage and was waging war with obsolete airplanes. Seeing the writing on the wall, Col. Gen. Ernst Udet, the chief of air armaments, drank two bottles of cognac on November 17, 1941. He then telephoned his mistress in a state of hysteria. "I can't stand it any longer!" he cried and then shot himself. He was officially reported as having been killed in a crash while testing a new airplane. Goering cried like a small child at Udet's funeral but later blamed him for the destruction of the *Luftwaffe*.[23]

Erhard Milch succeeded Udet in all of his offices and took energetic measures to restore the *Luftwaffe* to its former position, but he could not make good four years lost to mismanagement and neglect. For the air force, the future looked grim indeed. In mid-1942, for example, as it prepared for the summer offensive, the *Luftwaffe*'s strength in the East stood at 2,750 combat airplanes, out of a total of 4,262 in the entire air force. More than 64 percent of the *Luftwaffe*'s combat aircraft were now on the Eastern Front, and the Red Air Force still outnumbered it by at least three to one.[24]

To reach even this strength, Gen. Hans Jeschonnek, the chief of the General Staff of the *Luftwaffe*, had to dip into the training establishment once more. This time, he sent fighter training units and their instructor pilots to the front. Adolf Galland, who had succeeded the late Werner Moelders as the general of fighter forces,[25] protested this decision and called upon the chief of the *Luftwaffe*'s General Staff to increase the number of fighter training units, instead of decreasing them. "If you reduce them now instead of forcing them up, you are sawing off the branch on which you are sitting," he warned. Jeschonnek listened quietly without interrupting. He did not question the validity of Galland's arguments. When the fighter general had finished, Jeschonnek spoke "without vehemence, presumption, or demagogy." He told Galland that he understood the seriousness of his decision, but the rapid annihilation of the Soviet Union was an essential prerequisite for the continuation of the war. This was Hitler's goal for the summer offensive of 1942, and all forces, including the *Luftwaffe*, now had to be concentrated for this decisive blow. "He was fully aware of the deathly crisis in which the *Luftwaffe* stood because of the war in the East," Galland recalled.[26] He also realized that if the gamble failed, the *Luftwaffe*'s training branch would probably not be able to furnish enough replacement fighter pilots for the Western Front—or for the defense of the Reich. He sent the fighter squadrons east just the same. Victory over the Soviet Union in the summer offensive of 1942 had priority over all other considerations.

There were more German victories, but by early September 1942, the powerful German 6th Army was bogged down in street fighting in Stalingrad. Its long, exposed flanks were protected on the northwest by the Italian 8th and Romanian 3rd Armies, while its southern-southwestern flank was shielded by Hermann Hoth's weak 4th Panzer Army, which was intermixed with the even weaker 4th Romanian Army. The overall Axis commander, Col. Gen. Baron Maximilian von Weichs, the commander in chief of Army Group B, was not unaware of the threat to the 6th Army's flanks and pointed out the dangers to OKH. By the second week in November, he was convinced that the Russians were going to launch major offensives against both of his flanks. Even Hitler was concerned. On November 9, he said, "If only the front were held by German formations, I wouldn't lose a moment's sleep over it. But this is different. The 6th Army really must make an end of this business and take the remaining parts of Stalingrad quickly."[27]

This, however, the 6th Army could not do.

On November 19, the Soviets launched a major offensive against the 3rd Romanian Army, northwest of Stalingrad. To stop it, Weichs committed his only reserves: Lt. Gen. Ferdinand Heim's XXXXVIII Panzer Corps. Heim, however, had only one German division, the 22nd Panzer, which was a mechanical wreck. It had more than 100 tanks, but only 42 would start on November 19. The Soviets struck the 3rd Romanian Army with more than a million men and 900 tanks along a forty-mile front. They had 900 tanks, supported by 13,500 guns and 1,115 aircraft. The Romanian forces collapsed completely, and Heim was lucky to

THE STALINGRAD ENCIRCLEMENT

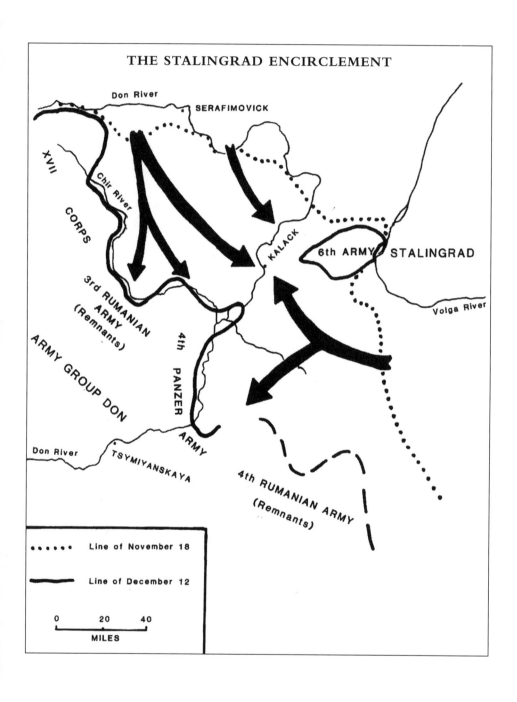

Don River

SERAFIMOVICK

XVII

Chir River

CORPS

KALACK

6th ARMY   STALINGRAD

3rd RUMANIAN
ARMY
(Remnants)

4th

Volga River

PANZER

ARMY GROUP DON

ARMY

Don River

TSYMIYANSKAYA

4th RUMANIAN ARMY
(Remnants)

• • • • •   Line of November 18

————   Line of December 12

0   20   40

MILES

escape across the Chir River with a remnant of his command. Hitler promptly had him thrown into prison.

The next day, November 20, the Soviets hit Weichs's southern flank in equally overwhelming force. Once again, the Romanians ran away, allowing the Russians to split the 4th Panzer Army in two. Hoth escaped to the south with the 16th Motorized Division. His other three German divisions, including the elite 29th Motorized Division, fought their way to the north into the rapidly forming Stalingrad Pocket, along with Schwelder's IV Corps Headquarters.

On November 21, both Soviet spearheads pivoted ninety degrees. They linked up two days later, completing the encirclement of the 6th Army. Some 230,000 German soldiers were surrounded.

To rescue the 6th Army, Hitler turned to what many experts consider the best general Nazi Germany produced during World War II: Field Marshal Erich von Manstein.[28] His Headquarters, 11th Army, was upgraded to Army Group Don on November 22, transferred from Army Group North (where it was preparing to attack Leningrad), and inserted between Army Groups B and A. It was activated on November 27.

Initially, Manstein had only a handful of battered and understrength German infantry divisions and a few practically useless Romanian formations. He was charged with the task of rescuing the 6th Army at Stalingrad while simultaneously preventing the Soviets from capturing Rostov and thus cutting off Army Group A (the 1st Panzer and 17th Armies) in the Caucasus and Kuban. He faced ten Soviet armies; a tank army; four air armies; several independent tank, mechanized, and cavalry corps; and hundreds of smaller units—not counting the seven armies encircling Stalingrad. With the help of reinforcements rushed to him by Hitler and OKH, Manstein used his incredible reservoir of military genius to check the Soviet spearheads within fifteen miles of Rostov while at the same time assembling a potent force to relieve Stalingrad, even though he was outnumbered by at least seven to one.

Manstein's relief forces included the 6th, 17th, and 23rd Panzer Divisions, which were under the command of Gen. of Panzer Troops Friedrich Kirchner's LVII Panzer Corps.[29] Only the 6th Panzer, which had just completed a rebuilding program in France, was at anything close to full strength. Manstein had Kirchner secretly assemble his forces south of Stalingrad, which was the last thing the Soviet generals expected.

When he attacked with 230 tanks on December 12, he took the Russians completely by surprise, although they reacted quickly and rushed reinforcements to the threatened sector. Kirchner pushed to within thirty miles of the Stalingrad perimeter, and his 11th Panzer Regiment alone destroyed 400 tanks in three days.[30] At night, his vanguards could see the the muzzle flashes from the guns firing on Stalingrad.

Kirchner was unable to break the back of the Russian defenses, however; the relief attempt made slow progress after December 17 and was finally halted on December 23. Manstein, meanwhile, called upon Paulus to break out of the pocket and head for the LVII Panzer Corps' vanguards on December 19, but Paulus was not willing to do so without Hitler's permission, which was not forthcoming. Kirchner was now under attack by hundreds of Soviet tanks and armored vehicles, and on December 26, he was forced to fall back. After this, Manstein left the 6th Army out of his calculations. By the end of the year, the LVII Panzer Corps was in full retreat, and the Soviets were again threatening Rostov.

CHAPTER 2

Manstein Restores the Southern Flank

THE RETREAT BEGINS

The Soviets completed the encirclement of Stalingrad on November 23, 1942. Not only had they surrounded the 6th Army, but they had completely destabilized the Eastern Front. By November 27, they had pushed thirty-four divisions across the Don River. To oppose them, Manstein had the equivalent of only three German divisions to cover more than 200 miles of front. Gen. Kurt Zeitzler, the chief of the General Staff and de facto head of OKH, did what he could to help Manstein and dispatched the 3rd Mountain, 7th and 15th Luftwaffe Field, 306th and 336th Infantry, and 6th, 11th, and 17th Panzer Divisions to the Don Front, but it took them quite some time to arrive.

On December 16, the Soviets, who were 125 miles from Rostov, resumed their drive on the city by launching a massive attack on recently upgraded Army Detachment Hollidt* and Army Group B. In Hollidt's zone, the Soviet 7th Tank Corps struck two Romanian divisions, which promptly ran away, but Hollidt, who had detected the Russian build-up, quickly committed the German 294th Infantry Division and the fourteen remaining tanks of the 22nd Panzer Division to the battle and temporarily halted the Soviets. The following day, how-

---

* An army detachment (*Armee Abteilung*) was a status between a corps and an army group.

ever, Hollidt's neighboring unit, the 8th Italian Army, was routed, completely exposing his left flank. Meanwhile, on Hollidt's southern flank, the Soviets established several bridgeheads on the west bank of the Chir on December 18.

Gen. of Infantry Karl Adolf Hollidt was a veteran infantryman noted for his selflessness. During the next few days, he conducted a series of well-executed withdrawals, and by using all of his considerable skills, he was able to both save his command and delay the Russian advance, although he was not able to halt it. Col. Gen. Baron Maximilian von Weichs's Army Group B was less fortunate. His Italian contentgents panicked, and his weak German forces, under Gen. of Infantry Hans von Salmuth's 2nd Army, were mauled by three Soviet armies.[1] By December 19, the Soviets had opened a thirty-mile gap between Hollidt and Army Group B and had committed four tank corps and a motorized corps in a general pursuit to the southwest.

On December 20, OKH transferred the XXX Corps Headquarters (now designated Army Detachment Fretter-Pico) from Army Group North to Army Group Don, with orders to protect the Donetz crossings, rally the Italians, cover Manstein's left flank, and reestablish contact with Army Group B. All the new command had, however, was one fresh German infantry division and elements of the 3rd Mountain Division. Obviously, the new commander, Gen. of Artillery Maximillan Fretter-Pico, did not have sufficient forces to carry out his tasks. On December 20, the right flank of Army Group B—the Italian Celere and Sforzesca Divisions—collapsed, as did two Romanian divisions on Manstein's left, and the gap between Army Groups B and Don grew to 100 miles.

By December 23, Manstein could no longer ignore the deteriorating situation on his northern flank. He transferred the 11th Panzer Division from the 4th Panzer Army to Army Detachment Hollidt, and in order to hold Rostov, he diverted the 6th Panzer Division from the LVII Panzer Corps to the Rostov sector. This maneuver effectively ended the Stalingrad relief attempt. Meanwhile, Hoth's 4th Panzer Army was desperately trying to hold its positions north of Rostov against heavy attacks by three tank and motorized corps.

Stalin was not through, however. On December 30, he committed two new armies to the attack against Army Detachment Fretter-Pico: the 5th Tank Army (50,000 men, 72 tanks, and 900 guns) and the 5th

Shock Army (71,000 men, 252 tanks, and 814 guns).[2] They struck along a thirty-mile stretch between Oblivskaya and Rychkovsky, bypassed Millerovo, and drove on the Donetz crossings; meanwhile, three armies that had previously been besieging Stalingrad struck Army Detachment Hollidt and the left wing of the 4th Panzer Army. Hollidt threw Maj. Gen. Hermann Balck's 11th Panzer Division into the breach, and Hitler ordered Lt. Gen. Baron Hans von Funck's 7th Panzer Division to be held at Rostov in case a last-ditch defense of the city was necessary.[3] Manstein pressed clerks, supply troops, and administrative personnel into ad hoc units for a final defense of the city.

The situation by now was truly desperate. On New Year's Day, 1943, the Russians were only fifty-five miles from Rostov, and three Russian armies were advancing on the city along both banks of the Don. That same day, in a dazzling piece of fanatasy and self-deception, Hitler announced that he was sending the 1st, 2nd, and 3rd SS Panzer Grenadier Divisions and the Grossdeutschland Panzer Grenadier Division[4]—all under the newly formed SS Panzer Corps—to relieve Stalingrad. This maneuver would take at least six weeks to complete. Army Groups Don and B were to hold their present positions until then. Manstein, of course, realized that this was out of the question and that the situation was hopeless for the 6th Army, which no longer played a part in his calculations.

During the first week of January 1943, the Soviet 3rd Guards Tank Corps broke through and raced along the southern bank of the Don in the gap between Hollidt's right flank and the left flank of Hoth's 4th Panzer Army. On January 7, the Soviet corps' forward units pushed to within twenty miles of Rostov. Manstein was working in his office in his forward command post when his aide, Captain Annus, burst in.

"Sir, Soviet tanks have crossed the Don only twelve miles from here and are making straight for us!" he cried excitedly. "Our Cossack covering parties have been overrun. We've nothing left."

"That so?" Manstein replied, calmly regarding his aide. "We've got all sorts of things left, Annus." He ordered the captain to scrape together whatever he could find and reminded him that there was a tank repair shop nearby. It was bound to have a few more or less operational tanks. The field marshal ordered Annus to collect whatever he could use, organize the staff company and support units in Rostov for combat, and go out and defeat the Soviets. The army group headquarters was not going to take to its heels, and he was not going to be bothered by any of it. "I'll leave you to cope with this little disturbance!"[5]

Captain Annus did as he was told. His ad hoc combat group took the Soviets by surprise and threw their spearhead back across the river. The crisis passed.

This incident was typical of Manstein and of the entire southern sector of the Eastern Front in the winter of 1942–43. By shifting his panzer units now to the south, now to the north, Manstein, Hollidt, and the other German commanders were able to halt the Russians, cover Rostov, and continue their retreat to the Donetz during the second week of January. The well-led Army Detachment Fretter-Pico was also fortunate. It extricated 14,000 troops who had been encircled at Millerovo and then successfully retreated behind the Donetz between January 15 and 19. Hollidt also fell back behind the frozen river but, like Fretter-Pico, was closely pursued by the Russians. Meanwhile, Manstein took Balck's 11th Panzer Division from Hollidt in order to counter the Russian threat to Rostov and protect the rear of the 4th Panzer Army. Balck counterattacked and pushed the Soviet spearheads back across the Manich River and away from Rostov, but on January 23, four Russian armies attacked Fretter-Pico on the Donetz. Several of the attacks were beaten off, but the 1st Guards Army drove across the Aydar River and crossed the Donetz west of Voroshilovgrad, effectively outflanking Army Group Don.

By now, even Hitler began to doubt his own decision to leave Army Group A in the Caucasus. Typically, however, he did not reverse himself, but rather opted for a half-measure. On January 27, he ordered the 1st Panzer Army transferred to Army Group Don, along with a panzer division, an infantry division, and two security divisions. He also promised Manstein that the SS Panzer Corps, which was on its way from France to Russia, would begin a counteroffensive from the Kharkov area on February 12. Manstein immediately ordered Gen. of Cavalry Eberhard von Mackensen, the commander of the 1st Panzer Army, to take over the sector of Army Detachment Fretter-Pico.[6] He also ordered the units Hitler had released to rush to Rostov as quickly as possible in order to get them out of the narrowing bottleneck before the Soviets could close it.

To the north, Army Group B was still attempting to shield Army Group Don's left flank on the Krasnaya River, but it had very little with which to do it. In all, the Soviet Southwest Front* alone had 325,000 men and 360 tanks, with the 1st Guards and 25th Tank Corps (another 300 tanks) on the way to join them. The Italian 8th and Hungarian 2nd Armies had collapsed, and Army Detachments Hollidt, Fretter-Pico, and Lanz had only 160,000 men and 100 tanks combined, although the SS Panzer Corps (another 200 tanks) was now beginning to arrive from France.[7]

On January 28, 1943, a new headquarters, Army Detachment Lanz, was created under the command of Hubert Lanz, who was promoted to general of mountain troops that same day.[8] On February 1, the detachment took over the southern flank of Army Group B and was given the mission of protecting Kharkov and the northern flank of Army Group Don. Its forces initially included Corps Cramer (the 168th Infantry and Grossdeutschland Panzer Grenadier Divisions) and the SS Panzer Corps, most of which had not yet arrived from the West.[9] Clearly, Lanz had an impossible mission.

That same day, the Russians attacked the remnants of Army Group B with the newly created Popov Group under Gen. Markian M. Popov, which included four tank corps and a rifle corps. The German forward positions were quickly overwhelmed, and there was nothing in reserve. Popov surged into the German rear, crossed the Donetz, and headed west for Slavyansk at the junction of Army Groups B and Don.

On February 5, the Russians took Izyum in the deep left flank of Army Group Don. An advance of seventy more miles would allow the Soviets to cut both of Manstein's main railroads and essentially leave the army group without supplies. To check the Soviet juggernaut north of Kharkov, Weichs had only three understrength infantry divisions, the Grossdeutschland Division, and the Deutschland SS Panzer Grenadier Regiment from the "Das Reich" Division. It was obviously not strong enough to prevent the Soviets from enveloping Army Detachment Lanz at Kharkov and then rolling up the flank of Army Group Don. The army group was no longer strong enough to secure the area assigned to it for its covering mission, as Weichs frankly reported to Fuehrer Headquarters. Manstein's right flank was also in serious trouble. Army Detachment Fretter-Pico had only three infantry divisions, and the strongest of these—the 335th Infantry—had only 3,500 men. Both of Fretter-Pico's

---

* A Soviet front was the equivalent of a German army group.

armored divisions—the 19th and 27th Panzers—were burned out and had a combined strength of only fifteen tanks and seven assault guns.[10] Manstein estimated that Army Groups B and Don were outnumbered eight to one and asked for permission to retreat.

Hitler responded by sending a fast Condor airplane to fly Manstein to Fuehrer Headquarters at Rastenburg. Without preliminaries, Hitler personally assumed sole responsibility for the disaster on the Volga. "I alone am responsible for Stalingrad," he said. "I could perhaps aver that Goering gave me inaccurate information on the supply-carrying capabilities of the *Luftwaffe*, and could thereby unload part of the responsibility on him. But he is the man I myself have appointed as my successor. I therefore cannot burden him with the responsibility for Stalingrad."[11]

The field marshal was taken aback by such honesty from Hitler. He had intended to ask the dictator to lay down command of the *Wehrmacht* and appoint a qualified professional (i.e., himself) in his place. Instead, he now only asked Hitler to appoint a military deputy. Hitler responded evasively, so Manstein got down to specifics. He requested permission to withdraw behind the Mius. This sparked a four-hour debate, but in the end, Hitler relented, probably because his confidence in his own military capabilities had been temporarily shaken by the loss of a quarter of a million men at Stalingrad.

Of this meeting, military historian Dana V. Sadarananda writes:

> The meeting . . . also demonstrates the moral courage and sheer physical strength needed when discussing operational matters with Hitler. Indeed, there were only a handful of generals who had the will to stand eye to eye with Hitler to argue their point to a favorable decision. During the meeting, Manstein sought only one decision on operational matters. After four long hours, Hitler gave in, but only after exhausting every argument against Manstein. It is not difficult to imagine how much longer this meeting might have lasted if Manstein had had more to discuss. . . .
>
> Manstein displayed considerable skill and determination in his arguments with the dictator. . . . Manstein refused to be distracted by side issues, returning again and again to the matter at hand despite Hitler's efforts to the contrary. The result was a timely decision to withdraw to the Mius.[12]

By the time Manstein left, however, Hitler had all but decided to relieve the field marshal of his command at their next meeting. Before he returned to the front, Hitler asked him to delay his retreat as long as possible. Before he gave up more territory, Hitler wanted to try an offensive solution first.

On or about February 3, Hitler had declared Kharkov a fortress. Lanz had promptly objected on the grounds that the city was not fortified and that he had no troops with which to hold it. Hitler responded by summonding him to Fuehrer Headquarters, and on February 6, the same day he met with Manstein, Hitler personally gave Lanz two missions: hold Kharkov and counterattack to the southwest with the two divisions of the SS Panzer Corps. The next day, Hitler sent Weichs a warning that no more excuses for not attacking with the SS Panzer Corps would be accepted. Meanwhile, though, both SS divisions had been tied down in heavy defensive fighting northeast of Kharkov. Instead of attacking, they were forced to evacuate Belgorod and Kursk on February 9. Manstein began his retreat that same day. Army Detachment Hollidt and the 4th Panzer Army covered 100 miles in nine days, closely followed by the Russians.

Hundreds of miles to the south, Army Group A had already retreated from the Caucasus and had evacuated the Maikop oil fields from January 23 to 30. (Hitler had relinquished the post of commander in chief of Army Group A in favor of Kleist on November 22, 1942. Gen. of Cavalry Eberhard von Mackensen had succeeded Kleist as commander of the 1st Panzer Army.) Rostov fell on February 14, and the 17th Army—the only army left in Kleist's army group—swung its left flank back to the Sea of Azov. It now held a continuous line on the Taman Peninsula from the Sea of Azov to the Black Sea, in a position called the Kuban Bridgehead. It was, Hitler said, to be used as a jump-off point for another attempt to conquer the Caucasus once Germany was ready to resume the offensive.

Meanwhile, Lanz's counterattack began on February 11 and was initially successful; however, by nightfall on February 13, the northern flank of the SS Panzer Corps had been forced back to the suburbs of Kharkov. The following morning, Hitler ordered that Kharkov be held at all costs, even if the counterattack had to be temporarily halted. Later that day, he took Army Group B out of the line and out of the German order of battle in the East. It was eventually deactivated on July 10, and Field

Marshal Weichs went into Fuehrer Reserve. (Army Group B's staff was not disbanded but rather was sent to Munich, where it was eventually taken over by Field Marshal Erwin Rommel for use in northern Italy.) The Second Army was assigned to Army Group Center, and Army Detachment Lanz was attached to Army Group Don, which Hitler redesignated Army Group South on February 12. Kharkov was to be held at all costs, he commanded.

Kharkov was the major city of northeastern Ukraine and the fourth largest city in the Soviet Union after Moscow, Leningrad, and Kiev. It was attacked by three armies of the Voronezh Front—about 200,000 men and 300 tanks. (The other two armies of the Voronezh Front had taken Kursk to the north.) Lanz met the Kharkov offensive with three infantry divisions, the Grossdeutschland Division, and the Deutschland SS Regiment—50,000 men in all, with each division holding a frontage of almost ten miles.[13] Even with the SS Panzer Corps added, Lanz was still outnumbered two and a half to one.

Lanz conducted a skillful retreat to the outskirts of the city and delegated the responsibility for holding it to one of Hitler's favorite commanders, SS Gen. Paul Hausser, the former commander of the "Das Reich" Division, who had lost his right eye during the drive on Moscow in 1941. Hausser, however, was no Nazi yes-man incapable of independent thought.[14] By noon on February 15, Hausser's corps was almost surrounded by two Soviet armies. Ignoring Hitler's hysterical instructions, Hausser ordered his troops to withdraw to the southwest at 1 P.M. By the time the last of them fell back, their escape corridor was only one mile wide.

General Lanz, Hausser's immediate superior, was horrified by his actions. At 3:30 P.M., he signaled Hausser: "Kharkov will be defended under all circumstances!"[15] Hausser ignored this order as well. The last German rear guard left the city on the morning of February 16. Hausser had saved the 1st and 2nd SS Panzer Grenadier Divisions, as well as the army's Grossdeutschland Panzer Grenadier and 320th Infantry Divisions.

Hitler reacted to this piece of insubordination in typical fashion. A scapegoat had to be found for this latest disaster on the Eastern Front, but Hausser—an SS officer and a holder of the Golden Party Badge—was not a candidate for public disgrace. Instead, on February 20, Hitler sacked Hubert Lanz, who had annoyed him with his earlier warnings, but who had, in fact, been the very officer who, in the end, had insisted that Hitler's order be obeyed. Contrary to usual practice, however, Lanz was not premanently retired but was given command of the XXII Mountain Corps a few days later. He was succeeded by Gen. of Panzer Troops Werner Kempf, the former commander of the XXXXVIII Panzer Corps, and his former command was redesignated Army Detachment Kempf.[16]

Meanwhile, to the south, General Mackensen's 1st Panzer Army took charge of the zone of Army Detachment Fretter-Pico, which again became the XXX Corps. Mackensen made his main stand at Slavyansk, which was defended by Funck's 7th Panzer Division. The battle began on February 3 when the 7th Panzer was attacked by vastly superior Soviet mobile forces; Funck's men, however, inflicted heavy casualties on the Russians and held their positions. The Reds surrounded the city but could not take it. Funck turned back attack after attack for days. He was still holding his positions on February 16.

While the 7th Panzer Division held up much of the Southwest Front's armor, Army Detachment Hollidt and the 4th Panzer Army occupied their positions behind the Mius on February 18. West of Kharkov, in the zone of Army Detachment Kempf, the situation also stabilized. Here, Erhard Raus, the veteran ex-commander of the 6th Panzer Division, took charge of the ad hoc Corps Raus, which consisted of the 168th Infantry and Grossdeutschland Panzer Grenadier Divisions and the 167th Infantry Division, which had just arrived from garrison duty in the Netherlands. With his reinforcements, Raus was able to destroy fifty-five Soviet tanks and slow their advance to a crawl. Throughout its zone of operations, the Voronezh Front had overextended itself by its rapid advance and was having serious supply problems; as a result, Army Detachment Kempf was able to check its advance, except for a few local gains.

Elsewhere, however, the situation remained extremely precarious. By now, Manstein's tank and motorized units had been in more or less constant combat for weeks and were now divisions in name only. The 6th Panzer still had sixty tanks and ten assault guns, and the 7th Panzer had thirty tanks and eleven assault guns, but the rest were in very bad shape. The 11th Panzer had twenty-eight tanks; the 5th SS Panzer Grenadier Division "Viking" had eleven; the 16th Panzer Grenadier had ten; the 19th Panzer had eight tanks and seven assault guns; and the 23rd Panzer had only eight tanks left.[16] Manstein had only two railroads with which to supply the 1st Panzer Army, Army Detachment Hollidt, and the 4th Panzer Army. Far in his rear, the Soviets' Group Popov advanced through terrain the Germans considered impassable and cut the first of the railroads, the Dnepropetrovsk-Stalino, at Krasnoarmeyskoye on February 13, and by February 19, the 1st Guards Army was nearing Sinel'nikovo, twenty miles east of Dnepropetrovsk and the Dnieper River. If the Soviets could seize the Dnieper crossings and cut the railroad running through Zaporozhye, they would severe the lifeline of Army Group South.

Despite the constant retreats since November 1942, Army Group South was not a defeated force. It had suffered heavy casualties, but it had retreated skillfully, and its morale was unbroken. Now it had been reinforced with several divisions from the 1st Panzer Army. It had also considerably shortened its front by retreating to the Mius, thus freeing several mobile units, and it had gotten control of the SS Panzer Corps as well. On the other side, the Russians had followed the line of least resistance and had gained vast amounts of territory, but they had done so without decisively defeating Manstein. Now they were at the end of a long supply line, and the German field marshal was planning a counteroffensive. The first step was to convince Hitler. This would not to be an easy task since Manstein wanted to abandon even more captured territory before counterattacking.

Hitler and his entourage—including Jodl; Zeitzler; Theodor Morell, his personal physician who filled him with dangerous drugs; his personal cook; and others—arrived at Manstein's headquarters at Zaporozhye on the afternoon of February 17. Lt. Alesander Stahlberg, Manstein's aide, described Hitler, "His appearance shocked me. His skin was slack and yellowish, he was unshaven and the lapels of his double-breasted grey uniform tunic were spotted, apparently with food stains. . . . Hitler looked like a used-up man."[17]

During their first meeting, Manstein informed Hitler that he wanted to take the SS Panzer Corps out of the Kharkov area, move it to Krasnograd, and use it to attack to the southwest; at the same time, the 4th Panzer Army would assume control of the mobile reserves to the south. It would attack to the north, linking up with the SS Panzer Corps. These forces, Manstein said, would crush the Soviet forces advancing in the gap between the 1st Panzer Army and Army Detachment Kempf. Once this was accomplished, Kharkov could be recaptured. This plan was diametrically opposed to Hitler's ideas; he wanted to use the entire SS Panzer Corps to retake Kharkov once the 3rd SS Panzer Grenadier Division "Totenkopf" had arrived from France.

As Manstein talked, he became so engrossed in the military situation that he did not look at anyone and was oblivious to the world around him. Lieutenant Stahlberg recalled:

> Hitler's jaw muscles began to move . . . for minutes on end . . . more and more vigorously. It looked almost as if one of his choleric outbursts was on the way . . .
>
> However, nothing of the kind occurred . . . . When the presentation was over, Hitler cleared his throat and made one or two indifferent comments, such as, yes, that was interesting, but it all seemed to him very risky . . . [which] proved yet again that Hitler was not capable of strategic thinking. He simply would not see that in view of the massive numerical superiority of the Soviets, our only chance was to shift decisively to mobile warfare. What constantly astonished me was Hitler's incapacity to learn from such an outstanding military expert as Manstein. I saw Hitler ultimately as a small-minded man, riddled with complexes. . . .
>
> The briefing . . . ended with a certain sense of relief: at least Hitler had not interfered with operations. That alone was a success in Manstein's eyes.[18]

Hitler and Manstein met again on February 18. To Lieutenant Stahlberg, the dictator appeared to be "a completely different Hitler . . . in no way comparable with the man of . . . the day before. The dropping, failing figure was suddenly transformed into an upright, brisk and vital apparition. . . . Drugs must have been at work here."[19] By this time, Soviet armor was only thirty-six miles east of Zaporozhve, with no major German forces between them and the headquarters of Army Group South. There was now a 110-mile gap between the right flank of Army Detachment Kempf (west of Kharkov) and the left flank of the 1st Panzer Army through which the Soviet 1st Guards and 6th Armies were advancing to the south and west. By now, there was no question that the Soviets intended to drive through the gap to the Dnieper, just as Manstein had said.

By this point in the war, it was unusual for Hitler to visit a headquarters this far forward. He was quickly absorbed in planning with Manstein and forgot all thought of dismissing him; in fact, he was converted by the marshal and became enthusiastic about the operation. On February 19, he ordered Kleist and Richthofen to evacuate as many troops as possible from the Kuban and give them to Army Group South. By March 6, this number amounted to 100,000 men, although they arrived without heavy weapons or equipment.

The headquarters of the 4th Panzer Army turned its front over to Hollidt on February 17 and quickly moved to Dnepropetrovsk, from which it was to direct the southern prong of Manstein's offensive. The field marshal gave Hoth control of the XXXXVIII Panzer Corps (6th and 17th Panzer Divisions) and the SS Panzer Corps ("Das Reich" and "Totenkopf" SS Panzer Grenadier Divisions). In the meantime, the 1st Panzer Army had already taken control of the XXX Corps, the XXXX Panzer Corps (7th Panzer, 11th Panzer, and 5th SS Panzer Grenadier Divisions), and Lt. Gen. Hermann Breith's weak III Panzer Corps (62nd and 333rd Infantry, 8th and 19th Panzer, and 8th Luftwaffe Field Divisions).[20] In all, Hoth and Mackensen would have approximately 225 tanks and assault guns, but only three infantry divisions.

Manstein's plan was fairly simple: the XXXXVIII Panzer Corps would attack from the south and the SS Panzer Corps from the northwest to crush the Soviet 6th Army between them. Simultaneously, the XXXX Panzer Corps of the 1st Panzer Army would advance northward on the inner (eastern) flank of the XXXXVIII Panzer Corps in an effort to cut off and destroy Group Popov. The map on the next page shows this battle as Manstein planned it and as it actually evolved.

The Russians, meanwhile, charged blindly forward into the trap. They had, it will be recalled, won an unbroken series of victories since November 1942, and their senior generals were intoxicated with the heady taste of victory. They believed that the Germans were beaten and that the pursuit would continue indefinitely. In fact, they thought Manstein was trying to get behind the Dnieper. They had no idea that their prey was about to turn on them. Incredibly enough, Manstein's

MANSTEIN'S MIRACLE ON THE DONETZ

1: OSTROGOZHSK

2: KHARKOV

3: SINEL'NIKOVO

4: PAVLOGRAD

5: LOZOVAYA

6: KRASNOARMEYSKOY

7: SLAYANSK

8: KRASNOGRAD

9: NOVOMOSKOVSK

- – – – LINE OF JAN. 13
- –·–·– LINE OF FEB. 4
- – – – LINE OF FEB. 19
- ——— LINE OF MAR. 25
- ● AXIS POCKETS

0   25   50
MILES

ARMY GROUP CENTER
•Orel

BRYANSK FRONT

Livny

Kursk
▲

Kastornoye

38 ARMY

2 ARMY

VORONEZH FRONT

BREAK-OUT

ARMY GROUP B

40 ARMY

1
2 HUNG. ARMY
8 ITALIAN ARMY

Sumy

ARMY GROUP SOUTH

•Belgorod

ARMY DETACH. KEMPF

2

3 TANK ARMY

6 ARMY

SOUTHWEST FRONT

3 RUM. AR.

SS PANZER CORPS

•8

Izyum

RUMANIAN

•9

•5

4 Pz ARMY

3

Dnepropetrovsk

1 Pz ARMY

MOBILE GROUP POPOV

•6

Stalino

ARMY DETACH. HOLLIDT

ARMY GROUP DON

Zaporozhye

1 Pz ARMY

DNIEPR R.

4 Pz ARMY

Taganrog

Rostov

SOUTH FRONT

•Melitopol

Mariupol•

SEA OF AZOV

offensive was in its fifth day before Nikolai F. Vatutin, the commander of the Southwest Front, realized what was happening, and Stavka did not grasp the true situation until some time after that. By then, it was too late to prevent Manstein from scoring a smashing victory.

The SS Panzer Corps, on the right flank of Army Detachment Hollidt, began its attack at dawn on February 19, striking due south from Krasnograd into the rear of the 1st Guards and 6th Armies. It achieved complete surprise and, advancing rapidly, took Novo-Moskovsk the next day and Pavlograd the day after that, eliminating the threat to the Dnieper crossings and trapping sizable Russian forces south of the Samara River. On February 23, the 3rd SS Panzer Grenadier Division "Totenkopf" attacked to the east, overrunning several Soviet spearheads in the process. At the same time, the 6th and 17th Panzer Divisions of the XXXXVIII Panzer Corps (on the right flank of the 4th Panzer Army) attacked to the north against Group Popov. Meanwhile, on the eastern edge of the gap, Mackensen ordered Funck to evacuate Slavyansk in order to free the 7th Panzer Division for the attack. This was accomplished on February 17. Two days later, Mackensen struck Group Popov with such speed and force that the Russians were taken completely by surprise. Using the 7th and 11th Panzer Divisions and SS Lt. Gen. Felix Steiner's 5th SS Panzer Grenadier Division "Viking" (recently arrived from the Caucasus), he trapped most of Group Popov in a large pocket at Krasnoarmeyskoye. The Russians tried desperately to escape the sudden encirclement. Popov broke out but was quickly pursued by the XXXX Panzer Corps. Because of a shortage of fuel, he decided to make a stand at Barvenkovo to the north. Manstein turned his attention to the southern flank of the Voronezh Front, west of Kharkov. On February 25, he ordered the 1st Panzer Army to take Petrovskoye and Izyum and close the Donetz crossings. The 4th Panzer Army was instructed to attack to the northeast, then due north, along the railroad to Kharkov.

The SS Panzer Corps and XXXXVIII Panzer Corps tore apart the Russian 6th Army, while Henrici's XXXX Panzer destroyed the 4th Guards Tank Corps and surrounded Group Popov in the Barvenkovo area. Here, four tank corps were destroyed by Funck's 7th Panzer Division and Balck's 11th Panzer. Their tasks were made possible only because the Soviets had outrun their supply lines before the Manstein offensive began, and most of Popov's tanks ran completely out of fuel.

Even so, Russian resistance was bitter, and the battle continued until February 28, when scattered remnants of Group Popov broke out and escaped in the direction of Izyum. They left behind 251 tanks, 125 anti-tank guns, 73 heavy guns, and hundreds of other weapons, vehicles, and pieces of equipment.[21]

On February 24, Vatutin at last realized that his spearheads were trapped, but it was too late for his countermeasures to be effective. On February 26, Lozovaya fell and the 4th Panzer Army turned for the Donetz. On February 28, the 6th Panzer and 17th Panzer Divisions smashed the 1st Guards Cavalry Corps west of Izyum, and the "Viking" and 7th Panzer Divisions reached the southern bank of the Donetz. Meanwhile, the III Panzer and XXX Corps of the 1st Panzer Army joined the attack, retook Slavyansk, and pursued the Russians across the Donetz.

On March 1, the Soviet 3rd Tank Army tried to restore the situation by counterattacking due south toward Lozovaya. After being pounded by Stukas from the 4th Air Fleet, it ran straight into the "Totenkopf" and "Das Reich" SS Divisions. The next day, the 1st SS Panzer Grenadier Division "Leibstandarte Adolf Hitler" joined the battle, and the 3rd Tank Army was soon surrounded by the three SS divisions. When the battle ended two days later, only the remnants of the 6th Guards Cavalry Corps managed to escape to the north; two tank corps had been annihilated.

Even before this battle ended, Manstein ordered Hoth to begin the attack toward Kharkov while Mackensen advanced to the Donetz east of Petrovskoye. The panzer troops hurried to carry out their orders because the snow was already melting and soon the spring thaw would make all movement impossible. Over the next five days, the 4th Panzer Army advanced fifty miles and, on March 5, was ten miles south of Kharkov, where it made contact with Army Detachment Kempf, at last closing the gap in the German lines. That day, Hoth's army destroyed three more Soviet rifle divisions and three tank brigades of the 3rd Tank Army in a small pocket at Krasnograd, where the Russians lost an estimated 12,000 killed. The 4th Panzer Army reported the capture of 61 tanks, 225 guns, and 600 motorized vehicles.[22] Meanwhile, the 1st Panzer Army reached the Donetz all along its front. Several Soviet bridgeheads remained, but German commanders decided to deal with them in more favorable weather.

Hoth planned to break Soviet lines west of Kharkov and then to fall on the city from the north. The attack began on March 8, when the SS Panzer Corps broke through Russian defensive positions on a wide front. As Hausser neared Kharkov the next day, he decided to take it via a coup de main from the west. Hoth ordered him to stick to the original plan, but the SS general again disobeyed orders and attacked the city with one division from the west, supported by a second attack from the north. This decision began several days of bitter fighting in the city. When it was finally secured on March 18, the three SS divisions had suffered 11,500 casualties. Twenty thousand Soviets had also been killed, wounded, or captured. Hausser's reputation suffered considerably during this battle because Kharkov could almost certainly have been taken without such heavy losses; Hoth, however, decided not to bring formal charges against him.

After the SS invested Kharkov, Soviet resistance west of the Donetz collapsed. The 40th and 69th Armies of the Voronezh Front tried desperately to escape across the river but were overtaken by the Grossdeutschland Division, which split them in two on March 15. The Grossdeutschland was then joined by the hard-marching 167th and 320th Infantry Divisions, and they trapped the bulk of the 69th Army in the Udy Pocket. The 1st SS Panzer Grenadier Division also continued to advance, pushed aside the 2nd Guards Tank Corps, and retook Belgorod on the east bank of the Donetz on the morning of March 18 after four hours of fighting. It then turned west and, in coordination with Group Raus, helped liquidate the Udy Pocket. Many of the Soviet soldiers trapped here managed to escape, but they lost all of their equipment and heavy weapons.

Manstein wanted to cross the Donetz in order to shorten his line. On March 21, however, he met with Hoth, who persuaded him to halt because the soldiers were exhausted. Besides, Hoth pointed out, he would rather hold a longer defensive line on a river than a shorter line in open terrain, with a river at his back, especially since the thaw was beginning. Manstein officially declared his great counteroffensive at an end on March 23. In thirty-three days, he had turned the tables on the Red Army. In a brilliant operation, he had eliminated the threat to Army Group South, stabilized the Eastern Front, and destroyed the Soviet 6th Army, 3rd Tank Army, and Group Popov in the process. The Soviet 1st

Guards, 40th, and 69th Armies had also been wrecked. Total Russian losses during the offensive amounted to more than 46,000 killed and 14,000 captured. Some 1,200 artillery pieces and more than 600 tanks had also been captured or destroyed. (The relatively low number of prisoners is a reflection of three factors: the bitterness of the fighting, the fact that the Germans were low in infantry and could not hold all points on the walls of the pockets, and the February weather that forced the Germans to spend their nights in the villages, where there were stoves, allowing many Russians to escape after dark.)

Manstein had regained the initiative for the *Wehrmacht* and brought the German Army back to about the same line it had held in the summer of 1942.[23]

CHAPTER 3

The Defeat of the German Navy

BACK TO THE ATLANTIC

In the spring of 1942, a new type of U-boat made its appearance in American waters: the U-boat tanker, or "milk cow." These supply submarines displaced nearly 1,700 tons and carried 700 tons of fuel, the bulk of which was used to refuel other U-boats. They also carried food, spare parts, medical personnel, and replacement technicians. The "milk cows" were slow, hard to control, and they had no torpedo tubes and almost no armament. Without them, however, the German submarine campaign in the south would not have been very effective. With them, Karl Doenitz's captains were able to spread destruction and terror along the shipping lanes from the coasts of Trinidad and Guiana to Cape Town. Admiral Doenitz was still not satisfied. His U-boats were sinking only an estimated 800,000 tons of shipping per month,[1] but the Americans alone were building an estimated 15,000,000 tons of shipping per year (1,250,000 tons per month).[2] Therefore, the Allies were actually increasing their shipping reserves, despite the best efforts of the U-boats.

In June, as shipping in the Caribbean began to decrease and convoying and air patrol activities there intensified, the U-boat Command began to order submarines to the Gulf of Mexico, where ships continued to sail alone or without escort. The other U-boats returned to their old hunting grounds on the convoy routes between Canada and England. During the second "happy time," they had sunk some 500 ships, including dozens of tankers. Doenitz, however, had never regarded Washington's unpreparedness as more than a temporary condition. As soon as the American defenses improved, he returned to the Atlantic, where the convoys were still outside the range of protective depth-charge-carrying land-based airplanes.

The Battle of the Atlantic began again in earnest in early May, when Lt. Hans-Peter Hinsch in *U-569* spotted a westbound convoy and summoned five other submarines to the area. This wolf pack sank seven ships in the first night of the attack and would have devastated the convoy had bad weather not intervened. A few days later, they attempted to attack a second convoy, this one bound for America, but were beaten off by its escorts. At the same time, Erich Topp sank five ships from a convoy bound for England from Gibraltar; none of the other four U-boats in this wolf pack were able to break through the defenses of the escorts.[3]

By May 1942, the tonnage sunk per day by the average U-boat had fallen to about one-tenth of the figure for 1940. The submarine continued to be a major threat to the Allies, however, because thirty submarines, complete with trained crews, were coming out of the training establishments every month—thanks mostly to Adm. Hans-Georg von Friedeburg, Doenitz's second in command and the organizational genius who invented the "endless belt" system of training and replacement.[4]

Meanwhile, destroyers escorting convoys began to attack U-boats with such accuracy that Doenitz started to suspect they might have radar. In addition, several submarines had been lost in the Bay of Biscay, the last leg of the homeward journey. All had apparently been destroyed by airplanes that suddenly appeared out of the clouds, sun, or darkness at an altitude of 150 feet. In June, three more submarines were seriously damaged by mysterious British air attacks. In July, the U-boats lost 15 percent of their operational force. Doenitz did not know that the British were using "Leigh Lights" (invented by Squadron Cmdr. H. de V. Leigh of RAF Coastal Command) in conjunction with airborne radar to spotlight and sink surfaced U-boats as they returned to base at night. To counter the threat, the U-boats were equipped with Metox radar search receivers (called "Biscay crosses"), which were effective early-warning devices against airborne radar. The early Metox receivers could be quickly disassembled as the U-boat prepared to dive; later models fea-

tured a waterproof aerial that could be left on the bridge by a diving U-
boat. As a result, only four U-boats were destroyed in August—a month
during which the German submarines sank 108 Allied ships (about
650,000 tons).[5] In September, the U-boat arm lost only 6 percent of its
operational force and sank another 650,000 tons of Allied shipping.

THE BATTLES OF THE MURMANSK RUN

The convoy battles of the Murmansk Run had their genesis on June 22,
1941, when Hitler invaded the Soviet Union. Although there was no
great sentiment in the United States for aiding Communist Russia, President Franklin D. Roosevelt quietly released the maximum possible
amount of military hardware to the Soviets. At the end of September
1941, the so-called Moscow Protocol was signed, obligating the United
States and Great Britain to supply the Soviet Union with specific
amounts of war materiel, including airplanes, tanks, artillery, metals,
petroleum products, industrial equipment, and food. Every effort was
made to deliver the needed supplies and equipment to Russia. During
1942, the western Allies delivered 1,880 airplanes, 2,350 tanks, 8,300
trucks, 6,400 other motorized vehicles, and 2,250 pieces of artillery to
the Soviet Union. By the end of the war, the Americans alone had delivered more than $11 billion worth of supplies and equipment to the
Russians, and Britain had also delivered considerable amounts.[6] American vehicles in particular were of decisive importance on the Eastern
Front, for they enabled the Russians to equal and finally exceed the Germans in mobility—the very element that made the *blitzkrieg* effective
and made it possible for Hitler to win his victories.

The problem, from the Allies' point of view, was how to get the supplies and equipment to the Soviet Union. The most direct route, through
the Black Sea, was dominated by the Turkish Straits, and Istanbul
adherred to a policy of strict neutrality. This route was therefore closed.
By far the shortest and quickest remaining route from the industrialized
cities on the east coast of the United States to the Soviet Union was via
the North Atlantic–Iceland–North Cape–Barents Sea–Murmansk route
(or, alternatively, through the White Sea to Archangel). The sailing time
between Iceland and Murmansk was only ten days. This route also had
the advantage of a port that did not freeze over in the winter because,

despite its northern location, Murmansk was kept ice-free year round by an offshoot of the Gulf Stream. The major disadvantage of the Murmansk route, of course, was the nearness of Nazi-held territory. Still, since time was the essential factor and since the other routes were closed or not yet fully developed, the vast majority of the supplies sent to the Soviet Union had to go via the northern (Murmansk) route during the critical years of 1941, 1942, and the first half of 1943.

Fortunately for the Allies, the Germans were uncharacteristically slow in recognizing the importance of this lifeline. In 1941, approximately 110 merchant ships made the Murmansk Run, and only one or two were lost.[7] This situation gradually began to change at the beginning of 1942. By then, it was obvious that Gen. Eduard Dietl's 20th Mountain Army was not going to be able to capture Murmansk, despite the fact that it had reached a point only thirty miles from the city. At the same time, Hitler had decided to concentrate the remnants of his surface fleet in the Norway area because of the preceived threat of an Allied invasion there. By this time, all that remained of the surface fleet was the battleship *Tirpitz* (the sister ship of the *Bismarck*), the battle cruiser *Scharnhorst*, the heavy cruisers *Admiral Hipper* and *Prinz Eugen*, the pocket battleships *Admiral Scheer* and *Luetzow* (which had been officially reclassified heavy cruisers in 1941), four light cruisers, and a handful of destroyers.

Between January and March, U-boats sank several ships, and in the next four convoys each way, twenty-seven ships were sunk. Then, at the end of May, Allied convoy PQ16 sailed for Murmansk with thirty-four ships and a strong escort. By this time, Col. Gen. Hans-Juergen Stumpff's 5th Air Fleet in Norway had received some reinforcements, but its performance was disappointing. In a six-day air and sea battle, PQ16 lost only seven ships sunk and several damaged. The attacks sent 770 vehicles, 147 tanks, and 77 aircraft to the bottom of the Arctic Ocean, but the convoy delivered 2,507 vehicles, 321 tanks, and 124 aircraft to Stalin's docks at Murmansk.[8]

By now, the Allies were heavily engaged against the U-boats in the Atlantic and were unable to provide enough escorts for the Murmansk convoys. Hitler was now planning his summer offensive of 1942 and wanted to deprive the Soviet Union of badly needed aid at this critical time, so he sent strong air and naval reinforcements to Norway. The 5th Air Fleet was reinforced to a strength of 103 Ju 88 bombers, 42 He 111 torpedo-bombers, 15 He 115 float planes/torpedo-bombers, 30 Stukas, eight Condors, 22 Ju 88 reconnaissance airplanes, and 44 Blohm and Voss 138 (BV 138) reconnaissance seaplanes. Hitler intended to slaughter the next convoy.

Convoy PQ17 left Iceland on June 27 with thirty-five merchant ships and a few escort vessels. At this time of year, the Germans had the additional advantage of the long days of the Arctic summer. The first attack took place on July 4 and scattered the convoy; then the *Luftwaffe* and the U-boats began to hunt down the cargo ships one by one. Eight of them were sunk by airplanes and nine by U-boats, with seven being shared kills. The eleven survivors hid along the coast, and the last of these finally reached Archangel several weeks later. They delivered 896 vehicles, 164 tanks, and 87 aircraft to Stalin's armies; however, PQ17 lost 3,350 vehicles, 430 tanks, 210 airplanes, 100,000 tons of other cargo, and 24 ships—a total of 143,977 tons of shipping. The materiel lost was roughly equal to the Red Army's losses in the battle of encirclement at Uman.[9] It was a major disaster for the Allies.

Not lost on Hitler was the fact that the surface fleet had not accounted for a single ship. By the time PQ17 was sighted, most of the fleet was in Norwegian waters: the *Tirpitz* and *Hipper* were at Trondheim, and the *Luetzow* and *Scheer* were at Narvik. Only the *Scharnhorst* and *Prinz Eugen* were absent. The fleet began its advance on the convoy on July 1 under the command of Adm. Otto Schniewind, who had been the Fleet Commander since Admiral Luetjens went down with the *Bismarck*.[10] The ships had bad luck from the beginning. The *Luetzow* ran aground in heavy fog, and three destroyers hit an uncharted belt of rocks and had to be left behind. Then Hitler and the High Command of the Navy hesitated and did not give the disgusted Schniewind the operational go-ahead until July 4. Even then, the Office of the Chief of Naval Operations admonished him: "Do not hesitate to terminate operations if the situation becomes doubtful. Do not permit an enemy success against the nucleus of our fleet."[11]

Schniewind was at sea for three days. He ventured out into the Arctic Ocean, intercepted radio messages that indicated that the Royal Navy had heavy forces in the area, and, in accordance with his orders, returned to base without firing a shot. This operation, he correctly reported later, had "aptly demonstrated that without some offensive spirit, warlike operations cannot be carried out with hope of success."[12]

The PQ17 disaster forced the Allies to suspend convoy operations to Murmansk and Archangel until October, when the longer polar nights offered the ships better protection. This time, they also sent an aircraft carrier with the escorts. Convoy PQ18 had forty cargo ships and seventy-seven escorts. Stumpff attacked it with everything he had in what was considered one of the fiercest air-sea battles of the war. The *Luftwaffe* suffered heavy losses but sank thirteen merchant ships; the twenty-seven ships that did arrive in Murmansk carried enough materiel to equip an entire Soviet tank army.[13]

PQ18 was the last convoy to come under heavy *Luftwaffe* attack. The Allies invaded North Africa on November 8, and the Ju 88 and He 111 torpedo-bombers were transferred to the Mediterranean. The Allies had learned the lesson of PQ17 well; never again would they send out a convoy without major capital ships and aircraft carriers. As a result, Germany lost the battles of the Murmansk Run. In all, 15,000,000 of the 16,500,000 tons of American supplies dispatched to the Soviet Union reached their destination—most of it by way of Murmansk. These supplies included 13,000 tanks, 135,000 machine guns, tens of thousands of vehicles, and thousands of modern airplanes.[14] Even so, losses continued to mount in the sea lanes to Murmansk. The fifteen ships of convoy QP14 ran into a wolf pack off the coast of Spitsbergen and lost four cargo vessels and an escort. Because of the heavy losses, the Allies sent no further major convoys in 1942. They did, however, try a "Trickle Movement" under which fast merchant ships steamed to Murmansk individually or in pairs; only five of the thirteen ships bound for Russia made it. Ships bound for home did much better; only one of twenty-three westbound ships was sunk.[15]

In summary, from August 1941 to the end of 1942, twenty-one convoys sailed for Russia. Of the 301 ships in these convoys, 248 arrived, and 53 were lost. Of the 232 ships returning home in sixteen convoys, 216 arrived, while 16 were lost.[16]

THE FALL OF GRAND ADMIRAL RAEDER

By the end of 1942, the Murmansk route was losing its importance as the Allies improved the transportation system in Iran and more and more tonnage was shipped to Russia via the less vulnerable Persian Gulf. Even so, the Murmansk Run continued. The next convoy was divided into two parts: JW51A and JW51B. JW51A and its sixteem ships arrived without incident, delivering 100,000 tons of war materiel to Stalin. JW51B, however, sailed from Scotland on December 22 and was intercepted on December 31 by Vice Adm. Oskar Kummetz, the commander of Warship Group 2 and commander in chief of cruisers, who controlled the *Hipper*, the *Luetzow*, and six destroyers.[17] Kummetz had just received an order from Adm. Kurt Fricke, the chief of staff of German naval operations, stating, "Discretion to be exercised in face of enemy of equal strength owing [to the] undesirability of submitting cruisers to major risk."[18] Kummetz interpreted this order to mean that he was supposed to play it completely safe.

The convoy was escorted by the 17th Destroyer Flotilla, five destroyers under Capt. Robert St.V. "Rupert" Sherbrooke, Royal Navy. Also near the convoy were the cruisers *Sheffield* and *Jamaica*, under the command of Rear Adm. Robert L. Burnett, whose task was to provide extra protection to the convoy, just in case the German surface fleet ventured out. The engagement, known as the Battle of the Barents Sea, began at 9:15 A.M., when the German destroyer *Friedrich Eckoldt* opened fire on the British escorts. Admiral Kummetz signaled Berlin that a battle had begun, but then, in accordance with his orders, he did not try to break through the destroyer screen because he would have to place his cruisers at risk to do so. As a result, by 11:00 A.M., the convoy was on the verge of escaping, despite the overwhelming superiority of Kummetz's forces. The admiral seemed to have second thoughts about obeying the timid orders from Berlin and launched an attack with the *Hipper* around 11:15 A.M. By 11:30, the British destroyer *Achates* was on fire and sinking when Admiral Burnett suddenly arrived on the scene with his two cruisers and struck the *Hipper* below the water line with a 6-inch shell. Rather than engage this new enemy, Kummetz broke off the battle (in accordance with orders) at 11:37 A.M. Meanwhile, in the snowy and foggy weather, Capt. Alfred Schemmel, the commander of the German destroyer flotilla, was aboard the *Friedrich Eckoldt*. He decided to join the two large ships in the distance, which he took to be the *Hipper* and one of her escorts. Too late did he realize that the silhouettes were Admiral Burnett's cruisers. The *Eckoldt* was blasted at close quarters by no fewer than seven salvos and sank in the icy water with all hands on board.

Meanwhile, back at the Wolf's Lair, Adolf Hitler was beside himself with worry and anger. He was always extremely nervous when the fleet was at sea, and he was already deeply upset about the 6th Army's situation at Stalingrad. Now he had to wait for hours for word about his warships. Kummetz maintained radio silence as he retreated, which meant that no one knew the status of the ships. As New Year's Eve wore on, worry and anger turned to fury. Hitler lashed out Adm. Theodor Krancke, the naval liaison officer at Rastenburg, who tried unsuccessfully to convince him that Kummetz was keeping silent to avoid giving away his position.[19]

Hitler did not sleep a wink that night. Then, as New Year's Day dawned, he received his first news of the battle from his information bureau, which had received its information from a British news agency. Worse still, the report stated that a strong German naval task force had been checked and driven off by much weaker British escort forces. Furthermore, a German destroyer had been sunk and a cruiser badly damaged, against the loss of a single British destroyer.

When he learned all of this, Hitler became completely furious. Even so, at 5 P.M., he still had not received a word from his own navy. Completely enraged, he called in Krancke and gave him a blistering reprimand, which ended with an announcement: he had decided to scrap the entire surface fleet, which was useless anyway, and to have their big guns converted into coastal defense batteries.

"That would be the cheapest victory Britain could possibly win!" the admiral snapped.

This remark only made Hitler angrier. He repeated his decision and demanded that Admiral Raeder report to him in person. Krancke hurriedly telephoned Raeder, who was not in. Two hours later, Raeder sent word that he was ill and could not appear. Before he saw Hitler, he wanted to know what he had happened and to give Hitler time to cool down.

This Adolf Hitler did not do. When the grand admiral finally arrived at the Wolf's Lair on the evening of January 6, Hitler raved at him for an hour and a half—a ninety-minute monologue of uninterrupted abuse. After this tirade, which Raeder later described as "completely spiteful," the grand admiral asked to speak to Hitler privately. After Keitel and the two stenographers left the room, Erich Raeder asked to be relieved of his command. He was, he said, responsible for the conduct of the navy, and in view of Hitler's opinion of it, he no longer felt he was a suitable officer for this post.

Hitler at once changed his tone. He did not mean to condemn the entire navy, he said, only the heavy ships. He begged Raeder to stay on, but the grand admiral—who considered the surface fleet his life's work—had been too deeply hurt and insulted to even consider it. "My authority has been shaken," he said. "I absolutely decline to remain in office."[20] He asked that the changeover take place on January 30—the tenth anniversary of the Nazi seizure of power—so that it would appear that he had voluntarily stepped down on his own to make room for a younger man. Hitler saw that he could not repair the damage he had done and eventually agreed to Raeder's conditions. The dictator asked only that Raeder suggest two possible successors. He recommended Gen. Adm. Rolf Carls, the commander in chief of Naval Group North, or Karl Doenitz.

Like Raeder himself, Carls was an officer of the old school and a "big ship" man. Predictably, Hitler chose Karl Doenitz. Raeder was given the honorary position of inspector of the navy and retired to Berlin, where he was arrested by the Russians at the end of the war. Doenitz was named grand admiral and commander in chief of the navy on January 30, 1943. He was also given an unofficial token of Hitler's esteem: a check for 300,000 Reichsmarks. He immediately set about "cleaning house" in the navy and getting rid of "Raeder men." Among the first to go was Rolf Carls, who, as fleet commander in the 1930s, had been one of Doenitz's biggest supporters; now, however, he represented a potential threat to the new grand admiral, so he had to go. He was not alone: at least twenty-two admirals were retired within a few weeks of Doenitz's assumption of command of the navy. Other "Raeder men" were transferred away from Berlin. Although these people were generally not promoted again, they were allowed to remain on active duty. Somewhat surprisingly, Adm. Kurt Fricke, the chief of staff of naval operations, was among these officers. He was named commander in chief of Naval Group South.

Doenitz's friends and those considered competent by Doenitz naturally received rewards, promotions, and assignments of greater responsibility. Most—but not all—of these men were in some way associated with the U-boat branch. For example, Vice Adm. Otto Backenkoehler, the chief of the Torpedo Office in the Naval Armaments Office of OKM, was promoted to admiral and named chief of the Naval Armaments Office. Vice Adm. Georg von Friedeburg, the second in command of the U-boat arm, was promoted to admiral and named commander of U-boats.[21] Capt. Eberhard Godt, the chief of U-boat operations, was promoted to rear admiral, as were Capt. Karl Hoffmann and Capt. Ernst Kratzenberg of Doenitz's staff. Hans-Erich Voss, the captain of the heavy cruiser *Prinz Eugen*, was promoted to rear admiral and replaced Krancke as naval representative and liaison officer to Fuehrer Headquarters—a post that would lead to further promotions for Voss. Finally, Doenitz apparently felt that he owed a debt of gratitude to Capt. Erich Schulte-Moenting, the chief of staff to the commander in chief of the navy, for interceding on his behalf with Admiral Raeder. He was not only retained at his post, but was promoted to rear admiral.[22]

Doenitz initially agreed with Hitler that the surface fleet should be disbanded. Upon mature reflection, however, he realized that this move would be a serious mistake. As long as Germany had a fleet "in being," Britain had to keep strong forces available to deal with it, even if it just sat in port. If the fleet were paid off, these forces would be released for use against Germany's ally, Japan; worse still, they could be used as convoy escorts. Hitler was surprised by Doenitz's change of heart. He held to his own position—that the surface fleet was useless—but on February 26, 1943, he gave Doenitz six months to prove him wrong. They would discuss the matter again at the end of that time, Hitler said.

There were no further discussions. Hitler had long considered Karl Doenitz an outstanding example of a good National Socialist officer. As grand admiral, Doenitz was a loyal and often enthusiastic supporter of Adolf Hitler, habitually backing the Fuehrer on every possible occasion, including those which were militarily senseless (so long as the situation did not involve naval units). He also issued propaganda statements echoing Goebbels, Goering, and others; lavishly praised Hitler at every opportunity; called for fanatical resistance; advocated ground offensives in highly inappropriate situations; and made sure that the navy was ideologically "pure" (i.e., pro-Nazi). Whether he knew of the mass murders of the Hitler regime is still the subject of debate, but he did use slave labor in his naval construction programs and was at least outwardly friendly with Heinrich Himmler. If this kind of officer wanted to keep the surface fleet "in being," Hitler was prepared to let the matter slide.

THE DEFEAT OF THE WOLF PACKS

Meanwhile, the wolf packs had returned to the Atlantic. They sank 108 ships (more than a half a million tons) in August 1942 and another 98 ships (485,000 tons) the following month. However, in September, for the first time, a British convoy sailed with an auxiliary aircraft carrier equipped with old Swordfish airplanes. When the Allies constructed enough of these, they would eliminate the gap in the North Atlantic, and there would be little hope for the U-boats. This time had not yet arrived in October 1942, and the German submariners sank 93 more ships (more than 600,000 tons). In November, this figure climbed to 117 ships (700,000 tons), including 15 ships in a single night. With the help of their "milk cows," German undersea raiders were able to roam farther afield than ever before, appearing in places no one suspected they could reach, places where Allied defenses were weak to nonexistent. Lt. Cmdr. Karl-Friedrich Merten in *U-68*, for example, rounded the Cape of Good Hope and penetrated into the Indian Ocean, where he found good hunting and easy prey. On October 8 alone, he sank 4 ships. The next day, he sank two more. His total reached 9 ships (61,600 tons) on this one cruise before he had to return to home base.[23] Lt. Carl Emmermann in *U-172* sank 8 more (59,800 tons) at the same time, and Cmdr. Wolfgang Lueth in *U-181* sank 12 ships (58,381 tons) in a single raid into the Indian Ocean between November 3 and December 2, 1942.[24]

Allied shipping losses declined to 336,000 tons (sixty-one ships) in December, but only because of poor winter weather. The German submarine command entered the fourth year of the war with confidence, despite the fact that it had lost 105 U-boats since the conflict began. January 1943 was also a month of gales and heavy seas, but the U-boats still managed to sink thirty-seven ships (200,000 tons), including eight out of nine ships in a tanker convoy, which were destroyed in a week-long running battle between Trinidad and the Canary Islands. Another 360,000 tons (sixty-three ships) were sunk in February, but with the return of better weather in March, U-boats sank an estimated 780,000 tons of shipping. (Actual Allied losses were only about two-thirds of this figure. This is because it was natural for U-boat captains to overestimate the size of their victims' ships. They were also now having to dive quickly and rarely had a chance to actually observe the results of their attacks. Often, the only indication they had of success was the sound of a detonating torpedo.) Even so, Anglo-American shipping losses were very serious. Between March 17 and 19, convoy SC122 lost eight ships (47,000 tons) out of fifty-one in the convoy. HX229 lost thirteen ships (93,500 tons) out of forty between March 16 and 19, and a delighted Hitler decorated Grand Admiral Doenitz with the Oak Leaves to the Knight's Cross. German casualties had also been high. Nineteen U-boats were lost in February and fifteen in March—more than 13 percent of the total force at sea.[25]

April was another month of hard fighting. The Allies lost sixty-four ships (344,680 tons), but fifteen submarines failed to return. U-boat losses were now on the verge of exceeding production, but Doenitz still escalated the battle. In May 1943, the full weight of Allied technology was at last brought to bear on the U-boat arm. Fifty-eight British and American vessels (299,428 tons) were sunk, but a shocking total of forty-one U-boats were destroyed. No single event, invention, or innovation defeated the wolf packs; rather, they were defeated by a cumulation of new inventions, improved devices, perfected antisubmarine tactics, increasingly experienced Allied officers, sailors, and merchant marines, and a lavish expenditure of Allied industrial and human resources in a concerted crusade to drive them from the sea. Their images were picked up and their positions located by high-frequency direction finders, radar-equipped destroyers, radar-equipped airplanes, sophisticated radio-interception equipment, and all manner of other electronic devices. U-boats were sunk by long-range bombers flying out of surface bases, by catapult-launched fighters, by new and improved Hedgehog depth-charge projectors, by new U.S. and RAF antisubmarine patrols, and by auxiliary aircraft carriers (the "escort carriers"). They were sunk as they maneuvered to attack, they were sunk as they crash-dived, they were sunk when they came up at night to recharge their batteries. They were sunk by bombs, depth-charges, ramming, and combination attacks. U-boats returning to their bases were sunk in the Bay of Biscay by Liberators, Flying Fortresses, Boeings, and Beaufighters. Usually, there were no survivors. For the first time, the previously exemplary morale of the German submariners began to falter.

Admiral Doenitz did not wait until the end of the month to admit defeat. On May 24, he withdrew his decimated wolf packs from the North Atlantic. It is a measure of his influence with Hitler that the Nazi dictator accepted this decision—effectively an admission of a strategic defeat of the first magnitude—without a word of protest or reproach.

Doenitz's strategy for the rest of the war was to (1) build more U-boats; (2) continue the submarine war, mainly in the "softer" sectors, such as the Caribbean or the area southwest of the Azores; and (3) press for and await new scientific developments which would again shift the balance in favor of Germany. He continued to periodically send submarines to the North Atlantic, but never again with appreciable success. U-boats continued to go out and sink enemy ships, but now the seas were almost as dangerous for them as for their targets—and sometimes even more so. From June through August 1943, for example, the Allies lost only sixty freighters but sank seventy-nine U-boats. From May 1943, it was no longer completely accurate to refer to the German submarines as "the U-boat threat." The German submarine—and indeed the entire German Navy—had been reduced to the status of a nuisance weapon. The U-boat threat had been eliminated.

CHAPTER 4

Tunisgrad

Erwin Rommel, the "Desert Fox," had just started to retreat from his catastrophic defeat at El Alamein when another disaster befell the Axis: Allied forces landed on the coast of French North Africa in November 1942 and quickly neutralized French resistance. Rommel and his Afrika Korps were now caught between two fires and were no longer capable of dealing with either. These Allied landings, code-named Operation Torch, set the stage for yet another debacle, this one on the magnitude of Stalingrad. Indeed, the German people privately referred to the ensuing disaster as "Tunisgrad."

OPERATION TORCH

Operation Torch involved three separate but coordinated assaults made by 107,453 soldiers ferried up to 4,500 miles in 111 transports and escorted by more than 200 warships. In accordance with the plan, the Western Task Force, led by U.S. Maj. Gen. George S. Patton Jr., hit the beaches near Casablanca with 40,000 men and 250 tanks and quickly overran French Morocco. Meanwhile, U.S. Maj. Gen. Lloyd R. Fredendall's Central Task Force seized Oran, and the Eastern Task Force under U.S. Maj. Gen. Charles W. Ryder went ashore near Algiers.[1] The map on page 51 shows the Allied landings and the subsequent German reaction.

The French Army in North Africa—which numbered 150,000 men in fourteen divisions—outnumbered the Allies by more than 40,000 men but offered little more than token resistance, which ended on November 11. Then, on November 15, Gen. Sir Kenneth A. H. Anderson's 1st British Army began to advance from Algiers to Tunis, 380 miles away, to complete the conquest of French North Africa and cut Rommel's escape route.

The Germans had no troops in French North Africa and, unlike Mussolini, did not expect the invasion armada to land here. The *Abwehr*, the German intelligence service, wrongly (as usual) expected the landings to take place in the south of France or at Dakar in western Africa. There was panic in Berlin and Rastenburg when the truth became known. When the Allies landed, Germany did not have a single ground combat soldier in Tunisia, and Rommel's rear was completely undefended.

The terrain between Algiers and Tunis differs from that of the Western Desert. The Atlas Mountains and their subsidiary ranges stretch from Morocco to Tunis and generally run quite near the coast. The land is broken, rugged, and occasionally forested; the climate is wet; the passes between the mountains are few and easy to defend; and the heavily cultivated coastal valleys become impassable to vehicles in times of heavy rain. The map on page 52 shows the main surface features of the Tunisian Bridgehead. In addition, Tunisia was almost devoid of good roads in 1942, and winter is the rainy season in the Mediterranean. It was raining when the Allies began their advance to the east on November 15, and the drive on Tunis soon deteriorated to a crawl and a struggle against the elements.

THE GERMAN BUILDUP AND THE OCCUPATION OF VICHY FRANCE

Rommel immediately grasped the significance of the landings. That night, November 8–9, in the camp of the 164th Light Afrika Division, in a state of great bitterness, he gave voice to his fears. "The campaign in Africa is lost," he bluntly told Maj. Gen. Carl-Hans Lungershausen. He went on to say that if Mussolini and Hitler did not realize it and take immediate actions to save Panzer Army Afrika, it would be captured, and there would be nothing left with which to defend Italy from the next invasion.[2]

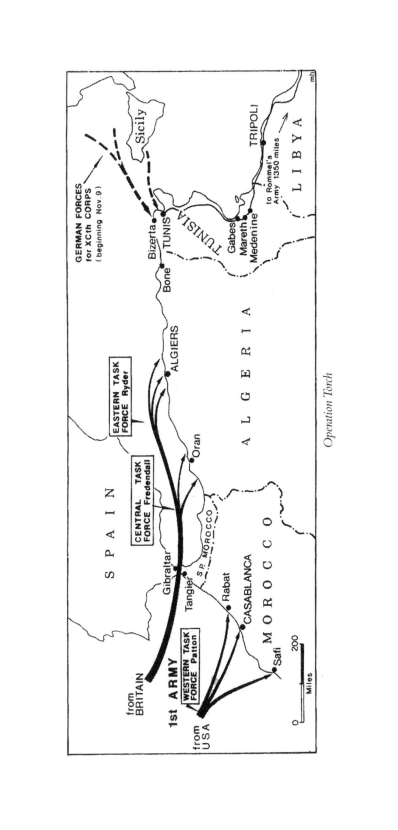

Operation Torch

Tunisia

The Desert Fox suggested an African Dunkirk: every possible man must be evacuated to defend Italy and southern France against an Allied invasion of southern Europe. Hitler's reaction was just the opposite. On the day of the landings, he telephoned Field Marshal Albert Kesselring, the supreme commander in the Germans' southern theater (*Oberbefehlshaber Sued*, or OB South), at his headquarters near Rome and asked him what he could send to Tunisia. Kesselring replied that other than a few paratroopers, all he had was his own staff company. "Send everything you can across," Hitler ordered.[3]

Hitler was furious at the token nature of French resistance. Realizing that he could expect little more effort if the Allies landed in France itself, he signaled Paris and instructed Field Marshal Gerd von Rundstedt, now the commander in chief in the west (formerly Army Group D), to occupy Vichy France.

At 7 A.M. on the morning of November 11, the German 1st Army and Army Detachment Felber (formerly LXXXIII Corps), under the command of Col. Gen. Johannes Blaskowitz and Gen. of Infantry Hans Felber, respectively, crossed the border. Except for the rebuilt 7th Panzer and 1st SS Panzer Division, their order of battle was not impressive, but the 100,000-man army of Vichy France did not resist. That afternoon, the 4th Italian Army began to move into the French Alps, while smaller Italian forces sailed for the island of Corsica. By the morning of November 14, the operation was complete, except in the Toulon sector. Here Admiral Raeder made a special arrangement with the French Navy. Toulon remained the center of a neutral zone, and the French fleet refrained from all hostile acts against the Axis. This uneasy stalemate existed until November 27, when, on the orders of Adolf Hitler, Sepp Dietrich's I SS Panzer Corps crossed into the neutral zone. In response, the French fleet scuttled itself, sinking sixty-one ships totaling 225,000 tons.[4]

On November 11, while Rundstedt's troops were sweeping through Vichy France unopposed, the "Green Devils" of Lt. Col. Walter Koch's 5th Parachute Regiment boarded forty Ju 52s at the *Luftwaffe* bases in Naples and Trapani and flew toward Tunis. There was high tension as they approached the airfield because no one knew what kind of reception they would meet. How would the French forces in Tunisia react to the occupation of Vichy France? Thousands of French troops were dug in and ready all around the airfield, but they did nothing.

Meanwhile, Gen. of Panzer Troops Walter Nehring, the former commander of the Afrika Korps, received orders to take charge of the defense of Tunisia.[5] Although he had not yet fully recovered from the injuries he had suffered at El Alamein and the wound in his right arm was still open, he immediately headed for the front. When he arrived, he found that his entire command consisted of Koch's regiment, Major Witzig's 11th Parachute Engineer Battalion (which had just landed at Bizerta), and a few infantrymen who had been brought in by sea. Nehring's corps headquarters (the XC) did not exist. His entire staff consisted of himself and his aide. For transport, he had to rely on the taxicabs of Tunis.

In the meantime, two top diplomats arrived from the Wilhelmstrasse: Ambassador Rudolf Rahn and Consul-General Friedrich Moellhausen. Rahn, now the "political representative" to Tunis, met with Adm. Jean Esteva, the French governor-general, and persuaded him to maintain strict neutrality. In accord with this agreement, Esteva ordered Gen. Georges Barre, the French ground forces commander in Tunisia, to withdraw his division from the airport area, and the German buildup continued in relative safety. The next day, German forces starting landing in force at Bizerta. Following orders from Esteva, the French port commander, who had 14,000 men at his disposal, did nothing to stop them.

Meanwhile, Nehring asked Barre to confer with him in Tunis, but the French general refused. He wanted to speak with Gen. Alphonse Juin, his superior in Algiers, before he took any action. Nehring, however, was anxious to meet the Allies as far west as possible, so at 1 P.M., Moellhausen tried to get Barre to clear the routes leading to Algeria. Barre did not refuse, but he did not agree either. Since every delay benefited the Allies, Ambassador Rahn gave Barre just six hours to comply with Nehring's request. If he did not, the ambassador warned, Nehring would have to take military action. Still the French did nothing. At 11 P.M., the *Luftwaffe* bombed what was thought to be Barre's command post. German artillery opened up twenty minutes later, and Koch's paratroopers began to advance. The French general ordered his men to return fire, and the French and Germans were in combat against each other after an interval of more than two years.

Despite the odds against them, Koch's elite paratroopers soon defeated the poorly armed and ill-equipped Frenchmen, who retreated to the west toward the Americans and British. By the middle of the month, Nehring's troops had occupied all of the key points in all of the major cities of Tunisia, including the vital ports of Tunis and Bizerta. By now, there were more than 5,000 German troops in Tunisia, with the equivalent of a new battalion arriving every day. The first tanks of the 10th Panzer Division were on their way from France, and the Germans had established a secure base along the coast and air superiority over western Tunisia. Meanwhile, the British 1st Parachute Battalion (the "Red Devils") seized Beja, a key road junction about ninety miles west of Tunis, and linked up with Barre's division, which was retreating from the east. Because of rainy weather and poor roads, the main British assault forces were unable to cover the distance from Algiers to Tunis before Nehring barred the road to the Tunisian capital.

The critical northern sector of the Tunisian bridgehead was entrusted to Col. Walter Barenthin, a famous parachute engineer who controlled the Barenthin Glider Regiment, the bulk of Koch's regiment, Witzig's 11th Parachute Engineer Battalion, and various miscellaneous units. Barenthin was attacked by Anderson's vanguard, which consisted of the British 78th Infantry Division with elements of the British 6th Armoured and U.S. 1st Armored Divisions in support. After Barenthin repulsed several attacks during the last week in November, Lt. Col. John K. Waters's battalion of the U.S. 1st Armored Division broke through Barenthin's thin front and overran Djedeida, the forward German airfield on the road to Bizerte. The ground here was too wet for the airplanes to take off, and fourteen Messerschmitt fighters and twenty-four Ju 52s were destroyed, against a loss of two Americans killed. Only a few Germans escaped the disaster. The U.S. armor pushed to within six miles of Tunis, and on November 30, Eisenhower announced to Washington that the fall of Tunis and Bizerta was imminent. He was premature. Nehring checked the American Stuart tanks with a battery of 88-millimeter guns—his last reserves.[6] After losing twenty tanks, the Americans retreated to Djedeida.

The Allies made several attempts to take Tunis and break Nehring's line, but they failed each time. Finally, much to Nehring's relief, strong tank elements of Lt. Gen. Wolfgang Fischer's 10th Panzer Division arrived in Tunis and Bizerta on November 29. Also off-loaded from these ships were the first three PzKw VI Tiger tanks of Major Luder's 501st Heavy Panzer Battalion. The Tigers were superior to any armored vehicle yet seen in Africa. Modeled on the Soviet tanks, the Tigers weighed more than fifty tons and had a very effective long-barreled 88-millimeter main battle gun. No Allied tank could match it in one-on-one situations.

By the end of November, Nehring had reorganized his command. His northern flank was now the responsibility of the newly formed Division von Broich (under Col. Baron Friedrich von Broich); his center belonged to the 10th Panzer Division; and his left was held by the Italian Superga Division.[7]

Now that he had superiority in armor, Nehring decided to expand the dangerously shallow bridgehead by launching an offensive of his own. On December 1, Colonel Koch struck at the Allied spearheads in the Tebourba sector, while General Fischer launched a brilliant counterattack in the Djedeida area, where the Allied vanguard barely escaped encirclement. Anderson's forces lost more than 1,000 men captured, 29 guns and 40 mortars captured or destroyed, 55 tanks destroyed, and 300 other motorized vehicles captured or destroyed.[8] The German advance could not be stopped until after Fischer captured the critical Djebel el Ahmera position, known to the Arabs as Red Hill and soon to be commonly known to the Allies as Longstop Hill. Although its 900-foot elevation was not as impressive, it was nevertheless of critical military importance because it barred the Allies' path down the Medierda Valley. Without Longstop Hill, Tunis—which was only twenty-five miles away—could not be taken.

By the first week of December, Nehring had about 17,000 Germans and 12,000 Italians. He had held the Tunisian bridgehead, but only barely. Nehring also saw no prospects for a long-term Axis victory in Tunisia and felt that the best course of action would be to abandon Africa altogether. Because of this opinion, Capt. Alfred Ingomar Berndt, Goebbels's agent in North Africa, denounced him as a defeatist, and Goebbels called him "an outspoken pessimist,"[9] and Kesselring complained that he "drew the blackest conclusions" from the American raid on the Djedeida airfield on November 26.[10]

Kesselring—always an extreme optimist—requested that a new panzer army headquarters be established, which meant that Nehring could be superseded by a higher-ranking officer. Hitler agreed and went one step further by relieving Nehring of his command on December 4. The XC Corps was upgraded to the 5th Panzer Army, and Nehring was sent to the Eastern Front and replaced by Juergen von Arnim.

THE GREAT RETREAT

Field Marshal Erwin Rommel was desperately trying to get the remnants of his army out of Egypt. He realized that he had to reach Mersa el Brega on the Gulf of Sirte before Montgomery did; otherwise, he would be trapped in the Cyrenaican bulge, just as Field Marshal Wavell had trapped and destroyed the Italian 10th Army in the winter campaign of 1940–41. Rommel was fortunate that Montgomery pursued him in a hesitant, almost leisurely fashion—or else he probably would not have been able to save more than a small fragment of his army.

As they fell back across western Egypt and into Libya, Rommel and his men ate half-rations, endured attack after attack from the fighter-bombers of the RAF, and engaged in bitter rearguard actions with the pursuing columns of the British 8th Army. Physically and mentally exhausted, they passed familiar places: Mersa Matruh, Sidi Barrani, Sollum, Halfaya Pass, Capuzzo, and Bardia were all abandoned, never to be recaptured, and memories of past victories came back to haunt them. During the night of November 12–13, they gave up Tobruk, the scene of one of their greatest victories. Fortunately for the army, Maj. Gen. Karl Buelowius, who had replaced the wounded Colonel Hecker as chief of the panzer army engineers, proved to be a genius in the retreat. He blew up the Coastal Road wherever it crossed difficult terrain, destroyed bridges, scattered mines everywhere, and placed booby traps in the most unsuspected places. Simply adjusting a picture, for example, could cause an entire house to disintegrate in a deafening explosion. As a result, the British became more and more cautious, which was all that saved Panzer Army Afrika. On November 15, all of the German divisions except the 90th Light were immobilized because they were totally out of diesel and gasoline. They remained immobile throughout November 16 and could easily have been destroyed by an aggressive enemy. They did not move until November 17, when they finally received an issue of fuel.

After abandoning Benghazi on the morning of November 19, Panzer Army Afrika installed itself behind the Mersa el Brega position, more than 600 miles from Gabes, the southern anchor of 5th Panzer Army. This excellent line was behind a 10-mile-long salt marsh, which Montgomery would find very difficult to outflank. By now, Rommel had retreated 800 miles since El Alamein, and it was the British who had outrun their supply lines. The pursuit temporarily came to a halt.

On November 26, Rommel turned temporary command of the army over to Gen. of Panzer Troops Gustav Fehn, who had assumed command of the Afrika Korps on November 13, and flew to East Prussia, confident that Hitler's failure to understand the true situation in North Africa was because he had been receiving overly optimistic reports from Kesselring and the Italians.[11]

Rommel believed that once he briefed Hitler on the true state of affairs, he would draw the correct military conclusions and accept Rommel's position—that North Africa must be evacuated—as long-range policy. Little did Rommel know that his status at Fuehrer Headquarters had changed. He was no longer the conquerer of Benghazi and Tobruk or the hero of Cherbourg, Battleaxe, Knightsbridge, the Gazala Line, and a dozen other hard-fought battles. Now he was just another professional soldier who had been defeated and thus had let Hitler down.

Rommel arrived at Rastenburg at 4 P.M. on November 28 and was ushered into Hitler's presence an hour later. "How dare you leave your theater of command without my permission!" Hitler snapped as soon as he saw the Desert Fox. Rommel ignored the warning signs and calmly briefed the silent Hitler on the realities of the military situation in Tunisia and Libya. He concluded that the abandonment of North Africa must be accepted as long-term strategic policy.

At this, Hitler exploded. For the first time, Rommel was treated to the same kind of abuse that Keitel experienced almost every day. He screamed in fury, called Rommel a defeatist, and accused his men of cowardice. He had shot generals who had made the same sort of suggestions about the Eastern Front, Hitler bellowed; he would not yet do this to Rommel, but he had better be careful. Rommel ignored this threat and proceeded to try to explain the reasons for his defeat at El Alamein.

Hermann Goering, who was also present, played the role of Hitler's mouthpiece, and the two veteran politicians verbally ganged up on the soldier. Rommel still could not be intimidated and again asked to be allowed to withdraw the panzer army to Italy so that he could defend the continent against Eisenhower's anticipated invasion.

"I no longer want to hear such rubbish from your lips," Hitler responded very coldly. He stated catagorically that Tunis would be defended just as Stalingrad would be. The invading Allied armies would be defeated in Tunisia, not in Sicily. Rommel tried to argue, but Hitler cut him off again. North Africa would not be evacuated, he ordered. Out of control again, Hitler raved on and on about how his decision to hold at all costs had saved the Eastern Front in 1941–42, and now he expected his orders to be ruthlessly obeyed in North Africa as well.

Rommel interrupted and asked whether it was better to lose Tripoli or the Afrika Korps. Hitler replied that the Afrika Korps did not matter. It would have to fight to the bitter end. Instead of being cowed, Field Marshal Rommel invited Hitler or some of his entourage to come to North Africa to show them how to do it. "Go!" Hitler roared, now completely unglued. "I have other things to do than to talk to you!"

Rommel saluted and walked out. Hitler, perhaps realizing that he had gone too far, came running after him. He put his arm around Rommel's shoulder and asked the Desert Fox to excuse him because he was very nervous at that time. He assured Rommel that everything would be all right. He asked the field marshal to visit him the following day, when they would have a calm discussion of the matter. He added that it was unthinkable that the Afrika Korps would be destroyed.[12]

As promised, Hitler was in a better mood the next day. He turned to Goering and ordered him to see to all of Rommel's supply needs. This opened up a trying three days for the field marshal, in which he had to put up with Goering's alternating flattery, megalomania, and verbal abuse. Goering, in fact, had the mistaken impression that there were easy laurels to be gathered in Africa and had ambitions of replacing Rommel with one of his own officers. Rommel later called Goering his bitterest enemy. They met with Mussolini and Kesselring, but Goering did nothing to help the Afrika Korps and agreed with Kesselring that a further retreat was out of the question. Erwin Rommel was glad to return to the front.

ENTER GENERAL ARNIM

In the meantime, Juergen von Arnim arrived in Tunisia.[13]

Arnim distinguished himself as a divisional commander on the Eastern Front in the fall of 1941. He fought in the last stages of the Battle of Kiev, in the Battle of Vyazma-Bryansk, and in the early stages of the drive on Moscow. In early November, he was promoted to general of panzer troops and was given command of the XXXIX Panzer Corps, then in the vicinity of Tikhvin. Arnim directed a step-by-step retreat through a frozen wilderness in temperatures as low as sixty degrees Fahrenheit below zero, in the face of massive Soviet attacks. Casualties were heavy, but Arnim managed to install his corps behind the Volkhov River, which he held into 1942.

Arnim's last major assignment on the Eastern Front was to rescue the German garrison at Kholm, which he accomplished just in the nick of time on May 1. After that, his sector was relatively inactive until November 30, 1942, when he received a call from Maj. Gen. Rudolf Schmundt, the chief of the Army Personnel Office (*Heerespersonalamt*, or HPA), an office in which Arnim had many friends. Arnim was ordered to report to Fuehrer Headquarters in East Prussia for an important new assignment.

When he arrived at the Rastenburg airstrip on December 4, Schmundt and Jodl informed him that he had been promoted to colonel general and named commander of the newly created 5th Panzer Army. He was introduced to his new chief of staff and deputy commander, recently promoted Lt. Gen. Heinz Ziegler, whom he had never met before, and then was briefed on the situation in North Africa and Tunisia by Keitel and Hitler. As usual, Hitler was full of promises. He pledged to send Arnim three panzer divisions and three motorized divisions, including the elite Hermann Goering Panzer Division. He also promised the new colonel general that he would receive plenty of supplies. His mission was to eventually drive the Allies from Algeria and French Morocco.

When Arnim arrived in Tunisia on December 8, Fischer and the 10th Panzer Division were already engaged in pushing back the Allies to enlarge the bridgehead, and by December 10, the British 1st Army had lost 41 guns, 72 tanks, and 1,100 men taken prisoner. Combat Command B (CCB) of the U.S. 1st Armored Division lost 18 tanks, 41 guns, and 150 vehicles—all mired in the mud and left behind. On December 13, Arnim signaled Berlin that the Allied forces in the Tebourba-Mateur area had been more or less destroyed and that the 5th Panzer Army was going over to the defensive. He initially retained Nehring's dispositions and reinforced the Italians with the German 47th Grenadier Regiment.

On the night of December 22–23, General Anderson launched a major attack on Longstop Hill in preparation for a decisive offensive against Tunis. Anderson assigned this task to the just-arrived British 1st Guards Brigade and the 1st Battalion of the U.S. 18th Infantry Regiment. The 1st Guards included the 2nd Battalion of the Coldstream Guards and the Grenadier Guards, two of the oldest units in the British Army, with traditions dating back nearly 300 years.

The struggle was bitter, and the assault commander, Maj. A. P. S. Chichester, was mortally wounded; nevertheless, the Coldstream Guards took the hill from a battalion of Col. Rudolf Lang's 69th Panzer Grenadier Regiment of the 10th Panzer Division. Significantly, the Guards took only a few prisoners, most of whom were wounded—an indication that German resistance was far from broken. It began to rain at 1 A.M., and two hours later, it began to pour, just as the 1st Battalion of the U.S. 18th Infantry Regiment began to arrive to relieve the Coldstream Guards—a tricky operation in the best of times, but especially at night, in the rain, and with green troops (as the Americans were). The relief had only just been effected when Lang launched his counterattack, sweeping the inexperienced Americans from the hill. The commander of the 1st Guards ordered the Coldstream Guards to retake the position and reinforced them with elements of the 9th Armoured Brigade, but by now, the rain had turned the Tunisian soil into an extremely sticky mud. The Germans, drawing on their experiences in Russia, had modified their tanks and tracked vehicles, while the British and American tank tracks were still too narrow, and either bogged down or threw a track in heavy mud. As a result, no Allied tanks or mechanized vehicles could get closer than 3,000 yards to the hill, and the attack failed.

The main attack of the British V Corps also failed. In the "bloody djebels," the German paratroopers took every advantage of the excellent defensive terrain and shot Gen. Charles Allfrey's spearheads to pieces. The Hampshires, for example, went into action with 800 men and returned with 6 officers and 194 men—100 of whom had not even been engaged. The rain and supply problems also had a paralyzing effect on operations.[14]

To get a better grasp on the situation, Eisenhower went forward himself. He recalled:

> Rain fell constantly. We went out personally to inspect the countryside over which the troops would have to advance, and while doing so, I observed an incident which, as much as anything else, I think convinced me of the hopelessness of an attack. About thirty feet off the road, in a field that appeared to be covered with winter wheat, a motorcycle had become stuck in the mud. Four soldiers were struggling to extricate it, but in spite of their most strenuous efforts succeeded only in getting themselves mired in the sticky clay. . . . We went back to headquarters, and I directed the attack to be indefinitely postponed. It was a bitter decision.[15]

Elsewhere, Rommel was having his own problems. For a variety of reasons, the Italians, Goering, and Kesselring were all intriguing to get rid of him, but he continued to be as outspoken as ever. Rommel's supply staff and Arnim's staff got together and, on January 8, estimated that it would take 150,000 tons of supplies per month to keep both armies supplied in the Tunisian bridgehead. Four days later, Kesselring told Hitler that OB South could supply the two armies with 60,000 tons of supplies per month. Apparently, neither he nor Hitler thought to compare this figure to the demand.[16]

Montgomery, in the meantime, had reestablished his supply lines, replenished his reserves, and attacked the Mersa el Brega Line on December 15. His plan was to pin down Rommel's front with two divisions while Freyberg's 2nd New Zealand Division swung far to the south in order to get behind Rommel and reach the Coastal Road in his rear, cutting off the entire Panzer Army Afrika. Rommel's reconnaissance airplanes spotted the maneuver, however, and the Desert Fox managed to execute another skillful withdrawal, this one with the approval of Commando Supremo, which was justifiably concerned that the nonmotorized (or "marching") infantry might be captured. It was not, and

Rommel fell back to Buerat (200 miles east of Tripoli), which Hitler ordered him to defend to the last. The Italians succeeded in getting Hitler to change his mind, and Commando Supremo even agreed to let Rommel retreat to the Mareth Line, the old French fortifications just across the Tunisian frontier, provided he delayed the Allies here for two months. Rommel refused to guarantee this, but he did send Col. Hans-Georg Hildebrandt's 21st Panzer Division to Tunisia to help Arnim repulse any Allied attempt to reach the coast before Panzer Army Afrika could enter the bridgehead. This is exactly what the Allies had in mind.

Stretching south of Tunis and running generally parallel to the coast toward Gafsa is a mountain chain, the Eastern Dorsal, which reaches elevations of 4,500 feet and is especially abrupt and rugged on its eastern face. To traverse this barrier, a general needed to control the openings in the mountain wall: the Maknassy Gap, Faid Pass, and the Fondouk and Pichon defiles. If Rommel were not to be denied entrance into the Tunisian bridgehead, the Axis would have to control at least one of these major passes.

During December, Nehring and later Arnim had been forced to entrust their southern flank to the unreliable Italian Superga Division. In early January, three French divisions, reinforced with the British 6th Armoured Division, all under Gen. Alphonse Juin, began an offensive against the Superga. By January 14, they had pushed the Italians back and had occupied the entire Western Dorsal range—including the two main passes, Sbiba and Kasserine—and had seized most of the Eastern Dorsal mountain range, putting the Allies in a position to push on to the coast, cut off Rommel from Tunisia, and isolate Panzer Army Afrika.

Accordingly, on the fourteenth, Arnim ordered a limited objective attack, code-named Operation *Eilbote* ("Express Messenger"), to restore the situation. By this time, he had been reinforced with Col. Friedrich Weber's 334th Infantry Division and elements of the Hermann Goering Panzer Division. For the operation, Arnim assembled a battle group consisting of elements of the 334th Infantry and 10th Panzer Divisions, plus the 501st Heavy Panzer Battalion, which included seventeen Tiger tanks. The battle began on January 18. The British generally held their positions, but the ill-equipped French were forced back. Arnim's forces recaptured the Fondouk Pass, took 4,000 prisoners, and destroyed or captured 24 tanks, 55 guns, 27 antitank guns, and 228 vehicles. Arnim did not break off the offensive until the night of January 23–24, and only then because of supply shortages.

Meanwhile, the 21st Panzer Division had arrived in southern Tunisia. On January 30, Arnim threw it into a surprise attack on the Faid Pass, where it surrounded and overwhelmed the French garrison, capturing 1,047 men, 25 armored cars, and 15 antitank guns in the process. Colonel Hildebrandt then successfully beat back an attempt by the U.S. 1st Armored Division to retake the pass. A few days later, Arnim launched another surprise attack against the French, which had been reinforced with elements of the U.S. II Corps, and scored yet another local victory. A French brigade was destroyed, more than 1,000 French soldiers were captured, and the U.S. 168th Infantry Regiment of the U.S. 34th Infantry Division lost nearly 1,100 men. Arnim had thus secured his left flank and significantly enlarged the Tunisian bridgehead, just as Rommel was about to arrive with the bulk of his army.

The last phase of the war in Libya began on January 15, 1943, when Montgomery forced Rommel out of his Buerat positions and began his drive on Tripoli. Rommel fell back toward the Mareth Line, and on January 19, Buelowius blew up the city's port installations and blocked the harbor. Montgomery accepted the city's surrender on January 23, as the remnants of Panzer Army Afrika retreated toward the Tunisian border. The last German rear guard crossed the Tunisian frontier on February 12, 1943. A page in history had turned. Italian North Africa no longer existed.

"UNCONDITIONAL SURRENDER"

Several days earlier, on January 14, another momentous event took place when the Casablanca Conference convened at Anfa, a suburb four miles south of the French Moraccan city. At this meeting, the Allies adopted the peripheral (i.e., Mediterranean) strategy favored by Churchill and Gen. Sir Alan Brooke, the chief of the Imperial General Staff, over the direct-approach strategy favored by the chief of staff of the U.S. Army, Gen. George C. Marshall, whose plan for an invasion of France in 1943 was scrubbed in favor of an invasion of Sicily. On January 24, as the conference was winding down, President Roosevelt staged a media event during which he told reporters: "Prime Minister Churchill and I have determined that we will accept nothing less than the unconditional surrender of Germany, Italy and Japan." He went on to suggest to one correspondent that this conference might be called the "Unconditional Surrender Conference."

As his less astute colleague rattled on, Churchill sat there stunned. Roosevelt had not bothered to inform him that he was going to make this announcement. Did the American president have any idea what the implications of his remarks would be?

Apparently not. As historian Charles Wilmot later wrote,

> To those whose minds ran along these lines, "Unconditional Surrender" seemed to be an appropriate demand to make of an enemy who waged "Total War." This point of view was not unreasonable in the light of past experience, but it was one thing to form this resolve in secret for ultimate enforcement; it was quite another to proclaim it to the enemy in advance.
>
> By doing this, the Anglo-Saxon powers denied themselves any freedom of diplomatic maneuver and denied the German people any avenue of escape from Hitler. Ten months before Casablanca, Goebbels had written . . . "The more the English prophesy a disgraceful peace for Germany, the easier it is for me to toughen and harden German resistance." After Casablanca, Goebbels had delivered into his hand a propaganda weapon of incalculable power.[17]

Gen. Albert C. Wedemeyer, the chief of the War Plans Office and perhaps America's greatest strategic thinker at the time, agreed. Later, he wrote, "Our demand for unconditional surrender naturally increased the enemy's will to resist and forced even Hitler's worst enemies to continue fighting to save their country. The courage of despair imbued the German armed forces with a heroic spirit until the very end."[18]

The Roosevelt pronouncement undoubtedly cut the ground out from under the German resistance, which was even now plotting to assassinate Hitler and overthrow the Nazi regime. Gen. of Infantry Georg Thomas, the chief of the economic branch of OKW, for example, refused to play any further role in the conspiracy on the grounds that it no longer made any sense.[19] The unconditional surrender declaration also undercut the Italian dissidents in Rome, who were preparing to overthrow Mussolini and take Italy out of the war. It also had its effect on the *Landser*, the ordinary German soldier. "Unless those terms are softened," Brooke told Churchill, "the German Army will fight with the ferocity of cornered rats."[20]

Prophetic words indeed, as the U.S. forces at Kasserine Pass were about to find out.

THE BATTLE OF KASSERINE PASS

The arrival of Field Marshal Rommel's Panzer Army Afrika fundamentally changed the situation in North Africa, if only temporarily. For the moment, there were two Axis armies in Tunisia and only one Allied army (the British 1st). Montgomery's 8th Army had advanced 1,500 miles since November and, because of its logistical problems, would not be ready for another major offensive for some time. Therefore, Rommel reasoned, it would be possible for the two Axis armies to join forces, crush Anderson's army, and perhaps even conquer Algeria and Morocco before Montgomery could intervene. More likely, he felt he could at least defeat Anderson and enlarge the Tunisian bridgehead. With this in mind, he met with Kesselring, Italian Gen. Giovanni Messe, and Juergen von Arnim at the *Luftwaffe* base at Rennouch, Tunisia, on February 9.[21]

Arnim and Rommel had last met in 1925, when they were both captains. They had not liked each other then, and now they could barely stand each other. Arnim was a stiff, aristocrat Prussian and the product of a long line of soldiers. Rommel was the descendant of a lower middle class family from Swabia in southern Germany and was the son and grandson of schoolteachers. In addition, Rommel was outspoken (sometimes to the point of tactlessness), and despite the fact that he was three years younger than Arnim, Rommel was very much his senior in rank—a fact that provoked jealousy in the aristocratic, snobbish, and class-conscious older man.

Strategically, Field Marshal Kesselring was thinking along the same lines as Rommel. His plan envisioned the total destruction of the Americans. According to Kesselring, Rommel would attack the Americans to the south at the oasis town of Gafsa, while Arnim would do the same to the north at Sbeitla. Once through the mountain passes to the east, the German armor would sweep north, heading for the port of Bone on the Mediterranean Sea. At best, this operation would result in the total destruction of Anderson's army; at the very least, it would give Germany a major victory—something it badly needed after Stalingrad.

Arnim also wanted to go on the offensive, but not on the scale envisioned by Kesselring and Rommel. Finally, a compromise was reached, by which two virtually independent operations would be conducted: Arnim in the north would launch *Fruehlingswind* ("Spring Wind") against Sidi Bou Zid, while Rommel would conduct *Morganluft* ("Morning Wind"), an advance along the Gafsa-Feriana-Kasserine line.

The details of the offensive were worked out shortly thereafter. According to Rommel, the final plan called for Arnim to push through Faid Pass to Sidi Bou Zid to complete his hold on the Eastern Dorsal. In the initial attack, the 10th and 21st Panzer Divisions would be under the command of General Ziegler. Once he cleared the Faid area, Arnim would return the 21st Panzer Division to Rommel, along with the 10th Panzer Division and the 501st Heavy Panzer Battalion. Arnim was then to drive northward from Pichon, while Rommel was to strike at Gafsa-Tozeur, destroying the U.S. II Corps and possibly exploiting his attack as far as Tebessa. Arnim, however, wanted only to strengthen his hold on the Eastern Dorsal from the Pichon defile to the Maizila Pass. No agreement was reached, but both Rommel and Kesselring thought that they were all in full agreement and that the larger solution had been adopted.

Because of continuing heavy rain, Arnim's offensive was postponed until February 14, and Rommel's attack was rescheduled to begin the next day. In all, the combined Axis strike forces totaled 100,000 men: 74,000 Germans and 26,000 Italians. They had fewer than 300 tanks. The U.S. 1st Armored Division alone had 300 tanks.[22]

At 4 A.M. on Sunday, February 14, two battle groups of the 10th Panzer Division—well supported by Stuka dive-bombers and Messerschmitt fighters and spearheaded by the Tigers of the 501st Heavy Panzer Battalion—roared through Faid Pass and struck Brig. Gen. Raymond E. McQuillan's Combat Command A (CCA) of the U.S. 1st Armored Division and Colonel Drake's 168th Infantry Regiment. The first American armor they met was Colonel Waters's battalion, but the 37-millimeter guns of his Stuart tanks were useless against the 75-

millimeter and 88-millimeter guns of Arnim's PzKw IVs and Tigers. The American battalion was quickly smashed, and Waters, who was the son-in-law of General Patton, was a fugitive, as was most of his unit.

As the panzers advanced, panic seized some of the American units. The 2nd Battalion of the 168th Infantry lost more than half of its 600 men. The panzer grenadiers overran the headquarters of the 168th Infantry Regiment, capturing Colonel Drake and most of his staff. General McQuillan was slow to react. Almost five hours after the German attack began, he threw the 2nd Battalion of the 1st Armored Regiment into the battle. Soon forty-four of its fifty-one Shermans were destroyed. These thirty-ton tanks had a fatal flaw: they had a thinly protected gasoline engine, and one shot from the experienced panzer troops could turn them into blazing coffins. By the end of the battle, the American forces had been slaughtered. The 168th Infantry Regiment had started the battle with 189 officers and 3,728 men; when it was over, it had only 50 officers and 1,000 men left, and one battalion had not even been engaged. Two supporting artillery battalions were also overrun. CCA had lost 52 officers and 1,526 men, including 3 colonels missing and presumed dead. Between Faid Pass and Sbeitla lay forty-four burning tanks, fifty-nine halftracks, twenty-six guns, and a number of trucks.

At dawn the following day, Maj. Gen. Orlando Ward, the commander of the 1st Armored, launched an ill-conceived counterattack with the bulk of his reserve: Col. Robert I. Stack's Combat Command C (CCC), spearheaded by Lt. Col. Jim Alger's armored battalion of fifty-four Shermans. CCC was initially pounded by the Stukas, which severely disrupted the American attack. It did not get started again until 12:40 P.M., when it advanced in parade-ground formation. Again it was attacked by the Stukas; then it ran into a pincer attack and was caught between the 10th and 21st Panzer Divisions, which struck with almost 100 tanks. Colonel Alger's Sherman was knocked out, and he was taken prisoner. Stack's infantry fought well, but by 6 P.M., it was also in retreat. Alger's battalion had only four tanks left. The survivors of CCC just barely escaped to Djebel Hamra.

Meanwhile, at dusk, Rommel's forces moved forward, led by Col. Otto Menton's 288th Special Purposes Group. The group had originally been trained for duty in Iran but had been attached to the 90th Light Division instead. Menton struck toward the oasis of Gafsa but found it abandoned, signaling back to Rommel that the U.S. II Corps was retreating. An excited Desert Fox immediately telephoned Arnim and outlined his new plan. He would push on to the next village, Feriana, where the road forked and gave him two alternatives: he could strike north to Tebessa in Algeria or northeast through Thelepte to Kasserine, where he could link up with the 5th Panzer Army driving from Sbeitla. Then there was a chance that they could push on as far as Bone and the coast, crushing the Allies. Thinking he had Arnim's full support, Rommel ordered Menton to send a heavy reconnaissance force, backed by assault guns, toward Feriana. He was to probe ahead of the village, if possible, so that Rommel could see which route was best suited for his daring new plan.

On the other side of the lines, Anderson authorized Gen. Lloyd Fredendall, the commander of the U.S. II Corps, to withdraw. The American corps commander ordered Colonel Stark, the commander of the 26th Infantry Regiment of the 1st Infantry Division, to cover the retreat of the 1st Armored Division and delay the Germans for at least twelve hours. The 19th Engineer Regiment under Col. Anderson T. W. Moore and Combat Command Reserve (CCR) were also placed under Stark's command. If he were forced back, Fredendall ordered, he was to withdraw to Kasserine, which was to be held at all costs. Meanwhile, Anderson sent two British brigades to Fredendall's assistance: the 1st Guards to secure the undefended pass at Sbida and Brig. Charles Dunphie's 26th Armoured, which was ordered to take up positions in the general vicinity of Kasserine.

Arnim continued his advance by ordering the 21st Panzer to take Sbeitla and the 10th Panzer to attack toward Fondouk. He refused to release the 21st Panzer to Rommel as planned on the grounds that Rommel had already taken his objective (Gafsa) and the 21st was still engaged in the vicinity of Sidi Bou Zid. Ziegler now began to prove that he was not a competent handler of armor. Despite his initial victories, he was slow and hesitant in the pursuit. The Allies completed the evacuation of the Eastern Dorsal during the night of February 17–18, and Ziegler pursued them in an almost leisurely fashion. This lack of initiative angered Rommel, who later observed, "The Americans had as yet no practical battle experience, and it was now up to us to instill in them from the outset an inferiority complex of no mean order."[23] Ziegler, a career artillery and staff officer of no great ability, was not the commander to do this.

Rommel took Feriana and Thelepte on February 17, captured twenty tons of aviation gas and thirty tons of lubricants that the Americans had failed to destroy, and was already planning to take Tebessa. That morning, he signaled Arnim and asked if he would also be willing to advance that far. It was midnight before he received an answer: Arnim would send no troops forward of the crest of the Eastern Dorsal because of the difficulty in maintaining them. Rommel was furious; he felt that Arnim was letting the Americans escape. All of the dangers inherent in violating the principle of unity of command now became painfully evident. The African theater badly needed an army group headquarters to direct all operations, but the Italian High Command recoiled at this notion because that commander would have to be the senior German officer in the region, Field Marshal Rommel. Now the Axis cause paid the full price for their shortsightedness.

For Rommel, February 17 had been a bad day all the way around. The capable Major General Liebenstein, who had replaced the wounded General Fehn as commander of the Afrika Korps, had himself been severely wounded by a mine and was replaced as acting commander of the Afrika Korps (and the Battle Group Afrika Korps) by the senior surviving officer, General Buelowius. Although the records are somewhat unclear on this point, Col. Gerhard Franz, the capable chief of staff of the Afrika Korps, was apparently wounded as well. He was evacuated back to Europe on February 15 and was not able to return to active duty until August. In any case, the Afrika Korps had to replace both its commander and chief of staff in the middle of this battle. In addition, General Fischer, the brilliant commander of the 10th Panzer Division, had bled to death on February 5, after his vehicle hit a mine which blew off an arm and both of his legs. He had been replaced by the less capable Broich, a career cavalry officer.

Although he was a great combat engineer, Buelowius would prove to be deficient as a panzer leader. The quality of Rommel's subordinate commanders had, in fact, declined markedly since 1942, with the loss of such talented commanders as Nehring, Georg von Bismarck, Ritter Wilhelm von Thoma, Ludwig Cruewell, Gustav von Vaerst, and others. The loss of extremely capable staff officers—Albert Gause, Siegfried Westphal, F. W. von Mellenthin, Franz, and others—also significantly contributed to the performance of Rommel's army, which was not up to the standards it had set in previous campaigns. Finally, Rommel's own health had significantly deteriorated since early 1942, and this affected his performance. His leadership in the Kasserine campaign was sometimes not as dynamic as it had been in the past.

The following day, February 18, Rommel continued his advance and forced the evacuation of the Thelepta airfield, the main Allied air base in the 1st Army's southern sector. Thirty-four inoperative airplanes had to be destroyed. Rommel signaled Kesselring at 2:30 P.M. and asked that the 10th and 21st Panzer Divisions be placed under his command and moved rapidly to the Thelepte area for a continuation of the advance toward Tebessa (about forty-five miles northwest of Thelepte) and into the rear of the British 1st Army. Two hours later, Kesselring gave his provisional approval while he met with Mussolini to obtain final approval. A little later in the day, Kesselring placed Rommel in command of all mobile forces of the Afrika Korps, plus the 10th and 21st Panzer Divisions. Rommel immediately ordered an all-out attack on Kasserine for the following morning. That evening, he ordered a bottle of champagne—a most unusual request for him—and said, "I feel like an old cavalry horse that has suddenly heard the bugles sound again."[24]

Rommel's elation was short-lived. The next morning, a dispatch arrived from Commando Supremo confirming the transfer of the panzer divisions to his command but setting Le Kef as his primary objective. Le Kef was about 100 miles due north of Thelepte, well in the rear of the French XIX Corps. Rommel wanted to attack to the northwest, not due north. He believed that the northern route of advance would carry him into the area where the Allied reserves were strongest, instead of outflanking them to the west, as the Tebessa plan would do. Events proved that he was exactly right: the Allies had only the relatively weak CCB to cover Tebessa. By attacking due north, toward Thala and Le Kef, Rommel was advancing too close to the enemy's front and in exactly the place Alexander and Anderson expected him. Either route he chose, he would have to clear the Kasserine Pass, where the Americans were desperately trying to rally and make a stand. Rommel headed for it with the bulk of his forces.

The Kasserine Pass was shaped like the letter X and was barely 800 yards wide at its narrowest point. It was not impregnable, but it was dangerous to the Germans because it could easily be mined and an attacker could be restricted to the roads. Fredendall had already asked that all of the mines available in North Africa be sent to the Kasserine Pass as quickly as possible, and Eisenhower complied with this request with remarkable speed. Colonel Moore and his 1,400 engineers constructed a triple belt of antitank and antipersonnel mines behind which Colonel Stark was to make his stand. All of his troops were new to combat, however, and many were already slipping away to the rear.

At 4:50 A.M. on February 19, Rommel attacked the Kasserine Pass with Battle Group Afrika Korps under General Buelowius, but without success. Meanwhile, the 21st Panzer Division was checked at Sbiba, which was strongly defended by the Allies. Rommel was furious at Colonel Hildebrandt, the commander of the 21st, who took four hours to cover fifteen miles before he ran into significant opposition and was checked in a minefield. Rommel ordered him to push west and then north against the American infantry. Hildebrandt set off in the pouring rain with twenty-five PzKw IVs and some motorized infantry and smashed a troop of the 16th/5th Lancers, which was equipped with Valentine tanks and hopelessly outgunned by the panzers. Later that afternoon, however, Hildebrandt blundered into a trap, and his little battle group was shot to pieces by the U.S. 151st Field Artillery Battalion. He retreated, leaving behind about thirteen tanks.[25]

At the same time, the 10th Panzer Division advanced slowly, but it was only at regimental strength because Arnim had withheld half of the division, as well as the Tiger tanks upon which Rommel had been counting. Arnim had shown that he was incapable of looking beyond his own zone of operations. That evening, Rommel ordered the 10th Panzer to shift its axis of advance and follow Buelowius through the Kasserine Pass.

On February 19, Gen. Harold R. L. Alexander activated his Headquarters, 18th Army Group. Now the British 1st and 8th Armies were under a single ground commander. Alexander's first orders were simple: there would be no retreat from the Western Dorsal Mountains.

On the afternoon of February 19, the defenders of the Kasserine Pass were hit with Hitler's latest "wonder weapon": a six-barrelled, electrically operated mortar called the *Nebelwerfer*, which could lob an eighty-pound shell up to four miles. The high-pitched whine of this weapon further undermined American morale, which fell even lower after nightfall. "What happened during the night of February 19–20 cannot be clearly reconstructed from the record," Blumenson wrote later. The Germans launched a night attack, and by daylight, one battalion of Stark's force had ceased to exist, and some of the other units were shaky.[26]

Rommel wanted to launch his main attack against the Kasserine Pass on the morning of February 20, but it was slow in developing. Rommel went up to the front personally and demanded that Broich, the commander of the 10th Panzer Division, explain why he had stopped. Broich explained that he was waiting for the motorized infantry to come up and cover his advance. "Go and fetch the motorcycle battalion yourself!" Rommel roared, losing his temper. "And you are to lead it into action too!"[27] His words had the desired effect; the PzKw IVs of the 10th Panzer Division advanced into the pass without waiting for the motorized infantry, although the Panzer Grenadier Regiment Afrika and the 5th Italian Bersaglieri Regiment soon joined the battle.

The American defense quickly collapsed. Colonel Moore's headquarters was soon overrun, and all contact between the 19th Engineers and Stark's command post was lost. Several American engineer companies panicked, and the rapidly advancing panzers cut off elements of the U.S. 1st Infantry and 1st Armored Divisions in the northwest entrance to the pass. Gore Force, a reinforced British battalion at the north end of the pass, counterattacked the 10th Panzer with its Valentines, which were led by Major Biebly. Most of the obsolete infantry tanks were quickly destroyed, Biebly was wounded, and Gore Force began to retreat. By late afternoon, the Germans had pushed to within 200 yards of Stark's command post, and the colonel was forced to abandon it. Except for Gore Force and a few other pockets of resistance, Stark's command had been destroyed.

Major Bielby launched a desperate counterattack, but his tank soon took a direct hit, killing him instantly. The gunners of Gore Force fired their 6-pounder antitank cannon into the panzers over open sights, and six American Grants from the 1st Armored Division tried to cover the withdrawal of the British. Four of them were quickly knocked out by the PzKw IVs. Gore Force was completely overwhelmed. The last three Valentines were knocked out, and all but one of the 6-pounders were destroyed. By nightfall, the Kasserine Pass was open, and the Arabs were stripping the bodies of the dead. Rommel could now continue his advance via three directions: west against Tebessa, north against Le Kef via Thala, or northwest and then north to attack Le Kef via the Sbeitla-Sbiba Road. The Desert Fox sent Buelowius to probe against the American defenses to the west, while the 10th Panzer Division under Broich drove on Thala and the 21st Panzer Division under Hildebrandt headed for Sbiba.[28]

Despite this victory, Rommel's offensive was now making progress only in the center and only very slowly. On his left flank, Buelowius's probes toward Tebessa had been turned back by CCB and elements of the U.S. 1st Infantry Division. On his right flank, the 21st Panzer Division, under the less than effective Colonel Hildebrandt, had been decisively halted just south of Sbiba by the 1st Guards Brigade and the reinforced U.S. 18th Infantry Regiment. Rommel, in fact, threatened to relieve Hildebrandt of his command but did not, possibly because he had no one better qualified with whom to replace him. The colonel's tenure as commander of the 21st Panzer would nevertheless not be a long one.

February 22 was another day of rain. At dawn, Colonel French-Blake accidentally led the remnants of the 2nd Lothians into the laager of the 10th Panzer Division, which promptly blew away seven Valentines in seven minutes. The 2nd Lothians were virtually wiped out, but their appearance in the middle of his division had its effect on Broich, who had learned from the pro-Nazi Arabs that three battalions of artillery from the U.S. 9th Infantry Division had reinforced strong elements of the British 6th Armoured Division at Thala and that the 1st Guards Brigade was hurrying toward Thala from Sbiba. He was convinced that a major Allied counterattack was in the making. This last report was not true, but the Allies were obviously concentrating their considerable reserves against Panzer Army Afrika, and Rommel's offensive was clearly bogging down. As a result, Broich went over to the defensive.

While the 90th Panzer Artillery Regiment exchanged shellfire with Irvin's guns, Rommel came to the front and made his decision. It had been raining for three days, and the advance had slowed to a crawl; CCB was nearing the battlefield to his rear; a war of maneuver was impossible in the Tunisian mud; and his troops had enough fuel for only 180 miles and had very little ammunition. That afternoon, Kesselring and his chief of operations, Col. Siegfried Westphal, arrived and met with Rommel in his command truck.[29] He told them that there was no chance of success-fully continuing the offensive as far as Bone and that he believed now was the time to break off the attack and concentrate in southern Tunisia in an effort to catch the 8th Army off balance and defeat Montgomery while he was still assembling his forces. Kesselring and Westphal were aghast; they wanted him to continue and tried to persuade him, but Rommel could not be convinced. He was tired, sick, exhausted, and just plain worn out. He spoke of the weather, troop exhaustion, and Arnim, who had withheld the Tigers and several infantry battalions, robbing him of the momentum necessary to continue the offensive. In the end, Kesselring and Westphal gave up and left. Rommel began his retreat that night. The 16th Infantry Regiment of the U.S. 1st Infantry Division and CCB—the only unit of the 1st Armored Division which was still intact—reoccupied the Kasserine Pass on February 24.

During the battles that have collectively come to be known as the Battle of the Kasserine Pass, the Germans had lost 201 killed, 536 wounded, and 252 missing—a total of 989 casualties. They had also lost 14 guns, 61 motorized vehicles, 6 half-tracks, and 20 panzers. They had captured 4,026 prisoners, 61 tanks and half-tracks, 161 motorized vehi-cles, 36 guns, 45 tons of ammunition, and huge amounts of fuel, lubri-cants, and other equipment. The U.S. II Corps alone had lost about 300 killed and 3,000 wounded, as well as 183 tanks, 194 half-tracks, 208 pieces of artillery, and 512 trucks and jeeps—more than 20 percent of its combat strength. The British and French had also suffered significant casualties. The German offensive had been a brilliant local success, but it had fallen far short of a strategic victory because of a lack of cooperation on the part of Arnim and a lack of unity of command. Ironically, on Feb-

76 BLITZKRIEG NO LONGER

ruary 23, Commando Supremo created Army Group Afrika and appointed Erwin Rommel its first commander in chief. Had this step been taken two weeks earlier, much greater results might have been achieved.

OXHEAD AND MEDENINE

While the Desert Fox was retreating from the Kasserine Pass, Juergen von Arnim prepared to launch Operation *Ochsenkopf* ("Oxhead"). Arnim never bothered to consult with Rommel about the offensive, which began on February 26. (He did, however, send a staff officer to inform Rommel of his plans, which the Desert Fox described as "completely unrealistic." He erroneously blamed Commando Supremo for the plan, but they were just as shocked as Rommel when they saw it.[30]) Arnim struck along a broad front with Corps Weber: the 334th Infantry Division, Battle Group Schmid of the Hermann Goering Division, Division von Manteuffel (formerly Division von Broich), and half of the 10th Panzer Division, including the 501st Heavy Panzer Battalion. The attack was directed by Maj. Gen. Friedrich Weber, whose objectives were Gafour, Teboursouk, and Beja; simultaneously, Col. Baron Hasso von Manteuffel launched a weaker offensive aimed at Djebel Abiod.[31] Oxhead was too broad in scope and lacked enough focus to be successful. The brunt of the attack fell on the newly arrived British 46th Infantry Division, but it also involved major attacks against the 78th Infantry Division and the ad hoc Division Y.

On the first day of the offensive, Battle Group Lang, under Colonel Lang of the 69th Panzer Grenadiers, attacked the 5th Hampshires and 155th Battery of Royal Artillery about twelve miles northeast of Hunt's Gap. After a twelve-hour battle, the defenders were overrun, and only about 130 British soldiers escaped, but they destroyed or damaged forty panzers in the struggle. These casualties were out of all proportion for the limited gains. Oxhead was like that all along the line; it achieved none of the spectacular results predicted by Arnim. On February 28, Rommel ordered it to succeed and end; however, bitter fighting occurred in the Hunt's Gap sector, which covered Bela, until March 5 and in Manteuffel's sector until the end of the month.

By March 1, Lang was only about a mile from Hunt's Gap but had just five operational panzers left. He had lost so much armor that the troops had nicknamed him "Tank Killer." Weber had had enough and ordered Lang to go over to the defensive. Rommel was especially angry that the Tiger battalion had been committed to a marshy valley, where the tanks had bogged down and fifteen of the nineteen monstrous PzKw VIs had been destroyed by British artillery and antitank gunners.

During Operation Oxhead, Arnim captured 2,500 prisoners against a loss of just over 1,000 German casualties; however, he lost seventy-one panzers, against a British loss of only sixteen tanks and thirty guns. "Had his [Oxhead] effort been coordinated with Rommel's drive at Kasserine, a strategic victory in Tunisia would undoubtedly have been won," military historian Martin Blumenson wrote later.[32] To make matters worse, the divisions Rommel needed to launch his attack against Montgomery at Medenine were delayed a week by Oxhead. On February 26, Monty had only two divisions opposite the Mareth Line. By March 6, he would have the equivalent of four divisions, with nearly 400 tanks, 350 guns, and 470 antitank guns.

Rommel—now the commander in chief of Army Group Afrika—met with Messe and his divisional commanders on February 28 and ordered them to launch a spoiling attack against the 8th Army's outposts opposite the Mareth Line on March 6. (Italian Gen. Giovanni Messe had taken command of Panzer Army Afrika, which was now redesignated the 1st Italian-German Panzer Army.)

During the Battle of the Kasserine Pass, Monty had been asked to attack the outposts on the Mareth Line in order to relieve the pressure on Fredendall's forces. Against his better judgment, Montgomery had moved Leese's XXX Corps to Medenine to attack Rommel's screening forces. The Desert Fox was thus presented with the opportunity to attack two isolated British divisions before Monty could bring up the rest of his army.

Messe's plan called for the Afrika Korps, now under Lt. Gen. Hans Cramer, to move through the Matmata Hills and attack Medenine from the west and southwest while a mixed German-Italian combat group launched a pinning attack from the Mareth Line. Rommel did not like the plan, but he was convinced by his panzer commanders that it was the best that could be devised under the circumstances. Unfortunately for the Germans and Italians, British radio intercepts gave Montgomery early warning of what was going to happen. He brought up the 2nd New Zealand Division and reinforced the XXX Corps with three armored brigades. By the time Rommel struck, Montgomery's forward defensive forces were more than a match for him.

Medenine was Rommel's last battle in Africa. It was also his worst. Monty's defenses were bristling with 6-pounder antitank guns when the panzers appeared out of the mists on the morning of March 6. So great was the carnage that Montgomery had to commit just a single squadron of Shermans all day long; the rest of his armor was never engaged.

"The attack had been launched too late," Rommel commented later. He listed his own losses as "tremendous," including forty panzers completely destroyed. The cruelest blow, however, was the knowledge that he had not been unable disrupt Montgomery's preparations. "A great gloom settled over us all," he recalled.[33]

THE END IN AFRICA

On March 9, Rommel flew to Rome to personally argue his case for another limited retreat to Kesselring and Commando Supremo. Once in the Eternal City, he realized that they did not expect him to ever return to Africa. He flew on to Rastenburg, where he presented his arguments to Hitler, who was not really listening to him. When Rommel finished, Hitler instructed him to take sick leave in the Austrian Mountains. Juergen von Arnim took charge of Army Group Afrika on March 9. Gustav von Vaerst, a desert veteran who had been promoted to general of panzer troops on March 1, assumed command of the 5th Panzer Army, and Col. Fritz Bayerlein became the German chief of staff of the 1st Italian-German Panzer Army.

Arnim's cause in Tunisia was hopeless from the beginning, and he seemed to realize it. He had about 350,000 men, of which 120,000 were combat troops. Two-thirds of the fighting troops were German, as were one-third of the support troops. He faced more than 500,000 Allied soldiers, including more than 250,000 combat troops. He had barely 200 operational tanks to face 1,800 Allied tanks, backed by more than 1,200 guns and 1,500 antitank guns. He was defending 387 miles of frontage—far too much for his depleted divisions. The average company sector was 2.5 miles long, and his artillery density was less than one gun per mile.[34] If he were to hold the bridgehead, Arnim knew, he would first have to be allowed to withdraw to a much shorter front. He would also have to be adequately supplied.

The long-awaited Allied offensive began on March 17, when the U.S. II Corps (three reinforced divisions) attacked Gafsa. The British and French had jokingly called the Americans under Fredendall "our Italians." Under Maj. Gen. George S. Patton Jr., who had taken command of the corps on March 6, the II was no longer a joke. Patton took Gafsa from the 10th Panzer Division on the first day of his offensive, which he characteristically styled Operation Wop. The next day, he took El Guettar, despite the fact that Arnim had committed the 21st Panzer Division to the sector. Between them, however, the 10th and 21st Panzers had 110 tanks and were able to slow Patton's drive to a crawl.

With two of the three German panzer divisions committed to the north and the 15th Panzer Division (which had only 32 operational tanks) in army group reserve, Messe was justifiably nervous about his sector. As of March 20, the 8th Army outnumbered him approximately 160,000 to 80,000 in men, 743 to 142 in tanks, 692 to 450 in guns, and 1,033 to 244 in antitank guns (excluding 408 Italian antitank guns). Many of his tanks were nearly useless Italian vehicles. In addition, the Allies had 755 fighters, fighter-bombers, and tank-destroyer aircraft against 129 German airplanes in southern Tunisia, of which only 83 were operational. There were also about 40 obsolete Italian airplanes in the south. In addition, Bayerlein, Messe's German chief of staff, directed his forces almost as if he were an independent commander and presented the Italian general with *fait accomplis*. This was a direct violation of the principle of unity of command; besides, Messe was a much more capable commander than Bayerlein, even if he was Italian. Despite his many handicaps, Messe was able to check Montgomery for four days—a masterpiece of defensive fighting. At last, however, the Allied numerical superiority threatened to crush his armies, so Arnim ordered the evacuation of the Mareth Line to begin on the night of March 25–26. Between March 25 and 29, Messe, helped by Montgomery's slow pursuit, con-

ducted a brilliant withdrawal to the Wadi Akarit position, his Italian
infantry covered by the mobile formations of the Afrika Korps and German light divisions.

Kesselring ordered Arnim to hold the Akarit position and sent his
chief of staff, Westphal, to Tunisia to "explain" the order to the Prussian.
This led to another exchange of harsh words on March 30. Westphal
accused the army group of always "squinting over its shoulder."
Yes, Arnim confessed, that was true; it was squinting for the sight of
supply ships that never arrived. "We are without bread and ammunition,
as was Rommel's army before," he snapped. "The consequences are
inevitable."[35]

Arnim's supply lines had practically collapsed. His army group
needed 120,000 tons of supplies per month. In March, it received 43,125
tons and lost 41.5 percent of its supplies en route. In April, Army Group
Afrika would receive only 29,233 tons, with about the same percentage
lost en route. In March, Allied surface vessels, submarines, airplanes, and
mines sank thirty-six German and merchant ships. In April, another
thirty-three cargo ships were lost, and in May, a straggling thirty-nine
vessels were sunk on their way to North Africa. Arnim received only
about 3,000 tons of supplies that month.

Kesselring's 2nd Air Fleet had already lost the Battle for North
Africa because it could no longer protect Arnim's supply convoys from
Allied airplanes, submarines, and naval mining operations. Maj. Hermann
Grasser, the commander of the 2nd Group of the 51st Fighter Wing
(II/JG 51), recalled: "At first the Americans lacked experience. Then we
had a chance to surprise them and compensate for their numerical superiority with our experience and tactics. But with time they got experience, and we were thereafter unable to do anything."[36]

As the American fighters gained experience, they shot down more
and more German bombers. By the end of 1942, because of the high
losses among air crews and the deterioration in training standards at the
flight schools, the effectiveness of German bomber attacks had already
dropped appreciably, and many new and inexperienced crews had to be
committed to the battle. These men were inadequately trained and
proved to be completely unable to locate their targets. Some of them
could not even find their way back to their bases, and Maj. Gen. Martin
Harlinghausen, the commander of the II Air Corps, was forced to with-

draw his bomber units to the Italian mainland. This, in turn, released Allied air units for attacks against Axis naval convoys. By March 30, the 1st Italian-German Army's vehicles had only six-tenths of an issue of fuel left (i.e., enough to drive each vehicle about forty miles), with none left in the supply dumps. Vaerst's army was in even worse condition. It had rations for only six days and fuel totalling only three-tenths of an issue, with virtually none left in reserve. Merchant shipping losses reached 75 percent by late April.[37]

Messe's last units fell back into the Wadi Akarit positions on March 30. In the meantime, Hitler, Commando Supremo, and OB South continued to pour even more reinforcements into Tunisia, further stripping Sicily and southern Europe of their defensive forces. In April, Battle Group Hermann Goering was reinforced until its strength exceeded 11,000 men, and the 999th Afrika Division arrived in Tunisia. It was commanded by Maj. Gen. Kurt Thomas, the former commandant of Fuehrer Headquarters, and was unique in more than one way. The numeral "999" was the *Wehrmacht*'s designation for a penal unit, and most of the men in this unit were former political prisoners, many of whom enlisted—or were forced to "volunteer"—from concentration camps. It would fight surprisingly well in the days ahead.

The battle for Wadi Akarit began at 1 A.M. on April 6 with a massive artillery bombardment against the 1st Italian-German Army. Three British infantry divisions attacked about 4:30 A.M. The 50th Infantry was checked, but the 51st Highland advanced rapidly against the Trieste and Spezia Divisions, and the 4th Indian took 4,000 prisoners. Lt. Gen. Brian Horrocks, the commander of the British XXX Corps, requested that Montgomery commit the X Corps at 8:45 A.M., but Monty hesitated, giving Maj. Gen. Count von Sponeck time to counterattack with his 90th Light Division and partially close the gaps.[38] Montgomery did commit the X Corps at noon, but it was unable to break through. Meanwhile, Cramer and the Afrika Korps held Patton more or less in check near El Guettar, but only by committing their last reserves. The Axis line was holding—just barely—as night fell.

That night, Arnim gave Messe permission to retreat to the Enfidaville position, 150 miles to the north. When Montgomery delivered his main attack the following day, it hit thin air: the 1st Army was gone. Later that day, the American spearheads linked up with the 8th Army, completing the encirclement of the Tunisian bridgehead, while the RAF's Desert Air Force pounded the Afrika Korps, the 90th Light and 164th Light Afrika Divisions, and their Italian allies, causing heavy casualties.

The 1st Italian-German Panzer Army reached the Enfidaville position on April 11. It was hardly an ideal defensive position, but it was the best one Messe had left. A lull then descended on the North African front while the Allies prepared to launch their final attack on the shrinking bridgehead.

The Allies' "final attack" began on April 22 and met fierce resistance from the German and Italian divisions, who realized that their backs were against the wall. By now, the Allies had approximately 350,000 combat troops and 1,400 tanks. The nine German divisions—the backbone of the 100-mile-long defensive line—had barely 60,000 men and fewer than 100 tanks, only 45 of which were operational. The Manteuffel Division, for example, had only 8,000 men with which to defend forty-five miles of front. It was struck by the U.S. II Corps, now under Omar Bradley, which had 95,000 men. Nevertheless, the division held most of its positions and turned back the American attack, earning Baron von Manteuffel his promotion to major general on May 1. Meanwhile, the British IX Corps struck with massed armor (360 tanks) and penetrated eight miles but was halted when Arnim committed his only substantial reserve, the 10th Panzer Division, which had only thirty tanks left. Montgomery, who attacked with three divisions, was also checked in bitter fighting. Resistance was as fierce in the Italian sectors as in the German.

Although Army Group Afrika was not broken through, its main defenses were penetrated in several places. By April 25, the army group was down to its last one-fourth issue of fuel (enough for a move of fifteen miles) and barely enough ammunition for three days of combat. The Allied offensive had clearly been slowed by now, however, so Alexander allowed it to halt in some sectors but continued it in others. It now assumed the character of a limited-objective offensive, designed to keep the pressure on Arnim. On April 26, Longstop Hill was finally captured by the British 78th Infantry Division. Fighting continued to be heavy. On April 28, the British took Djebel Bou Aoukaz but were counterattacked and dislodged by Col. Josef Irkens, the commander of the 8th Panzer Regiment.

Bradley also kept up his attacks, and on the night of May 1–2, Man-teuffel's division conducted a skillful withdrawal to a defensive line east of Mateur, only fifteen miles from the port of Bizerta. The defense was now perilously lacking in depth. In addition, Allied airplanes seemed to be everywhere. During the week from April 22 to 29, Allied air forces flew more than 5,200 sorties in support of the British 1st Army alone, shooting up every conceivable target of opportunity. One Allied fighter-bomber shot up a staff car and severely wounded the driver. As the passenger—a lieutenant colonel of the General Staff—tried desperately to pull the driver out of the burning vehicle, the airplane made another strafing run. This time the driver was killed, and the colonel—Count Claus von Stauffenberg, the operations officer of the 10th Panzer Division—was desperately wounded. He was evacuated back to Europe, where surgeons were able to save his life, but not his left arm or left eye. When he finally did return to active duty, Colonel von Stauffenberg was a man with a mission: he intended to rid the world of Adolf Hitler.

The *Luftwaffe* pilots—or what was left of them—continued to fight bravely, and half of the tanks the Allies lost during the last week in April were destroyed by Ju 88 bombers and Hs 129s and Me 210s in ground-attack missions. They also shot down fifty Allied airplanes, against a loss of twenty-five of their own. But there simply were not enough of them left to make a difference.

On April 29, Alexander ordered the offensive halted, and a lull descended over the Tunisian battlefield on April 30. Alexander resupplied his units, regrouped, and prepared for his second "final attack." Arnim tried to reinforce the 5th Panzer Army with the Afrika Korps, but his plans were largely spoiled because many of the panzers did not have the fuel to make the move. The situation had become so desperate that his supply staffs were distilling fuel from low-grade Tunisian wines and liquors—an idea that actually worked.

Everyone except the fanatically optimistic Kesselring seemed to realize that the fate of Army Group Afrika was sealed. On one pretext or another, Arnim sent back to Europe any of his senior officers who wished to leave. Weber departed, as did Hans-Georg Hildebrandt (now a major general). Manteuffel was wounded and sent off, and Bayerlein also left. General Ziegler, who had proven to be no great asset, did not hesitate to accept a new appointment in Europe, and Arnim himself sent Gause back to Italy on May 4 on the pretext that he was needed at a conference. *Luftwaffe* Maj. Gen. "Beppo" Schmid of the Hermann Goering Division was ordered to fly out of the pocket by Goering, a personal friend, on May 9. Maj. Gen. Kurt Thomas, the commander of the 999th Afrika Division, tried to fly out on May 5, but his airplane was shot down and crashed into the Mediterranean, killing him instantly.

On the other hand, several distinguished officers who were given the chance to leave elected to remain with their troops and at their posts. Col. August-Viktor von Quast, Vaerst's chief of staff, refused to go, as did Col. Heinz Pomtow, the chief of operations of the army group. Others who refused to go included Maj. Gen. Baron von Liebenstein, the commander of the 164th Light Afrika; Baron von Broich, the commander of the 10th Panzer; Count Theodor von Sponeck, the commander of the 90th Light; and Willibald Borowietz, the last commander of the 15th Panzer Division, who was promoted to lieutenant general effective May 1. Meanwhile, Maj. Gen. Fritz Krause[39] replaced Weber as commander of the 334th Infantry; Buelowius took command of Division von Manteuffel; and Bayerlein was succeeded as German chief of staff of the 1st Italian-German Army by Col. Anton Markert.

The last offensive began at 3 A.M. on May 6. In two hours, 16,632 shells fell on the German forces facing the British 4th Infantry Division alone. The main Allied thrust came in the valley south of the Medjerda River, where Arnim had massed almost all of his remaining armor—sixty tanks under the control of the 15th Panzer Division—which faced four British divisions, two of them armored. The German armor began to give way at noon, and by nightfall, the British had advanced twelve miles—half the distance to Tunis. That night, Arnim signaled Rome that the 15th Panzer Division had been destroyed and that only excessive Allied caution could prevent Tunis from falling the next day.[40]

Juergen von Arnim continued to fight on but had lost control of the battle. The 7th British Armoured Division entered Tunis at 3:15 P.M.—almost the exact moment the U.S. 9th Infantry Division entered Bizerte. The French XIX Corps took Pont du Fahs despite fierce resistance from the 999th Afrika Division, which even resorted to rolling boulders down on them. Mass surrenders, however, were already beginning. At 10 A.M.

on May 9, the U.S. II Corps cornered Vaerst and what remained of the 5th Panzer Army staff, which surrendered before noon. Arnim and his staff joined Cramer and the staff of the Afrika Korps while Messe continued to hold his line against the 8th Army. An order arrived from Hitler: Army Group Afrika was to fight to the last bullet. Arnim interpreted this order in his own way. This was a tank battle, he declared, and the last bullet in a tank battle was the last tank or cannon shell.

One by one, the veteran divisions signed off. On May 12, the Afrika Korps and the headquarters of Army Group Afrlka capitulated, but Arnim refused to surrender all of the Axis troops still at large on the grounds that he was out of radio contact with most of his units. This refusal made little difference. At 12:20 P.M. on May 13, Messe and his two chiefs of staff, Gen. Alberto Mancinelli and Colonel Markert, surrendered the 1st Italian-German Panzer Army. Later in the day, Major General Liebenstein surrendered the last Axis unit, the 164th Light Afrika Division, to General Freyberg.[41] At 1:16 P.M., General Alexander signaled Churchill: "Sir, it is my duty to report that the Tunisian campaign is over. All enemy resistance has ceased. We are masters of the North African shores."

Axis losses in Tunisia were crippling. The 18th Army Group estimated that it captured 157,000 Germans and 86,700 Italians—a grand total of 244,500 prisoners of war. The U.S. official history placed the total at an estimated 275,000 while the British official history placed the total at 238,243. Martin Blumenson, the great American military historian, put the total at 200,000 captured.[42] The lowest estimate was that 94,000 Germans were captured.[43] By any estimate, at least 200,000 Axis troops fell into Allied hands. German civilians called the disaster "Tunisgrad," a play on Stalingrad. Those whose sons were captured, however, were happy that their children had been taken prisoner by the British and Americans rather than by the Soviets. In any case, the Third Reich had lost some of its best units, including the legendary Afrika Korps, three of its best panzer divisions (the 10th, 15th, and 21st), the well above average 164th Light Afrika Division, most of the elite Hermann Goering Panzer Division, and the truly outstanding 90th Light Division. Now the Third Reich had almost nothing left with which to defend southern Europe, except unreliable Italian divisions. Axis-occupied Europe was exposed to invasion from the Pyrenees to the Balkans. Eisenhower, on the other hand, had an entire army group, which he could use most dangerously. The question that dominated Axis strategic thought after the fall of Tunis was where and when Eisenhower would next employ his forces.

Luftwaffe Lt. Gen. Martin Harlinghausen (left) with Field Marshal Erhard Milch, the state secretary for aviation and Goering's second in command. Harlinghausen was a pioneer in the field of attacking ships but was less successful commanding II Air Corps in Tunisia. He never held another major appointment and ended the war in a minor territorial command.

A Panzer Mark IV (PzKw IV) tank captured by the British in North Africa. USAMHI

Field Marshal Erwin Rommel, "the Desert Fox." Initially very successful, he was the first commander of Army Group Afrika in Tunisia.

Field Marshal Guenther von Kluge, the commander of Army Group Center on the Eastern Front, 1941–43.

Adolf Galland, general of fighter pilots, 1941–45. He later had a falling out with Goering and was demoted to the command of a jet fighter wing. Wounded on April 26, 1945, he was still in the hospital when the Americans captured him on May 6. Galland had 104 kills to his credit. USAMHI

Field Marshal Erich von Manstein, commander of Army Group South, considered by most of the German officer corps to be their best commander. Hitler sacked him in April 1944.
NATIONAL ARCHIVES

Field Marshal Walter Model, "the Fuehrer's Fireman." As an army and army group commander, he was given only the most dangerous and difficult assignments. USAMHI

Lt. Gen. Fridolin von Senger und Etterlin, the German liaison officer to the Italian 6th Army in Sicily. After successfully directing the evacuations of Corsica and Sardinia, he was given command of the XIV Panzer Corps, which he led in Italy for the rest of the war.
USAMHI

Gen. of Infantry Karl Adolf Hollidt, commander of the XVII Corps and Army Detachment Hollidt on the Eastern Front. Promoted to colonel general on September 1, 1943, he commanded the reconstituted 6th Army from March 5, 1943, until Hitler sacked him on April 8, 1944. AUTHOR'S COLLECTION

A German forward observer on the Eastern Front. This lieutenant had been wounded at least three times. NATIONAL ARCHIVES

A Ju 88 bomber. This aircraft was also used as a night fighter. AIR UNIVERSITY

The Eastern Front during the spring thaw. NATIONAL ARCHIVES

A Luftwaffe mortar crew. Air force troops were used extensively in ground combat in 1942 and 1943, but the experiment turned out to be a failure. NATIONAL ARCHIVES

A Messerschmitt Me 109 fighter.

Hitler and Field Marshal Wilhelm Keitel, commander in chief of the High Command of the Armed Forces, 1938–45. USAMHI

A pair of Heinkel He 111 bombers. Although obsolete by 1940, the He 111 remained the standard Luftwaffe bomber throughout the war. NATIONAL ARCHIVES

Soviet infantry in the attack, 1943. USAMHI

A StuG IV assault gun. Built on the chassis of an obsolete PzKw III, it was cheap to manufacture and highly effective. By January 1944, these guns had destroyed 20,000 tanks on the Eastern Front.
NATIONAL ARCHIVES

A German reconnaissance battalion, circa 1943. By 1943, many of the reconnaissance battalions of the infantry divisions were equipped with bicycles. NATIONAL ARCHIVES

Col. Gen. Hermann Hoth, who commanded the 3rd Panzer Group, 17th Army, and 4th Panzer Army on the Eastern Front. Sacked by Hitler in November 1943 for being a defeatist, he was never reemployed. NATIONAL ARCHIVES

Hitler shakes hands with Col. Gen. Kurt Zeitzler, chief of the General Staff, 1942–44. Known for his incredible energy, Zeitzler would have a nervous breakdown in July 1944. NATIONAL ARCHIVES

Grand Adm. Karl Doenitz, commander of the German U-boat branch (1938–43) and commander in chief of the German Navy (1943–45). NATIONAL ARCHIVES

Hermann Goering and Benito Mussolini inspect an Italian honor guard, February 1942.

NATIONAL ARCHIVES

German ski troops on the Eastern Front, circa 1943. NATIONAL ARCHIVES

German troops in the snows of Russia, circa 1943. NATIONAL ARCHIVES

Luftwaffe Field Marshal Albert "Smiling Al" Kesselring, commander in chief of OB South in Tunisia, Sicily, and Italy, 1943–45.

NATIONAL ARCHIVES

A railroad demolished by German troops.

NATIONAL ARCHIVES

SS Gen. Paul Hausser, commander of the 2nd SS Panzer Division "Das Reich" and the II SS Panzer Corps on the Eastern Front. NATIONAL ARCHIVES

A U-boat under attack by a U.S. naval cutter, 1942. After scoring some impressive victories, the German submarines were decisively defeated in the Battle of the North Atlantic in May 1943. USAMHI

Col. Gen. Heinrich von Viet-inghoff with an American intel-ligence officer, 1945. Vietinghoff led the 88th Panzer Battalion (part of the Condor Legion) in Spain, 5th Panzer Division in Poland, XIII Corps in France, and XXXXVI Panzer Corps and 9th Army in Russia. He distinguished himself as the commander of the 10th Army in Italy (1943–44). NATIONAL ARCHIVES

Italian dictator Benito Mussolini (left) confers with German Foreign Minister Joachim von Ribbentrop, 1938. NATIONAL ARCHIVES

CHAPTER 5

The Bombing Intensifies

THE DETERIORATION OF THE *LUFTWAFFE*

"The *Luftwaffe* had grown too quickly for enduring strength," Col. Adolphe Goutard wrote after the war.[1] No one on the Allied side, however, realized how vulnerable it was. "From 1939 until 1944, no foreign estimate had correctly assessed the strength of the *Luftwaffe*," General Rieckhoff wrote. "No one suspected how low it really was." He added, "Sooner or later every bluff is called!"[2]

Richard Suchenwirth called training "the Step-Child of the *Luftwaffe*."[3] *Luftwaffe* training wings were in combat from September 1, 1939, the first day of the war. (Appendix E shows a table of *Luftwaffe* aviation units, strengths, and the ranks of their commanders.) Between 1939 and 1943, Goering and Hans Jeschonnek, the chief of the General Staff of the *Luftwaffe*, raided the training establishment to obtain transports and transport instructor pilots, as well as fighter and dive-bomber instructors and aircraft. Jeschonnek was especially guilty as he gradually changed the ratio of combat aircraft to trainers, transports, and reconnaissance aircraft. When the war broke out, this ratio was fifty-seven to forty-three. By 1942, it stood at seventy-five to twenty-five, and in 1944, it reached eighty-eight to twelve.[4] By 1944, British fighter pilots were receiving 360 hours of flight training before being sent to the combat wings, and American fighter pilot trainees were receiving 40 hours more than that.

New *Luftwaffe* fighter pilots were being sent to the squadrons with only 160 hours of flight time.[5] Then they were committed to battle in obsolete airplanes, facing numerically superior American and British pilots with more than twice their training and experience and flying modern aircraft. The results were predictable: the *Luftwaffe* began to suffer higher combat losses and more accidents, especially upon landing. The quality of new *Luftwaffe* pilots continued to deteriorate throughout the rest of the war.

AIR ATTACKS ON THE REICH

Similarly deteriorating was the *Luftwaffe*'s military domination over the skies of the Reich itself. In January 1943, the U.S. Army Air Corps[6] made its first major bombing raid over the Reich and attacked the U-boat base of Wilhelmshaven. The raid was partially successful, and the U.S. 8th Air Force lost only three of the ninety-one aircraft participating in the daylight strike.[7] The Wilhelmshaven raid set a precedent that would remain almost uninterrupted until the end of the war: the Americans, who had vastly superior bombsights, would engage in precision daytime bombing while the British concentrated on nighttime raids against area targets. Even though this strategy evolved by accident, the techniques of nighttime area bombing and daytime precision bombing were to prove a lethal combination for Nazi Germany.

The RAF resumed its nocturnal activities in January and February 1943, and RAF raids gradually increased in number, accuracy, and severity.[8] On March 2, 1943, Bomber Command dropped 600 tons of bombs on Berlin, starting 1,700 fires in the city, killing 700 civilians, and leaving 35,000 homeless. "The western parts of Berlin remind one of the front," Herr and Frau Bausch wrote to their son, a lieutenant on the Eastern Front. "We now call [the suburb of] Wilmersdorf 'Sodom and Gomorrah.'"[9] The day after the raid, many people were openly wondering if the attack was sent by God to punish Berlin for what was happening to the Jews.

The night of March 5–6 saw the beginning of what was later dubbed the Battle of the Ruhr. The *Luftwaffe* met the Allied bomber streams with an assortment of technologically obsolete aircraft, all of which had been designed before the war. They were also short on trained pilots and aircrewmen, since many of their best instructors lay dead in the snows of Russia. The bill for Jeschonnek's shortsighted policies was now coming due with monstrous interest. The first Allied attack struck Essen with 442 heavy bombers, devastating 160 acres of the city and destroying or seriously damaging three-quarters of the buildings on another 450 acres. Essen would be attacked four more times during the Battle of the Ruhr.[10]

The British had by now discovered that fire was a more effective area-bombing weapon than explosives. They accompanied the magnesium stick bombs with liquid incendiary bombs containing a mixture of gasoline, rubber, and a viscous material or bombs made up of oil, liquid asphalt, and magnesium, a kind of synthetic lava that was more difficult to extinguish than conventional bombs.[11] The *Luftwaffe* countered by introducing new tactics, by activating new flak units and fighter wings, and by bringing old ones back from the fronts for the defense of the Reich. By early 1943, the Reich's defenses were much stronger and included three night-fighter divisions, four flak divisions, two searchlight divisions, and three flak brigades. Nevertheless, the overall situation in the air only continued to grow worse.

Although the Allies concentrated against the Ruhr in March 1943, they did not limit their attentions to Germany's major industrial district. True, they blasted Essen, Duisburg, Duesseldorf, Geisenkirchen, Wuppertal, Dortmund, and Bochum, but they also struck Berlin, Aachen, Stettin, Pilsen, Munich, Stuttgart, Frankfurt am Main, and Nuremberg in strength. Hamburg was subjected to its first heavy bombing that month, and Nuremberg was set ablaze by 800 tons of bombs on March 8. The next day, Munich was heavily bombed, and on March 11, Stuttgart was attacked. On the night of March 15, Essen was raided again, and the vital Krupp steelworks and armaments center was heavily damaged.

The raids continued until March 30, when the *Luftwaffe* finally handed the RAF a significant defeat. That night, 700 British bombers set out for Nuremberg. Gen. of Night Fighters Joseph Kammhuber's planes did not engage them until after their fighter escorts reached the limit of their fuel range and turned back for home. Then German fighters struck the unescorted British bomber formations and shot down ninety-five airplanes. Another dozen were so badly shot up that they later crashed or crash-landed in England. These heavy losses forced British Air Marshal

"Bomber" Harris to temporarily suspend his attacks, although not for long. During the Battle of the Ruhr, Bomber Command had flown 18,506 sorties and lost 872 aircraft. Another 2,126 had been damaged, for a high total casualty ratio of more than 16 percent. Still, British production had proceeded at such a pace that the RAF had almost 200 more bombers at the end of the battle than when it began.[12]

The temporary halt of massive British bombing did not stop them from launching minor or harassment raids, especially with their Mosquito bombers. These wooden-framed aircraft were faster than any German fighter and were at least as maneuverable. They were employed in several roles during World War II but were most effective as a nuisance bomber, robbing the already tired German worker of his rest and serving as a constant reminder that the enemy might strike anytime, anywhere— a fact that soon had its effect on German civilian morale.

American precision bombing also continued, mainly on the fringe of German airspace, but gradually extended inland. U.S. bombers blasted the Renault factory in Paris, the port of Naples, and the Erla aircraft factory and the engine works in Antwerp, followed by Palermo, Catania, and Messina in Sicily, Tunis (several times), Lorient, Brest, Naples (several more times), and Saint-Nazaire. On April 17, more than 100 American heavy bombers attacked the Focke-Wulf factory at Bremen but met strong fighter opposition and lost fifteen airplanes shot down.[13] The British were also back in action, bombing Essen again. Throughout May, the Allies launched violent attacks on the Ruhr and other German and German-held cities. The Americans bombed the former Ford and General Motors plants at Antwerp on May 4 and 14 and attacked the submarine yards at Kiel on May 14. These raids were followed by bombing strikes against the naval installations on Helgoland, the marshalling yards and airfields at Emden, the naval base and submarine construction works at Wilhelmshaven, the naval yards at Flensburg, and the submarine pens along the French coast. Most of these targets were subjected to multiple raids. In the meantime, the RAF dropped another 1,500 tons of bombs on Duisburg, Dortmund, and other cities, while a special "dam busting" squadron blew up two dams supplying much of the water to the Ruhr. Several British Mosquitoes carried out a daylight raid on the Zeiss optical factory at Jena in the center of the Third Reich without suffering a single casualty.[14]

The Allied attacks intensified in the last week of May. Dortmund took another 2,000 tons of bombs on the twenty-third, and Duesseldorf was hit by about the same force on the twenty-fifth. Wuppertal was attacked two days later, and 2,450 civilians were killed and about 118,000 left homeless in fifteen minutes of stark terror. Wuppertal-Barmen was struck with sticks of high-explosive bombs mixed with canisters full of phosphorus that burst into flames as they pierced right through the houses to the ground, leaving, as one German woman recalled, "a blazing trail throughout their passage. . . . It was impossible to extinguish the burning chemical, especially as it caused major conflagration on all floors simultaneously." As a result, residents had no chance of saving their homes. In the streets, one half-crazed woman repeated her story again and again to anyone who would listen. She had three small children and faced the alternative of carrying two to safety or letting the entire family perish together. She saved two of the children from their burning home but was filled with remorse about the third, whose cries still rang in her ears.

Many people caught in the raid jumped into the Wupper River with their clothes on fire, and a large number of them drowned. News of the latest disaster spread throughout Germany, and the bureaucracy even waived its beloved red tape. The people of Wuppertal-Barmen were "given free rail passes, special food and clothing coupons, and every help available," one resident recalled. She went to the Elberfeld station with her children and asked for tickets to Godesberg. They were given the tickets but did not have to pay for them, even though they did not say they were victims of the raid. "Our bandages, tangled hair, blotchy faced, scorched eyebrows, and the wild look in our eyes were our passwords wherever we went. That morning, we could tell at a glance by the expression on people's faces whether they had been through the ordeal or not." This particular woman, who had been burned, was awarded the Wounded Badge, a medal normally reserved for soldiers, and was granted a state pension of twenty marks a month for life.[15]

Back in the ruins of Wuppertal, survivors left messages and/or addresses on the walls of the ruins. These were often the only clue homecoming soldiers had as to the whereabouts of their relatives—or whether they were alive or dead.

The experience of Wuppertal was by no means unique; in fact, it was becoming more or less typical, as the cities of Germany became battlefields. On June 11, another 2,000 tons of bombs were dropped on Duesseldorf, and another 100,000 people were left homeless. The next day, 1,500 tons of high explosives and incendiaries were dropped on Bochum, and Oberhausen was severely bombed the day after that. In the third week of June, the RAF deposited 2,000 tons of bombs on Krefeld, 1,640 tons on Muelheim and Oberhausen, another 1,660 tons on Wuppertal, and 1,300 tons on Gelsenkirchen. In two attacks, 8,000 civilians were killed in Wuppertal alone, and still the raids continued. Cologne was pounded again on the night of June 28–29, when 540 British bombers dropped 1,614 tons of high-explosive and incendiary bombs on the city, killing 3,460 people and leaving 400,000 homeless in sixty terrifying minutes.[16]

On June 22, 182 U.S. heavy bombers launched a precision-bombing run on the chemical works at Huls in the Ruhr and badly damaged one of the Reich's most important synthetic rubber plants. The U.S. 8th Air Force also smashed aircraft factories at LeMans and Nantes; however, the American air effort over Europe was severely limited for the rest of the summer because several fighter and heavy bomber groups were transferred to the south to bolster the Allied air effort in the Mediterranean. In May and June 1943, the British Bomber Command launched sixteen major raids against the cities of the Third Reich, most of them in the Ruhr. Dortmund was hit twice with 3,500 tons of bombs. Almost 4,000 tons of bombs fell on Duesseldorf in just two raids. Cologne was hit twice, as was Bochum, with each city being struck with more than 2,000 tons of bombs. Of the Dortmund raid of May 24–25, Goebbels wrote in his diary:

> Destruction . . . is virtually total. Gauleiter [Albert] Hoffmann informed me that hardly a house in Dortmund is habitable. . . . The fact is that the Royal Air Force is taking on one industrial city after another, and one need not be a great mathematician to prophesy what a large part of the industry of the Ruhr will be out of commission.[17]

Hitler ordered the fighter defense of the Reich increased again on July 2, 1943. The veteran 3rd Fighter Wing "Udet" was recalled from the Russian Front. The 2nd Group of the 27th Fighter Wing (II/JG 27) was transferred from Italy to Weisbaden, and the 2nd Group of the 51st Fightering Wing "Moelders" (II/JG 51) was moved from Sardinia to Germany to defend the Munich area. Other groups followed shortly thereafter. By autumn, there were five fighter divisions in Germany, with another two assigned to Hugo Sperrle's 3rd Air Fleet for the defense of occupied Europe. Goering also strengthened the Reich's flak defenses. By early 1944, there were no fewer than twelve flak divisions guarding German and associated airspace, as opposed to the equivalent of five in late 1942. The table below shows the flak arm's order of battle in early 1944. Note that only eight of Germany's twenty extant flak divisions were at the front, while 60 percent guarded the airspace over Germany or German-occupied territory. This was a terrible drain on the front and, coupled with the transfer of dozens of fighter squadrons to other theaters, enabled the Red Air Force to gain air parity in several sectors.

ORDER OF BATTLE OF THE FLAK ARM BY DIVISION, EARLY 1944

Flak Division	Area of Responsibility
1st	Berlin
2nd (Mtz)	Russian Front
3rd	Hamburg
4th	Duesseldorf
5th	Southeastern Europe
6th (Mtz)	Russian Front
7th	Cologne
8th	Bremen
9th	Russian Front
10th (Mtz)	Russian Front
11th (Mtz)	Southern France
12th (Mtz)	Russian Front
13th	France (around Caen)
14th	Leipzig
15th (Mtz)	Russian Front
16th	France (around Lille)
17th (Mtz)	Russian Front
18th (Mtz)	Russian Front
21st	Southwestern Germany
22nd	Western Germany

Note: The 19th and 20th Motorized Flak Divisions had been destroyed in North Africa in May 1943.

Goering, as usual, did not blame himself for the mounting numbers of disasters, but rather the "cowardice" of the German fighter pilots—an assessment with which no Allied bomber crewman would agree. Goering also made the very serious mistake of trying to counter terror with terror and increased German bomber production at the expense of fighter production. As a result, he was unable to defend against the next onslaught, which proved to be one of the most powerful of the war.

THE DESTRUCTION OF HAMBURG

The Battle of Hamburg began on the night of Sunday–Monday, July 24–25. The attacks began when dozens of British bombers disrupted German radar by dropping millions of strips of tinfoil (called "chaff"). These had a multiplying effect because the strips fell slowly and were frequently carried aloft by updrafts. The chaff was followed by an even deadlier Allied innovation, the bomber stream. Prior to Hamburg, the British bombers had approached the German targets in formation, usually within visual contact of each other. Now, however, they came toward the target on a narrow front in no definite formation and usually out of visual contact with each other. The German night-fighter defense was simply unable to cope with the British tactics.[18] There were 740 heavy bombers in the first stream, but only a dozen were shot down. Much of the city was burned to the ground, and 1,500 civilians were killed. The streets were filled with rubble, and many fire trucks lost their tires trying to get to burning buildings. Others simply had to be left to burn, and even the central police station burned down. Fire engines were brought in from Luebeck, Kiel, and Berlin to help fight the blazes.

A second RAF raid took place early in the morning of Sunday, July 25, followed by a harassing raid on Tuesday, July 27. To the more astute, these attacks indicated that the danger was not yet over, and thousands of citizens left the city for safer parts. The really devastating raid did not come until the night of July 27–28, when British bombers dropped 2,300 tons of bombs on the second city of the Reich. About half of these were incendiaries, half high explosives. Air raids were nothing new to Hamburg by the middle of 1943; the attack of July 25 was the city's 138th of the war, according to the count of the city's chief of police. The city was not at all unprepared: its fire department had 305 new fire engines (excluding the reinforcements it had received from other cities),

935 portable power pumps, 49 fire boats, and some 200 miles of fire hose—enough to extend from Hamburg to Berlin.

Nothing, however, could have prepared the city for this raid, which involved 722 bombers. Nature was also working against the fire fighters because north-central Germany was in the grips of a drought, and the Hamburg fire department had been fighting blazes caused by the previous raids for three days and was now seriously low in water. The first waves of bombers killed many of the firemen and ruptured water mains. The weight of the bombs dropped in the early-morning hours of July 28 was approximately the same as the raid of July 25, but the results were far more catastrophic because of the atmospheric conditions. The temperature was abnormally high (ninety degrees Fahrenheit), and the moisture content of the air was very low (about 30 percent). The heat caused by the incendiaries and the ensuing fires was so intense that artifical firestorms were created. "The air brought in from the areas surrounding the major fires attained cyclonic force," historian Earl Beck wrote later. "Ground-level Hamburg became the fire pan of a gigantic oven." Smoke rose to observable heights of four to five miles, and many firemen simply gave up fighting the uncontrollable conflagrations and concentrated on extricating trapped survivors instead. Tens of thousands died in the heat and flames. Temperatures in the firestorms reached 700 degrees Fahrenheit in places, and even the asphalt on the streets caught fire.

Two nights later, the RAF repeated the performance, dropping more than 2,000 tons of high-explosive and incendiary bombs. That night, the *Luftwaffe* shot down only twenty-eight bombers as Hitler's second largest city died. Hundreds of buildings were blown apart or burned to the ground, and dozens of firemen, volunteer fire fighters, civil defense workers, and rescue personnel were killed, along with hundreds of civilians. The worst incident occurred when the exit of the public air raid shelter of the Karstadt department store was blocked and 370 people perished from carbon monoxide poisoning. Thousands more people—many of whom had lost everything except the clothing on their backs—fled the city in terror and spread panic and demoralization as they went.[19]

Fear not only gripped the average citizen; it spread to the leaders of the Third Reich as well. After visiting Hamburg, Field Marshal Erhard Milch, the inspector general of the *Luftwaffe*, momentarily lost control and, on August 2, bluntly cried to Joseph Goebbels, "We have lost the war."[20] "Hamburg . . . put the fear of God in me," Albert Speer recalled.

On August 1, he informed Hitler that armaments production was collapsing and that Hamburg-like raids on six more major cities would bring Germany's armaments production to a halt. "You'll straighten all that out again," Hitler replied lamely.[21]

That weekend, the RAF attacked Remscheid and Duesseldorf, and 120 American four-engine bombers blasted the Fieseler-Storch works at Magdeburg, where the excellent German short-range reconnaissance airplanes were produced, on July 28. The RAF further disrupted the German war effort during the night of Saturday, July 31, by dropping thousands of leaflets on Berlin. They threatened the capital with the same treatment as Hamburg and urged the Germans to evacuate all women and children from the city at once. The next day, Berlin's railroad stations were besieged by mobs of people trying to get out of the city, and panic gripped the capital of the Reich.[22] The British, however, did not launch a major raid against Berlin; instead, on Monday, August 2, they attacked Hamburg for the last time.

Thunderstorms prevented more than half of the bombers from reaching the target area, and those that did drop their bombs scattered them everywhere, but this relative failure mattered very little. The city was already devastated. In the four night raids of July 24–August 2, Hamburg suffered as much destruction as Great Britain endured throughout the entire war. The death total could only be estimated, but 50,000 is a commonly cited figure. Another 40,000 people were seriously wounded, half of the city's factories were destroyed, more than 50 percent of Hamburg's houses were destroyed by explosion or fire, and more than a million homeless refugees fled into the interior of the Reich, spreading fear as they went. German war morale sagged notably for the first time. Fortunately for Nazi Germany, the Allies did not concentrate such air power against a single city again until 1945, when they fire-bombed Dresden.

Goering did not dare show his face in Hamburg after the raid. He merely sent a letter of condolence to Gauleiter Karl Kaufmann and the population. The Gauleiter never published it because it would have caused a riot.[23]

THE AIR BATTLE OF BERLIN

The enormous quantities of tin foil the RAF dropped during the Battle of Hamburg effectively neutralized General Kammhuber's radar systems, so the German night fighters soon adopted the "Wild Boar" (*Wilde Sau*) tactics invented by Maj. Hans-Joachim "Hajo" Hermann. They were based on the idea that the Allied night bombers could be silhouetted by lighting target areas with flares, searchlights, and flak. Then freelance single-engine fighters, flying at high altitudes, could attack the bombers from overhead, relying exclusively on visual sightings. Kammhuber was not at all in favor of the new free-for-all tactics, which was a major factor in his eventual removal as general of night fighters.

Although more effective than the *Kimmelbett* system in which the night fighters did not leave their assigned sectors, the Wild Boar tactics did not halt the RAF bomber offensive. The "Battle of Berlin" began on July 24, 1943. During the first phase, which lasted until November 18, the Allies launched thirty-three major raids, concentrating on the capital but also bombing Bochum, Duisburg, Gelsenkirchen, Wuppertal, Leverkusen, Essen, Duesseldorf, and Remscheild in the Ruhr. They struck Hanover in more than 3,000 sorties and subjected Bremen, Kassel, Cologne, Frankfurt, Mannheim, Stuttgart, Munich, and Nuremberg to major aerial attacks. Targets in France were also subjected to precision bombing by the U.S. 8th Air Force (operating out of England), and Milan, Turin, and Genoa in Italy were victims of minor raids by the U.S. 15th Air Force (flying out of North Africa).[24]

Despite the considerable damage it caused, however, the British air offensive was failing in its primary purpose—destroying German morale. On December 23, 1943, Missie Vassiltchikov, a White Russian emigrant living in Berlin, wrote in her diary:

> It looks as if these ghastly raids are intended . . . [to break] the Germans' morale, but I do not think that much can be achieved that way. Indeed they are having the contrary effect. For amidst such suffering and hardships, political considerations become secondary, and everyone seems intent only on patching roofs, propping up walls, cooking fried potatoes on an upturned electric iron . . . or melting snow for water to wash with. Furthermore, at such times the heroic side of human nature takes over and people are being extraordinarily friendly and helpful to one another.[25]

Meanwhile, the 9th U.S. Air Force joined the European air war. Operating from bases in North Africa, it attacked the Ploesti oilfields on

August 1 and severely damaged the production facilities, but at a terrible price. Of the 178 B-24 Liberators involved, 50 were shot down, and 55 others were seriously damaged by the 1st Group of the 4th Fighter Wing (I/JG 4), the 4th Group of the 27th Fighter Wing (IV/JG 27), and the Bulgarian Fighter Regiment, which were operating out of Romania, Greece, and Bulgaria, respectively. On August 13, the Americans were more successful, devastating the Messerschmitt Aircraft Works at Wiener-Neustadt near Vienna. Then, on August 16, the Americans introduced shuttle bombing. Dozens of Flying Fortresses took off from England, bombed the Messerschmitt factory at Regensburg, and flew on to the American bases in North Africa before the *Luftwaffe* could react.

On the night of August 17, the British turned their attentions to Peenemuende, the center of German V-weapons research activities. Forty of the 597 heavy bombers which attacked the facility were shot down, but 700 workers were killed, including many almost irreplaceable technicians. Because of this one raid, the production of V-weapons was delayed an entire year. It was a major victory for the RAF, although the British did not fully appreciate it at the time.

After the Hamburg raid, Goering met with Milch, Col. Gen. Hubert Weise, Gen. of Fighters Adolf Galland, and several other officers of the *Luftwaffe* General Staff.[26] Even Col. Dietrich Peltz, the general of bomber forces, agreed that the bomber arm should relinquish its industrial priority at once so that Germany could produce more fighters. "Never before and never again did I witness such determination and agreement among the circle of those responsible for the leadership of the *Luftwaffe*," Galland recalled.[27] Personal animosity and ambition were set aside; everyone wanted to do everything possible to prevent a second national catastrophe of the scale of Hamburg. Albert Speer, the minister of armaments and munitions, joined Milch and Galland in opposing Hitler's policy of retaliation because it cost roughly nine times as much manpower and materiel to produce a bomber as a fighter. Even Hermann Goering was carried away. He rushed off to Fuehrer Headquarters to secure Hitler's permission for the *Luftwaffe* to give the highest priority to the defense of the Reich. Fighter production, he told Hitler, must be emphasized, even at the expense of bomber production.

There were apparently no surviving witnesses to the scene that followed in Hitler's bunker, but Goering emerged sobbing. Hitler had rejected any radical changes in the air war; there would be no switch from offensive to defensive tactics. Terror bombing against England would still be the answer to terror bombing against Germany. Furthermore, Hitler declared that he had lost faith in Goering and the *Luftwaffe*. Completely shattered, Goering begged for another chance. Hitler relented. "The Fuehrer made me realize our mistake," he moaned to Galland and Peltz. "The Fuehrer is always right. We must deal such mighty blows to our enemy in the West that he will never dare to risk another raid like Hamburg."[28] Goering ordered Peltz to direct the aerial counterattack on England and then hurried back to Rominten, East Prussia, to hunt. The air war would take its inevitable course down the road to total defeat. If Hermann Goering could not see this—or refused to admit that he saw it—Hans Jeschonnek finally saw it clearly. As a result, he took what he considered the appropriate step: he shot himself in the head on August 18.

CHAPTER 6

The State of the Wehrmacht, Spring 1943

The disasters of Stalingrad and Tunisia, coupled with the Japanese reversals in the Pacific and the rapid increase in the military strengths of the United States and Soviet Union, convinced most of the senior generals of the German Army that the Axis could not win the war. Stalemate, with the hope of a negotiated peace, seemed to many to be a realistic goal, and Manstein's victories on the Donetz left the initiative on the Eastern Front in the hands of the *Wehrmacht*. Meanwhile, the army took advantage of the Russian thaw—during which both sides were virtually immobilized—to regain much of its strength.

The winter campaign of 1942–43 had cost the Third Reich one of its best armies and had thrown the Germans back nearly 500 miles from the Volga; nevertheless, the *Wehrmacht* had shown a remarkable resiliency. Kharkov had been a magnificient victory and went a long way toward restoring German morale on the Eastern Front. There were ominous developments in other aspects of the war effort, however. Germany had failed to maintain its superiority in equipment and mobility vis-a-vis its enemies—a fact which was especially significant on the Eastern Front, where most of the Red Army had been equipped with American trucks that enabled it to make and exploit deep penetrations in the increasingly thin German line. Moreover, since Washington was providing trucks, jeeps, and other motorized vehicles for the Red Army, Soviet industry was able to concentrate on the manufacture of tanks and heavy weapons and further increase its numerical superiority over the *Wehrmacht* in these categories. (The United States also provided Stalin with Sherman tanks, but not many, since Soviet tanks were superior to the Sherman.) Historian Albert Seaton wrote:

> The German Army, once the best equipped in the world, within a space of two years was relegated to the position of an out-of-date force, indifferently provided with obsolescent equipment. The German equivalent to the Red Army quarter-ton jeep for commander or messenger remained the horse. The counterpart of the Studebaker or Dodge six-wheeled drive truck was the horse-drawn panje wagon. The efficiency of German field formation staffs and the quality of the German fighting soldier were still superior to those of the Red Army, yet . . . the German Army, once the pride of the Reich, had become one of the poorer armies in the world.[1]

In terms of equipment, Germany would be at a strategic disadvantage for the rest of the war. This fact is well reflected in tank availability statistics. Germany had invaded Russia with 3,300 tanks, but by January 23, 1943, it had only 495 operational panzers on the entire Eastern Front.[2] By June, German repairmen had more than 2,000 panzers operational on the Eastern Front, but many of these were mechanically shot and subject to breaking down under the slightest pressure. In addition, the Soviet T-34 and KV tanks were superior to the main German battle tanks, the PzKw III and IV, and by the end of 1942, the Soviets were manufacturing around 2,000 tanks a month. German production of the PzKw IV, on the other hand, did not exceed 100 per month until October 1942.[3]

Hitler decided to do something about the deterioration of the German panzer arm in early 1943, following the surrender of Stalingrad. On February 17, after the details of the negotiations were handled by intermediaries, he had Heinz Guderian summoned to Fuehrer Headquarters at Vinnitsa, where he was offered the post of inspector of panzer troops. Guderian, however, had his own ideas and his own conditions. Most significantly, his inspectorate would be an independent organization, subordinate only to Hitler himself. It would not take orders from Zeitzler,

OKH, OKW, or Col. Gen. Fritz Fromm's Replacement Army and would have the status of an independent army command.

The artillery officers at OKW, led by Alfred Jodl, succeeded in aborting Guderian's attempt to absorb the assault gun branch, which remained part of the artillery, but Guderian got everything else he wanted. The panzer inspectorate was made responsible for the organization, training, and technical development of the panzer arm, which now included all panzer troops, all panzer grenadier units, all motorized infantry with the panzer and panzer grenadier divisions, the heavy *Panzerjaeger* tank destroyers, the panzer and motorized reconnaissance battalions, all dismounted antitank gunners, and armored railroad troops. In the vital fields of equipment design, development, and industrial production, Guderian was responsible to no military authority except Hitler. Finally, all motorized schools and training installations came under the new panzer inspectorate, and a new commander of panzer troops (*Kommandeure der Panzertruppe*) was assigned to each *Wehrkreis*. The Replacement Army remained responsible for allocating new recruits and draftees to the panzer arm. This naturally led to a great deal of friction between the Home Army and the panzer arm, between Fromm and Guderian.

"Guderian had been elevated to a position that was of hardly less importance than that of Jodl and Zeitzler," Seaton wrote later.[4] Unfortunately, these three men disliked each other intensely. The result was a further fragmentation of the German High Command. Jodl and Zeitzler were already at each other's throats more or less constantly, sometimes quarrelling bitterly over a single division, while Guderian could not work well with any superior officer. To make matters worse, Hitler was visibly tiring and showing symptoms of a nervous disorder, which was no doubt aggravated by drug abuse and severe stress. He had no one to blame for this except himself, since he had set up this irregular system of command and government. He was constantly besieged by bickering and backbiting officials and generals, each intent on presenting his own view of a particular situation or dispute to Hitler. Directly subordinate to Hitler in his capacity as Supreme Commander were OKW, OKL, OKM, OKH, the panzer inspectorate, and the Waffen-SS. However, since the army group commanders knew that Zeitzler had little real authority, they often bypassed him and presented their problems directly to an increasingly exhausted Hitler. Also directly responsible to Hitler was an entire host of Nazi Party officers, Gauleiters, ministers, diplomats, bureaucrats, government officials, representatives of his allies, and other officials. More and more, Hitler took to delegating his civilian responsibilities to Goebbels, Himmler, or the ever-present Martin Bormann. As his military problems increased, Hitler—as often as not—handled them by making empty promises and giving in to the last person to whom he spoke (unless, of course, one of his pet projects was involved). In other cases, he simply made snap decisions based on intuition or inadequate information or fell back on the rigid formula of "hold at all costs" or "not one step back." As the war progressed, he increasingly resorted to the technique of simply putting decisions off—sometimes indefinitely.

This method of leadership had a particularly disastrous impact on the German Army. Plans that should have been made in a systematic manner often had to be thrown together overnight. Movements, especially retreats, that could have been conducted in a leisurely manner had to be executed in great haste, often involving unneccessary casualties and the loss of heavy equipment. All too often, decisions to retreat were postponed until it was too late for the units involved to escape at all. In short, German strategic leadership was in shambles by the spring of 1943, and any semblance of unity of command, in either the army or the armed forces, had simply ceased to exist.

In terms of tactical and operational leadership, the German Army maintained its superiority over all of its enemies, especially in the East. The problem the *Wehrmacht* and the other ministries faced in early 1943 was twofold: (1) obtaining the personnel necessary to handle the equipment that was available, and (2) producing the equipment necessary to sustain the fight. To accomplish this, the Germans resorted to drastic measures. In June 1942, for example, they created a special staff under the command of Gen. of Infantry Walter von Unruh, a *Pour le Merite* winner in the First World War. Responsible only to Hitler, Unruh and his staff were given the authority to transfer individuals to the Eastern Front—orders which could be revoked only by Hitler. Naturally, a visit from Unruh and his men was greeted with terror in the rear echelons, which dubbed them "hero snatchers."

Unruh succeeded in reducing the number of men in rear-echelon units, but while his efforts were considered worthwhile, they were not decisive because he and his staff concentrated more on sending individuals to the combat zone, rather than on eliminating entire rear-area formations and branches of government. Other steps were necessary. These included reducing the number of exemptions for workers in the industrial and agricultural sectors and recruiting formerly unwanted Germans and sending them to the front in penal battalions. The Germans also resorted to the forced recruitment of ethnic Germans (*Volksdeutsche*) and reshaped the services to thin out men for combat duty. They reorganized their formations to allow for more frontline combat power and significantly increased the number of machine guns in an infantry company by arming platoons with machine pistols (called "burp guns"). They also recruited women auxiliaries to free men for frontline duty, increased the use of allied troops, recruited Soviet prisoners of war and Soviet civilians as auxiliaries, and, on a more limited scale, began to recruit Russians, Ukrainians, Latvians, and other Soviet nationals into combat formations. As a result, the German armed forces reached its peak strength for the entire war in the summer of 1943.[5]

As of July 1, 1943, the German Army had a total of 4,480,000 men in 243 divisions (174 infantry, 23 panzer, 16 fortress, 12 panzer grenadier, 11 security, and 7 mountain divisions). Of these, 168 divisions (3,100,000 men) were stationed in the East, along with 2,269 of the army's 3,142 tanks and 997 of its 1,442 assault guns.[6] These figures are somewhat deceiving, however. Because of Hitler's irrational demands for more and more divisions, the army was continually raising new formations, but it was not allowed to rebuild, reequip, or properly maintain existing formations. As a result, the army was 616,000 men below establishment. Some panzer units, for example, had fewer than thirty tanks (less than a prewar battalion) and were thus divisions in name only. Some infantry divisions were at only regimental strength, and the term *Kampfgruppe* (battle group or combat group, abbreviated KG) was used more and more frequently to describe a burned-out and understrength division that had the approximate combat value of a regiment. Had OKH been allowed to merge these depleted units, it could have reestablished a reasonable ratio between men in combat units and men in administrative, service, supply, and support units. Hitler refused to allow this. "Hitler, the military illiterate, continued to view military strength in terms of numbers rather than in quality," Matthew Cooper, a historian of the German armed forces, wrote later.[7] Hitler insisted that the number of divisions remain constant, even if it meant continually diluting the fighting strength of the individual divisions. Naturally, the vast majority of the casualties in the combat divisions occurred in the combat elements (infantry, panzer, assault gun, and so forth), as opposed to the administrative and rear-area elements. Since they were not allowed reinforcements, the size of the administrative tails of these divisions were out of all proportion to their shrunken combat units. Many infantry divisions were reduced from nine to six infantry battalions—and some from three to two infantry regiments—while quite a few divisions created an ad hoc third infantry regiment by combining their engineer and reconnaissance battalions into a single battle group and using them as infantry—perhaps the best solution to the problem under the circumstances, but hardly a desirable one. Hitler's response to the problem was to refuse to face it; instead, he ordered that every division destroyed at Stalingrad be rebuilt, as well as four of the six destroyed in Tunisia. As a result, the quality of the German division continued to decline.

Naturally, although the quality of the German officer remained relatively high, the army was not able to maintain its prewar standards, which were incredibly high, and was not even able to maintain the standards of 1940. Between 1933 and 1943, the army's officer corps expanded sixty-four-fold. The army had 246,453 officers as of October 1, 1943, but more than 80,000 of these were physicans, medical officers, veterinarians, and other specialists. Qualitatively, the officer corps had devolved from a small, elite professional corps into a large people's officer corps (*Volksoffizierkorps*). Many of its members were from the older-age groups, but they were, generally speaking, intelligently used in the rear areas and in the *Wehrkreise*. The younger officers, however, fundamentally changed the character of the officer corps because there were so many of them and because most of them were National Socialists. Between 1939 and 1942, for example, almost 45 percent of all officer-candidates were members of the Nazi Party. The army had lost its homogeneity, some of its elitism and professionalism, and much of its nonpolitical character.[8] It had also lost a great deal of its political power and influence. When Adolf Hitler assumed the title of commander in chief of the army in December 1941, he had, in effect, abolished the post. The army, therefore, had no representative at Fuehrer Headquarters and in the upper echelons of the government, such as the *Luftwaffe* had in Goering, the navy in Raeder (and later Doenitz), and the SS in Himmler. As a result, other branches of the service and even organs of the party were able to make inroads into areas that were formerly the province of the army.

THE LUFTWAFFE

By the spring of 1943, the *Luftwaffe* was in dire straits in all active sectors, including the Eastern Front. In Russia, its aviation units were outnumbered five to one by the Red Air Force, but the German pilot was still definitely superior to his Russian opponent—whenever there were German forces in a particular area, that is. The quality of the German aviator was also declining, mainly because of Jeschonnek's unsound training policies and his disastrous use of the training wings. As a result, newly trained aviators were sent to the Eastern Front, where their chances of survival were greater. Even so, these poorly and incompletely trained German pilots did not have a very long life expectancy, even by the depressing standards of that theater.

Aviation units were certainly not the only type of *Luftwaffe* formations in existence in 1943. There were about two dozen flak divisions and brigades, and the best of these were in action on the Eastern Front, where they were often used as antitank units in the combat zone. They destroyed hundreds of Allied airplanes, tanks, and motorized vehicles, both in North Africa and in Russia. German parachute units also fought on all active theaters in the war and distinguished themselves in a dozen different campaigns, even though they were used almost exclusively as infantry units after the bloodletting on Crete. With considerable justification, one paratrooper compared using airborne troops as infantry to mopping a barracks floor using champagne instead of water, since it cost considerably more to train them, but at least they did perform exceptionally well in combat. The other major type of *Luftwaffe* infantry unit, the *Luftwaffe* field division, contributed very little to the German war effort.

In the fall of 1942, it became obvious that the aviation, support, and service branches of the *Luftwaffe* were bloated and that the large number of ground troops they controlled was far in excess of their needs or combat value. Hitler, therefore, ordered the *Luftwaffe* to hand over 200,000 of its excess troops to the army. Hermann Goering would have none of it. With tears in his eyes, he went to Hitler and begged him not to turn good "National Socialist" *Luftwaffe* troops over to OKH, where they would be corrupted by reactionary attitudes. This approach touched a responsive cord in Hitler, whose irrational hatred for the army and its General Staff grew every day. As a result, in mid-September 1942, OKW issued an order for the formation of ten to twelve *Luftwaffe* field brigades. In theory, they were to support the army in land operations. Their equipment, however, was to be provided by the army, and Goering, who was still in charge of a large portion of the German war economy, saw to it that they were superbly equipped.

Allowing the creation of the *Luftwaffe* field divisions was a horrible mistake on Hitler's part, for his air force was not able to properly train these men for ground combat, and this needlessly cost thousands of men their lives. These new units also severely hamstrung the army, which eventually had to equip twenty-two *Luftwaffe* field divisions— enough to form three armies—and did not get a single reliable division in return.

The first of the *Luftwaffe* field divisions was created in September 1942. In mid-October, before it could complete its training, OKW ordered the formation of twelve more *Luftwaffe* field divisions. The Army Organizations Branch recorded in its war diary on October 25: "The requirement in load-carrying vehicles for 11 to 12 *Luftwaffe* divisions is approximately 6,000; the result will be to postpone, yet again, bringing four to five panzer divisions up to establishment."[9]

The *Luftwaffe* field divisions proved to be marginal or downright worthless in combat, where they suffered appalling casualties. By November 1943, Hitler was convinced that he had made a mistake, and the field divisions were transferred back to the army, although they retained their *Luftwaffe* field designations. As of March 1945, only four still existed. The following table shows the fate of the *Luftwaffe* field divisions.

THE *LUFTWAFFE* FIELD DIVISIONS

Number	Created	Sector	Fate
1st	1942	Leningrad	Suffered such heavy casualties that it had to be disbanded in early 1944.
2nd	1942	Army Group Center	Disbanded in early 1944.
3rd	1942	Army Group Center	Disbanded in early 1944.
4th	1942	Army Group Center	Destroyed at Vitebsk in July 1944.
5th	1942	Southern Russia	Suffered heavy casualties during the winter of 1942–43; then disbanded.
6th	1942	Army Group Center	Destroyed at Vitebsk in July 1944.
7th	1942	Army Group Don	Suffered heavy losses on the Upper Chir in winter of 1942–43; disbanded in May 1943.
8th	1942	Army Group Don	Suffered heavy losses on the Upper Chir; disbanded in May 1943.
9th	1942	Leningrad	Suffered heavy casualties in the retreat of February 1944; then disbanded.
10th	1942	Leningrad	Heavy losses in January 1944; subsequently disbanded.
11th	1942	Balkans	Surrendered to the Red Army at the end of the war.
12th	1942	Army Group North	Surrendered in Courland at the end of the war.
13th	1942	Army Group North	Suffered heavy casualties in January 1944; subsequently disbanded.
14th	1942	Norway	Surrendered in 1945; never engaged in combat.
15th	1942	Army Group Don	Suffered heavy losses at Taganrog; subsequently disbanded.
16th	1942	Holland	Committed to combat in Normandy; lost 75 percent of its men within hours; survivors assigned to 16th Volksgrenadier Division.
17th	1943	Le Havre, France	Destroyed by U.S. 1st Army on August 28, 1944; survivors assigned to 167th Infantry Division.
18th	1943	Northern France and Belgium	Destroyed in Mons Pocket; the few survivors were assigned to the 18th Volksgrenadier Division.

THE *LUFTWAFFE* FIELD DIVISIONS

Number	Created	Sector	Fate
19th	1943	Italy	Heavy losses in first battle; sent to Denmark; absorbed by 19th Volksgrenadier Division.
20th	1943	Denmark/Italy	Heavy losses in Italy in 1944; pulled out of combat zone; absorbed by 155th Field Training Division in 1945.
21st	1943	Army Group North	Surrendered in Courland at the end of the war.
22nd	1943		Never completely formed, probably because of the poor combat record of the earlier *Luftwaffe* field divisions.

Note: Four *Luftwaffe* field corps headquarters were formed in 1942–43. The I was disbanded in 1943 and never saw active field service. The II fought on the Eastern Front in 1943–44 and was disbanded in early 1944; part of its staff was used to form the I Parachute Corps. The III fought on the northern sector of the Eastern Front and was dissolved in October 1943. The IV was formed in the winter of 1942–43 and fought in the southern sector of the Eastern Front from 1943 to early 1944; transferred to the French Mediterranean coast, it took part in the retreat to Alsace and was redesignated as the XC Corps in late 1944.

Sources: OB 1945; Mitcham, *Hitler's Legions*, 427–38.

THE WAFFEN-SS

Of the Waffen-SS, Theodor Eicke, the first inspector general of concentration camps and the commander of the notorious "Totenkopf" SS Panzer Grenadier Division, said, "We don't carry weapons to look like the army but rather to use them when the Fuehrer and the movement are in danger."[10] Use them they did, especially Eicke. He used them on political opponents during the Weimar era, on Jews, homosexuals, Poles, Russians, and political and criminal prisoners—even on fellow Nazis, for it was Eicke and his adjutant who shot Ernst Roehm, the chief of the Brownshirts, in his cell in Munich in 1934. He also formed the "Death's Head" units from his concentration camp guards and led them until he was killed in action on the Eastern Front in February 1943. But Eicke's activities were only a part of the larger goal of the SS. During World War II, SS influence in internal, foreign, economic, police, and military affairs grew to the point where it seemed likely that Himmler's ultimate objective was nothing less than the re-formation of German society as a whole.[11]

Throughout the Nazi era, few areas were safe from attempts by the SS to extend its influence. After the war, for example, Albert Speer wrote an entire book subtitled "How Heinrich Himmler Schemed to Build an SS Industrial Empire."[12] In the armed services, however, Himmler's encroachment progressed only very slowly at first. Although Adolf Hitler definitely favored the SS over the army, the really massive expansion of the Waffen-SS did not begin until after the Battle of Moscow, when Hitler decided that the army and its General Staff had failed him. On March 1, 1942, he allowed Gottlob Berger to form the first *Volksdeutsche* division, the SS Volunteer Division "Prinz Eugen," which was later redesignated the 7th SS Mountain Division "Prinz Eugen." It was made up of ethnic Germans living in Yugoslavia and was used primarily against partisans in the Balkans. It was followed rapidly by an entire host of new SS divisions, several of which were German.

By the end of World War II, a total of forty SS divisions had been raised, although some had been dissolved or destroyed by then; twenty-seven of them were composed of foreigners. Thirteen SS corps headquarters and two army headquarters had also been formed. Long before this time, the SS took over the Opel Works and began producing vehicles with their own labor. Between July 1 and September 30, 1942, the Waffen-SS formations acquired twice their allocation of vehicles and received almost twice as many trucks, automobiles, and other motorized vehicles as the army did—much to the disgust of the General Staff.[13] The army was powerless to do anything about it because it was divided against itself. It had no separate commander in chief to represent it, and the General Staff's standing at Fuehrer Headquarters sank even lower as the German tide ebbed on the Eastern Front.

CHAPTER 7

Hitler's Summer Offensive

THE SITUATION IN THE EAST, EARLY 1943

Even after his amazing victories on the Donetz, Erich von Manstein knew that Germany had no choice but to go over to the strategic defensive in 1943; within this defense, however, he believed it would be possible to wear down Soviet strength by quick, powerful local offensives aimed at taking large numbers of prisoners but without capturing vast territories. He presented his views to Hitler in a memorandum he submitted in late February. As Manstein saw it, there were two options, which he labeled "forehand" and "backhand." The forehand option would entail preempting Stalin by launching a strong local offensive before the Red Army could attack. The backhand option would involve a duplication of the "Miracle on the Donetz": allow the Soviets to attack, fall back with the blow, conduct a mobile defense until the Red juggernaut wore itself out, and then launch an offensive of his own. Manstein favored the backhand option, but Hitler would not consider abandoning the Donetz Basin on the grounds that it would have unforeseen effects on the Turks and the Romanians. As a result, Manstein was forced to plan a forehand attack. Naturally, his attention was drawn to the Kursk salient.

Located due north of Kharkov, the Kursk bulge stuck into the German line like a clenched Russian fist. It had a total frontage of about 250 miles, but its base was less than 70 miles from north to south. The enemy forces in the bulge had been worn down in several months of continuous fighting, their combat strength was low, and their equipment was in poor condition. Manstein calculated that an offensive launched in early May—just as soon as the spring thaw had dried—would take the Russians by surprise and find them unprepared. In addition, the liquidation of the Kursk salient would eliminate the threat to the Orel salient, which was held by Army Group Center to the north of Kursk.

Manstein could provide the thrust against Kursk from the south, using the 4th Panzer Army and part of Army Detachment Kempf. The thrust from the north, however, would have to be carried out by Army Group Center, which had nothing in reserve; it was obvious that they were going to need more troops. Two sources immediately suggested themselves to General Zeitzler: the Demyansk "mushroom," which was defended by twelve divisions (100,000 men), and the Rzhev salient, which was held by the entire 9th Army. Remarkably, Hitler approved both operations.

The evacuation of Demyansk was brilliantly directed by Lt. Gen. Paul Laux, the acting commander of the II Corps. Beginning on February 17, he evacuated 1,200 square miles of territory in ten days in the face of five Soviet armies. He did not lose a single operational gun or vehicle, although 1,500 damaged vehicles, 700 tons of rations, and several hundred tons of ammunition had to be destroyed. All that was left behind for the Russians were 10,000 carefully prepared and attended German graves.[1] These were promptly bulldozed by the Soviets.

The evacuation of Rzhev—known as Operation Buffalo—began on March 1 and was also carried out flawlessly. The Soviets were not able to pursue effectively because of the huge number of mines the German engineers left behind and the places they left them. One intercepted Soviet message read: "I stable my horse and enter the house—and there is a big bang. Stable and horse are gone. Those damned Fritzes plant their mines anywhere except where we suspect them."[2] Such nasty surprises resulted in a very slow pursuit, and the divisions of the 9th Army and the left wing of the 4th Army fell back from phase line to phase line for sixteen days, carrying about 15,000 civilians with them. The forward German units retreated as much as 90 miles, abandoning Rzhev on March 3, Belyy on March 10, and Vyazma on March 12. When the operation was over, the German frontage in this sector had been reduced from 340 miles to a mere 110 miles, freeing an entire German army: four corps headquarters and twenty-one divisions (three of them panzer). Army Group Center had its forces for the Kursk offensive.

Model's 9th Army Headquarters was sent south to the Orel area, where it assumed command of the units scheduled to launch the northern pincer of the attack on Kursk.

THE NEW PANZERS CAUSE DELAYS

Hitler accepted the idea of the Kursk offensive and issued a detailed operation order (Number 6) to that effect on April 15. Dubbed Operation Citadel, it called for a pincer attack at the base of the salient. Model's 9th Army would attack from the north, while Hoth's 4th Panzer Army and Army Detachment Kempf of Manstein's Army Group South advanced from the south, as shown on the map on the next page. Each army would have to advance about thirty-five miles to close the trap. Unfortunately, the plan was already handed over to the Russians by the Lucy spy ring as early as the first week in April; in fact, copies of Operation Order Number 6 reached Zhukov and the other senior Soviet military commanders before it reached the German field army commanders. The offensive was thoroughly compromised before it began.

Once he knew what the Germans were planning, Zhukov devised a scheme to decisively defeat the *Wehrmacht*. He would check the German assault forces in the Kursk sector and, once they had spent their force, counterattack against the Orel salient to the north and against Belgograd to the south, encircling Model's 9th Army at Orel and inflicting upon Hitler a defeat greater than Stalingrad. In a sense, he was planning Manstein's backhand in reverse. He immediately began pouring troops, civilian workers, weapons, and supplies into the cauldron of Kursk. In May, it was still questionable whether he could reinforce the salient to the point where he could check the Germans; however, Hitler played into his hands by delaying the offensive again and again. It was more than ten weeks between the time Hitler issued the operations order and the actual beginning of the attack. During that period, Zhukov ran a half a million freight cars into the Kursk area, all loaded with men, weapons, tanks, and mines. By July 1, 20 percent of the entire Red Army was in the area of the Kursk salient, along with every fourth combat airplane

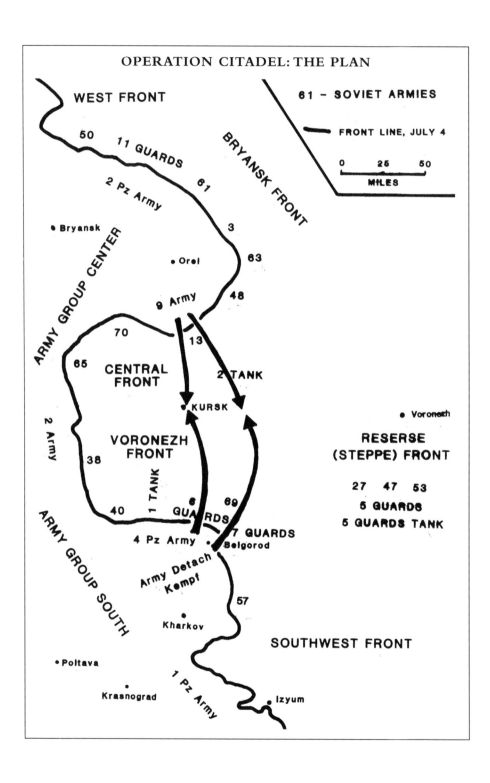

OPERATION CITADEL: THE PLAN

61 – SOVIET ARMIES

FRONT LINE, JULY 4

0   25   50

MILES

WEST FRONT

50

11 GUARDS

61

2 Pz Army

BRYANSK FRONT

• Bryansk

ARMY GROUP CENTER

• Orel

3

63

9 Army

48

70

13

65

CENTRAL
FRONT

2 TANK

• Voronezh

2 Army

VORONEZH
FRONT

RESERSE
(STEPPE) FRONT

38

• KURSK

27   47   53

1 TANK

5 GUARDS

5 GUARDS TANK

ARMY GROUP SOUTH

40

6
GUARDS

69

4 Pz Army

7 GUARDS
• Belgorod

Army Detach
Kempf

57

• Kharkov

SOUTHWEST FRONT

• Poltava

•
Krasnograd

1 Pz Army

• Izyum

and more than a third of Stalin's armor. Zhukov only awaited Hitler's attack.

Why did the Nazi dictator delay launching the Kursk offensive?

Adolf Hitler had always been fascinated with new military innovations, techniques, and weapons. He appreciated, for example, the theory of *blitzkrieg* and the value of the panzer branch long before many of his more conservative generals. In early 1943, he was aware of the defects of the obsolete German panzers, and he became convinced that only an influx of new, qualitatively superior tanks could win a major victory at Kursk. Three such tanks were already in the early stages of production: the PzKw V Panther and two versions of the PzKw VI Tiger, the Porsche model (known as the Ferdinand) and the Henschel. Unfortunately, series production of all three tanks was delayed, and Hitler kept putting off the offensive until the new tanks could be delivered to the panzer battalions.

Part of the problem was that Hitler constantly tinkered in matters of tank design, development, and procurement, so that heavy tank production soon degenerated into utter confusion. Another part of the problem was that no one in authority could seem to decide which of the Tiger tanks to adopt. The experts favored the Henschel model because it was clearly a better weapon. It weighed about fifty-six tons, carried 100 millimeters of frontal armor, and boasted a long-barrelled 88-millimeter main battle gun and two 7.92-millimeter machine guns. Its 88-millimeter gun was probably the best weapon of its type produced by any country in the Second World War.

The Porsche, on the other hand, was a flawed tank. It was actually manufactured by the Krupp Company and suffered from a number of design problems, the most serious of which was the fact that it had no secondary armament—i.e., it had no machine guns. Although its 88-millimeter main battle gun was excellent, it had no way of dealing with Russian infantry. There were actually cases during the Battle of Kursk when Porsche Tiger crewmen fired machine guns at Russian infantry over the side of the turret or through the main battle gun—an occurrence that was probably unique in the history of World War II. If Guderian's panzer inspectorate had been in existence when the Tiger was being designed, it is highly doubtful whether this defective model would have made it to the production lines at all.

The new Panther was a medium tank that weighed forty-five tons and had a very effective 75-millimeter main battle gun and three machine guns. Its designers copied many of the best characteristics of the Soviet tanks, and the General Staff considered it the best tank ever produced. After the war, many former panzer troops expressed the same opinion. For their time, they were probably right. Later models were, in fact, very mechanically reliable, and the Panther became an excellent combat tank. The first models, however, suffered the teething problems normally associated with such weapons, and the rushed nature of Panther production did not help matters. Hitler expected 250 PzKw Vs to be ready for battle by the end of May. Production and delivery fell far behind, and during a meeting in Berlin on May 10, Hitler postponed the Kursk offensive until June 12. Speer assured him that the production problems had been solved and that there would be more than 300 Panthers available for the offensive. Actually, by July 1, German industry was producing only a dozen PzKw Vs a week.

By the first week of May, several of the German generals were having second thoughts about the wisdom of launching Operation Citadel at all. On May 4, Hitler invited his top commanders to a conference at Munich to sort out the problems associated with the offensive. Alfred Jodl, OKW's chief of operations, had never favored Citadel and again called on Hitler to abandon the idea of an offensive in Russia (the OKH sector) in favor of bolstering the Mediterranean and Balkans (OKW sectors). Kurt Zeitzler, chief of staff of OKH, derided Jodl for his timidity and continued to lobby strongly for the offensive. OKW head Wilhelm Keitel, sensing that Hitler wanted to attack, voted to strike. Heinz Guderian, inspector general of the panzer troops, strongly opposed the offensive, as did Armaments Minister Albert Speer. Guenther von Kluge, the commander of Army Group Center, favored an attack and let his pathological hatred for Guderian get out of hand. He told Hitler that he intended to challenge Guderian to a duel and asked Hitler to serve as his second; Hitler refused to allow the duel to take place. The 9th Army's commander, Walter Model, wanted to delay the offensive until the heavier Porsche tanks could be delivered.

Hitler was impressed with Model's arguments and proposed waiting until June. Erich von Manstein, commander of Army Group South, objected on the grounds that the delay would benefit the Russians more than the Germans because they would have more time to recover from their defeats at the end of the winter and because Soviet tank production—already higher than that of the Reich—would cancel out any gains. Kluge agreed with Manstein and, perhaps miffed at Model, added that 9th Army was not in as bad a condition as its commander indicated.

The weight of opinion at Munich was clearly in favor of attacking, despite the delays—although the leading commanders felt there should be no more postponements. Model's arguments carried the day, and on May 6, Hitler announced that Citadel would be delayed until June 12.

Zeitzler and Werner Kempf immediately protested and called upon Hitler to reconsider, but he would not do so. He wanted Model to have the ninety Porsche Tigers that would be ready in June. Guderian continued to try to talk Hitler into cancelling the offensive altogether. On May 10, he asked Hitler why he wanted to attack in Russia at all that year. Keitel answered that they had to attack for political reasons. Guderian then pointedly asked Keitel how many people in the world even knew where Kursk was; no one, he suggested, cared whether they held Kursk or not. The panzer leader then turned back to Hitler and again asked why attack in Russia at all in 1943.

"You're quite right," Hitler responded, looking Guderian right in the eye. "Whenever I think of this attack, my stomach turns over."

"In that case, your reaction to the problem is the correct one. Leave it alone!"[3]

Hitler could not bring himself to leave it alone, nor could he speed up the production of his new tanks or solve the problems of the Panther or Tiger. In the meantime, Zhukov continued to flood the Kursk sector with reinforcements. By July 1, his forces included Gen. Markian Popov's Bryansk Front (six armies) and Marshal Vasilii Sokolovsky's West Front (seven armies), north and east of Orel; Marshal Konstantin Rokossovsky's Central Front (holding the northern face of the Kursk salient with five armies); Marshal Nikolai Vatutin's Voronezh Front (holding the southern face with six armies); and Marshal Ivan Konev's Reserve (later Steppe) Front (five armies in strategic reserve east of the Kursk salient). In addition, there were several independent rifle, motorized, tank, mechanized, and cavalry corps with the various fronts. By July 1, in the area of the Kursk salient alone, Zhukov had 1,337,000 men, 20,220 pieces of artillery, 3,306 tanks and assault guns, and 2,650 combat airplanes, according to official Soviet sources.[4] These figures are probably low.

Zhukov's defenses were by no means limited to these forces. His engineers also constructed six lethal fortified belts, all bristling with bunkers, machine-gun nests, antitank obstacles, trenches, miles of anti-tank ditches, and tens of thousands of mines. In the Central Front alone, the Soviets dug more than 3,000 miles of trenches and hundreds of miles of antitank ditches. Much of this work was done by 300,000 civilian workers, most of them women. In addition, some of the most intensive minefields in the history of the world were laid in the Kursk salient, averaging more than 5,000 antitank and antipersonnel mines *for each mile of defensive zone*.[5] And the Soviet defensive zone varied in depth from sixteen to twenty-five miles.

Against these incredible defensive belts and huge arrays of forces, Model and Manstein could bring only 900,000 men (570,000 of them in combat divisions), 10,000 guns and mortars, and 2,700 tanks and assault guns.

On June 12, Hitler again postponed Citadel, so that another three weeks' output of tanks would be available for the attack. At this point, Erich von Manstein categorically called for the cancellation of the offensive, and Lt. Gen. Adolf Heusinger and his OKH operations staff joined him in recommending that Citadel be abandoned.[6] It was too late for that: Citadel had assumed a life of its own. Zeitzler had convinced Hitler that the concentration of Soviet forces showed how important Kursk really was to them, and the staffs of both army groups had submitted their appreciations of the situation, which suggested that the Soviet buildup was a sign of a pending offensive, which could best be disrupted by proceeding with Citadel. Keitel and Kluge also continued to favor the offensive, as did much of the General Staff. Hitler ordered that the offensive begin on July 3. On June 20, he set the last "final date": July 5. The stage was set for the greatest tank battle in history.

THE BATTLE OF KURSK

During the first days of July, the German attack forces moved to their assembly areas. Hermann Hoth's 4th Panzer Army prepared to strike with Paul Hausser's II SS Panzer Corps and Gen. of Panzer Troops Otto von Knobelsdorff's XXXXVIII Panzer Corps.[7] Army Detachment Kempf was to advance to the east of the 4th Panzer Army to protect

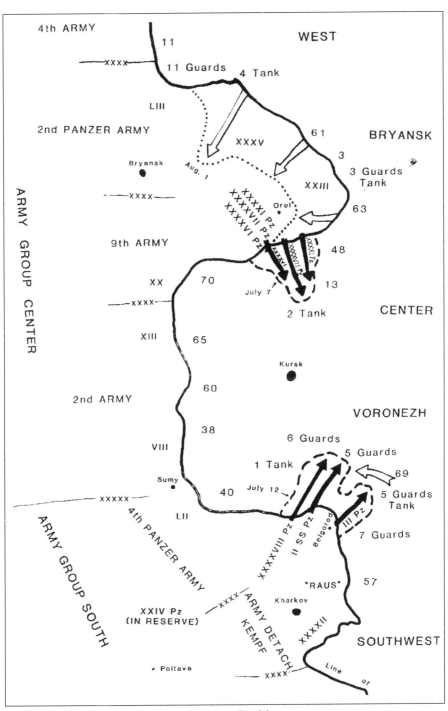

Operation Citadel

Hoth's right flank. Its main forces consisted of the III Panzer Corps, plus two infantry corps. Army Group South also had the XXIV Panzer Corps in reserve. All totalled, Manstein had 1,081 tanks and 376 assault guns. The table below shows the German order of battle for Operation Citadel. The map on the previous page shows the disposition of opposing forces, the maximum German advances, and the subsequent Russian Orel counteroffensive.

ORDER OF BATTLE OF THE GERMAN ARMY, BATTLE OF KURSK, JULY 7, 1943

ARMY GROUP CENTER: Field Marshal Guenther von Kluge

9th Army: Col. Gen. Walter Model

  XXIII Corps: Gen. of Infantry Johannes Friessner

    383rd Infantry Division

    216th Infantry Division

    78th Infantry Division

  XXXXI Panzer Corps: Gen. of Panzer Troops Joseph Harpe

    86th Infantry Division

    292nd Infantry Division

    10th Panzer Division

  XXXXVII Panzer Corps: Gen. of Panzer Troops Joachim Lemelsen

    9th Panzer Division

    2nd Panzer Division

    6th Infantry Division

    12th Panzer Division

  XXXXVI Panzer Corps: Gen. of Infantry Hans Zorn

    31st Infantry Division

    7th Infantry Division

    258th Infantry Division

    102nd Infantry Division

  XX Corps: Gen. of Artillery Rudolf von Roman

    72nd Infantry Division

    45th Infantry Division

    137th Infantry Division

    251st Infantry Division

2nd Army: Gen. of Infantry Walter Weiss[a]

  XIII Corps: Gen. of Infantry Erich Straube

    82nd Infantry Division

    340th Infantry Division

    377th Infantry Division

    327th Infantry Division

ORDER OF BATTLE OF THE GERMAN ARMY, BATTLE OF KURSK, JULY 7, 1943

VII Corps: Gen. of Artillery Ernst-Eberhard Hell

88th Infantry Division

26th Infantry Division

323rd Infantry Division

75th Infantry Division

68th Infantry Division

Reserve:

1st Slovak Security Division

ARMY GROUP SOUTH: Field Marshal Erich von Manseein

4th Panzer Army: Col. Gen. Hermann Hoth

LII Corps: Gen. of Infantry Eugen Ott

57th Infantry Division

255th Infantry Division

332nd Infantry Division

XXXXVIII Panzer Corps: Gen. of Panzer Troops Otto Knobelsdorff

3rd Panzer Division

Grossdeutschland Panzer Grenadier Division

11th Panzer Division

167th Infantry Division

II SS Panzer Corps: Gen. of Waffen-SS Paul Hausser

SS Panzer Grenadier Division "Leibstandarte Adolf Hitler"

SS Panzer Grenadier Division "Das Reich"

SS Panzer Grenadier Division "Totenkopf"

ARMY DETACHMENT KEMPF: Gen. of Panzer Troops Werner Kempf

III Panzer Corps: Gen. of Panzer Troops Hermann Brelth

168th Infantry Division

6th Panzer Division

19th Panzer Division

7th Panzer Division

Group Raus (XI Corps): Gen. of Panzer Troops Erhard Raus

106th Infantry Division

320th Infantry Division

ORDER OF BATTLE OF THE GERMAN ARMY, BATTLE OF KURSK, JULY 7, 1943

XXXXII Corps: Gen. of Infantry Franz Mattenklott

282nd Infantry Division

39th Infantry Division

161st Infantry Division

ARMY GROUP RESERVES:[b]

XXIV Panzer Corps: Gen. of Panzer Troops Walter Nehring

17th Panzer Division

SS Panzer Grenadier Division "Viking"

Notes:

a. Assigned a strictly defensive mission for Operation "Citadel."

b. As of July 11, 1943.

Source: Tessin, *Verbaende und Truppen,* 2:89, 125; 3:85, 226.

Model was set to sally forth with two infantry and three panzer corps—a total of 1,200 tanks and assault guns. His initial attack along a thirty-five-mile front was to be spearheaded by Gen. of Panzer Troops Joachim Lemelsen's XXXXVII Panzer Corps, with Gen. of Panzer Troops Joseph Harpe's XXXXI Panzer Corps on its left and Gen. of Infantry Hans Zorn's XXXXVI Panzer Corps on its right. Model's attack was supported by Gen. Paul Deichmann's 1st Air Division of Ritter Robert von Greim's 6th Air Fleet (formerly Luftwaffe Command East). Manstein's forces were supported by Hans Seidemann's VIII Air Corps of the 4th Air Fleet, which was now under the command of Col. Gen. Otto Dessloch, the former commander of the I Flak Corps.[8]

Most of the German divisions participating in Citadel were in the best shape they had been in since the early days of Operation Barbarossa, the 1941 invasion of the Soviet Union. The divisions had used the long lull in productive training exercises; many of their wounded veterans were now fully recovered and back at the front and were well rested and reasonably well equipped. Morale in the assault divisions was high. The *Luftwaffe* in the East was also in its best shape since 1941. It now had 2,500 airplanes in Russia—only a few hundred below its peak strength—and more than half of these would support Citadel. The Red air forces in the Kursk area, however, had also been greatly reinforced and included the 1st, 2nd, 3rd, 15th, and 16th Soviet Air Armies. They outnumbered the *Luftwaffe* at least three to one.

The leading German commanders adopted markedly different tactics for Operation Citadel. Model planned to rely on his infantry and artillery to breach the Soviet line; then he would commit his panzers. With the cooperation of General Kempf, Hermann Hoth, the proven master of mobile warfare, concentrated nine of Germany's best armored divisions along thirty miles of front.[9] For his attack, Hoth relied on a technique called the *Panzerkeil*, the armored wedge. In this type of attack, the German forces would advance in a succession of wedges, with the Tigers at the tip of the wedge, followed by the Panthers, with the PzKw IVs and IIIs to the flanks. Behind these tanks came the motorized infantry, and at the base of the wedge was the panzer artillery. Hoth hoped that driving a series of these wedges through the Soviet defensive lines would cause them to collapse.

In an effort to catch the Soviets by surprise, Hoth struck at the unusual hour of 3 P.M., instead of at dawn, on July 4—a day ahead of everyone else. He called this preliminary offensive a "reshaping" of his line. Knobelsdorff's XXXXVIII Panzer Corps steadily pushed back 6th Guards Army in moderate fighting. By nightfall, the XXXXVIII Panzer was in a much better position to begin the main offensive the following day.

Meanwhile, from prisoners and deserters, the Soviet High Command learned that a major offensive was imminent. At 10:30 P.M. on July 4, Vatutin unleashed a massive artillery bombardment of about 600 big guns on the German assembly areas. By 3 A.M., the bombardment had been extended across the entire front, disrupting the timing of the entire offensive. Even worse for the Germans, it began to rain without letting up that night, the earth turned into a quagmire, and small, insignificant streams turned into formidable defensive obstacles. Hoth nevertheless struck at dawn with everything he had along a twenty-mile front; he broke through Vatutin's first defensive belt within two hours. Disaster struck again when the II SS Panzer ran into a cleverly disguised minefield, and Vatutin's armies retreated to their second line without heavy losses, while their artillery pounded the panzers. On Hoth's right, Kempf's offensive gained ground only very slowly and was unable to keep pace with Hoth's panzer troops. To the north, Model lost about 100 tanks and self-propelled assault guns in the minefields, despite the fact that he committed only one of his armored divisions (the 20th Panzer) to the battle. Model's forward spearhead had gained about six miles, and most of his initial assault forces were still penned down in Rokossovsky's first defensive belt when night fell.

The German rear was also in chaos. The beginning of the Kursk offensive was the signal for the start of a partisan uprising in which an estimated 200,000 guerrillas took part. They ambushed German supply columns, blew up bridges, mined roads, sniped at sentries, attacked barracks and outposts, and completely disrupted the German railroad system, which was cut more than 1,500 times. The German railway engineer units worked day and night, and the security units did what they could, but the flow of ammunition and replacements to the front was reduced to a trickle.

July 6 was another day of unexpectedly slow progress for Model's 9th Army. Russian resistance remained fierce, but a sizable breach was achieved at Gnilets. Model promptly committed three panzer divisions to the attack under his personal leadership. Rokossovsky had anticipated just such a maneuver and met the attack with the 2nd Tank Army. Both sides were disappointed in the ensuing battle. The 2nd Tank Army failed to check Model and hold the first defensive belt, while Model failed to achieve the clean breakthrough he expected. By evening, the 9th Army had managed to push Rokossovsky's men back a maximum of about thirteen miles at a cost of more than 25,000 killed or wounded and about 200 tanks or assault guns knocked out or completely destroyed, and he still had not captured his initial objective, the town of Olkhovatka, less than a dozen miles from his jumpoff point. In addition, many bypassed Soviet snipers made life dangerous in the German rear. Gen. of Panzer Troops Erhard Raus's XXXXVII Panzer Corps, in the van of the advance, had been stopped in the low hills north of Olkhovatka, and Gen. of Artillery Johannes Friessner's XXIII Corps, on Model's left, was unable to protect its flank because of the stubborn defense the Soviets were putting up in the area north of Maloarkhangelsk. The scene was set for the decisive battle on the northern face of the Kursk salient.

During the evening of July 6, Rokossovsky ordered his tanks to dig in and defend the line between Maloarkhangelsk and Nikolskoye. Within this line, Model concentrated his assaults on the heights between

Ponyri and Molotychl, where the troops of two ruthless ideologies battled under a blistering sun for the next four days. Sometimes, the fighting was hand-to-hand. In one hour, a company of the 112th Panzer Grenadier Regiment lost all of its officers killed or wounded, but the attacks continued. "The Germans fought with an amazing spirit and drive, taking advantage of every break in the fighting, exploiting every weakness, meeting head on the worst of Soviet firepower when there was no other way to advance," historian Martin Caidin wrote later.[10] Rokossovsky countered by rushing three tank corps—the bulk of his reserves—into the battle. On July 8, Model committed his last tank reserves, Lt. Gen. Dietrich von Saucken's 4th Panzer Division, against the village of Teploye (near the western edge of the heights), which was already under attack from the 2nd and 20th Panzer Divisions.[11] The Russians had concentrated two infantry divisions, an artillery division, two tank brigades, and an assault gun brigade for the defense of the village. Even so, Model's troops overran Teploye and headed for the vital heights, which were defended by Rokossovsky's last immediate reserves, the 3rd Anti-Tank Brigade under Col. V. N. Rukosuyev. The battle continued to be fierce, but finally, the 33rd Panzer Grenadier Regiment of the 4th Panzer Division destroyed one of Rukosuyev's regiments and seized the critical heights. The Russians launched an immediate counterattack and retook the high ground. The determined grenadiers struck again and seized the heights, only to be pushed off by another Soviet counterattack. Once again the 33rd advanced, and once again pushed the Russians off the heights, only to be driven back by a fresh counterattack. The Soviets braced themselves for another assault, but there was no fourth attack. The 33rd Panzer Grenadier Regiment—and, indeed, the entire 9th Army—was finished.[12]

Model tried to resume his advance on the night of July 10–11, when he committed his last mobile reserves, Lt. Gen. August Schmidt's 10th Panzer Grenadier Division, to an attack on the village of Ponyri at the eastern edge of the ridge.[13] It failed in heavy fighting. Model's half of the offensive was over.

Meanwhile, Germany lost one of its best commanders. Col. Gen. Rudolf Schmidt had led the 1st Panzer Division in Poland and the XXXIX Panzer Corps in Belgium, France, and Russian. Later, he served as acting commander of the 2nd Army in the Battle of Moscow, before succeeding Guderian as the commander of the 2nd Panzer Army. He had distinguished himself in virtually every battle in which he had fought. During the first five days of the Battle of Kursk, his army protected Model's left flank and rear, covering the Orel salient. Yet he was relieved of his command on July 10. The reason was his brother, whom the Gestapo arrested for treason in early May 1943. While searching his possessions, they found his correspondence, which included several letters from the general. In them, Rudolf Schmidt gave vent to his true feelings, which were anything but friendly to the Nazi regime and very unflattering to Hitler. As a result, Schmidt was summarily discharged.[14] No successor was immediately announced, and as of July 12, the post of commander of the 2nd Panzer Army was vacant.

To the surprise of the senior Soviet generals, Manstein's attack proved to be much more difficult to deal with than the 9th Army's. Model's "infantry first" tactics, followed by the piecemeal commitment of his tank divisions, were much less effective than Hoth's panzer wedges, which wielded considerably more punch in terms of firepower and shock action.

Vatutin had correctly assumed that the main German assault would come in the Belgorod sector, so he placed his elite 6th Guards Army (Lt. Gen. Ivan M. Chistyakov) north of the city and the 7th Guards Army (Lt. Gen. Mikhail S. Shumilov) south of it. Behind the 6th Guards, he stationed Lt. Gen. Mikhail E. Katukov's 1st Tank Army, which had the task of barring the road to Oboyan, which, thanks to Lucy, the Soviet generals knew to be Hoth's initial objective. Hoth learned of the location of the 1st Tank Army from aerial reconnaissance reports, and he directed his main attack toward Prokhorovka, a town more than twenty miles east of Oboyan, which was not protected by significant Soviet reserves. By changing his initial objective, the brilliant panzer leader thus effectively rendered meaningless much of Vatutin's defensive plan on the first day of the battle.

The Germans also thwarted the Soviets' air attack plan on the first day of the invasion, although it was a close-run thing. With uncharacteristic boldness, the Red Air Force assembled 500 bombers, dive-bombers, and ground-attack aircraft from their 1st, 4th, and 16th Air Armies and flew for Kharkov in order to launch a preemptive strike against the German airfields, which were crowded with He 111s, Ju 87s, and Do 17s.

Fortunately for the *Luftwaffe*, the Russians did not know that the Germans had Freya sets, an early form of radar, which quickly picked up the massive formations. Seidemann's two fighter wings, the 52nd (Moelders) and the 3rd (Udet), scrambled immediately. In their hurry, some of the fighters did not wait for the bombers to vacate the runways but took off from taxiways instead. They intercepted the Russian bomber streams and, in what historian Musciano called "the largest and fiercest air battle of all time," shot down 432 Soviet airplanes and completely neutralized the threat. The *Luftwaffe* lost only twenty-six airplanes in the battle.[15]

Despite these early German victories, Soviet ground resistance was fierce. Even so, the XXXXVIII Panzer Corps broke through the 6th Guards Army in the direction of the Psel, and on Knobelsdorf's right, Hausser's II SS Panzer Corps broke through in the direction of Prokhorovka, spearheaded by a tank company of the Leibstandarte Adolf Hitler led by SS Lt. Rudolf von Ribbentrop, the son of the foreign minister. As Ribbentrop and his supporting SS panzer grenadiers overran position after position, Vatutin ordered Gen. Mikhail Katukov to halt him at all costs.[16] Katukov counterattacked with two mechanized infantry regiments, which were quickly slaughtered by the SS. "After two hours, all that was left of them was their regimental numbers," one witness recalled.[17] Farther west, the III Panzer Corps of Army Detachment Kempf crossed the Donets and headed north toward Rzhavets, but the 7th Guards Army was more successful in slowing down the Germans than its sister army.

The XXXXVIII Panzer Corps continued to make good progress on July 6 despite heavy but uncoordinated Soviet counterattacks and the "teething problems" its Panthers were experiencing. On July 7, the Grossdeutschland Division forced the 3rd Mechanized Corps back across the Pena River, the last defensible position south of Oboyan, despite losing one of its best commanders, Col. Erich Kahsnitz, the commander of the Grossdeutschland Fusilier Regiment, who was mortally wounded.[18] Meanwhlle, the 1st SS Panzer Division "Leibstandarte Adolf Hitler" reported that it had already destroyed 123 Soviet tanks, but its own losses were also high.

Soviet armored formations were also being blasted by a new German innovation: the tank-destroying airplane. Capt. Bruno Meyer of the *Luftwaffe* led four squadrons of Hs 129s, which were armed with 30-

millimeter cannons mounted below their fuselages, and destroyed dozens of Soviet vehicles. Another experimental detachment, this one consisting of Stukas armed with a 37-millimeter cannon under each wing, destroyed even more. The detachment commander, Capt. Hans-Ulrich Rudel, personally destroyed four Russian tanks in his first attack. By the end of the day, he had destroyed eight more.[19]

On July 8, the 3rd Mechanized launched a strong counterattack, spearheaded by forty T-34s, against the Grossdeutschlanders, but they were met by a Tiger detachment, which quickly shot them to pieces. Despite heavy showers, the Grossdeutschland continued its drive along the east bank of the Pena and seized the village of Verkhopenye, along with its damaged bridge, which the panzer engineers quickly repaired. On July 10, the XXXXVIII Panzer Corps pressed on toward Oboyan until it reached the high ground overlooking the town on the Psel River, the last natural barrier between Knobelsdorff and Kursk. For the first time in this battle, there were signs of panic in the Russian ranks. Vatutin committed most of his reserves to this sector in a desperate attempt to bar the road to Kursk. This is exactly what Hoth wanted him to do, for he had no intention of taking Oboyan. He ordered the XXXXVIII Panzer Corps to seize a crossing over the river in order to further deceive the Russians and then to wheel east toward Prokhorovka.

The XXXXVIII Panzer Corps had already accomplished much of its mission. In addition to forcing Vatutin into committing his main reserves in the wrong place, it had forced Zhukov into doing something he did not want to do: commit the 5th Guards Tank and 5th Guards Armies from Konev's Reserve Front to the fighting south of Kursk. However, despite the undeniable tactical skill with which he was handling this battle, Hoth's plan was also beginning to come unravelled, because there were simply too many Russians. One historian wrote:

> No matter how many men they lost, there seemed always to be fresh reserves. No matter how many tanks were destroyed in battle, the next morning brought waves of tanks from a seemingly inexhaustible supply. No matter how fiercely the *Luftwaffe* fought in the air, the following day brought waves of new Russian fighters and ground-attack planes . . . there was always more.[20]

Army Detachment Kempf was unable to gain any momentum, and as the II SS Panzer Corps advanced rapidly in the direction of Kursk, its right flank became more and more exposed. This fact did not escape Vatutin or Zhukov, and they ordered four armies to mount an all-out counterattack on July 12. In addition, German casualties had also been severe. Ribbentrop's company, for example, had started the battle with twenty-two tanks, but as dawn broke on July 12, only seven were still operational.[21]

The 1st Tank and 6th Guards Armies struck Knobelsdorff's XXXXVIII Panzer Corps on the Psel on July 12, starting a bitter but indecisive battle that lasted for several days. When it was over, the Grossdeutschland Division was down to a strength of 80 tanks; it had started the battle with 300. (Some of these losses, especially in the newer models, resulted from mechanical problems rather than enemy action.) The Soviets also suffered very heavy losses, and the battle ended as more or less a draw. Meanwhile, the Soviet 5th Tank Army attacked Hermann Breith's III Panzer Corps and quickly inflicted a sharp defeat on the Germans. The main Soviet attack was delivered against the II SS Panzer Corps by the 5th Guards Tank Army, which was led by the very able Gen. Pavel A. Rotmistrov. He had 850 tanks, most of them T-34s but also some KV-1s and two brigades of the new SU-85s, a heavy assault vehicle featuring an 85-millimeter gun on a T-34 chassis. Against this massive force, Hausser's three SS divisions had almost 700 tanks, 100 of which were Tigers. The Russians were fresh, with full complements of fuel and ammunition. Just as Rotmistrov had calculated, Hausser's advance carried him along the bank of the Psel, between the river and a railroad embankment in an area of gullies, ravines, and orchards.

Shortly after daybreak, the Red Air Force launched a surprise attack against the II SS, sending in wave after wave of Ilyushin Il-2 ground-assault aircraft. Then Rotmistrov ordered an all-out attack, similar to a wild cavalry charge of a bygone era. The two opposing sides were soon hopelessly mixed, and the battle degenerated into a wild melee. In this type of point-blank battle, the longer range and striking power of the Tigers' 88-millimeter guns were neutralized, while the faster T-34s had an advantage. At ranges of less than 100 yards, the 76-millimeter main battle guns of the T-34s were very effective, even against Tigers and Panthers. General Rotmistrov recalled later: "The bursts of gunfire merged into one continuous roar. Soon the whole sky was shrouded by the thick smoke of burning wrecks. On the black, scorched earth, the gutted tanks burnt like torches. It was difficult to establish which side was attacking and which side was defending."[22]

The confusion, huge clouds of dust, and lack of visibility also made it impossible for the *Luftwaffe* to intervene on behalf of the panzer divisions. Soon the battlefield was littered with burning tanks. Rudolf von Ribbentrop had already destroyed several Soviet tanks when his own tank was hit and his gunner badly wounded. Unable to fire because his opticals were damaged, Ribbentrop abandoned his panzer, commandeered another, and continued to fight, destroying several T-34s at a range of less than twenty-five yards. When the battle ended, he had only two tanks left.[23]

Ribbentrop's company had been virtually destroyed, but his losses were not unusual. When night fell, Hausser's troops were still in possession of the field, leading Goebbels' Propaganda Ministry to claim that the Germans had won a victory. They had done nothing of the kind. The SS had lost at least 350 tanks and possibly as many as 400, and most of the rest were damaged, in poor mechanical shape, and very short of ammunition. They had also lost about 10,000 men, including many veteran tank crewmen and panzer grenadiers. The Soviets lost about the same number of tanks and men, but they could afford it; Germany could not. Soviet Gen. Ivan Konev called it "the swan-song of the German armor."[24]

That afternoon, Hoth arrived on the battlefield and decided to continue the offensive, despite the disturbing news from other areas. The Allies, he knew, had landed on Sicily two days before, and the West and Bryansk Fronts had launched a massive offensive against the 2nd Panzer Army earlier that day. The next day, Hitler summoned Kluge and Manstein to Rastenburg and informed them that he had decided to call off Citadel because of the threat to the Orel salient (where Model was in danger of being surrounded), because of the Soviet buildup against Army Detachment Kempf and the 1st Panzer and 6th Armies, and because of the Allied landings in Sicily, which made it clear that the Italians would not fight, even in defense of their homeland. Italy was collapsing, Hitler said, and it had become necessary to create new armies to defend Italy and the Balkans. The divisions to form these armies would have to come from the Eastern Front.

Kluge agreed with this decision, but Manstein protested. Citadel, he said, had just reached its turning point in the zone of Army Group South, and if the 9th Army could resume its attack within the next few weeks, Germany might still win a major victory. He pointed out that Vatutin had committed all of his reserves, but he (Manstein) had not; in fact, he was presently moving his XXIV Panzer Corps out of reserve behind the 1st Panzer Army and into the Belgorod area, where it would be on hand for the final thrust on Kursk. In addition, the III Panzer Corps had finally broken through the 7th Guards Army on July 11. It had beaten the counterattacks of the 5th Guards Army the following day, and by nightfall on July 12, the III was advancing rapidly in the direction of the II SS Panzer Corps. By nightfall, it would have a considerable portion of the newly committed Soviet reserves trapped between itself and the right flank of the II SS Panzer Corps.

Manstein stood alone. Kluge declared that the 9th Army could not advance and, indeed, would have to withdraw to its original line of departure within the next few days. Although Hitler gave Manstein permission to continue his attacks for the purpose of winning a purely local victory, he gave Model command of both the 9th Army and 2nd Panzer Army (replacing Schmidt) and ordered him to close the breakthroughs of the Bryansk and West Fronts and reestablish the original front. The Battle of Kursk was over.

Although both Hoth and Kempf were shocked by the cancellation of the offensive, it must be concluded that Hitler's decision, for once, was the correct one. Kluge was right when he said that the 9th Army would not be able to withstand the Soviet offensive for weeks, as Manstein requested. In addition, although Manstein was accurate when he said that Vatutin had committed his reserves, he ignored the fact that Zhukov had not. It is inconceivable that the Soviet marshal would have allowed Manstein to bite off the Kursk salient when he had several reserve armies near at hand to prevent it. In fact, Manstein's own Army Group South was about to be subjected to the same type of offensive that Army Group Center was experiencing. On July 14, Hitler ordered the XXIV Panzer Corps to return to reserve behind the 1st Panzer and 6th Armies. The Soviet counteroffensive in this zone began only seventy-two hours later.

Soviet losses during the Battle of Kursk were very heavy. On July 5, they had 3,800 operational tanks; eight days later, they had less than

1,500. German losses were even more devastating, even if they did lose
fewer tanks. The exact numbers are not known because of the fluid
nature of the battle. There was no pause between Citadel and the battles
of the Orel salient, Belgograd, and Zhukov's massive drive on Kharkov
and the Dnieper, so German figures are fragmentary. We do know that
between July and October 1943, the German losses in the East exceeded
900,000 men.[25] Only about half of these could be replaced. Soviet figures are, as usual, almost useless. For example, Stavka reported the
destruction of 2,900 German tanks at Kursk—a remarkable statistic since
only 2,700 were engaged.

Citadel failed because it was badly conceived and poorly executed.
Manstein, arguably the greatest military commander of World War II,
undoubtedly fought his worst battle here. That the originator of the
Ardennes offensive of 1940, the conqueror of the Crimea and Sevastopol, and the architect of the "Miracle on the Donetz" could come
up with nothing less predictable than Citadel is, in retrospect, somewhat
astonishing. In Manstein's defense, however, it must be pointed out that
the delays that postponed the offensive from May to July cannot be laid
at his doorstep and neither can the fact that Soviet intelligence quickly
compromised the entire plan. Yet how he could maintain, even after the
war, that Hitler's halt order of July 13 robbed Germany of a major victory at Kursk defies explanation. In any case, Manstein was soon to
redeem himself.

On the other hand, Kursk was Hitler's last major offensive in the
East. Before this battle, the German Army had been winning tactically
and losing strategically. Germany would now lose most of its battles,
both strategically and tactically. Prior to Citadel, the Soviets had been
able to defeat the German armies only during the winter. The summer-
time defeat before Kursk sent shivers of alarm through every German in
the Reich. They would grow even more alarmed in the months ahead.
From Kursk on, all roads in Russia led to the west—toward Germany
and ultimate defeat.

CHAPTER 8

The Retreat Begins
in the East

The long retreat from Kursk to Berlin began on the morning of July 12, 1943. Confident that the German reserves were tied down in Operation Citadel, Popov's Bryansk Front and Sokolovsky's West Front attacked the northern face of the Orel salient. The 2nd Panzer Army, which was holding a 170-mile front with fourteen understrength divisions, could not prevent a quick breakthrough. Soon the Russians had created a seven-mile gap, which they continued to expand as the day wore on.[1] Before noon, Field Marshal Kluge was forced to send two divisions he had promised to Model to the 2nd Panzer's zone north of Orel. That afternoon and evening, the field marshal ordered Model to give up two panzer divisions and half of his Porsche Tigers, as well as artillery and rocket-launcher ("projector") units. All of these were hurried to the Orel salient, and still the Red flood could not be checked.

The following day, Hitler called upon Model to master the Orel crisis. "He became increasingly the man whom Hitler assigned to restore a critical situation or to bolster a wavering line," Manstein wrote later, "and his performance in the execution of these missions were [sic] extraordinary."[2]

When Model took over, the 2nd Panzer Army's front was broken in three places, and soon Russian forces were driving on the Bryansk-Orel Railroad, the lifeline of the 9th Army. Since neither the 2nd Panzer Army nor Army Group Center had anything left in reserve, Ritter von

Greim reinforced the 1st Air Division with the antitank squadrons of the VIII Air Corps and committed them to the battle against Soviet tanks. The air-ground battle lasted from morning to nightfall. Hundreds of Russian tanks were destroyed in low-level attacks, and the Soviet spearheads were all but wiped out. "For the first time in military history, the *Luftwaffe* has succeeded, without support by ground forces, in annihilating a tank brigade which had broken through," a delighted Model signaled.[3] During the Battle of Orel, the 1st Air Division performed at an almost superhuman level. It flew 37,421 sorties and shot down 1,733 Russian airplanes, against a loss of only 64 German aircraft. It destroyed or knocked out more than 1,100 Soviet tanks and 1,300 trucks and dropped more than 20,000 tons of bombs of Russian targets. In addition, the 12th Flak Division shot down 383 Soviet airplanes and knocked out 229 Soviet tanks and inflicted heavy losses on several Russian infantry units.[4]

There was no making up for the German weakness on the ground, however, and the offensive was far from over. Stalin hurled eighty-two rifle divisions, fourteen tank corps, twelve artillery divisions, and a number of independent tank brigades into the Orel fighting. In spite of the fact that Hitler, for once, allowed an elastic defense, the Germans had only twenty-eight infantry, eight panzer, and two panzer grenadier divisions in the Orel salient (i.e., in both the 2nd Panzer and 9th Armies)—a total of 492,300 combat soldiers, more than 100,000 support troops, about 1,000 tanks and assault guns, 7,000 pieces of artillery, and about 1,100 airplanes.

Facing the Germans were 1,286,000 Soviet soldiers, supported by more than 21,000 guns, 2,400 tanks, and more than 2,000 combat aircraft. By this point in the war, the Soviets' artillery was so abundant that they usually committed three to five artillery regiments for every regiment of infantry in their main attacks.[5] The German infantry divisions were slowly ground to bits. In addition, the *Wehrmacht* had only five divisions in reserve from Kirov to Kharkov—by no means enough to deal with three Soviet army groups. By July 20, Rokossovsky's troops had forced the 9th Army back to its original jumpoff points for Citadel and, by July 22, had pushed them out of these. They took what was left of Bryansk and effectively outflanked the rest of the Orel salient from the northwest. On July 30, the Soviets were threatening to trap much of the 2nd Panzer and 9th Armies east of Orel, and the roads leading out of the city were filled with German vehicles, all retreating to the west. They were continuously attacked by the Red Air Force, especially at "choke points," such as the Oka River crossings. Even so, the German infantry rearguards fought with grim determination. When the Russians finally took Orel on August 5, it was burning from end to end. All the factories had been destroyed, and almost all of the buildings were either totally destroyed or uninhabitable. The city had housed 100,000 people before the war.[6]

Model's armies were not the only ones under heavy attack in July and August 1943. From July 17 to 31, the Soviet Southwest and South Fronts struck the 1st Panzer and 6th Armies on the right flank of Army Group South. The 6th Army alone suffered 23,855 casualties between July 17 and August 6.[7] It also took 17,000 prisoners and destroyed or captured 700 Soviet tanks and 200 guns during the same period.[8]

With Hitler's permission, Model began the retreat to the Hagen positions immediately behind the Orel on August 1, just as the Soviet armies closed in on the city. Unfortunately, Walter Model believed in Hitler and his methods, and he carried out Hitler's scorched-earth policy without question. As the combat troops fought a delaying action, the rear-area units burned the rye crop, which was just ready for harvest, and herded up 250,000 civilians and their livestock and whatever personal possessions they could carry. They suffered immeasureably under the hot summer sun, and there were thousands of deaths as the peasants were herded west like so many cattle. Many divisions established special commands to destroy or confiscate everything of economic value in areas earmarked for evacuation. All villages, farms, windmills, and crops were burned. During the last three weeks in September, one such command in the Grossdeutschland Division evacuated 13,627 civilians and 9,268 head of livestock, destroyed 1,260 agricultural machines and 165 mills, and transported 1,392 tons of corps to the rear. All of the villages in its sector were burned to the ground.[9]

On August 6, with the 2nd Panzer and 9th Armies in full retreat, Vatutin—with the cooperation of Stavka—extended the Red offensive into the zone of Gotthard Heinrici's 4th Army, which he attacked with seven armies. His objective was Roslavl, a strategic city whose fall would finish the Hagen position before Kluge could occupy it. By the second week of August, the 4th Army was near the breaking point. The Russians charged forward with reckless abandon, using human-wave tactics, and the German machine gunners mowed them down by the thousand, but they kept on coming, often with their arms linked, drunk on vodka, and screaming, "Urrah, Urrah, Urrah!" One 4th Army officer estimated that Soviet casualties exceeded German casualties by a five-to-one ratio but that the Russian numerical superiority was ten to one.[10]

During the night of August 17–18, the last rear guards moved into the Hagen position. Model's retreat had been a major tactical achievement, especially when one considers that Stalin's objective was to encircle and destroy both the 2nd Panzer and 9th Armies. German losses had been heavy. Army Group Center lost the equivalent of fourteen divisions—a full one-fifth of its strength—in the retreat from the Orel salient to the Hagen line (a period of six weeks).[11] The *Wehrmacht* could no longer afford losses of this magnitude. The main Soviet offensive did not take place in this sector, however; it fell along the Donetz in the zone of Field Marshal Erich von Manstein's Army Group South.

During the third week of July, Army Group South deployed, north to south, the 4th Panzer Army, Army Detachment Kempf, 1st Panzer Army, and 6th Army. In all, the army group had 822,000 men and 1,161 tanks, only half of which were operational. It was opposed by an estimated 1,713,000 men and 2,872 tanks.[12] It held 250 miles of front, from just north of Belgorod to the Gulf of Taganrog. The Russians held several small bridgeheads on the southern bank of the Donetz, the one at Izyum being the most important. At the nearest point, a Soviet advance of only thrity miles would give them Kharkov, the fourth largest city in the Soviet Union. An advance of another 100 miles from Kharkov to Dnepropetrovsk would put them in position to cut off the 1st Panzer and 6th Armies east of the Dnieper River and isolate Army Group A in the Kuban and Crimea. In addition, the Soviet economy needed the coal, metal, and foodstuffs of the region, especially Ukraine. More than half of the Donetz's coal reserves lay between Stalino and the Mius, and the mines at Krivoy Rog in the great bend of the Dnieper accounted for more than 40 percent of Russia's prewar iron ore production. Finally, a major advance in southern Russia would have a significant impact on Germany's remaining allies, Romania and Hungary, and perhaps convince Turkey to join the war on the side of the Allies. The units of the Red

Army, therefore, gravitated to the southern sector of the Eastern Front for economic, political, and military reasons. So did the forces of Hitler's Reich. The stage was set for another series of battles on an immense scale.

The battles of the southern sector of the Eastern Front were indeed mammoth in the summer of 1943. Manstein and his subordinates—Hoth, Kempf, and the rest—shuttled their mobile reserves and panzer divisions rapidly from place to place in a bitter effort to check the Soviet tide. Gradually, however, the Soviets pushed the Germans back in desperate fighting. On August 7, the Red Army struck toward Kharkov, using several hundred tanks in a single wedge. They were met by the 128 Tigers and Panthers of the "Das Reich" SS Panzer Division, plus a battalion of the new Hornet tank destroyers, which were equipped with 88-millimeter guns. When the surviving Russians finally retreated, they left behind the hulls of 154 destroyed tanks.[13] Still the Russians kept on coming. They lost more than 80 tanks in a night attack on August 8–9, but they persisted with their assaults despite their losses. On August 12, Kempf signaled that he was at the end of his strength and intended to evacuate the city, but Hitler ordered that it be held. Kempf responded that to do so would produce another Stalingrad. He was relieved of his command on August 14 and replaced by Gen. of Infantry Otto Woehler. Army Detachment Kempf was redesignated as the 8th Army two days later.[14]

Woehler could not prevent the Soviets from nearly encircling the city before Hitler finally gave him permission to retreat. During the night of August 22–23, Kharkov changed hands for the fourth and final time during the war. Still the Russian attacks continued with unabated fury. The Hagen line was breached in August. Stalino fell on September 7. The Donetz was lost, and Army Groups Center and South fell back toward the Panther line and the Dnieper River, respectively. And still the battle continued.

The retreat was a brutal one. "No one wanted to become a Russian prisoner because we all knew this meant almost certain death," Pvt. Paul John von Ruhland recalled. The companies with the toughest assignments took to calling themselves *Himmelfahrtskommando* ("ascension command") because their soldiers "would travel very fast to heaven."[15]

As usual, the Germans put the Russian towns and villages to the torch as they retreated. One private first class wrote to a friend, "We've had to burn many villages down to the ground in order to destroy these haunts of the scum of human society and many a time we have had to 'erase' the male population. . . . But in handling these pariahs there cannot be any slackening. All mercy is out of place here."[16]

This kind of brutality was not one-sided. Soviet partisans were especially barbaric, and German soldiers dreaded the prospect of falling into their hands. The things some of them did to their captives almost defy description. They smashed prisoners' penises with hammers, decapitated them, and multilated their bodies to the point they could not be identified. The Germans retaliated in kind. "Every day we go out reconnoitering and ferreting out partisans," one wrote to a friend.

> Once we caught two . . . and brought them to our company. The things they had on them . . . glass grenades, explosives, hand grenades, fuses, detonators. . . . We got so mad we grabbed our whips and flogged them within an inch of their lives. Then we cross-examined them. . . . Then we took them and strung them up. What else could we do? They don't deserve any better treatment. That's how the days and weeks go by.[17]

"The morale among us gradually reached a point where a soldier wished or hoped for a major injury, if only to escape the horror and agony of war," Paul von Ruhland recalled.[18] A few even tried *Heimatschuss*—self-inflicted wounds called "back-to-mother shots." This was a dangerous business. A soldier found guilty of such an act usually faced death—and there were always plenty of volunteers for the firing squads because the men of the *Wehrmacht*, especially on the Eastern Front, had no sympathy for slackers in their ranks. "The fact that we fought harder and harder the longer the war dragged on might come as a surprise to many people," Hans-Ulrich Greffrath, a machine-gun squad leader in the Grossdeutschland Panzer Division, recalled later.

> We simply did our duty. We fought with ever-increasing defiance and bitterness . . . because of the terrible experiences we had at the front. We saw mutilated soldiers who had fallen into the hands of the Russians—soldiers without ears, without noses, without eyes. We knew we had to keep on fighting if we wanted to prevent this sort of thing from happening to our families at home.

Greffrath further stated that he never fought for Hitler. He fought for Germany—his home and fatherland. "I think all of my comrades did the same," he added.

Fight he did. After more than a year on the Eastern Front, Greffrath attended an officers' training course in Germany, but he returned in time to celebrate his twentieth birthday with his division just before the Battle of Kursk. Thirteen other lieutenants attended the party. Eight days after Citadel began, only two of them were still alive. Lieutenant Greffrath was wounded for the third time during the retreat of 1943 but was back with his division in the spring of 1944, when it was attacked by 420 Russian tanks. In three days, the Grossdeutschlanders destroyed 382 of them. Greffrath's luck had run out, however. His leg was shattered and had to be amputated, leaving a stump which no prosthesis could fit. "We didn't take our mutilations too seriously," he said later. "We were glad to be alive at all. Two months later, he celebrated his twenty-first birthday.[19]

The pace of the retreat to the Dnieper slowed after September 15, but for the Germans, the pattern on the Eastern Front did not change. It was still one crisis after another. Only the places and the names of the units changed. In mid-September, General Woehler reported that his rear-area troops now consisted exclusively of sole surviving sons and fathers of large families—the two categories Hitler had exempted from frontline duty. All the rest of the service troops had been sent to the front. Even so, one infantry division was down to a combat strength of 6 officers and 300 men. Exhaustion had given way to apathy, the 8th Army commander asserted; he predicted that the front would break if it were subjected to a heavy attack.

Hoth's 4th Panzer Army was in even worse shape. By this time, Army Group South was down to a rifle strength of only 1,000 men per infantry division. It had only thirty-seven such divisions to defend 450 miles of front—12 miles per division. Since a full-strength division could be expected to hold only 6 miles of front against a major assault and since Manstein's divisions had the strength of regiments, it was obvious to the rational observer that they would not be able to hold their positions against the Soviet onslaught. Manstein did not have any reserves of consequence, and his mobile forces were severely depleted. As of September 7, his panzer divisions had only 40 to 50 tanks, and there were only 257 tanks and 220 assault guns in the entire army group.[20]

Army Group Center was no better off. The average division in Walter Weiss's 2nd Army was down to a combat strength of 1,000 men, and by mid-September, the Russians were through the Hagen line and were expanding their Desna bridgeheads, while only the weak 4th Army barred the Red Army's path to Kiev and expected an attack at any time. As a measure of his desperation, General Weiss had to commit two security divisions—each with two regiments but little artillery—and an unreliable Hungarian division to cover his right flank.

On September 13, the Soviets began their drive on Smolensk. Kluge requested permission to retreat to the Panther positions, which would mean giving up more than half of the Russian territory held by Army Group Center. In preparation for this move, he ordered Model to pull his center back behind the Desna and gave Weiss permission to withdraw west of the river.

If anything, the odds against Manstein were worse than those Kluge was facing. By the second week in September, he was outnumbered approximately seven to one, and the 4th Panzer Army was in danger of immediate collapse. The Russians had split Hoth's army into three parts, and the Voronezh Front threatened to push him south, parallel to the Dnieper, leaving long stretches of the river exposed. Accordingly, Manstein ordered Hoth to break contact with the 8th Army on his right and swing his flank to the west in order to cover Kiev. That night, Hitler ordered both Manstein and Kluge to report to his headquarters in person the next day.

Early the next morning, Nezhin fell, and there was "near panic" at Fuehrer Headquarters. OKH now reversed itself completely, cancelled its hold-at-all-costs order, and urged Army Group Center to speed up its withdrawal in order to free four more divisions for Army Group South.

But the German line simply could not be held. Manstein was fortunate to escape across the Dnieper with his entire command. The frontline troops, as usual, conducted their retreat with courage and discipline, but there were signs of panic among supply and rear-echelon units, and many of the Nazi civil administrators ran away, taking with them what they had looted as well as items for their personal comfort. General Fretter-Pico described how the Nazi officials fled Dnepropetrovsk with a fleet of trucks, loaded down with furniture, food, and beds, while his XXX Corps could not move its bridging equipment because of a lack of transport. Fretter-Pico, for one, solved this problem by setting up road-blocks and requisitioning what he needed at gun point, ignoring the howls of the civilian administrators.[21] In any case, for Army Group South, the safety of the mile-wide Dnieper River had proven to be an illusion. In the last two and a half months, Army Groups South and Center had lost an average of 150 miles of territory along a 600-mile front, including some of the most valuable regions of the Soviet Union, and still the Red Army had not been stopped. The retreat continued, and another Russian winter was just around the corner.

CHAPTER 9

Decay and Disarray in the Mediterranean

THE DETERIORATING AXIS

The Rome-Berlin Axis was a reversal of a long standing historical trend and was never much more than a personal alliance between their two dictators, Hitler and Mussolini. In fact, the Germans and Italians are historic enemies. "The Dark Ages began when the savage vigour of the Germans broke up the system of Mediterranean civilization which the Romans had established," Elizabeth Wiskemann wrote, and a "tradition of conflict between Italy and Germany lingered on ever after through the centuries."[1]

The Hitler-Mussolini alliance did not exactly fill Germany's enemies with dread. During the Sudetenland crisis, for example, French Minister of Colonies Georges Mandel predicted that in case of war, "Germany will be beaten in six months without Mussolini; in three months with Mussolini."[2] Eight months later, Churchill expressed similar sentiments when he remarked, "There is a school of British strategists who hold that in a world struggle with Nazidom, it would be a positive advantage to have Italy as an enemy."[3]

Subsequent events proved the validity of this statement all too well. The Italian "volunteers" performed poorly during the Spanish Civil War, and the Italian Army did poorly in the fighting in the French Alps, in the Greek campaign, in Russia, and in the North African desert. One is reminded of the words Otto von Bismarck uttered six decades earlier:

Italy "has a large appetite but very poor teeth."⁴ This was certainly true of Fascist Italy in World War II.

"The sole significance for Germany of the active entrance of Italy into the war in the summer of 1940 was a heavy burden," Col. Gen. Heinrich von Vietinghoff commented later, adding:

> Hitler kept the faith with Mussolini as he did with almost no other human being, to the ruin of both men and of their two peoples. To help him, to support him . . . [Hitler] plunged into the African and Balkan adventures, without following any big over-all plan. Blinded by Mussolini's unquestionably considerable success in the domestic political field, he did not see—and *did not want* to see—how war-weary the Italian people were after the Abyssinian War, how little value his [Mussolini's] armed forces had, how incompletely equipped they were with all modern means.⁵

The Russian campaign marked a turning point in Mussolini's relationship with his own people. The Italian generals almost unanimously opposed the venture, as did the soldiers who served there. The ill-equipped Italian 8th Army was badly outclassed by the resurgent Red Army, which attacked it in overwhelming numbers in the winter of 1942–43. The Italian Army was slaughtered, 75 percent of its men were lost, and Mussolini's popularity at home plummetted.

Then came El Alamein, Operation Torch, and the loss of Libya. Like a gambler who does not know when to stop, Mussolini threw some of Italy's best divisions into the Tunisian bridgehead. Meanwhile, he continued to try to safeguard his own position. On February 6, 1943, just after the fall of Stalingrad, he dismissed most of his cabinet—the so-called "Ciano cabinet"—and replaced it with men whom he considered more loyal to him personally. He ousted Foreign Minister Galeazzo Ciano, his son-in-law, took over the foreign ministry himself, and appointed the mediocre Giuseppe Bastianini as his undersecretary for foreign affairs. In April, he acted on the advice of Heinrich Himmler and appointed Carlo Scorza secretary of the Fascist Party. Described as "an ambitious thug," Scorza sent gangs of Fascist hoodlums into the streets to harass and intimidate the general population.⁶ Unlike in past years, the opposition and citizenry struck back, and some of the Blackshirts were themselves beaten up or murdered in the night. Defeatism was already too widely spread for Scorza's methods to be successful, and unrest grew. Members of the pre-Fascist political parties began to meet cautiously. On May 1, several labor unions marched in May Day parades despite the official police ban, and unauthorized demonstrations were held. Mussolini was obviously losing control of the situation. He was now opposed by the Royalist Officers' Corps, the anti-Fascist political parties, the labor unions, the average citizen, and a growing number of dissident Fascists.

The collapse of the Tunisian bridgehead in May came as a severe shock to the Italians. "The loss of their last colony was a heavy blow to the Italian people," Kesselring's chief of staff recalled, "for it meant that all the energy and sacrifice which had been expended over a half a century in building up the colonial territories had been in vain. So vanished for many Italians the hope of a better future."[7]

"They were tired of a war which had been unpopular from the beginning," Maj. Gen. Burkhart Mueller-Hillebrand wrote later, "and yearned for peace at any price. . . . [After Tunisia], Mussolini's prestige was shattered."[8]

At the end of May 1943, Italy was, as historians Garland and Smyth wrote, "in the tragic and ridiculous position of being unable either to make war or to make peace."[9] Economically, Italy was a vassal state of the Third Reich, heavily dependent on Germany for coal, iron, oil, rubber, and other essential commodities. Its industrial production was inadequate for modern warfare, and its military hardware was hopelessly inferior to that of the Russians, British, or Americans, especially in tanks and airplanes. Of the 2,000,000 men in the Italian armed forces at the end of 1942, about 1,200,000 were serving in foreign areas, including Russia, North Africa, southern France, Corsica, Slovenia, Greece, Dalmatia, Albania, Montenegro, and the islands of the Aegean Sea. These included Italy's best-trained and best-equipped divisions. The worst units were at home and in the Balkans. Marshal Pietro Badoglio recalled "artillery divisions manning the coastal defences without artillery, with very few arms and with no transport."[10] The morale of these units was rock bottom—although Italian morale was generally bad everywhere.

Gen. of Infantry Dr. Edmund von Gleise-Horstenau, the German commander in Croatia, grumbled to a friend that he had never seen anything like the Italian 2nd Army. "The officers live by smuggling Jews, the NCOs smuggle arms, tobacco and salt, and the soldiers simply steal. They leave the mountains to the partisans." He predicted that if the Allies landed, the 2nd Army would not fight for twenty-four hours.[11] The Italian Air Force was in equally bad straits, and the Italian Navy, while still formidable on paper, had remained so only by religiously avoiding battle with the Royal Navy—except for the submarine branch, which performed so courageously that it is beyond criticism.

With his own armed forces in such hopeless disarray, one might think Mussolini would have welcomed German aid, especially after the fall of Tunisia. Mussolini, however, was influenced by Gen. Vittorio Ambrosio, the anti-German chief of Commando Supremo who had replaced Ugo Cavallero on February 1, and others and was basically ignorant of the state of his own forces. As he had told one of his generals years before, "If they [the Germans] get a footing in the country, we shall never be rid of them."[12] In early May 1943, when Hitler offered to send five mobile divisions with modern equipment, Mussolini would accept only three. This reply again provoked Hitler's fears about a possible Italian defection. On May 20, Hitler met with Rommel, Keitel, and Lt. Gen. Walter Warlimont (Jodl's deputy), among others, to discuss the Italian situation, and on May 22, OKW issued Plan Alarich, a contingency plan to be implemented if Mussolini's government collapsed. It called for the formation of an army group of thirteen to fourteen divisions under Field Marshal Rommel to rapidly assemble and occupy all of Italy. Later, when the political situation temporarily stabilized, the number of divisions earmarked for Alarich was reduced to eight, to be taken from Germany and OB West.

On May 22, Gen. of Infantry Enno von Rintelen, the chief OKW liaison officer in Italy and a man who knew how to deal with the Italians, obtained a firm commitment from Commando Supremo to accept four German divisions: a panzer grenadier division, eventually designated the 15th, to be reconstituted in Sicily by June 1; a panzer grenadier division, later designated the 90th, to be created by the expansion of the German brigade in Sardinia; the Hermann Goering Panzer Division, much of which had been destroyed in Tunisia, to be reconstituted on the mainland; and the 16th Panzer, a division largely destroyed at Stalingrad, to be reconstituted in France and then sent to Italy. The Italians also agreed to accept headquarters of the XIV Panzer Corps, led by Gen. of

Panzer Troops Hans Valentin Hube, to prepare the German troops for combat.

The senior German headquarters in Italy was *Oberbefehlshaber Sued*, or OB South (later OB Southwest), which was under the command of *Luftwaffe* Field Marshal Albert Kesselring, who was simultaneously the commander in chief of the 2nd Air Fleet until May, when Baron von Richthofen was given that post. After the fall of Tunisia, Kesselring believed that the Allies' next invasion would be launched against Sicily or Sardinia. Most of the members of Commando Supremo picked Sardinia as the most likely target and had some very convincing military reasons. First, it was a stepping stone to southern France. Second, Allied air forces based in Sardinia and Corsica, which could not be held if Sardinia fell, could bomb the entire Italian mainland and southern Germany. Third, Sardinia was the gateway to the Po River Valley, Italy's dominant agricultural and industrial region. Finally, the capture of Sardinia would effectively bottle up the Italian Navy in the Tyrrhenian Sea. Capturing Sicily, on the other hand, would not put the Allies within escorted bomber range of any important industrial targets, nor would it serve as a springboard for an invasion of central or northern Italy, as would Sardinia. In other words, Sicily was not a stepping stone to anywhere except southern Italy, which had little military value; it was therefore not seen as an important enough target to warrant an invasion of the magnitude the Allies were preparing.

Most of the Axis military experts agreed with Commando Supremo. Richthofen picked Sardinia, as did Kurt Student, the paratrooper expert. Italian Marshal Badoglio also picked Sardinia and later denounced the invasion of Sicily as "a severe strategic mistake." Supermarina, the General Staff of the Italian Navy, also anticipated an invasion of Sardinia, as did Admiral Doenitz and the German Office of the Chief of Naval Operations. Nevertheless, their view was far from unanimous. General d'Armata Alfredo Guzzoni, the former undersecretary for war, expressed as early as 1942 the opinion that the Allies would be wise to attack Calabria (the toe of the Italian boot). This move, he said, would cut off and trap all Axis forces in Sicily, which was virtually undefended. German Maj. Gen. Eberhard Rodt, the commander of the 15th Panzer Grenadier Division in Sicily, expressed the same view. Adolf Hitler and the OKW staff had another theory altogether. They thought the eastern Mediterranean was in greater danger than the west or the center and expected an invasion of Greece or the Balkans. This view was confirmed by "the man who never was."

Operation Mincemeat was a brilliant deception plan hatched in the fertile minds of Lt. Cmdr. Ewen Montagu of British Naval Intelligence and Flight Lt. Charles Cholmondeley, an Air Ministry intelligence officer. They had a British submarine release the body of Maj. William Martin of the Royal Marines in the Gulf of Cadiz so that the currents would wash it ashore near Huelva, Spain. Martin, an official messenger, had apparently drowned after his airplane crashed into the sea. Still handcuffed to his wrist was a briefcase, which the Spaniards opened. Inside were top-secret documents from London directing General Alexander to feint against Sicily while preparing to invade Sardinia. They also instructed Gen. Henry Maitland "Jumbo" Wilson, the commander in chief in the Middle East, to veil his invasion of Greece by faking an attack on the Dodecanese Islands. As Montagu predicted they would, the Spanish handed copies of the documents over to German secret agents. Soon they were in the hands of Adm. Wilhelm Canaris, the chief of the *Abwehr*, the German intelligence service. He forwarded translated copies to Adolf Hitler.

Major Martin never existed. Like the top secret documents, his identity was fake. The man in the Royal Marines uniform was actually a British civilian who died of pneumonia, the symptons of which resemble drowning. His body had been packed in dry ice for the submarine journey to the gulf.[13]

Hitler fell for Mincemeat hook, line, and sinker. On May 14, he expressed the view that "the discovered Anglo-Saxon order confirms the assumption that the planned attacks will be directed mainly against Sardinia and the Peloponnesus."[14] Therefore, during the summer of 1943, he dispatched the bulk of his reinforcements to Greece and southeast Europe. Before the end of May, OKW sent the 1st Panzer Division to Greece despite the bitter objections of Guderian, who rated this division "our strongest reserve."[15] By July 7, there were thirteen German divisions in the Balkans, mostly under the command of Col. Gen. Alexander Loehr's Army Group E (the upgraded headquarters of the 12th Army). OB South had just six at its disposal; only two of these were in Sicily, the real target of the invasion.

Just before Tunis fell, Col. Bogislaw von Bonin, the operations officer of the 5th Panzer Army, flew out of the pocket on May 8. When he
arrived in Rome, he was made chief of a special staff (*Einsatzstab*)
charged with organizing two German motorized divisions, one in Sicily
and one in southern Italy. At that time, Bonin recalled, "there was not
one battleworthy formation of the German Army in Italy, including the
islands."[16] The only German division-level headquarters existing in Sicily
at the time was the ad hoc Division Kommando Colonel Baade, which
had been formed in April to control the replacement (march) battalions
heading for Tunisia. Field Marshal Kesselring wrote later, "At the time of
the capitulation of Tunis, the outlook in Sicily, as everywhere, was very
black. I counted on the enemy's following up his victory, if not immediately, at least after the shortest possible breather. . . . Every day the enemy
gave us was a day gained, however, and gradually a striking force was
organized."[17]

Bonin and Ernst Baade reacted quickly to take advantage of the
Allied generosity. By June, they had converted these replacement battalions, supply troops, and miscellaneous troop units into the 15th Panzer
Grenadier Division. Many of their troops were Afrika Korps veterans
returning from the hospital.

On June 9, 1943, the colorful Colonel Baade, who sometimes went
into battle dressed in a Scottish kilt and carrying a broadsword, was
replaced as divisional commander by Maj. Gen. Eberhard Rodt, a veteran of the Eastern Front. Meanwhile, in Sardinia, the 90th Panzer
Grenadier Division was being formed under the command of General
Lungershausen with the assistance of Colonel Bonin, and the Hermann
Goering Panzer Division arrived in Sicily. Most of this unit had been
sent to Tunisia as part of Kampfgruppe Hermann Goering, which was
destroyed in May 1943. When Tunisia fell, the Hermann Goering lost
four grenadier battalions, two flak battalions, a panzer battalion, most of
its reconnaissance unit, part of its engineer battalion, and its signal and
medical battalions. Nevertheless, it was hurriedly reorganized and sent to
Sicily between June 20 and July 1.

Both German divisions in Sicily, therefore, had the characteristics of
hastily organized, improvised formations, which were indifferently
equipped and short of many technical specialists. The Hermann Goering
was especially deficient in leadership. The commander of the Hermann

Goering Panzer Regiment, for example, was a former bomber pilot who was grounded because he developed a nervous condition. Why he was given command of a panzer regiment is anyone's guess, but many of his peers were air force officers who were equally unqualified to direct a ground battle. The divisional commander, Lt. Gen. Paul Conrath, had fought on the Western Front in World War I but had spent the Weimar era as a police officer in Berlin. He had served in the flak artillery from 1935 to 1942 and had done very well; however, successfully commanding a motorized flak regiment in Russia and leading an understrength panzer division against the British and Americans were two different things, as Conrath found out in Sicily in 1943.

If the newly formed German divisions in Sicily were not the highest quality, the Italian divisions were much, much worse.

General d'Corpo Mario Roatta's 6th Army in Sicily included four field and six coastal defense divisions. Of the field divisions, only the Livorno (4th) Assault and Landing Division was fairly well trained and equipped, was two-thirds motorized, and included a fair number of light tanks. The Aosta (28th) and Napoli (54th) Infantry Divisions were both poorly trained and equipped, operating at reduced strength levels and suffering from low morale. The Assietta (26th) Infantry Division was also understrength and badly equipped, but it was better trained and had higher morale than the Aosta or the Napoli. All four of these divisions were very short in artillery ammunition, communications equipment, fuel, and other vital areas of supply.

The Axis first line of defense in Sicily was the six coastal defense divisions, which were made up almost entirely of Sicilians. Their morale was so low that they were almost at the point of disintegration—even before Allied bombing made things worse. Sicily first became a target during the Tunisian campaign when the Allies struck the island's cities in an attempt to disrupt the flow of supplies to North Africa. Catania and Messina were especially hard hit, and many residents fled into the interior because the Fascists had not constructed air-raid shelters. Hundreds of families were forced to live in huts and caves in the black lava fields around Mount Etna. Morale naturally fell to an all-time low, and Mussolini did not help when he referred to the Sicilians as "decadent people." The Allies moved to accelerate the rapid decline in Sicilian morale by dropping leaflets on the island pointing out the insensitivity of the

Fascist regime to their suffering and the futility of resistance. All of this naturally affected the morale of the Sicilian coastal defense units. Pvt. Alberto Testaecca, a gunner in an artillery unit near Syracuse, recalled:

> The Fascist government was rationing everything to the civilians, saying that the army must have the best of everything. Had it only been true! We only saw poverty, hunger, discomfort, and dirt. Always hunger. . . . The civilian population was exasperated; many prayed for the arrival of the Allies. We could not care less about [government] propaganda; there was no order; there was no discipline. We soldiers had to go into the villages to scrounge bread from the civilians, whilst the civilians came to the army camps with the same aspirations. But they were disappointed. They must have seen us with toes sticking out of our boots. Our horses could hardly stand.[18]

General di Divisione Achille d'Havet was sent to Sicily in 1943 to straighten out the "notoriously bad"[19] 206th Coastal Defense Division, but there was little he could do, other than send back reports stating that some of his soldiers could not fix bayonets because they were afraid of cutting themselves with their own weapons. Many of his officers had not seen active duty since they were lieutenants in World War I. They habitually took Sundays off to be with their families, who were not supposed to be in Sicily in the first place. When Prince Umberto inspected the division, he court-martialed several of them for "complete ignorance" of even the most basic elements of military etiquette and training.[20]

Unfortunately, the 206th was the rule, rather than the exception, for the coastal divisions in Sicily. "General Roatta stated quite openly that these units were not to be relied on," General Westphal recalled.[21]

Roatta worked very hard to prepare the island for defense, but he could do only so much, and he was hamstrung by the incompetence of the high command.[22] Many of his troops still had rifles manufactured in 1915; worse still, many of his troops were actually barefoot. Others considered themselves lucky to have sandals. The shortage of boots was so serious that training had to be curtailed in order to save footwear. There were huge quantities of boots available in the 6th Army's warehouses in Sicily, but they were all surplus too-large sizes, useless for most of the men. In Catalina, just across the Straits of Messina, there were several warehouses full of boots of the more normal sizes, but they could not be issued because the officials in Rome would not authorize it. Roatta also requested 160,000 tons of concrete per month to build obstacles, bunkers, strongpoints, and other fortifications and to put Sicily in a reasonable state of defense. He received only 7,000 tons a month. He also stated that he needed 8,000 tons of supplies per day to meet the minimum civil and military requirements of the island. He received only 1,500 to 2,000 tons per day.[23]

In the latter part of May, Roatta gave a speech during which he made a remark that was interpreted as a slight on Sicilian patriotism. With the gap between the Sicilians and the Italians already dangerously wide, Commando Supremo kicked Roatta upstairs and made him chief of staff of the army. On May 30, he was succeeded in command of the 6th Italian Army by sixty-six-year-old General d'Armata Alfredo Guzzoni.

Guzzoni seems an odd choice for this command. He had had a distinguished career, but he had never been to Sicily and had never expressed the slightest interest in the place. Guzzoni also fell far short of being an awe-inspiring character or a superb troop motivator, such as Rommel, Patton, or Montgomery. He was old, small of stature, heavy set, and known as a political "operator," like most Italian generals. Despite his appearance, however, he was one of the regime's most competent field commanders, as he was to prove in Sicily. To assist him, OKW named Lt. Gen. Fridolin von Senger und Etterlin chief of the German liaison staff in Sicily.

Senger was a devout Catholic and an officer known for his suave urbanity. On June 22, 1943, he was summoned to the Obersalzberg, where he was received by Adolf Hitler, who, Senger recalled, "was counting on Italy's defection in the near future" because of the intrigues of the royal court, social circles, the royalist General Staff, and others. He discussed at length the possibility of defending Sicily even without Italian help with the two divisions and 30,000 other Germans on the island (the extensive *Luftwaffe* ground organization, antiaircraft units, supply formations, and other units), and he concluded that "because they failed to cross over to Sicily immediately after their landing in North Africa, [the Allies] had already lost the Battle of the Mediterranean."[24]

Once this vague, rambling monologue ended, Senger ate breakfast with Lt. Gen. Walter Warlimont in the latter's apartment. Jodl's notoriously arrogant but highly competent deputy appraised the situation much more realistically than did Hitler. He told the veteran cavalryman that in case of an invasion, his best bet would be to transfer the majority of the German troops in Sicily to the mainland. He also commented on the improbability of salvaging most of the equipment.

Following a general situation conference, Senger spoke with Keitel alone. "He had received reports about the local Sicilian conditions from General Hube," Senger remembered, "and apparently considered a successful defense as hopeless as did General Warlimont."[25] After leaving Berchtesgaden, Senger met with Kesselring in Rome, where he found the optimism of the *Luftwaffe* marshal in sharp contrast to the realism of Keitel and Warlimont. Later, in an unpublished manuscript, he wrote:

> Many officers fighting in Africa (including Colonel Bonin) charged that Kesselring held far too optimistic views of the situation, as a result of which the influence of Rommel, who had better opportunities for a correct appraisal, had been unduly restricted. I found these charges confirmed to the extent that Kesselring obviously considered the possibility of successfully defending Sicily with far too much optimism.[26]

After visiting with Kesselring, Senger proceeded to Sicily, where he and his special staff would coordinate German forces for the defense of the island. The map on the facing page shows the major cities and paved roads on the island in 1943.

On June 26, Kesselring arrived at 6th Army Headquarters at Enna in the center of the island to discuss the detailed tactical and operational plans for the defense of Sicily with all the major German and Italian commanders. Col. Wilhelm Schmalz, the most competent commander in the Hermann Goering Division, was present, as were Senger, Rodt, Conrath, and others. Schmalz later recalled with envy the impeccably dressed Italian staff officers and their luxurious headquarters.

The atmosphere of the conference was cool from the outset. Guzzoni was as pessimistic about the general situation as Kesselring was optimistic. Guzzoni expected the Allied attack about the middle of July and doubted the outcome of the battle. Tactically, he had already assigned the defense of the western half of the island to the XII Italian Corps under Generale di Corpo Mario Arisio and given him the Assietta and Aosta

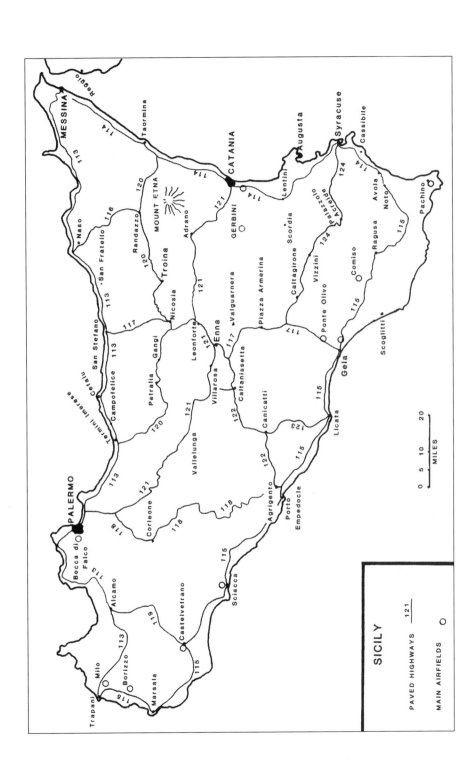

SICILY

PAVED HIGHWAYS ——121

MAIN AIRFIELDS ○

MILES
0 5 10 20

Divisions, three and a half coastal divisions, and the reinforced 104th Panzer Grenadier Regiment from the 15th Panzer Grenadier Division, which had been sent to the western half of the island at Kesselring's insistence in early June. Generale di Corpo Carlo Rossi's XVI Corps had the task of defending eastern Sicily with the Napoli Division and two coastal divisions. He placed the Hermann Goering Panzer Division and the bulk of the 15th Panzer Grenadier Division in reserve in southeast Sicily under the control of the XVI Corps. The Livorno Division was stationed nearby as part of the 6th Army's reserve. According to Guzzoni's plan, the Italians would delay the Allied invaders as long as possible until the Germans and the Livorno could launch a concentrated counterattack and throw them back into the sea.

Had Guzzoni been allowed to execute this plan, the U.S. 7th Army might well have suffered a major disaster, for his disposition could not have been more perfectly designed to counter the American landings if he had had a copy of General Patton's operations order. But Kesselring objected. He wanted to send the 15th Panzer Grenadier to the western end of the island to guard against an attack on Palermo while the Hermann Goering Division (part of which was still en route to Sicily) assembled at Caltagirone in the southeast. Kesselring also wanted another regimental group of the 15th stationed in the Catania sector on the east coast under a newly formed (and ad hoc) Brigade Schmalz. In other words, Kesselring wanted to scatter the 15th Panzer Grenadier— the best division in Sicily—all over the island.

Albert Kesselring was a forceful personality and a strong-willed, convincing man, while General Guzzoni was not. Rather, as Senger recalled, the Italian "was always conciliatory and prepared to moderate differences. With regard to the employment of German forces, Guzzoni was entirely willing, even against his own better knowledge, to adapt himself to Kesselring's wishes, since he realized that the German divisions were the backbone of the defense."[27]

In insisting upon this plan, Kesselring committed the greatest tactical blunder of the campaign. Coupled with Hitler's strategic ineptitude and the consistent outwitting of German military intelligence by the British intelligence agencies, Kesselring's decision robbed the 6th Army of its only chance to repel the invasion and so doomed the entire campaign to eventual failure. The naval fortress areas of Messina–Regglo, Trapani, and Augusta–Syracuse were the most strongly fortified and garrisoned places on the island, but they remained independent of the 6th Army's control. Ironically, the 15th Panzer Grenadier Division had already conducted counterattack drills against the very beaches on which Patton's forces would land within three weeks.

Luftwaffe Field Marshal Wolfram von Richthofen, the newly appointed commander in chief of the 2nd Air Fleet, also weakened the Sicilian defenses on the eve of the invasion. He had worked well with Kesselring when his VIII Air Corps was part of the latter's air fleet on the Western Front in 1940 and in Russia in 1941. Now, however, Richthofen was determined to act independently. He decided that the Allied invasion would come against Sardinia, and despite all of Kesselring's remonstrations, he moved the bulk of his fighters there. From mid-May until July 10, 1943, the number of aircraft in Sicily actually declined, from 415 to 175, in spite of the fact that the Mediterranean theater was receiving 40 percent of all German aircraft production—mainly Me 109 and FW 190 single-engine fighters.[28]

Luftwaffe fighter-pilot morale in the Mediterranean declined perceptibility from May through early July, a period in which they fought no fewer than twenty-one major air battles against vastly superior enemy forces. Goering recognized what was happening but did not see the cause. He brought great pressure on his fighter units and effectively neutralized all of Galland's efforts with the following order:

> Together with the fighter pilots in France, Norway, and Russia, I can only regard you with contempt. I want an immediate improvement in fighting spirit. If this improvement is not forthcoming, flying personnel from the commander down must expect to be remanded to the ranks and transferred to the Eastern Front to serve on the ground.

On June 25, Goering went one step further by issuing an order demanding that one pilot from each fighter group in the 2nd Air Fleet be court-martialed for cowardice in the face of the enemy. Several outraged group commanders, their Knight's Crosses dangling from their necks, turned themselves in for trial, forcing Adolf Galland, the general of fighters, to quietly sweep the matter under the rug. It had done nothing to improve morale.

On July 5, in his private diary, Col. Johannes Steinhoff, commander of a fighter wing, wrote of his pilots:

> I had long been aware that they had ceased taking unneccessary risks. . . . Now they only went for the easy kills—the solitary flier, the inexperienced pilot who had broken away from his formation, the crippled straggler. During the air battles over England, whatever the mistakes that had been made, things could hardly have come to such a pass. But now we were tired, worn out and dispirited.[29]

With their opposition deteriorating, the American twin-engine, twin-boomed P-38 Lightnings, which had been escorting bombers, began attacking ground targets in Sicily and southern Italy if they did not encounter enemy fighters in their escort duties. Trains were favorite targets, and so were trucks, wagons, and ground troops. German soldiers already dreaded the appearance of the Lightnings, and the "German glance"—a fugitive look over the shoulder for enemy airplanes—arrived in Europe. It would become commonplace among the frontline troops on the Italian and Western Fronts in the months ahead.

The Allies began their final, all-out air offensive during the last half of June, especially from July 1 on. Their objectives were to eliminate the Axis air forces and communications centers; isolate the Sicilian battlefield from the mainland; neutralize the railroads in Sicily and southern Italy in order to cut the 6th Army's supply lines and make it impossible to reinforce the island; and further lower Axis, especially Italian, morale. On July 9, the day before the landings, the Allied air forces had approximately 4,900 operational airplanes divided among 146 American and 113.5 British squadrons. That day, they launched twenty-one major air raids against airfields and other targets from Sciacca to Taormina. Gerbini and seven of its satellite fields were now unusable, as were Comiso, Catania, and Bocca di Falco. Palermo, Trapani, Cagliari, Messina, and others were also attacked and suffered varying degrees of damage. Castelvetrano had to be abandoned, and several other airfields were usable only in emergencies. Only Sciacca and Trapani–Milo were fully operational. The *Luftwaffe* had only about fifty operational airplanes left on the island as the Allied invasion force struck on July 10.

The air attacks on Sicily prior to the invasion set the pattern for things to come throughout Italy and western Europe in 1943, 1944, and 1945. The British and Americans had neutralized the U-boat threat and established naval superiority in the waters around Hitler's "Fortress Europe." They had also shown that they could effectively establish air superiority—and sometimes air supremacy—in any major zone they chose to attack. This pattern continued for the rest of the war. Allied forces would first establish air superiority; then their ground forces would land without opposition from the German Navy. Next, the well-supplied and superbly equipped ground forces, lavishly supported by their air forces, would slowly crush their outnumbered and usually ill-equipped German opponents, who suffered from supply shortages of every kind (largely because of the highly successful Allied blockade and the disruptive affect of Allied air attacks and aerial bombardments on supply lines, rear areas, and industrial production centers). Even before the first Allied soldier set foot on European soil on July 10, 1943, their leaders had devised the operational formula that would lead them to final victory.

CHAPTER 10

The Allied Invasion of Southern Europe

THE ALLIED PLAN

The Allied command system for Operation Husky, as the invasion of Sicily was code-named, was established at Casablanca and included Gen. Dwight D. Eisenhower as commander in chief of the Allied Expeditionary Force; Adm. Andrew B. Cunningham as naval commander in chief in the Mediterranean; Air Chief Marshal Arthur Tedder as commander in chief of Allied Mediterranean Air Forces; and Gen. Harold Alexander as commander in chief of the 15th Army Group and Eisenhower's deputy commander in chief. Alexander would be responsible for the overall command of the ground battle. His main forces consisted of the British 8th Army under Gen. Bernard Law Montgomery and the newly formed U.S. 7th Army under the command of Lt. Gen. George S. Patton.

The detailed Allied planning went poorly, however, and resulted in animosity between Patton and Montgomery, a friction that would continue throughout the war. No fewer than seven plans were presented and rejected before one was finally adopted. The time-consuming and ham-fisted Allied planning effort represented a significant victory for the Germans at a time when they had nothing with which to defend Sicily. Since the plan did not receive final approval until May 13, it could not be executed until July 10. Military historian Basil Liddell Hart wrote:

These delays in the planning were more regrettable since only one of the ten divisions to lead the invasion of Sicily was engaged in the final stages of the North African campaign, and seven of them were fresh entries. A landing in Sicily soon after the Axis collapse in Africa would have found the island almost naked of defense.[1]

This would not be the case on July 10. It should be noted here that many historians and military experts, then and now, consider the invasion of Sicily and the subsequent campaign in Italy to be a mistake on the part of the Allies. "I for one still think of the Mediterranean as a trap which prolonged the war in Europe by a year," Gen. Albert C. Wedemeyer, one of America's best strategic minds, wrote later. "It was a side show, and it cost many unnecessary lives." He added, "The decision to invade Sicily (which was to lead insensibly to further employment of Allied armies up the tortuous spine of Italy) inevitably sidetracked the main Normandy commitment, the really decisive operation, until 1944."[2]

Samuel Eliot Morison, the distinguished naval expert and historian, wrote that "ascending the Mediterranean ladder" would "consume more of our forces than of the enemy's, and delay the cross-Channel operation at least a year—as indeed it did."[3] British Field Marshal Wavell agreed. He felt that by adopting their Mediterranean strategy, the Allies had committed themselves to killing an octopus by cutting off tenacle after tenacle.[4]

"Once again, the oratorical powers of Churchill, instead of sound strategic thinking, were to influence the operations of the Allies," Wedemeyer moaned. He wished that Gen. Douglas MacArthur had been in a position of power in Washington because of his "strategic desire to go by the most direct route to critical areas which the enemy could not afford to lose for either psychological, economic, or military reasons. . . . MacArthur adhered to the root principles of military strategy, namely, concentrating for a decisive blow against the most critical target."[5]

THE LANDINGS

The final Husky plan called for Montgomery to land on the southern and eastern coasts of Sicily near Syracuse while Patton landed at Gela and covered his left flank. In all, 2,590 naval vessels would be used in the initial assault alone. They would bring ashore 115,000 British and Canadian and 66,000 American soldiers, 14,000 vehicles, 600 tanks, and 1,800 guns. It would be the largest amphibious operation in history—larger even than the June 6, 1944, landing on the coast of Normandy. Elements of two Allied airborne divisions were also scheduled to take part in the invasion.

The Sicilian landings took Hitler and the entire German command by surprise. Because of poor weather conditions, General d'Havet had failed to place the 206th Coastal Defense Division on alert, and it also was taken by surprise. Except for the Allied parachute drops and glider landings, which scattered British and American paratroopers all over the island, Operation Husky was a success everywhere. The British amphibious landings met only the most feeble resistance, which was quickly silenced, and by late afternoon, the British 5th Infantry Division was approaching Syracuse from the south. Meanwhile, an ugly chain reaction began in Vice Adm. Priamo Leonardi's Naval Fortress Area Syracuse-Augusta when a small German antiaircraft detachment withdrew to the north, apparently to join Brigade Schmalz. This had a demoralizing effect on the Italians, who soon panicked and were seized by a positively frenzied orgy of destruction. Despite the absence of a direct threat, they blew up fixed positions, gun emplacements, fuel tanks, and ammunition stockpiles. Hundreds of sailors and soldiers deserted and fled to the north.

Naval Fortress Area Syracuse-Augusta was the most massively fortified defensive position in all of Sicily. To defend the two ancient cities and twenty miles of coast, it had at least twenty-three coastal defense batteries (four of them of 6-inch caliber), five antiparatrooper batteries, dozens of reinforced bunkers, miles of barbed wire, mobile assault troops, minefields, armored trains, armored cars, hundreds of machine guns, and thousands of men. Yet when the British marched into Syracuse on the evening of July 10, they were unopposed, and they found the port undamaged. In their haste to escape, the Italians had neglected to destroy the harbor installations. Soon the British 5th Infantry Division was advancing to the north on a two-brigade front against the rapidly disintegrating Napoli Division. It was not halted until after nightfall when it ran into Brigade Schmalz (part of the Hermann Goering Division), which was rushing down from the north.

Colonel Schmalz realized that he could not stop the British with his meager forces, which were the only reliable troops between Montgomery and Messina. He had already decided to conduct a delaying action all the way to the Simeto River, just south of Catania. By then, he hoped, reinforcements would have arrived, enabling him to hold this line and keep the British armor from reaching the Catanian Plain; otherwise, there was a distinct danger that nobody would stop Montgomery before he reached Messina and bottled up the entire Axis garrison of Sicily.

Patton's spearheads landed on the unprotected beaches east and west of Gela. Unfortunately, all of the 7th Army's beaches were fronted by "false beaches": sand bars with enough water over them to float a small landing craft but not the heavier and critical LSTs (landing ships, tank) that carried most of the American armor, artillery, and heavy weapons. Between the false beaches and the real beaches lay "runnels," miniature lagoons deep enough to drown a tank or vehicle. Therefore, the U.S. Navy had to construct pontoon causeways from the LSTs in the deep water across the false beaches and the runnels to the landing beaches. All of this, of course, required time, during which the causeways and LSTs were exposed to air attack. There were only two LSTs available in the Gela zone, but one of these missed its destination in the high seas and darkness and ended up near Scoglitti, well to the south. The other was destroyed by a Me 109. As a result, Patton was not able to get a single operational tank onto dry land in the Gela sector on July 10.

THE COUNTERATTACKS

General Guzzoni ordered the Hermann Goering Division and Italian Mobile Group E (a battalion-size task force equipped with thirty Renault-35 tanks, which weighed only ten tons) to counterattack on the morning of July 10. Because of problems with American paratroopers, his inexperienced officers and men, and his own ineptitude, General Conrath did not attack until 2 P.M. Mobile Group E attacked in the morning, broke through American lines, and actually pushed into Gela, the principal city in the American sector. Because it had no infantry support, it was eventually forced to retreat by U.S. Rangers.

Shortly after the Italian tanks fled, a battalion of the 33rd (Livorno) Infantry Regiment marched across the plain and attacked the Gela perimeter from the west. They were almost in parade-ground formation, closely packed, showing great courage but no tactical skill. Historian Carlo D'Este noted that the advance was "reminiscent of nineteeth-century warfare" and a "sad illustration of the ineptitude of the Italian Army."[6] Had they advanced when the tanks of Mobile Group E entered Gela, the Americans would have been in deep, deep trouble; now, however, the Italian infantrymen were like sheep for the slaughter. The American Rangers opened up on them with mortars, captured artillery, rifles, and machine guns. Rank after rank went down. It was butchery. Soon the survivors fled, leaving behind a field covered with dead and wounded.

When Conrath finally did attack that afternoon, he advanced in two columns: Kampfgruppe Rechts (Right) and Links (Left). Kampfgruppe Rechts got nowhere. It was halted at Priolo by the U.S. Navy's big guns, and Colonel Urban, the former bomber pilot with the nervous disorder, quickly fell back. Conrath, who was accompanying Kampfgruppe Rechts, relieved Urban of his command and personally took charge of the task force but could not get the attack going forward again.

Approximately fifteen miles to the east, Kampfgruppe Links attacked through the dense olive groves against the left flank of the U.S. 45th Infantry Division. Spearheaded by its Tigers, Kampfgruppe Links overran the 1st Battalion of the U.S. 180th Regimental Combat Team (RCT) and captured its commander and most of its men. The battle group pursued the few survivors to the south, where they ran into the 3rd Battalion, 180th RCT. They were now only four miles from the 45th Division's beaches and behind the right flank of the 1st Infantry Division. The battle had reached a crisis, and it seemed for a moment that the 3rd Battalion was doomed to suffer the same fate as its sister. Then, for some unexplained reason, the Germans panicked and fled wildly to the rear, unpursued by the surprised Americans, who had, in fact, been losing the battle. Conrath, presented with a *fait accompli*, had no choice but to call off the battle at 4 P.M. He resolved to try again the next day.

Conrath spent much of the evening touring his units, relieving commanders, giving severe reprimands, and threatening to have people shot for cowardice. He reorganized the division into three columns by splitting Kampfgruppe Rechts in two and ordered them to counterattack at daybreak on July 11.

The Livorno and the Hermann Goering struck the U.S. 7th Army at 6:15 A.M. on the eleventh. Soon the entire sector from Gela to south of Biscari was a sea of smoke, blood, fire, and confusion. The U.S. 26th Infantry Regiment in the center of the 1st Infantry Division's line was mauled by the reinforced II Battalion of the Hermann Goering Panzer Regiment, which formed the right flank of Conrath's attack. All of the 26th's antitank guns had gone down with an LST, and the sixty medium panzers of the II Battalion rapidly overran an infantry battalion and pushed in the center of the 1st Infantry Division. Meanwhile, on the left flank of the German attack, the infantry-heavy Kampfgruppe Links broke through the front of what was left of the 180th RCT and, spearheaded by several Tigers, cut the Coastal Highway and drove the Americans back to Biazzo Ridge, only two miles from the beaches. In the center, Conrath himself led an attack against Hill 41, which was held by paratroopers and the 2nd Battalion of the 16th RCT. Conrath's battle group included twenty-one medium panzers, well supported by the Hermann Goering Panzer Artillery Regiment. Most of the men of the 2nd Battalion of the 16th RCT were recent replacements in battle for the first time, and the sight of a reinforced panzer battalion in the attack was too much for them. More than half of them broke and ran; the rest fought as bravely as the paratroopers, but they could not hold. The panzers overran the hill, crushing many Americans to death in their foxholes. Conrath then pursued the survivors to the south.

By 9:30 A.M., the Americans were being pushed back everywhere. Before noon, much of the U.S. 7th Army had been shoved back to its final defensive positions on the sand dunes south of the Coastal Road on the very edge of the invasion beaches. Here Patton had landed the 32nd Field Artillery Battalion as well as the 41st Armored Infantry Regiment and the 18th RCT from his floating reserve. By 11 A.M., the battle east of Gela degenerated into a free-for-all, and the Germans and Americans were too intermingled in close combat for the U.S. Navy to use its big guns. The panzers pushed to within 2,000 yards of the beaches and raked supply dumps and landing craft with their main battle guns. Conrath even signaled that the Americans were reembarking, but his jubilation was premature. The German attack was halted just in front of the American final defensive position by the gunners of the 32nd Field Artillery, the 16th Cannon Company, the heavy weapons of the 41st Armored

Infantry Regiment, and four Shermans, which the tankers and shore parties had finally managed to get off the beaches and onto the fringe of the coastal plain. Ten panzers were knocked out and several others damaged. The *Luftwaffe* tankers halted, then slowly fell back to regroup. This put a short distance between them and the Americans, so the navy immediately opened up with its heavy firepower, and the German retreat became faster and more disorganized. Although it did not degenerate into a rout, Paul Conrath was never able to get the attack going again. The Americans did not pursue, so the battle ended about 2 P.M. The Hermann Goering had lost ten Tigers and thirty to forty PzKw IIIs and IVs destroyed, for a total of forty to fifty tanks completely destroyed. The Hermann Goering Panzer Regiment lost at least a third of its tank strength on July 11, and about half of its tanks were at least seriously damaged. Thirty officers and 600 men were casualties.

With Patton breathing down their necks, the American engineers finally succeeded in repairing the Gela pier, and the Shermans at last began to come ashore in strength. In the meantime, to the east, Maj. Gen. Troy Middleton, the commander of the U.S. 45th Infantry Division, did not allowed the threat to his beaches to distract him from his primary mission: the seizure of Comiso airfield. He sent two infantry regiments forward to take it in a deep pincer movement. Italian resistance was weak, and the airfield fell at 4:30 P.M. The Americans captured 125 Axis airplanes—only 20 of which were operational—and 200,000 gallons of aviation fuel.

At dawn on July 12, the Battle of Sicily entered a new phase in the American zone. By now, Patton had enough tanks, artillery, supplies, and heavy equipment to go over to the offensive, and the battle turned into a pursuit—except in the Niscemi Road–Piano Lupo sector, where Conrath had decided to conduct his own private war. By now, Guzzoni had learned that Syracuse had fallen and that his left flank was on the verge of collapse. Colonel Schmalz desperately needed mobile reinforcements, which could come only from the Hermann Goering Division. Senger fully concurred with Guzzoni and urged Conrath to move his division to the northeast as quickly as possible.

An hour before dawn, the 2nd Battalion of the 16th RCT, accompanied by about a company of the ubiquitous migrant American paratroopers, had captured Hill 41 in the Piano Lupo sector. With incredible pigheadedness, Conrath decided to retake it, despite the fact that it no longer had the slightest military significance. He launched four frontal attacks against the hill—all poorly coordinated and lacking sufficient infantry support—and all were easily repulsed. That day Conrath issued a bitter order to his troops, stating that he had seen men "running to the rear hysterically crying because they had heard the detonation of a single shot." Once again, he threatened severe measures, including death sentences.[7]

Elsewhere, the Americans surged forward. By mid-morning, the Livorno—the best of the Italian divisions in Sicily—was in remnants, having lost more than half of its men and most of its combat units. On Patton's left flank, Maj. Gen. Lucian K. Truscott Jr. and his U.S. 3rd Infantry Division were also pushing forward, and soon they cut the Italian 207th Coastal Defense Division in half. Fortunately for the Italians, Col. Fritz Fullriede's 129th Panzer Grenadier Regiment was near at hand, holding a breaking position to the north. As the Italians retreated, Fullriede turned back the U.S. attacks and knocked out or disabled forty-three American tanks.[8] Only after nightfall did the 129th Panzer Grenadier follow the Italians and retire toward the new line. Meanwhile, Karl Ens came up with his 104th Panzer Grenadier Regiment.

PRIMOSOLE BRIDGE

While Patton's artillery was battling the panzers on the edge of the beaches and American Rangers were fighting Italian tanks in the streets of Gela, Montgomery was advancing to the north against decreasing Italian resistance. Alexander reported, "The Italian coastal divisions, whose value had never been rated very highly, disintegrated almost without firing a shot, and the field divisions, when they were met, were also driven like chaff before the wind. Mass surrenders were frequent."[9]

Meanwhile, Col. Wilhelm Schmalz conducted his delaying action with the sure touch that normally characterized the German tactical commander in the field. As he retreated, southeastern Sicily was in an uproar. Refugee columns clogged the roads heading north. They were joined by Italian deserters, most of whom were now dressed as civilians; many deserters took to robbing, stealing, and looting from fugitives and villagers. It was a sorry sight. Fascist officials fled, law and order broke down, and anarchy ruled the countryside. To make matters worse, the dust often made it impossible to tell the difference between refugee columns and Axis military formations from the air, and many fleeing civilians were strafed as a result, adding to the horror, misery, and confusion.

On July 12, Schmalz ordered his men to fall back north of Augusta, leaving the defense of the city to the incompetent Admiral Leonardi. The British entered the city that evening. Ironically, the Allied aerial bombardments had caused such severe damage that the capacity of the port was reduced to only 1,600 tons of cargo per day. That same day, the 1st Canadian Division entered Modica and captured several hundred prisoners, including General Achille d'Havet, the commander of the 206th Coastal. His capture signaled the end of his division. After the fall of Modica, a platoon of infantry, supported by a troop of tanks, turned south to clear the nearby village of Scicli. The Edmonton Regiment's unit diary reported that "the tanks fired three shots over the town, and 1,100 prisoners emerged from the hills and gave themselves up."[10] During the day and the following night, other units of the British 8th Army made similar progress.

In the meantime, the first substantial German reinforcements arrived in Sicily. From his OB South reserve, Kesselring sent Col. Wolfgang Maucke's 382nd Panzer Grenadier Regiment, which was a rebuilt "African" unit, and the Panzer Grenadier Battalion Reggio, which had been created from the 69th March Battalion. The most significant reinforcement was Col. Ludwig Heilmann's 3rd Parachute Regiment (1,817 men), which jumped into Sicily from more than 100 He 111s at 7 P.M. on July 12. The operation was risky, but as Kesselring observed, "the British fighters' rigid time-table gave us repeated opportunities to risk the move."[11] Group Schmalz would eventually be reinforced by most of the rest of the 1st Parachute Division, except for the 1st Parachute Regiment and the divisional headquarters. (Kesselring obviously had more confidence in Schmalz than in Lt. Gen. Richard Heidrich, the divisional commander.)

On the other side of the hill, Montgomery was as wlldy optimistic as Kesselring had been earlier. He believed that he had a chance to end the campaign in a matter of days. He felt that one British corps could cut behind the Germans by driving inland to Enna, trapping the Axis forces in central Sicily between the British and Americans. Following this triumph, the British corps, Leese's XXX, could make a left hook west of Mount Etna, possibly trapping the rest of the German forces between it and Dempsey's XIII Corps, which would by then be blitzing up the coast toward Catania and Messina.[12]

This was not a good plan because it was far too ambitious. Nevertheless, Alexander approved it, even though it meant taking Highway 124 away from the Americans. When he issued the orders at 8 P.M. on July 13, the U.S. 45th Infantry Division was within 1,000 yards of cutting the highway. Now it had to turn around, march to the rear, and reinsert itself into the battle west of the 1st Infantry Division. In effect, the order forced the U.S. II Corps to halt its offensive for several days, taking the pressure off of the Hermann Goering Panzer Division. It also divided Montgomery's main effort into two parts, violating the principle of mass, and sent the British XXX Corps into an area where armor could not be used effectively and which was out of the range of the Royal Navy. Furthermore, in the two weeks it would now require Patton and Montgomery to reach positions north of Mount Etna, the Germans would have time to deploy more than half of the 1st Parachute Division and the entire 29th Panzer Grenadier Division. The brilliant Hans Hube—the veteran commander of the XIV Panzer Corps—had taken charge of the battle on the Axis side and staged an extremely quick recovery, depriving the Allies of their chance to win a quick and decisive victory in Sicily.

Montgomery decided to break through to Catania by a combined land, parachute, and sea assault. He was sure that one more blow would send the Germans and their reluctant allies hustling back toward Messina in full retreat. "I shall be in Catania tonight!" he declared on the thirteenth.[13] There was little time to plan Operation Fustian, the airborne part of the assault. On the evening of July 13, the 1,856 "Red Devils" of Brig. Gerald Lathbury's 1st British Parachute Brigade boarded their airplanes at Kairouan, Tunisia. Their objective was the Primosole Bridge, a 400-foot-long structure standing about eight feet above the sluggish Simeto River. If they would capture the bridge and hold it until the spearheads of the XIII Corps reached it from the south, the British would be able to continue their rapid advance on Messina; if not, the Germans might be able to rally in the excellent defensive terrain to the north.

What the British did not know was that Maj. Werner Schmidt's 1st Parachute Machine Gun Battalion had landed in Catania that morning and that Colonel Heilmann had ordered it to defend the bridge, just in case the British tried an attack of this nature. As a result, the German gunners dug in on the edge of an orange grove 2,000 yards south of the bridge—well within machine-gun range of the main British drop zones. The few British paratroopers who landed where they were supposed to were quickly shot to pieces. Lathbury was still able to seize the bridge, but by the next morning, he had only 295 men with which to defend it—less than 16 percent of his assault force.

It should be noted here that a strange bond of comradeship existed between the German and British paratroopers fighting for the Primosole Bridge. The Red Devils, swinging helplessly from orange trees, were not shot or bayoneted in their harnesses, as one might expect in such a confused night battle; rather, the enemy paratroopers were allowed to disengage themselves and fall to the ground, where they were taken prisoner. Captives were not shot or even roughly handled but were instead treated almost as guests. Seriously wounded prisoners on both sides received priority medical attention, while lightly wounded friendlies awaited their turn without complaint. It was incredible behavior for the Second World War. "Marching" British infantry certainly did not receive such preferential treatment from the Germans, nor were Italian prisoners treated so politely by the Red Devils.

The British airborne landing caused such fear and panic in Generale di Divisione Carlo Gotti's 213th Coastal Defense Division that most of it was gone by morning. Many of the troops of Generale di Brigata Azzo Passalacqua's Port Defense Area E—the port defense troops of Catania— also fled, although some continued to fight until their city fell twenty-five days later.

The British relief force, the 50th (Northumbrian) Infantry Division and the 4th Armoured Brigade, slowly drove north against Brigade Schmalz. Montgomery's plan, which required them to advance twenty-five miles in less than twenty-four hours, simply exceeded their capacities. The 50th Infantry gained only ten miles on the fourteenth. The Shermans of the armored brigade were of no use whatsoever because the Germans blew up the bridges as they retreated. The infantry could cross the small rivers on foot, but the tanks simply had to wait until the engineers could come up and rebuild the bridges. This also took time. The British did not reach Lentini until the afternoon of July 14.

On Primosole Bridge, time ran out. After nightfall on July 14, Lathbury, who was almost out of ammunition, was forced to abandon the bridge and withdraw the remnants of his brigade to positions about 1,200 yards south of the river, where he was joined by the 4th Armoured Brigade the following morning. Meanwhile, Schmalz sidestepped to the west and, using secondary roads, retired across the Gornalunga River at Gerbini, which put him even closer to the flank of the Hermann Goering Division, which was finally coming up from the west. (They would link up on the morning of the fifteenth.) On the night of the fourteenth, a new German force dropped just north of the bridge—a battalion of Col. Erich Walters' 4th Parachute Regiment and Capt. Paul Adolff's 1st Parachute Engineer Battalion, as well as elements of the 1st Parachute Artillery Regiment. All of these units were placed under the command of Brigade Schmalz.

The British continued to attack Primosole Bridge for four more days. They succeeded in recapturing the damaged bridge but could not break through the main German line 3,000 yards to the north. By July 19, the British 8th Army had been checked.

The was no doubt in the mind of Maj. Gen. Francis de Guingand, Montgomery's chief of staff, why the offensive had been halted. It was because the German paratroopers had "fought with fanatical savagery."[14] General Alexander himself later called the men of the 1st Parachute Division "the best soldiers in the world." Pond recorded that even those who were taken prisoner "remained arrogant and hostile in the face of all threats and interrogations. . . . Spitting in the faces of their captors, some officers would not answer any questions, refusing to give even name, rank, and number."[15] General de Guingand wrote later:

> During the fighting across the Simeto, these incidents occurred. A wounded German was lying on a stretcher at a dressing station having his wounds dressed by one of our orderlies. Directly he recovered sufficient strength and turned over, seized the orderly's hand and plunged his teeth deep into it, shouting some Nazi invective. Another, when being interrogated by one of our officers, drew himself up to attention and spat deliberately into

his face. A third, who was wounded, managed to standup, pulled out his revolver, shouted 'Heil Hitler' and shot himself.[16]

De Guingand had a personal brush with one of the paratroopers. Albrecht Gunther, a twenty-eight-year-old lieutenant, had been brought to the 8th Army's chief of staff. Cut off behind British lines, Gunther had tried to get back to his unit by putting on civilian clothes, but he had been captured nevertheless. Gunther was a veteran of the Russian Front and had fought in Holland and France before that, but de Guingand did not know it. "He refused to give anything except his rank and name," the chief recalled. Finally, the exasperated chief of staff told Gunther that since he had been caught in civilian clothes, he could be shot as a spy under international law; in fact, that was what was going to happen to him. "His face never showed the least reaction," de Guingand recalled.

"That is quite understood," the young officer replied. "I took the risk and failed—I deserve it. Heil Hitler!" Gunther then saluted and walked away.[17]

De Guingand did not have Gunther shot. He sent him to a prisoner-of-war camp instead and released the story to the British Broadcasting Company in hopes that it might lead to better treatment of Allied POWs by the Germans.

THE DRIVE ON PALERMO

General Patton reintroduced the American forces as a factor in the battle much more quickly than either the Germans or British thought possible. Between July 13 and 16, he captured Agrigento, the gateway to western Sicily, as well as Porto Empedocle, a much-needed harbor, destroying the 207th Coastal Defense Division and capturing more than 6,000 men, 50 guns, and more than 100 vehicles in the process. In the meantime, he made a major decision: he would seize Palermo whether General Alexander liked it or not.

Western Sicily was defended by Generale di Corpo Francesco Zingales, who had replaced Mario Arisio as commander of the XII Corps on July 12. (Arisio had assumed command of the 7th Army on the mainland.) Zingales's command included the Aosta and Assietta Divisions, Generale di Divisione Giovanni Marciani's 208th Coastal Defense

Division, the ad hoc Mobile Group West (Mobile Groups A, B, and C under Colonel Rossi), Group Schreiber, and a few miscellaneous units. It now faced Patton's new command, Provisional Corps, which was led by Maj. Gen. Geoffrey Keyes, the deputy commander of 7th Army. Keyes controlled the 82nd Airborne, 3rd Infantry, and 2nd Armored Divisions—more than a match for Zingales's forces. At the same time, the 45th and 1st Infantry Divisions of Omar Bradley's II Corps were to advance northward on the far right.

Keyes jumped off at 5 A.M. on July 19 against weak resistance. "It was a pleasure march," Brig. Gen. Maxwell Taylor, the deputy commander of the 82nd Airborne Division, recalled later.[18] Mass surrenders were frequent, and the 3rd Infantry Division advanced fifty-four miles in thirty-three hours—on foot. Only the 1st Infantry Division made very slow progress, but that was because it was facing Lt. Col. Fritz Fullriede's 129th Panzer Grenadier Regiment. One by one, the small Italian mobile groups were overwhelmed. Group Schreiber was overrun and destroyed by American tanks near Alimena on July 21, and Patton's spearheads barrelled into the rear of the retreating Assietta and Aosta Divisions, destroying the Aosta's mortar battalion and overrunning several battalions of infantry. The 48th (Assietta) Artillery Regiment escaped with only one gun.[19]

By July 21, the 202nd Coastal Defense Division had "self-demobilized" (i.e., vanished), and the American vanguards captured 4,000 prisoners, almost without firing a shot. General Marciani went forward to try to rally his troops on July 22, but he was quickly captured by a patrol from the 82nd Reconnaissance Battalion, the vanguard of the 2nd Armored Division. The responsibility for the defense of Palermo devolved onto Generale di Brigata Giuseppe Molinero, who was himself captured a few hours later.[20]

Recognizing a hopeless situation, Molinero offered to surrender the city to Keyes, who promptly accepted. The formal capitulation ceremony took place at the Royal Palace at 7 P.M. that same day. Patton entered Palermo two hours later. That night, the city was swept by an orgy of rioting and looting.

Troy Middleton's 45th Infantry Division reached the northern coast of Sicily at Station Cerda east of Palermo at 9 A.M. on July 23 after advancing eighty miles in five days on foot. After reaching the sea, Middleton's Thunderbirds turned right along Highway 113 and advanced east until they were stopped near Campofelice by Col. Max Ulrich's 15th Panzer Grenadier Regiment, the vanguard of Maj. Gen. Walter Fries's 29th Panzer Grenadier Division. Here Middleton halted to await resupply and reinforcements from the rest of the 7th Army.

Meanwhile, western Sicily was quickly cleared by the U.S. 82nd Airborne Division. Provisional Corps (the 82nd Airborne and 2nd Armored Divisions) settled down to garrison duties until it was dissolved on August 20. During its race through western Sicily, it had captured 189 guns, 359 vehicles, 45 tanks, and thousands of Italian soldiers. It had also significantly improved the status of the American army, which was taken far more seriously by the British after this rapid victory.

Hitler's enemies: Joseph Stalin, Franklin D. Roosevelt, and Winston Churchill. NATIONAL ARCHIVES

Adm. Wilhelm Canaris, chief of the Abwehr (right), speaking with a German general and his aide. Canaris was a almost total failure as head of German military intelligence.

Hermann Goering (left) and Field Marshal Albert Kesselring at Fuehrer Headquarters.
NATIONAL ARCHIVES

A German mountain artillery unit in Italy, circa 1944. NATIONAL ARCHIVES

SS Gen. Theodor Eicke, commander of the 3rd SS Panzer Division "Totenkopf." A very brutal man, Eicke was the former commandant of Dachau and inspector general of concentration camps. He was killed in action on the Eastern Front in February 1943. NATIONAL ARCHIVES

A Panzer Mark III (PzKw III) tank, 1943. NATIONAL ARCHIVES

Hitler speaks with Field Marshal Baron von Richthofen while Gen. Kurt Student (second from right) and Col. Gen. Hans Jeschonnek, chief of the General Staff of the Luftwaffe (far right), look on. Seeing the handwriting on the wall, Jeschonnek committed suicide in August 1943. NATIONAL ARCHIVES

A German infantryman takes cover behind an armored vehicle, Eastern Front, circa 1943.

A German machine gunner looks down on the Dnieper River, 1943. NATIONAL ARCHIVES

Axis airplanes strafe U.S. naval vessels off the coast of Gela, Sicily, July 11, 1943. USAMHI

Members of the staff of the Italian 6th Army march from the Hotel Belvedere in Enna, Sicily, toward the POW camps, July 1943. These men had several days to escape but did not do so. NATIONAL ARCHIVES

Italian prisoners of war talking with an American private of Italian descent, 1943. NATIONAL ARCHIVES

These German airplanes were on their way to the forward squadrons when they were destroyed on their railroad cars by Allied fighter-bombers in Sicily, July 1943. USAMHI

American heavy artillery on the move, Sicily, July 1943. USAMHI

The graves of German soldiers killed near Troina, Sicily, August 1943. An American convoy is seen in the background. Note the rough nature of the barren terrain, which the German defenders used to maximum advantage, both in Sicily and in Italy. NATIONAL ARCHIVES

German prisoners of war being interrogated, July 24, 1943. The POWs were members of the 29th Panzer Grenadier Division. NATIONAL ARCHIVES

An American Sherman tank, part of the elite U.S. 2nd Armored Division, entering Palermo, Sicily, July 22, 1943. The Sherman was considered inferior to most German panzers in World War II.

A German PzKw VI Tiger tank, probably the most feared German ground weapon in World War II. This particular Tiger belonged to the 1st SS Panzer Regiment of the 1st SS Panzer Division "Leibstandarte Adolf Hitler," which distinguished itself on the Eastern Front in 1943.

*Hans Valentin
Hube.*

*Italian soldiers surrendering, 1943. Many Italians were happy to be leaving the war; German POWs
were a more sullen lot.* NATIONAL ARCHIVES

A former member of the Afrika Korps is being processed into the POW camps. NATIONAL ARCHIVES

An American soldier looks out over Messina, the strategic objective of the Sicilian campaign. The Italian mainland can be seen in the background. NATIONAL ARCHIVES

Victor Emmanuel III, king of Italy. Born in Naples in 1869, he was king from 1900 to 1946, when he abdicated in favor of his son, Umberto II. NATIONAL ARCHIVES

The Italian delegation signs the instruments of surrender at Cassibile, Sicily, September 3, 1943. Left to right: Maj. Gen. Walter "Beatle" Smith, Eisenhower's chief of staff; Cdre. Roger M. Dick, Royal Navy, Admiral Cunningham's chief of staff; Maj. Gen. Lowell W. Rooks, Eisenhower's operations officer; Captain de Haan, Strong's aide; Brig. Gen. Giuseppe Castellano, the Italian representative; and Consul Franco Montanari of the Italian Foreign Office. Brig. Kenneth W. D. Strong, Eisenhower's chief intelligence officer, is directly behind Castellano. NATIONAL ARCHIVES

In too much of a hurry to get to Messina, this German half-track fell from the bridge into this dry river bed. The graves of the crew can be seen in the upper portion of this photo.
NATIONAL ARCHIVES

American infantrymen advance through a demolished road in Italy, 1943. NATIONAL ARCHIVES

The U.S. Liberty ship Robert Rowan *explodes after suffering a direct hit from a Luftwaffe bomb off the coast of Gela, Sicily, 1943.* NATIONAL ARCHIVES

The Allied fleet off the coast of Sicily puts up antiaircraft fire against the Luftwaffe, July 10, 1943. The following evening, it did the same thing to aircraft transporting the U.S. 504th Parachute Infantry Regiment. NATIONAL ARCHIVES

A Tiger tank. NATIONAL ARCHIVES

A Tiger tank destroyed by U.S. naval gunfire in Sicily, 1943. NATIONAL ARCHIVES

"We need you at the front!" A German recruiting poster, circa 1943. USAMHI

CHAPTER 11

The Fall of Fascism and the Loss of Sicily

THE FALL OF BENITO MUSSOLINI

Ever since his rise to power in 1922, there had been those who would have deposed Italian dictator Benito Mussolini. These men, however, did not represent a significant threat to his regime until the Italian Army suffered its first serious defeats. As the tide of the war turned inexorably against Italy, more and more people in high places turned against Mussolini. Many of these dissents were within the leadership caste of the Fascist Party—from men of wealth, rank, and privilege who opposed much of what Mussolini was doing, such as losing the war. Mussolini did not realize the extent of the opposition until it was too late.

On Wednesday, July 21, Benito Mussolini played into the hands of the conspirators by scheduling a meeting of the Fascist Grand Council for 5 P.M. on the twenty-fourth. The reason for the call was low morale and weakening within the party. To rectify this situation, Party Secretary Carlo Scorza had planned a whole series of mass meetings in the major Italian cities, where top Fascist speakers would whip up public support for the war effort. To Scorza's surprise, several of the leaders refused to participate. These men, instigated by Dino Grandi, met with Mussolini to explain their dissatisfaction and asked the dictator to call the Grand Council into session. Apparently thinking he could use the meeting to restore party morale and under the illusion that he was still in control of the situation, Mussolini agreed to their request.

203

On July 24, Kesselring and his chief of staff, Siegfried Westphal, visited Mussolini in the Palazzo Venezia, the famous fifteenth-century palace which had housed the Austro-Hungarian Embassy until World War I. Contrary to custom, the dictator kept the Germans waiting half an hour. Mussolini then emerged and "with jovial excitement" asked Kesselring, "Do you know Count Grandi? He just visited me. We have spoken out our minds, we are moving along the same line. He is completely loyal to me."[1]

"I often had occasion to think of this remark later," Westphal wrote, "particularly as I had formed the impression before this that judgment of character was not one of Mussolini's strong points."[2]

At 2:40 A.M. the following morning, the Fascist Grand Council—led by Grandi and Ciano—voted nineteen to eight (with one abstention) to turn command of the armed forces over to the king. The resolution was tantamount to a vote of no confidence and was effectively an invitation for Mussolini to resign, but he did not. He met with the king later that day at Villa Savoia, the royal residence on the outskirts of Rome. The monarch "accepted" Mussolini's resignation, and as he left the palace, the ex-dictator was met by a squad of *carabinieri*, which arrested him. The stunned Mussolini neither resisted nor protested. He was hurried into an ambulance and spirited away to an unknown location.

The conspirators of the Fascist Grand Council did not intend that the party should give up the reins of power, but they had unleashed forces far beyond their control. At 5 P.M., Marshal Pietro Badoglio was ushered into the king's presence and was named premier of Italy. Unfortunately for Italy, the coup had resulted in a weak, inexperienced, and inefficient government under a timid and indecisive monarchy. The seeds of disaster had been planted.

Conspicuous by his absence from the list of new cabinet ministers was Count Dino Grandi. He sat in his office all day on July 25, awaiting an inviation to head a new government—a call that never came. "Grandi had overlooked a centuries-old Savoy tradition," historian Melton S. Davis wrote later, "betrayal of those who helped the House."[3]

News of Mussolini's overthrow and arrest was broadcast from Rome that evening, along with official proclamations from Badoglio and the king. There was dancing in the streets as the Italian people sang, paraded in jubilation, and wept for joy. They thought the overthrow meant the end of the war. Mobs attacked Fascist Party offices, desecrated Fascist statues and monuments, and tore down every Fascist symbol they could find, including those on the lapels of private citizens. There were incidents of Fascist militiamen being caught before they could get home to change. They were stripped, ridiculed, and sent home in their underwear. "Fascism fell . . . like a rotten pear," Badoglio wrote later.[4] Gen. Alfred Jodl agreed. "The fact is, the whole Fascist movement went pop, like a soap bubble!" he exclaimed to Adolf Hitler.[5] By dawn the next day, not a Fascist emblem was to be seen, and all the Fascist leaders had gone underground or into hiding. It was as if Mussolini, his party, and their axis with Hitler had never existed.

But it had existed, and as Adolf Hitler declared, it would exist again.

Lost in the excitement of July 25–26 was the fact that none of the conspirators had, as of yet, bothered to contact the Allies, so Italy was not in a position to either surrender or make peace with the Americans or British. In fact, Italy's handling of the negotiations was almost unbelievably inept. Badoglio's own hand-picked foreign minister was not even on the scene; he was still in Turkey. No one had thought to summon him to Rome so that he could assume his critical post immediately after the coup, just as no one had bothered to establish a diplomatic channel beforehand through which the Italians could contact the Allies. This lack of foresight was to exhibit itself again and again for the next several weeks. Judging from the leisurely Italian reaction (and that of the Allies as well), one would assume that the Italian government felt it had all the time in the world to plot and implement its course of action. Just the opposite was true. Despite the warning signs, which Hitler had recognized, the fall of Mussollni had taken the German leader by surprise. But the time period during which Italy could successfully extricate itself from the Third Reich and defect from the Axis was exceedingly brief.

Hitler's reaction to the collapse of Fascism bordered on panic. He soon recovered, though, and pretended that he was deceived by the declarations of loyalty sent to Berlin and Rastenburg by Badoglio and King Victor Emmanuel. "Undoubtedly in their treachery they will proclaim that they will remain loyal to us," Hitler told his staff. "Of course they won't. . . . We'll play the same game while preparing everything to take over the whole area with one stroke, and capture all that riff-raff."[6] He recalled the Desert Fox from the Balkans and put him in charge of German forces earmarked for commitment in northern Italy. The mission of Rommel's Army Group B was to gradually infiltrate divisions into Italy in order to cover Hube's rear and seize control of the country when the time came.

On the other hand, Field Marshal Kesselring was taken in by Badoglio's protestations of loyalty to the Axis, as were Ambassador Mackensen, General Rintelen, Admiral Canaris, and Baron Richthofen. Hitler chuckled when he heard the field marshal's views. "Kesselring is too honest for the men down there, for those born traitors," he commented.[7] Adolf Hitler was not—he had played this game before.

On the other side of the hill, the overthrow of Mussolini also took the Allies by surprise. It was impossible for them, as yet, to state even the most basic terms of peace with Italy, other than unconditional surrender. "The Allies even lacked a set of armistice terms for an Italy offering to surrender," the U.S. official history noted.[8] President Roosevelt's reaction was ambiguous, as was Winston Churchill's. On July 27, the British prime minister told the House of Commons, "We should let the Italians . . . stew in their own juices a bit." Neither he nor Roosevelt seemed to appreciate that time was of the essence if a German occupation of Italy was to be forestalled. At the moment, Italy was in a political power vacuum, but this situation was transitory. Nature abhors a vacuum, whether it is physical or geopolitical, and Adolf Hitler could not be counted upon to remain inactive forever. The only person on the Allied side who seemed to grasp this was Dwight D. Eisenhower, who realized immediately that the Allies had an opportunity that would never present itself again. Via radio broadcasts, he urged the king to make immediate contact for the purpose of arranging an armistice. He also drew up a set of armistice terms and asked for authority to negotiate the Italian surrender on behalf of the Allies. Eisenhower was prevented from acting by his superiors, who decreed that he could not fix general terms without the approval of both the British and American governments. Eisenhower promptly requested such authority, but it was not forthcoming, and the opportunity was lost. If they were not going to let Eisenhower negotiate the surrender, they should have at least empowered someone—even a single team of diplomats and politicians—to do so, but they did not. As a result, the Allies could not speak with one voice, they would not even attempt to contact the Italians, and their surrender terms remained inflexible.

To make matters even worse, the Allied political leaders tipped their hand to Hitler. On July 28, Churchill made a speech to the House of Commons, in which he stated that nothing short of "wholesale unconditional surrender" could prevent Italy from being "seared and scarred and blackened from one end to the other."[9] The next day, he spoke to Roosevelt on the transatlantic telephone. The two leaders gossiped gaily about the "imminent armistice with Italy," with total disregard for security, completely unaware that the conversation was being monitored by SS intelligence experts. Hitler received a transcript of the conversation the next day. From it, Hitler deduced that Roosevelt was in secret contact with the king but that several weeks would pass before Italy could defect because the terms of the armistice had not yet been worked out.[10] Hitler now knew that he did not have to take any chances; he would be able to gradually infiltrate his units into Italy without provoking a joint Italian-Allied reaction. He also knew that Hube could continue his campaign in Sicily, confident that his rear was not in danger—at least for the moment. He was free to fight a prolonged delaying action, inflicting as many casualties on the Allies as possible while simultaneously tying down their best divisions and planning a controlled, phased evacuation of the island. This is exactly what he did.

After several preliminary attacks, the main Allied offensive began on August 1. From the German point of view, the most dangerous Allied attack was delivered by George S. Patton along the northern coastal road. This sector was defended the 29th Panzer Grenadier Division, which was led by Maj. Gen. Walter Fries, an officer who had lost an arm and a leg on the Eastern Front. He was as competent and determined as Patton.

The Allied effort to dislodge Hube and force him to give up his bridgehead involved a number of division-size battles. Their relatively small scale did not detract from their fierceness. Campofelice, Tusa Ridge (called "Bloody Ridge" by the Americans), San Fratello, San Stefano, Nicosia, Agira, Regalbuto Ridge, Centuripe, Adrano (Aderno), and others were bitterly contested and produced heavy casualties on both sides, but especially to the attackers.[11] On the other hand, Allied fighter-bombers were flying close-support missions for the infantry, causing heavy losses to the German units, especially in terms of vehicles. On August 2, for example, the 1st Canadian Division forced the Hermann

Goering Panzer Engineer Battalion to retreat in full daylight. The fighter-bombers pounced on the Goerings, destroyed about forty vehicles on the road between Regalbuto and Adrano, and eliminated the battalion as an effective combat force.

Patton's attacks in the northern coastal sector were the most dangerous because they were the most innovative. Unlike the more conventional Montgomery, Patton used sea power and attempted to cut off the 29th Panzer Grenadier from the rear and then destroy it; if successful, this operation would have unhinged Hube's entire front, opened the road to Messina, and perhaps ended with the destruction of the entire XIV Panzer Corps. The problem was that the naval forces supporting Patton did not have enough landing craft to transport more than a reinforced infantry battalion into the German rear. Even so, at 3:15 A.M. on August 8, the 2nd Battalion of the 30th Infantry Regiment landed near Sant' Agata and cut off Fries's rear guard, killing or capturing 350 Germans and destroying or capturing 5 panzers, 2 Italian tanks, and perhaps 100 other vehicles in the process. Another landing at Brolo on August 11 was less successful; the 2nd Battalion was smashed and narrowly managed to escape after losing all of its supporting tanks and artillery pieces. Vice Adm. Friedrich Ruge, the German naval commander in Italy, was unimpressed by the American amphibious efforts. He commented that he did not see why this sort of operation had not been attempted earlier, more frequently, and on a larger scale. He was right on all three counts.

Brigade Schmalz finally retreated from the Primosole Bridge sector and evacuated Catania on the night of August 5–6 and then fell back to positions around Acireale. After a twenty-three-day battle, the British entered Catania on August 6. As the British and Americans pursued the Germans to the north, though, the brilliance of Hube's strategy became apparent. As the XIV Panzer Corps withdrew into the apex of the triangle formed by northeastern Sicily, its front became shorter and shorter; therefore, Hube was able to take troops out of the front line and send them back to the mainland without reducing the density of his frontline strength. To Monty (and later Patton), on the other hand, a shrinking front was a major disadvantage because they were forced by geography to pull units out of the line since they no longer had the space to employ their full combat strength.

HITLER MOVES IN ON THE ITALIAN MAINLAND

While Hube was tying down an entire Allied army group in Sicily with his one panzer corps, Hitler, Rommel, and others were capturing Italy. The process would not be complete by the time Hube finished his evacuation, but it would be so far along by then that it was irreversible. Actual operations on the mainland were initially directed by Gen. of Mountain Troops Valentin Fuerstein, as Hitler forbade Rommel himself to go south of Munich, at least for the time being.

During the last week in July, Rundstedt's OB West was ordered to transfer four divisions to Rommel while the II SS Panzer Corps was ordered from the Eastern Front to Army Group B, although only one of its three divisions was actually sent. At the same time, General Student and his XI Air Corps were sent to central Italy to assume command of the 3rd Panzer Grenadier and 2nd Parachute Division, which were already in the Rome area, and Kesselring was ordered to suspend further troop transfers to Sicily.

The German divisions entered Italy one by one, starting with the 26th Panzer Division. When the 44th Infantry Division attempted to enter via the Brenner Pass on the morning of July 31, Italian Lt. Gen. Alessandro Gloria refused to let it pass and made it clear that he would use force to prevent it, if necessary. Armed Italians faced armed Germans, and a pitched battle seemed a very real possibility, even though Gloria must have known that he could not win it. His XXXV Corps had only one division, the Tridentina (2nd) Alpine, and it was rebuilding after being smashed on the Russian Front the previous winter.

It was Badoglio who backed down. After two days of intense and often frantic negotiations between the senior members of his armed forces and the Italophile Field Marshal Kesselring and General Rintelen, he allowed the Germans to enter unopposed for two reasons: first, he placed great hopes in Rintelen's ability to convince Hitler of Italy's continued loyalty, and (more realistically) he viewed any attempt on the part of the Italians to resist the *Wehrmacht* by force of arms to be doomed from the outset—unless they received significant military assistance from the Allies.

On August 2, the German 44th and 305th Infantry Divisions poured across the Alps and into northern Italy. Simultaneously, the airlift of the

2nd Parachute Division to Rome continued at full speed, and more units were on the way.[12] The next day, OKW sent Gen. of Mountain Troops Ludwig Kuebler's LXXXVII Corps (two infantry divisions) to the Ligurian coast and the 94th Infantry Division through the Mount Cenis Pass. The 1st SS Panzer, 2nd SS Panzer, and 65th Infantry Divisions also began to enter northern Italy, and the 60th Panzer Grenadier and 715th Infantry Divisions "reinforced" the southern coast of Italian-occupied France, followed by two more infantry divisions. Commando Supremo accepted the new divisions without protest. Its efforts now centered on keeping the Germans as far as possible from the Italian capital and the main naval base at La Spezia. The Italian fleet was one of the few negotiating chips left to the Badoglio government.

In the meantime, Rintelen flew to Rastenburg and presented Badoglio's case to Hitler, with predictably fatal results to his own military career. "This is the biggest piece of impudence in history!" Hitler cried. "Does the man [Badoglio] imagine that I will believe him?"[13] Although he did not tell Rintelen, Hitler had already intercepted messages suggesting that Badoglio was lying and was attempting to negotiate with the Allies.

The Italian peace feelers to the Allies were conducted with an ineptitude that typified the Badoglio government. They finally chose Marquis Blasco Lanza d'Ajeta, a Ciano man and an inept diplomat of relatively low rank, to make contact with the Allies, but without authority to actually conduct negotiations. To demonstrate Italy's "good faith," d'Ajeta was to give the Allies the entire German order of battle in Italy, along with information on the divisions expected to enter the country.[14]

The emissary met with Sir Ronald Campbell, the British ambassador to Lisbon, on August 4. Historian Melton S. Davis wrote later:

> In one single short meeting the Italians managed to suggest that they did not consider peace with the Allies important enough to send someone of stature, that they were capable of lying to the Allies just as they were to the Germans, and that they wanted to initiate talks on equal terms although, by their own admission, they were incapable of maintaining order in their own country. In addition, they asked for nothing less than the second front in Europe, which Stalin had been vainly demanding for some time.[15]

Winston Churchill was unimpressed by the Italian peace feelers. "Badoglio admits he's going to double-cross someone," he cabled Foreign Minister Anthony Eden on August 9, and he did not want to be the victim.[16] Allied diplomacy nevertheless seemed paralyzed. The Allies did not reply to the Italian feelers until August 13; then they demanded unconditional surrender in accordance with the Casablanca pronouncement.

Badoglio's attempts to hoodwink Hitler were equally fruitless. During the week of August 13, the troops of Rommel's Army Group B poured into Italy while, in the zone of Kesselring's OB South, the 2nd Parachute Division consolidated its positions north and south of Rome, and elements of the 26th Panzer Division reinforced the 3rd Panzer Grenadier at Lake Bolsena in a position to threaten the Italian capital from the north. No major German units had moved south of Rome in some time. The table below shows the order of battle of the German forces in Italy during the third week of August—a marked contrast to their situation on July 25. By this time, the XIV Panzer Corps had joined them, and the Sicilian campaign was over.

GERMAN ORDER OF BATTLE IN ITALY, SECOND HALF OF AUGUST 1943

Army Group B: Field Marshal Erwin Rommel

LI Mountain Corps: General Feurstein
- 65th Infantry Division
- 305th Infantry Division

LXXXVII Corps: General von Zangen
- 76th Infantry Division
- 94th Infantry Division

II SS Panzer Corps: SS General Hausser
- 24th Panzer Division
- 1st SS Panzer Division "Leibstandarte Adolf Hitler"

Army Group Reserve
- 44th Infantry Division
- 71st Infantry Division
- Brigade Doehla

XI Air Corps
- 3rd Panzer Grenadier Division
- 2nd Parachute Division

GERMAN ORDER OF BATTLE IN ITALY, SECOND HALF OF AUGUST 1943

OB South: Field Marshal Albert Kesselring

10th Army: Colonel General Vietinghoff

  XIV Panzer Corps: General Hube

    15th Panzer Grenadier Division

    Hermann Goering Panzer Division

    16th Panzer Division

  LXXVI Panzer Corps: General Herr

    29th Panzer Grenadier Division

    26th Panzer Division (+)

    1st Parachute Division (-)

  90th Panzer Grenadier Division (forming in Sardinia)

  SS Brigade "Reichsfuehrer SS" (in Corsica)

Note: The 3rd and 4th Parachute Regiments of the 1st Parachute Division were attached to the 26th Panzer Division.

Source: Molony, 5:213.

THE EVACUATION OF SICILY

While Rommel's divisions were infiltrating into northern Italy, Hube was preparing to evacuate his XIV Panzer Corps back to the mainland. His delaying actions had been brilliant, but the bridgehead was becoming dangerously restricted. The weight of the Allied attack was at last beginning to tell on his units, and Calabria and southern Italy were still vulnerable to an Allied amphibious landing, since they were defended only by the 16th Panzer Division and a few miscellaneous battalions. Kesselring, therefore, asked for reinforcements; failing that, he requested permission to evacuate Sicily. Jodl emphatically objected to any reinforcements for southern Italy. As was frequently the case when confronted with opposing strategies, Hitler vacillated. On August 5, he rejected Kesselring's appeal for reinforcements, but he could not make up his mind to evacuate Sicily.

He never did. That order came from Field Marshal Kesselring on August 8. Earlier that day, General Senger reported that the situation in Sicily was serious, if not exactly critical. German combat units had been depleted by almost a month of heavy fighting, half of the panzers had been lost, and the grenadiers were outnumbered at least six to one and possibly as much as ten to one. Realizing the four divisions in Sicily were in danger, Kesselring signaled Hube that he could begin the evacuation when he felt it was appropriate.

Hube's plan for the evacuation of the island (Operation *Lehrgang*) called for the XIV Panzer Corps to retreat to Messina in stages by night. He designated five general lines of resistance, which were to be held for one day each and then abandoned that night. Once the evacuation began, however, operations went so well that he added an extra day in order to get more equipment and supplies off the island.

On August 10, Hube directed that the operation begin on the night of August 11–12. It started on schedule and generally went according to plan. Alexander did not even learn that it had started until August 14, when the Germans broke contact with the 8th Army all along the line. By that time, the 15th Panzer Grenadier Division was already on the mainland, as was much of the Hermann Goering Division. Patton tried to cut off the German retreat with another amphibious landing on the morning of August 15, but on this occasion, Fries was too fast for him. To Patton's embarrassment, the landing took place behind Truscott's spearheads—that is, behind American lines.

The evacuation of Sicily ended on the morning of August 17. At 5:30 A.M., the two one-armed generals, Hube and Fries, boarded a ferry and left, to be followed forty-five minutes later by the last vessel carrying the last of the rear guard—a battle group from the 29th Panzer Engineer Battalion, augmented by elements of the II Battalion of the Hermann Goering Panzer Regiment. During Operation *Lehrgang*, Hube and his subordinates evacuated 39,569 German troops, including 4,444 wounded, along with 9,605 vehicles, 94 guns (excluding those of Group Baade), 47 tanks, 1,100 tons of ammunition, 970 tons of fuel, and 15,700 tons of other equipment and supplies. In addition, more than 12,000 Germans, 4,500 vehicles, and nearly 5,000 tons of supplies had been sent back to the mainland before *Lehrgang* began; most of these were nonessential supply and service support units. OKW put the total number of Germans who left the island at 60,000. Even the British official history labeled Operation *Lehrgang* "brilliantly successful,"[17] and Vietinghoff later declared that Hube's evacuation of Sicily was "of decisive significance for the entire later course of the campaign in Italy," correctly adding that his most valuable forces in the Italian campaign came from Sicily.[18] The Italian ferry service had also done fairly well during *Lehrgang*, evacuating 62,182 men, 41 guns, 227 vehicles, 1,000 tons of ammunition and fuel, and 14 mules.

During the Battle of Sicily, the Italian 6th Army had lost 147,000 men, and Hube's German units lost about 12,000 killed or captured[19]—although Allied propagandists soon elevated this figure to 32,000 or more. Actual German losses, including wounded, probably totalled about 20,000—roughly the same as Allied losses.[20] German equipment losses were high, especially in motorized vehicles. Many German units reequipped themselves by taking vehicles from the Italians, sometimes at gunpoint.

Hube's achievements during this campaign were remarkable. From a peak strength of 60,000 men, his panzer corps, marginally assisted by a few extant Italian units, tied down the U.S. 7th and British 8th Armies for more than a month. These Allied armies had a peak strength of 217,000 and 250,000 men, respectively. Although facing twelve Allied divisions with three understrength German divisions and most of a fourth, Hube managed to tie up an entire Allied army group while Hitler funneled division after division into Italy and effectively neutralized the immediate threat to his southern flank. Hube then managed to escape with his corps intact in spite of clear Allied superiority on the ground and overwhelming superiority in the air and on the sea.

After the fall of Tunisia in May and again after the fall of Mussolini on July 25, Hitler's southern flank seemed to be on the brink of collapse. But the Allies opted for the cautious strategy, instead of the bold push, which would have caused Hitler's house of cards in the Mediterranean to fall apart completely. As usual, when given the chance, the Germans recovered quickly. The Allies would still be fighting in Italy a year and a half later. The next Allied invasion would obviously come against mainland Italy. This time, the Germans would not be fighting a delaying action in an attempt to stave off disaster; this time, they would be trying to wipe out an entire Allied invading force—and with a reasonable chance of success. The Allies had missed their opportunity in the central Mediterranean.

CHAPTER 12

Cracking the Floodgates: The Russian Front from 1943 to Early 1944

THE PROBLEM OF MEN AND SPACE

The German forces on the Eastern Front were in critical condition in the latter part of 1943. Colonel Stauffenberg, now on the staff of the Replacement Army, observed, "Losses are considerably higher than the replacements which can be furnished from home. The strength of the field army is sinking by the equivalent of an army corps a month. . . . We are heading for a military collapse."[1]

A major part of the problem in the East was simply one of men and space. When Hitler invaded Russia in June 1941, the German forces advanced from Poland on a line approximately 438 miles long. By the end of the year, they had advanced more than 625 miles and held a frontage of about 1,125 miles. During this time, the infantry strength of the infantry division had fallen by 33 percent, and artillery strength was down 25 percent. The average strength of the infantry divisions in the East, therefore, had fallen to less than 70 percent of their establishment. During that same period, the combat regiments of the panzer divisions had lost 50 percent of their men and 65 to 75 percent of their material; they were down to only 35 percent of their original strength. According to General Zeitzler, the strength of the German armies in the East had fallen from approximately 140 divisions to the equivalent of only 83 divisions. This was one of the main reasons for the defeats of December 1941.[2]

This density of men and space was also a major reason for Hitler's defeat in the Caucasus and Stalingrad battles. During the summer of 1942, Hitler's divergent offensives increased the frontage on the southern sector from 375–425 miles to about 1,250 miles, forcing him to deploy unreliable foreign armies on the flanks of the 6th Army. In September 1942, Zeitzler submitted a report to Hitler pointing out the dangers of the situation. It concluded, "There are too few men in too wide a space. This is in need of change if a disaster is to be prevented. There are two solution for a change, either bring more men into this space or give up space. There will hardly be more men available form the army at home. Consequently, the space must be reduced."[3]

Hitler, Zeitzler recalled, rejected this report, "bluntly, flatly, and furiously."[4] Manstein offered a third solution—a flexible, mobile defense with operational freedom for the commanders—but Hitler rejected this alternative as well. Hitler learned very little from the Stalingrad catastrophe, and the situation grew even worse, both in the East and the West. By the end of 1942, the Eastern Front was roughly 1,800 miles long, and the Atlantic Wall, extending from the eastern tip of the Netherlands to the Pyrenees, encompassed about 1,250 miles. The total frontage that the German divisions had to cover was 3,125 miles, excluding the Norwegian coast (1,250 miles), the north and west coasts of Denmark (250 miles), and the coasts of the Balkans, the Mediterranean islands, and North Africa, as well as the front in Finland. By any measurement, the frontage the German troops had to defend was fantastic. As early as July 1942, some of the divisions of Army Group Center had to cover as much as 40 miles of front, at a time when 6 miles was the maximum a reasonably strong division could be expected to hold against a determined attack. In August 1943, one army on the southern sector of the Eastern Front had fewer than 160 men per mile of front, and another corps had only 138 men per mile (i.e., 8 or 9 men per 100 yards). "The German defense bow was overstretched—a very thin string which, if struck sharply at any place, was bound to break," Zeitzler wrote later. "In this phase of the Second World War, enemy offensives had relatively quick and far-reaching success."[5]

On January 13, 1943, Hitler took a number of steps to improve the manpower situation at the front. He extended the total mobilization measures to all men between the ages of sixteen and sixty-five and to all women between ages seventeen and forty-five. The number of reserve occupations was reduced, and all men between sixteen and sixty were now subject to the German draft. The ensuing loss of manpower to German industry was to be made up by using women and foreign workers. The number of foreigners working in the Reich, voluntarily or otherwise, had already increased from 3,000,000 in 1941 to 4,200,000 in 1942; now it grew even more rapidly. By May 1943, there were 5,254,000 foreigners employed in the Reich, while, according to Keitel, 11,000,000 others were "working for Germany" in the East and 20,000,000 were doing the same in France. (The French were largely involved in the production of consumer goods, which freed German industry to concentrate on war production.) The abolition of many small business firms also increased manpower availability.[6] On the other hand, the mass murder of the Jews continued unabated, denying a major potential reservoir of skilled labor to the German war effort. Hitler considered this an acceptable loss.

Zeitzler and OKW also took measures to increase the number of men available for frontline duty. The Home Army abolished many of its subordinate units, and unit staffs were cut by 10 (and later 20) percent. The use of prisoners of war as an auxiliary labor force freed 260,000 German soldiers, while women were assigned to noncombat military duties, freeing 20,000 more men for the front. The establishments of all rear-area units were also reduced. In all, these measures provided an extra 560,000 men by September. Hitler further increased the number of divisions available to both OKW and OKH by dividing the functions of the reserve divisions. They were sent to France, the Balkans, or Russia with their training elements, leaving their replacement units behind. They operated against partisans until they were inevitably drawn into combat on either the Eastern or Western Fronts, where they generally performed well, but most of them were eventually destroyed. Several of the field training divisions, which belonged to the army groups and not to the Replacement Army, were also thrown into combat in a similar manner and were quickly destroyed because their troops were only partially trained and because they lacked equipment and heavy weapons.

To replace the departed reserve divisions, the Home Army had to reorganize again, and each *Wehrkreis* created one to three new replacement divisions. Each military district also had a panzer or motorized replacement command of approximately brigade strength or higher and often a special administrative division staff as well. It is a testimony to the resilience and flexibility of the Home Army that its operations were only temporarily disrupted. Finally, in an effort to get even leaner fighting organizations by reducing the number of divisional supply troops by 60 percent, the Home Army created the "Type 44 Division." It was designed to become the standard infantry division in the East and consisted of six infantry battalions (instead of the nine in the 1939 division) and had a total authorized strength of 12,700 men, of whom more than 1,400 were Russian *Hilfswillige*. The supply troops amounted to only 1,455 men.[7] Few of the Type 44 divisions ever reached their authorized strength. The German Army never fully solved the personnel problems caused by the vastness of the territory it had to defend and Hitler's irrational refusal to disband burned-out divisions.

THE ORGANIZATION OF THE REPLACEMENT ARMY, 1943

Wehrkreis I (Koenigsberg)
   406th Replacement Division (Koenigsberg)
   461st Replacement Division (Bialystok)
   Panzer Command I (Koenigsberg)
Wehrkreis II (Stettin)
   402nd Replacement Division (Stettin)
   Mobile Troop Command II
Wehrkreis III (Berlin)
   433rd Replacement Division (Frankfurt/Oder)
   463rd Replacement Division (Potsdam)
   Grossdeutschland Replacement Brigade (Cottbus)
   Panzer Command III (Kuestrin)
Wehrkreis IV (Dresden)
   404th Replacement Division (Dresden)
   464th Replacement Division (Chemnitz)
   Panzer Command IV (Dresden)
Wehrkreis V (Stuttgart)
   405th Replacement Division (Strassborg)
   465th Replacement Division (Ludwigsburg)
   Panzer Command V (Stuttgart/Zuffenhausen)

THE ORGANIZATION OF THE REPLACEMENT ARMY, 1943

Wehrkreis VI (Muenster)

176th Replacement Division (Bielefeld)

526th Replacement Division (Wuppertal)

406th Special Administrative Division Staff (Muenster)[a]

Panzer Command VI (Coesfeld)

Wehrkreis VII (Munich)

407th Replacement Division (Augsburg)

467th Replacement Division (Munich)

Panzer Command VII (Munich)

Wehrkreis VIII (Breslau)

408th Replacement Division (Breslau)

432nd Replacement Division (Kattowitz)

178th Motorized Replacement Division (Liegnitz)

Wehrkreis IX (Kassel)

409th Replacement Division (Kassel)

Panzer Command IX (Erfurt)

Wehrkreis X (Hamburg)

180th Replacement Division (Verden)

190th Replacement Division (Neumuenster)

410th Special Administrative Division Staff (Hamburg)

Panzer Command X (Hamburg)

Wehrkreis XI (Hanover)

471st Replacement Division (Hanover)

411th Special Administrative Division Staff (Hildesheim)

Panzer Command XI (Magdeburg)

Wehrkreis XII (Wiesbaden)

172nd Replacement Division (Mainz)

462nd Replacement Division (Metz)

Panzer Command XII (Landau)

Wehrkreis XIII (Nuremberg)

193rd Replacement Division (Prague)

423th Replacement Division (Nuremberg)

Wehrkreis XVII (Vienna)

177th Replacement Division (Vienna)

487th Replacement Division (Linz)

417th Special Administrative Division Staff (Vienna)

Panzer Command XVII (Vienna)

Croatian Training Brigade (Stockerau)

a. Used to train *Landesschuetzen* troops.

THE ORGANIZATION OF THE REPLACEMENT
ARMY, 1943

Wehrkreis XVIII (Salzburg)

  418th Replacement Division (Salzburg)

  438th Special Administrative Division Staff (Klagenfurt)

Wehrkreis XX (Danzig)

  152nd Replacement Division (Graudenz)

  Feldherrnhalle Motorized Replacement Brigade (Danzig)

Wehrkreis XXI (Posen)

  192nd Replacement Division (Rostock)

Panzer Command XXI/II (Kalisch)

Manpower shortages were not the only problem the *Wehrmacht* faced at the beginning of 1944; there was also a serious shortage of officers, especially in the combat arms. The German Army's view of war and its leadership doctrine was outlined in the *Truppenfuehrung* ("Command of Troops") training manual, which was first published in 1936. It stated:

> Personal influence by the commanding officer on his troops is of the greatest importance. He must be located near the fighting troops.
>
> A divisional commander's place is with his troops. . . . During encounters with the enemy, seeing for oneself is best.
>
> Commanders are to live with the troops and share with them danger, deprivation, happiness, and suffering. Only thus can they gain a real insight into their troops' combat power and requirements.[8]

The German officer corps took the leadership doctrine expressed in the *Truppenfuehrung* very seriously, which explains much of the success it experienced during the Second World War. At the tactical and operational levels of warfare (corps and below), no officer corps in the world performed as well that of the Third Reich. This doctrine also explains the high casualty rates it suffered. The losses of field- and company-grade officers below the rank of senior colonel had been even heavier, causing a severe strain on the officer training system of the army. By 1942, General Schmundt, the chief of the Army Personnel Office, had opened several new training schools and had instituted a new promotions policy, stressing combat experience over seniority and education. The results were quite successful. In 1943, 45,870 new officers were commissioned, as opposed to 7,000 in 1942. The quality of new second lieutenants declined somewhat because Schmundt pegged the maximum allowable failure rate for the officer training schools at 20 percent. Even these measures were not enough to remedy the situation, and losses continued to exceed commissionings. On September 5, 1944, for example, the German field armies were short 13,000 officers, and officer casualties that month averaged 317.5 per day.[9]

Schmundt tried very hard to do justice to the officers at the front and promote them in relation to their involvement in frontline operations. "The ideal divisional commander was to be a young, battle-experienced, vigorous officer of character and with heart," Foerster wrote.[10] Later, after July 20, 1944, no one over the age of forty was allowed to command a regiment unless he held at least the Iron Cross, 1st Class, and colonels could be promoted to major general only after serving a year of frontline duty. Because of the exigencies of the war, even General Staff training standards had to be lowered—although they remained high. There were now three stages. First, a candidate did on-the-job training, progressively serving on the staff of a division, corps, army, and army group. Next came a series of short, specialized courses on armor, artillery, engineering, and other areas. Finally, the candidate was sent to the War Academy, where he was taught how to lead a division in combat. Instead of three years, however, the entire process took less than a year by 1944 and consisted of three and a half months of on-the-job training, two months of specialized schools, and four months of formal instruction at the War Academy, which had been moved from Berlin to Hirschberg, a town in the Sudeten Mountains. All training in the social graces—which had been considered important in peacetime—had been eliminated by now.[11] General Staff officers were badly needed at the front, where the situation was desperate.

THE KUBAN AND THE FALL OF KIEV

Against all odds, Field Marshal Kleist's Army Group A had survived. It had been isolated in the Kuban at the beginning of February 1943, with only the XXXXII Corps in the Crimea and the 17th Army in the Kuban: a total of only about 400,000 men, excluding a few Romanian units, which were mostly in the Crimea. It was opposed by the Soviet Transcaucasus Front (three armies) and the North Caucasus Front (four armies). Kleist also controlled the rebuilt 6th Army under Col. Gen. Karl-Adolf Hollidt in the southern Ukraine, north of the Crimea.

Despite its dangerous and strategically useless position, Hitler would not authorize Army Group A to evacuate the Kuban peninsula until September 3. The evacuation began during the night of September 15–16. Over the next three weeks, Kleist and his naval commander, Vice Adm. Ernst Scheurlen, ferried 227,484 German and Romanian soldiers, 72,899 horses, 28,486 Russian auxiliaries, 21,230 motor vehicles, 27,741 horse-drawn vehicles, and 1,815 guns across the Kerch Straits and into the Crimea. The evacuation was completed on October 9. The Soviets attempted to disrupt it by launching several heavy attacks, supported by armor, but they were repulsed with heavy losses. The 17th Army, now under the command of Gen. of Engineers Erwin Jaenecke, even succeeded in evacuating its supplies and damaged equipment. All it had to leave behind was the fodder for its horses.[12]

Meanwhile, Manstein was trying to hold Kiev, the capital and major city of Ukraine. Throughout September, the 4th Panzer Army on the left flank of Army Group South held the city against growing Russian pressure. The Soviets held two major bridgeheads on the flanks of the city, one at the mouth of the Pripyat above Kiev and a second below it at Bukrin. During the first week of October, they established two more bridgeheads. Army Group South was simply unable to deal with every threat posed to it all along its overextended front. As of early October, Manstein had thirty-seven divisions, but they had an average combat strength of only 1,000 men each. This meant that they could deploy only 80 men per mile of front. A major part of the problem was Hitler's insistence that Army Group South and 6th Army hold the Dnieper bend, which covered twice the straight-line distance from Kiev to the coast and thus required twice as many troops to defend it. Hitler also insisted that the Zaporozhye bridgehead on the eastern bank of the Dnieper be held, which required even more men.

On October 15, another Soviet offensive began. Konev's 2nd Ukrainian Front had massed four armies in its bridgeheads below Kremenchug and attacked the 1st Panzer Army's weak screening forces with twelve rifle divisions. By dawn the next day, Konev had three armies across the river, and the 5th Guards Tank Army was driving toward Krivoy Rog deep in the rear of the 1st Panzer Army. Mackensen, the commander of the 1st Panzer Army, mishandled the battle and was forced to abandon Dnepropetrovsk in considerable haste on October 23; he barely managed to get his troops out of the city in time.

Manstein effectively took over the battle on October 24, when he transferred the headquarters of Gen. Ferdinand Schoerner's XXXX Panzer Corps to the 8th Army on the northern flank of the Krivoy Rog thrust and ordered it to counterattack across the Soviet spearheads with three panzer divisions, while the 11th Panzer Division tried to block the Soviets east of Krivoy Rog. The result was another brilliant local victory. The Russians entered the outskirts of Krivoy Rog on October 25 but were checked by Col. Wend von Wietersheim's 11th Panzer Division in heavy fighting. The XXXX Panzer attacked on October 27 and smashed the 5th Guards Tank Army, which was thrown back twenty miles by October 30. Most of two mechanized corps and nine rifle divisions were shattered, and the Soviets left behind 10,000 dead and 5,000 prisoners. More than 350 Soviet tanks and 350 guns were captured or destroyed.

Manstein's victory stabilized the southern sector, but only temporarily. At this point in the war, committing the panzer divisions at one point automatically exposed several other weak points somewhere else. In this case, the 6th Army, which was on the northern flank of Kleist's Army Group A, and the 4th Panzer Army, which was on the northern flank of Army Group South, were left to face a series of major Soviet offensives with insufficient resources. After the evacuation of the Kuban, Kleist had struggled to keep open the escape route of the 17th Army in the Crimea. Hitler refused to allow him to evacuate the peninsula despite the fact that it was in imminent danger of being cut off.

As of October 9, Army Group A had sixteen German divisions—thirteen of them with 6th Army and three with the 17th Army. They faced the four armies of Tolbukhin's 4th Ukrainian Front.[13] Seven Soviet armies had been freed by the evacuation of the Kuban but had not yet been committed to battle elsewhere. Worse yet, to cover the Perekop Isthmus, the 6th Army was forced to defend on the Nogay Steppe, one of the most barren stretches in Russia, which provided neither cover nor natural defenses. The attacks began on September 20, but the most bitter fighting took place in the Melitopol sector, beginning on October 9. Tolbukhin massed forty-five rifle divisions, three tank corps, two guards mechanized corps, and 400 batteries of artillery along twenty miles of front. He had 800 tanks against the 183 panzers and assault guns that Col. Gen. Karl Adolf Hollidt's 6th Army could muster. The Soviets finally reached Melitopol on October 12, but the 6th Army turned the city into a fortress and forced the Soviets into bitter house-to-house fighting. Melitopol finally fell on October 23. Two days later, the Russians cut the 6th Army in two.

By October 2, even Antonescu, the Romanian dictator, appealed to Hitler to abandon the Crimea. He did not want to lose seven more divisions. Hitler replied that the peninsula must be held because, if it were abandoned, the Russians could use it as an air base to bomb the Romanian oilfields and as a staging area for landings on the Romanian and Bulgarian coasts. Kleist had no choice but to instruct Jaenecke to hold the Crimea despite the latter's strenuous—indeed insubordinate—objections. (Kleist decided not to relieve him of command only because doing so would reinforce Hitler's negative view of the "traitorous" generals.) On November 1, the Soviets reached the Perekop Isthmus, and the 17th Army was isolated in the Crimea. The northern wing of the 6th Army fell back into a large bridgehead south of Nikopol on the southeastern bank of the Dnieper bend. Hitler ordered that Nikopol be held at all costs. In the meantime, much to Hitler's annoyance, Field Marshal Kleist continued to call for the 17th Army to be evacuated from the Crimea by sea.

To the north, yet another disaster occurred when the 4th Panzer Army was attacked by several Soviet armies supported by thousands of guns and tanks. The 4th's commander, Colonel General Hoth, dealt with the attacks with his usual tactical skill, but he had only one mobile division, the 20th Panzer Grenadier, in his entire army. This time, tactical skill would not be enough.

Hoth turned back two Soviet attempts to take Kiev in October 1943. Then, on November 3, a mammoth Soviet artillery preparation of 2,000 guns (more than 500 guns per mile) struck his lines opposite the southern bridgehead, followed by massed attacks by six infantry divisions and a tank corps. This sector was defended by Gen. of Artillery Ernst-

Eberhard Hell's weak VII Corps, which did not have a single panzer unit. By November 5, the VII Corps was under attack by thirty infantry divisions, supported by 1,300 tanks. The Russians finally broke through, and two tanks armies poured into the hole. The 60th Army broke out of the Yasnogorodka bridgehead to the north, and Hoth's front north of Kiev collapsed. There was fighting in the streets of Kiev during the night of November 5–6, and the last German troops left the city the following morning, retreating to the south. The major city of Ukraine and the third largest city in the Soviet Union was back in Stalin's hands.

Hitler responded in typical fashion: he blamed the defeat on the commander. On November 15, he sacked Hermann Hoth and replaced him with Gen. of Panzer Troops Erhard Raus. Hoth was never reemployed. Germany had lost one of its best and most experienced armored commanders.[14]

Heavy fighting continued throughout November and December 1943. Hitler continued to insist that every inch of ground be held while the German Army continued to be pushed slowly back. By rushing their panzer and panzer grenadier divisions from crisis point to crisis point, Manstein, Raus, Hube (who had replaced Mackensen as commander of the 1st Panzer Army), and the other German generals managed to avoid a major disaster, but just barely. All of Manstein's demands for freedom of action were rejected or ignored, as were Hube's and Woehler's calls for a general withdrawal. Finally, Manstein flew to Rastenburg for a showdown with the dictator. The confrontation took place on January 4, 1944, and it was acrimonious. Manstein forcefully critiqued Hitler's military leadership in the East, and Hitler tried to stare him down, but without success. Manstein recommended—for the third time—that Hitler appoint an OB East, like Kesselring in Italy (OB South) and Rundstedt in France and the Low Countries (OB West). Hitler turned him down and told Manstein that not even he, *der Fuehrer*, could get the generals to obey his orders. Did Manstein believe he could do better? Yes, Manstein replied honestly, his orders were always obeyed. Hitler, taken aback, brought the meeting to an abrupt end, but not before informing the field marshal that he could expect nothing more in the way of reinforcements until after the British and American invasion had been repulsed. Manstein returned to the front empty-handed.

CHERKASSY

While Manstein argued with Hitler, Stavka committed part of it reserves to the north. On January 10, the Russian 1st Tank Army broke through between the XXXXI Panzer and III Panzer Corps; simultaneously, the Soviet 40th Army broke through between the III Panzer and VII Corps and pushed to the outskirts of Uman. Manstein reacted by bringing up the 1st SS Panzer and 18th Artillery Divisions and assigned them to Lt. Gen. Hans Gollnick's XXXXVI Panzer Corps, thus restoring its striking power.[15] Early on the morning of January 24, it struck out of the corps front west of Vinnitsa, with the objective of regaining contact with the III Panzer Corps and encircling the Soviet 1st Tank Army. This operation had barely begun when, on January 25, Zhukov launched a massive two-prong offensive employing six Soviet armies. The northern prong broke through along the XXXXVII Panzer–XI Corps boundary while the southern thrust tore through the 389th Infantry Division, which averaged only one infantryman for every fifteen yards of front. The Soviets developed these attacks rapidly, and on the afternoon of January 28, the spearheads joined hands at Shpola and surrounded the XI and XXXXII Corps west of Cherkassy. Some 56,000 German troops, including their Russian auxiliaries, were trapped. Gen. of Artillery Wilhelm Stemmermann, the commander of the XI Corps, at once took charge of the pocket, which included the 88th, 57th, 389th, and 72nd Infantry Divisions, the 5th SS Panzer Division "Viking," Corps Detachment B, and the independent SS Assault Brigade "Walloon," a Belgian volunteer unit. Of these units, only the 72nd Infantry Division was still fully fit for combat. Despite the depleted state of his forces, Hitler ordered Stemmermann to hold at all costs.

That same day, to the south, the XXXXVI Panzer and III Panzer Corps linked up, surrounding the bulk of the 1st Tank Army. Hube immediately pulled the 17th Panzer Division out of this battle and ordered the rest of III Panzer Corps to disengage and head for Cherkassy as soon as the trapped Russians were under control. The entire panzer corps, which was led by the very capable Gen. of Panzer Troops Hermann Breith, was heading for the pocket by January 31. Meanwhile, the 1st Tank Army's pocket had been crushed; it lost 700 tanks and assault guns, as well as 8,000 killed and 5,436 captured when the pocket collapsed. The rest of its men were fugitives, trying to find their way back to friendly lines any way they could.

Manstein issued his relief orders on February 1. On February 3 or 4, the III and XXXXVI Panzer Corps were to attack toward Cherkassy, converging on its western rim. Breith's III Panzer included four panzer divisions, and the XXXXVI Panzer had five. The problem was that all nine were already in combat and had to disengage. This, of course, took time, and the Germans were unlucky. There was a blizzard blowing on February 1. On February 3, the weather turned unseasonably warm, and the *rasputitsa*—the spring thaw—set in without warning.

By February 6, the XXXXVI Panzer Corps was under heavy attack and could advance no farther. The III Panzer Corps, which was twenty miles away from the perimeter, continued to crawl slowly through the mud against stiff Soviet resistance. On February 10, Hube ordered Breith to begin his final push the next day, even if he had to leave his tanks behind. The next day, the 1st Panzer Division penetrated to Lisyanka on the narrow but deep Gniloy Tikich River. Here it halted, having run out of gas. The mud had caused the panzers to consume three times their normal rate of fuel. Two days later, the corps struggled forward again, and despite furious Soviet counterattacks, it managed to get the 1st Panzer Division and Heavy Panzer Regiment "Baeke" across the river. The Baeke Regiment alone had destroyed 400 Soviet tanks in three weeks, but it had only six operational Tigers left.

The relief units regrouped and refueled on February 14 and attacked again the next day. The 1st Panzer gained a little more ground but could not take Hill 239, which commanded the terrain on the southwest edge of the Russian encirclement. By now, Soviet attacks had reduced the pocket to an area of only six miles. That night, Stemmermann was told that he would have to cover the last five miles to Hill 239 on his own.

The breakout began at 11 P.M. Using only knives and bayonets, the spearheads quickly overcame the Russian outpost line. Two of the three regiments in the first wave met little resistance and reached German lines at about 5 A.M. on February 17, but the SS assault regiment was diverted to the east by Russian resistance and ended up having to swim the swift Gniloy Tikich. It lost all of its equipment—even its rifles—and hundreds of its men drowned. Others suffered frostbite or serious illness because of their dip in the cold Russian river.

The second wave had more problems than the first. Stemmermann had ordered that only tanks, assault guns, self-propelled artillery, prime movers, and ambulances be carried in the breakout, but many ignored his order and drove their trucks. The result was stuck vehicles and huge traffic jams. Then, at about 7 A.M., Stemmermann was killed by an anti-tank shell. All order quickly disappeared, and an "every man for himself" situation developed. Thousands who tried to swim the river were drowned, and the rear guard (the 57th and 88th Infantry Divisions) was sacrificed. General Lieb and his chief of staff swam the river late that afternoon and were among the last to get away. In all, 30,000 men escaped out of 56,000. Eleven thousand were captured, and the rest were killed or died of exposure. Virtually all of the equipment was lost, and the XI and XXXXII Corps were finished as effective combat units. Manstein sent all of the survivors back to Poland to recuperate. Some of these men were also "permanent losses." How many had to endure amputations of fingers, toes, and limbs because of frostbite is not known, but the total was likely very high.

THE ESCAPE OF THE 1ST PANZER ARMY

In January and February 1944, the Russians lost almost 4,000 tanks and more than 3,500 guns in their attacks against Army Group South. They still outnumbered Manstein's 400 panzers and assault guns by a ratio of four to one. Meanwhile, Hitler introduced a new and irrational tactical concept: the fortress. A fortress commander was directly responsible to the army group commander and had only one mission—hold the fortress or fight to the last man. He could not retreat without Hitler's personal consent and had extraordinary powers, such as command of all units within the fortress, including those of other services or of the SS, and he could impose the death penalty. Usually, the fortress commander was the father of a large family, which he knew would be arrested if he failed to do his "duty." On March 8, Hitler designated twenty-six cities and towns on the Eastern Front as "fortresses" or "fortified places."

The new concept angered Ewald von Kleist, who had just about had it with Adolf Hitler and the Nazis and who, like Manstein, was becoming increasingly outspoken. On March 4, the Soviets struck the 6th Army with overwhelming force. On March 8, Kleist bluntly informed OKH and Hitler that the 6th Army could not hold the Soviets forward of the Bug, and it was high time that higher headquarters stopped rejecting every proposal put forward by the army group. On March 12, he announced that Army Group A, which now included the 6th Army, was moving into Bessarabia "in spite of the Fuehrer and in spite of Antonescu [the Romanian dictator]." Hitler reluctantly gave approval to the retreat across the Bug, but it was already too late as the Soviets had pushed through the disintegrating right flank of the 8th Army and had crossed the river along a 100-mile front. They quickly encircled half of Hollidt's six divisions near Nikolaev; all three broke out, but they left many of their guns and vehicles behind stuck in the mud.

Disaster after disaster overtook the units of the German army groups in the south. On March 11, the Russians broke through the 1st Panzer Army, smashed the XXXXVI Panzer Corps, and poured into the area between the Bug and the Dnestr. By mid-March, it was obvious that the Soviets were trying to surround the 1st Panzer Army, but Hitler refused to sanction a timely withdrawal. The panzer army was encircled on March 26.

Hube now had only two choices: break out to the west and north-west across two Russian tank armies and two major rivers and over unfavorable terrain or break out to the south, where Manstein held a bridgehead over the Dnestr at Khotin and the enemy forces were thought to be less strong. Hube wanted to head south, but Manstein ordered him to break out to the west across the rear of the Russian 1st Tank and 4th Tank Armies. He wanted to prevent the panzer army from being pushed into the Carpathians; moreover, the Dnestr was a mile wide at Khotin and was almost at flood stage. He doubted if the army could make it across the river there.

The breakout attempt began on March 26. Hube had ten divisions, three of which were panzer. He created a "floating pocket," with his combat forces on the outer rim and his "soft-skinned" vehicles, supply units, German civilians, and refugees in the center. He also made a practice of attacking the Russians at night whenever possible to take advantage of the inexperience of the green Ukrainian draftees that made up perhaps 40 percent of Zhukov's encircling forces.

Manstein's choice had been the right one. Zhukov had stationed his reserves to swamp the 1st Panzer Army as it drove south; the breakout to the west took him by surprise, and it was too muddy for him to change his dispositions quickly. As Hube moved west, *Luftwaffe* transports resupplied him daily, sometimes with air drops. On March 29, he secured two bridgeheads over the Zbruch River, and his spearheads drove for the Seret. Zhukov, meanwhile, desperately drove his armor north to establish a line west of the Seret and maintain the encirclement. Hube was too fast for him and crossed the Seret despite the blizzards. On April 4, he defeated two Russian tank corps near Chortkhov and took the town. The next day, the II SS Panzer Corps attacked toward the east from the right flank of 4th Panzer Army. On April 6, the 1st Panzer Army and the II SS Panzer Corps linked up at Buchach on the Strypa River, and the encirclement was broken. By April 10, the entire army was across the Strypa, and Hube was being hailed as a hero throughout Nazi Germany. By this time, both Manstein and Kleist had gone. Hitler sacked them on March 30.[16]

Manstein was succeeded by Walter Model while Ferdinand Schoerner was named acting commander of Kleist's old army group. A few days later, on April 5, Army Group South was redesignated Army Group North Ukraine, and Army Group A became Army Group South Ukraine. Three days after that, Hitler relieved Hollidt of the command of the 6th Army and replaced him with Gen. of Panzer Troops Maximilian de Angelis.[17] To make matters worse, Hans Valentin Hube—one of the few generals Hitler was pleased with—died in an airplane crash on April 21, the day after he had been promoted to colonel general. He had just left Fuehrer Headquarters and died within five miles of Berchtesgaten. Hitler had already earmarked him for command of Army Group South Ukraine. He was temporarily succeeded by Gen. of Infantry Kurt von der Chevallerie. Col. Gen. Erhard Raus assumed permanent command of the army on May 1, and Josef Harpe, the commander of the 9th Army since November, replaced Raus as the commander of the 4th Panzer Army. Gen. of Infantry Hans Jordan, the commander of the VI Corps, was named acting commander of the 9th Army.

THE CRIMEAN DISASTER

The loss of Manstein and Kleist—whom even Hitler called "master tacticians"—augured ill for the future of the Eastern Front. This fact was borne out in less than a month. Thirty days after Schoerner assumed command of Army Group South Ukraine, he no longer held a foot of Ukrainian territory and felt that he had done well to save the 6th and 8th Armies from total disaster. The 3rd Ukrainian Front, supported by an entire corps of artillery, struck on April 5 and broke through completely. Odessa fell, and there were scenes of panic during this retreat, even among German troops. The Romanian rail system collapsed, and hundreds of trains were trapped in Odessa. The Dnestr line was breached by April 14, and the 6th and 8th Armies fell back into Romania. They finally halted on the Prut, although almost everyone knew that this stop was only temporary.

On the morning of April 8, Tolbukhin's 4th Ukrainian Front launched massive attacks against the Perekop Isthmus on the northern end of the Crimea. Gen. Rudolf Konrad's XXXXIX Mountain Corps (three infantry divisions) held firm, but the 10th Romanian Division on its right flank completely came apart, and Jaenecke was forced to order his 17th Army to fall back toward Sevastopol on April 10. Simultaneously, Gen. of Infantry Karl Allmendinger's V Corps, which held the Kerch sector with two German infantry divisions and two Romanian divisions, also fell back, pursued by twelve Soviet divisions. On April 11, Hitler belatedly authorized the 17th Army to retreat all the way to Sevastopol, but he insisted that the city be held indefinitely. On April 16, the army fell back into the Sevastopol defenses. It had executed a difficult retreat of 150 miles in the face of an enemy that had superior mobility and which outnumbered it ten to one. Now Jaenecke had only five German divisions to defend twenty-five miles of frontage, and these divisions were all *kampfgruppen* at only about a third of their normal strength. The table on the next page shows the order of battle of the 17th Army in April 1944.

Zeitzler, Schoerner, and Jaenecke all called for the evacuation of the Crimea. During the evening situation conference of April 21, however, Schoerner made a terrible blunder. He told Hitler that the 17th Army could not hold Sevastopol unless it was reinforced. Hitler immediately promised to do so. Schoerner had been outmaneuvered by the master politician. Now that he had Hitler's promise to reinforce the garrison, he had no choice but to try to hold the fortress. Hitler's reinforcements turned out to be two battalions of infantry totaling 1,300 men, fifteen antitank guns, ten mortars, and four howitzers.

ORDER OF BATTLE, 17TH ARMY, CRIMEA, APRIL 1944

17th Army: Colonel General Jaenecke[a]

V Corps: General of Infantry Allmendinger[b]

    73rd Infantry Division: Major General Boehme (captured, May 13)

    98th Infantry Division: Major General Reinhardt

XXXXIX Mountain Corps: General of Mountain Troops Conrad[c]

    50th Infantry Division: Major General Sixt (wounded, May 1)[d]

    111th Infantry Division: Major General Gruner (killed, May 12)

    336th Infantry Division: Major General Hagemann (wounded, May 10)

    Mountain Infantry Regiment "Crimea"

9th Flak Division: *Luftwaffe* Lieutenant General Pickert

I Romanian Mountain Corps:

    1st Romanian Mountain Division

    2nd Romanian Mountain Division

    3rd Romanian Mountain Division

Romanian Cavalry Corps:

    2nd Romanian Cavalry Division

    6th Romanian Cavalry Division

    9th Romanian Cavalry Division

    10th Romanian Infantry Division

    19th Romanian Infantry Division

Army Reserves:

    191st Assault Gun Brigade

    297th Assault Gun Brigade

    275th Army Flak Battalion

    279th Army Flak Battalion

---

a. Replaced by General Allmendinger, April 30.
b. Succeeded by Lieutenant General Mueller, May 3.
c. Succeeded by General of Artillery Hartmann, May 2.
d. Succeeded by Colonel Betz, himself killed on May 9.

Source: Buckner, *Ostfront 1944*, 140.

On April 28, Hitler summoned Jaenecke to Berchtesgaden and promised him "generous" reinforcements. Jaenecke soon learned that "generous" meant four battalions of half-trained recruits. He then requested that the 17th Army be subordinated directly to OKH (i.e., Hitler himself). In response, Hitler relieved him of his command and replaced him with Allmendinger.[18] Konrad, the commander of the XXXXIX Mountain Corps, was also sacked and replaced by Gen. of Artillery Walter Hartmann, who had already lost an arm and a leg on the Eastern Front. Lt. Gen. Friedrich-Wilhelm Mueller, a strong Nazi, replaced Allmendinger as commander of the V Corps.

The Russians began their final assault on Sevastopol on May 5. On the northern side of the pocket, the Saxons of Maj. Gen. Wolf Hagemann's 336th Infantry Division particularly distinguished themselves by repulsing dozens of Soviet attacks from five Russian rifle divisions in thirty-six hours of unrelenting combat. On the eastern face of the pocket, the understrength 73rd Infantry Division was unable to hold. Hitler finally authorized the evacuation of Sevastopol on May 9, but it was too late. Resistance was crumbling, the troops were pinned down at the front, and the Red Air Force completely dominated the skies. The last resistance ended on May 13. Only 26,700 of the 64,700 men in Sevastopol were evacuated, and 29,000 German soldiers were captured. Hitler ordered that neither Jaenecke nor Allmendinger were to be given another command until their conduct in the defense of the Crimea could be investigated by a court-martial. Both were placed in Fuehrer Reserve and never reemployed. Jaenecke was discharged from the service in January 1945 after he wrote a letter to Hitler calling upon him to end the war. Given Hitler's opinion of him, he is lucky that he was not sent to a concentration camp or shot out of hand.

THE SIEGE OF LENINGRAD, 1943–44

The siege of Leningrad had started in September 1941, and Stalin had been trying to raise it since December of that same year. As of the beginning of 1943, he had been unable to reestablish a land connection to the city, and supplies had to be ferried across Lake Ladoga. The German situation was not rosy either because their hold on the southern sector of Lake Ladoga was not firm; in fact, all they held was a narrow salient around Schluesselburg, tenaciously defended by Gen. of Infantry Ernst von Leyser's XXVI Corps of Col. Gen. Georg Lindemann's 18th Army, and it was in danger of being cut off as soon as the Neva River, which covered its left flank, froze.[19] Leyser's sector was called "the bottleneck" because it was so narrow. It was extremely heavily fortified.

On January 12, 1943, the long-expected Soviet offensive began. A dozen Russian divisions (about 120,000 men) attacked Leyser's five understrength divisions. The Soviets were supported by 100 guns and mortars per mile of front, as well as by the air forces of the Leningrad and Volkhov Fronts. Despite the weight of the Russian attack, Leyser's divisions gave ground very slowly, inflicting heavy casualties on the attackers every step of the way. It took the Volkhov Front five days to link up with the Leningrad Front, although they had to cover just ten miles. Cover it they did, however; on January 17, land contact between Leningrad and the outside world was reestablished for the first time in seventeen months. In the process, the 41st and 277th Infantry Divisions of Leyser's corps had been virtually destroyed.

The German hold on the city had only been loosened, not broken. The new lifeline was only six to seven miles wide, and all of it fell within range of German artillery. The Soviet attacks continued until early April but could gain no further ground. Stalin was nevertheless so pleased that he awarded 19,000 decorations.

The Leningrad and Volkhov Fronts tried to break the siege again in mid-July 1943 with a series of costly frontal attacks against Mga. This offensive was poorly coordinated and badly directed, and in spite of their material and numerical superiority (the Russians had 1,052 tanks in the Leningrad sector, as opposed to 49 in all of Army Group North), the Russians could not push back the 18th Army. During the last two weeks of the battle, the offensive degenerated into a series of random attacks by division-size units or smaller. It was finally cancelled on August 23, having accomplished nothing.

Hitler and OKH neglected Army Group North throughout 1943, when it was looked upon as a reservoir of reserves into which they could dip when the situation in other sectors became desperate. Several of Kuechler's best divisions were diverted to Army Group South or Center, and they were replaced by unreliable *Luftwaffe* field divisions—if they were replaced at all. The following table shows the decline in Army Group North's strength between January 2, 1942, and October 10, 1943. Note that Kuechler lost four of his five mobile divisions and all of his panzer units. In fact, as of September 15, 1943, there were only seven operational tanks in the entire army group. In short, Kuechler now held one of the weakest positions on the Eastern Front. He was opposed by three Russian fronts: the Leningrad, Volkhov, and Northwest.

DIVISIONS IN ARMY GROUP NORTH, JANUARY 2, 1942–OCTOBER 10, 1943

Date	Inf	Pz	Mtz	Mtn	Jaeger	Lw Fld	Tng	Secu	Total
22 Dec 42	33	2	3	2	3	4	1	3	51*
1 Jan 43	30	0	2	1	3	4	1	3	44*
9 Apr 43	31	0	2	1	3	6	1	3	47*
7 Jul 43	32	0	2	1	3	6	1	3	48*
10 Oct 43	30	0	1	1	3	4	1	3	43**

* Excludes the 2nd SS Brigade and 17th Police Regiment.
** Excludes SS Brigade "Latvia."

Source: Kriegstagebuch des OKW, 2:1,396–97; 3:7, 260, 734, 1158.

Kuechler realized that the Russians were building up for another offensive in the Leningrad sector. General Lindemann and his 18th Army intelligence staff were confident that they could repulse it, as they had beaten back the previous three, but Kuechler did not think they could hold again. He had already been planning a retreat to the Panther Line more than 100 miles to the west for months. By the end of 1943, tens of thousands of construction workers, both Reich Labor Service and Russian, had built 6,000 bunkers, laid 125 miles of barbed-wire entanglements, and dug 25 miles of trenches and 25 miles of antitank traps. Construction material was arriving at a rate of more than 100 car-loads a day, and 50,000 construction workers were busy improving the lines of communication from Riga and Dvink forward. Hitler, however, refused to authorize the withdrawal to this position, largely because Lindemann was confident that he could hold his lines. To make matters worse, OKH transferred one of Kuechler's best divisions—the East Prussian 1st Infantry—to Army Group South on December 29.

On January 14, the Leningrad Front attacked the 18th Army's left flank with forty-two infantry divisions and nine tank brigades, and the Volkhov Front struck its right flank with eighteen infantry and fifteen tank divisions. At the same time, the 2nd Shock Army tried to break out of the Oranienbaum bridgehead and into the 18th Army's rear. The Soviet plan was soon obvious: conduct a pincer movement on Luga to surround the 18th Army and destroy it by double envelopment. Simultaneously, the 2nd Baltic Front pinned down the 16th Army with heavy attacks so that it was soon fighting for its existence and could not send reinforcements to its sister army.

Lindemann met the Soviet winter offensive with five *Luftwaffe* field and thirteen understrength army and SS divisions. Some of his divisions occupied up to 25,000 yards of frontage. The 18th Army's line resembled the old trench lines from World War I, and the German defense was bitter and stubborn. Soviet losses were staggering, but they kept on coming. The battle seemed to be going Lindemann's way for the first three days, but then Soviet numerical superiority began to tell. The German divisions were simply being pounded to pieces by wave after wave of Russian attacks. The battlefield was littered with Russian dead and lighted at night by burning tanks, but Stalin's manpower reserves seemed inexhaustible, and no sooner would one attack be broken than a fresh wave would enter the battle. There were incidents of hand-to-hand fighting in the trenches. Some German divisions lost all of their regimental commanders and were reduced to strengths of 500 men. The 18th Army was literally being overwhelmed.

On the morning of January 17, Lindemann finally asked for permission to retreat, but Hitler would not allow it. The following morning, Lindemann reported that his battlefronts east of Oranienbaum and west of Leningrad were on the verge of collapse and that two of his divisions were in danger of being annihilated. That evening, Kuechler signaled OKH that he intended to retreat that night, whether Hitler approved or not. Hitler did approve, but only after Zeitzler told him that the retreat was already in progress. Hitler still would not allow a general withdrawal to the Panther positions.

Kuechler's withdrawal of January 18 effectively ended the siege of Leningrad. It had lasted 900 days, during which the *Wehrmacht* had destroyed 1,000 factories and inflicted $80 billion worth of damage. An estimated 1,000,000 Russian civilians also died during the siege, mostly to starvation.

Field Marshal Kuechler's courageous action came none too soon. After four days of continuous heavy combat, three German infantry divisions finally collapsed, leaving a huge gap in the German line south of Leningrad. The Soviet 42nd Army poured through and, on January 19, linked up with the 2nd Shock Army at Peterhof, cutting off Lindemann's rear guard, which was soon overwhelmed and destroyed. By January 20, the 18th Army was in danger of having both of its flanks enveloped. Kuechler again asked permission to retreat, but Hitler refused. In the meantime, the Red Army had cut the 18th Army's main supply route, broke the army into three pieces, virtually destroyed the 28th Jaeger Division, smashed several other units, and captured Mga, along with eighty-five German guns. Finally, on January 30, the field marshal went to Fuehrer Headquarters, where Hitler at last approved a retreat to the Luga, but with the provision that this line must be held. This would have been possible had the order been given three days before, but not now. The 18th Army had lost 14,000 men killed, its infantry strength had been reduced from 58,000 to 17,000 men,[20] and only its 12th Panzer and 58th Infantry Divisions were still intact. Col. Curt-Ulrich von Gersdorff, the Ia of Army Group North, protested that the order would be impossible to carry out since one of the gaps was now thirty miles long and the Russians were already across the Luga at two points. Kuechler asked Zeitzler to tell Hitler that the Luga line could not be held. He obviously did so: Kuechler was summoned to Fuehrer Headquarters for the noon situation conference the next day, January 31, where he was relieved of his command.[21] He was replaced by Col. Gen. Walter Model. (Model, incidentally, was named acting commander only; Hitler had already earmarked him to succeed Erich von Manstein as commander in chief of Army Group South.)

Model was rapidly earning the reputation as "the Fuehrer's Fireman" because he was used only in the most critical situations. He conducted the retreat to the Luga, where he introduced his *Schild und Schwert* ("Sword and Shield") policy, which stated that retreats were tolerable, but only if they paved the way for a counterstroke later. This was a brilliant piece of psychology because it made withdrawals palatable to Adolf Hitler. Staffs were frequently amazed by Model. Hitler would sack a commander for suggesting a retreat; then Model would arrive, and Hitler would approve anything he recommended. A week after he arrived at the headquarters of Army Group North, Hitler sent Model a dispatch instructing him to request permission to retreat to the Panther Line as soon as he felt it was necessary.

Walter Model desperately tried to hold the Luga River line east of the Panther positions, even though, as of February 6, the average 18th Army division had a strength of only four weak infantry battalions. It simply could not hold. Model reluctantly gave the order to retreat to the Panther position on February 12. To cover his northern flank, he created

Army Detachment Narva (the LIV and III SS Panzer Corps) under the command of Gen. of Infantry Johannes Freissner.[22] The Russians tried to reach the Narva before Freissner could complete his retreat and did in fact establish a bridgehead across the river. Freissner counterattacked immediately, cut the bridgehead in half, and eliminated it as a threat to the Panther Line. Army Group North completed its retreat to the Panther on March 1, but the Russians pursued rapidly. From March 1 to 10, the Leningrad, Volkhov, and 2nd Baltic Fronts launched repeated heavy attacks all along the front. By this time, the weather had turned against the Russians. The spring thaw had set in, and the 16th Army reported that the Russian tanks were sinking up to their turrets in the mud.

The Panther Line fully lived up to Kuechler's expectations. Stalemate set in on the northern sector of the Eastern Front.

CHAPTER 13

The Italian Defection and the Battle of Salerno

ITALY PREPARES TO DEFECT

While Manstein, Kuechler, and others attempted to stem the tide in the East, the Americans and British were preparing to enter the mainland of Europe.

On August 16, the day before General Hube completed the evacuation of Sicily, Eisenhower decided to launch Operation Avalanche, the main invasion of Italy, on September 9. Its target would be a twenty-mile stretch of beaches south and west of Salerno, just south of Naples, which was at the maximum range of Allied fighter protection. Prior to the main invasion, the British 8th Army would land in Calabria just across the Strait of Messina on the "toe" of Italy and drive north toward Salerno along the west coast of Italy. The Allies hoped that as a result of a quick success at Salerno, they could cut off significant German forces in southern Italy, push through the Sorrento Hills, and capture Naples before the Germans could react effectively.

On the other side of the line, Kesselring ordered Senger to evacuate the islands of Sardinia and Corsica. There were one and a half German divisions on these two islands: the rebuilding 90th Panzer Grenadier Division, the SS Panzer Grenadier Brigade "Reichsfuehrer-SS," and a few miscellaneous units—40,000 men in all. Senger accomplished his mission between September 11 and October 5, using the same boat flotillas Hube had used to evacuate Sicily. He later commented, "The capture of these islands would probably have been much easier than that of Sicily and the enemy would have had here an advanced base for their next jump to approximately the Livorno area [on the Italian mainland]. At this point, the Allies could have thus forced a landing some 600 kilometers [375 miles] farther north than at Salerno."[1]

Senger did not consider this operation too risky, given the Allies' strength. Fortunately for the Germans, Allied strategy in the Mediterranean was unimaginative, to say the least.

On the morning of September 3, the British 8th Army—supported by massive air strikes, the huge guns of three Royal Navy battleships, and thousands of shells from more than 600 pieces of field artillery—landed at Reggio on the Italian peninsula. Initially, the British met no German resistance, and the only casualty they suffered was one soldier who was severely bitten by a local mule. The 8th Army began advancing north through rugged mountainous terrain featuring narrow, winding roads with dozens of bridges and tunnels. It was a combat engineer's dream, and the Germans took maximum advantage of it. Salerno was still about 200 miles away.

That same day, after protracted negotiations, the Badoglio government agreed to surrender to the Allies. The secret surrender ceremony took place at Cassibile at 5:15 P.M.

THE ARMISTICE

As dawn broke on September 8, the Germans had no idea that the invasion would begin in less than twenty-four hours. They were not badly deployed to meet it, but their plans and dispositions were certainly not perfect. In northern Italy, north of the Pisa-Rimini line, lay the eight divisions of Field Marshal Erwin Rommel's Army Group B.[2] Its missions were to protect the rear of OB South and seize northern Italy in case of an Allied invasion. It was not directly involved in repulsing the invasion.

South of the Pisa-Rimini line lay OB South. Its main force was Col. Gen. Heinrich von Vietinghoff's 10th Army, which had been activated on August 17, the day Sicily fell. It consisted of the XIV Panzer Corps (two panzer divisions), which was deployed in the Salerno-Naples area, and Traugott Herr's LXXVI Panzer Corps (the 29th Panzer Grenadier and 26th Panzer Divisions), which were in Calabria. Part of this corps was waiting for the main invasion, and smaller elements were delaying the advance of the British 8th Army. Herr also controlled the 1st Parachute Division, most of which was in Apulia in the heel of Italy. One parachute regiment was in Calabria. The 15th Panzer Grenadier Division was in army reserve on the Garigliano River south of Rome.

In addition to the 10th Army, OB South controlled several other major formations, the most important of which was the XI Air Corps (the 3rd Panzer Grenadier and 2nd Parachute Divisions) in the vicinity of Rome. It also directed the recently organized 90th Panzer Grenadier Division in Sardinia and the SS Brigade "Reichsfuehrer SS" in Corsica. The table below shows the order of battle of the German forces in Italy on September 8, 1943.

GERMAN ORDER OF BATTLE, ITALIAN THEATER OF OPERATIONS, SEPTEMBER 8, 1943

Army Group B (Field Marshal Rommel): Northern Italy
  LXXXVII Corps
    76th Infantry Division
    94th Infantry Division
    305th Infantry Division
    24th Panzer Division
  LI Mountain Corps
    SS Panzer Division "Leibstandarte Adolf Hitler"
    65th Infantry Division
    44th Infantry Division
    Brigade Doehla
  Corps Witthoeft
    71st Infantry Division
    Smaller Units
OB South (Field Marshal Kesselring): Central and Southern Italy
  10th Army
    XIV Panzer Corps: Salerno
      16th Panzer Division
      Hermann Goering Panzer Division
      15th Panzer Grenadier Division
    LXXVI Panzer Corps: Calabria
      29th Panzer Grenadier Division
      26th Panzer Division (-)

GERMAN ORDER OF BATTLE, ITALIAN THEATER OF OPERATIONS, SEPTEMBER 8, 1943

Army Reserve:
    1st Parachute Division (-): in Apulia*
XI Air Corps: Rome Area
    3rd Panzer Grenadier Division
    2nd Parachute Division (+)
    90th Panzer Grenadier Division (Sardinia)
    SS Brigade "Reichsfuehrer-SS" (Corsica)

---

* Two battalions of the 1st Parachute Division were attached to the Hermann Goering Panzer Division

At noon that day, Allied bombers blasted Frascati, where Kesselring had his headquarters. The field marshal left his office just as a bomb exploded outside his glass veranda. The attack continued for an hour. OB West and Richthofen's 2nd Air Fleet were smashed, but most of the bombs fell in the Roman suburb. Kesselring crawled out of the wreckage shaken but not seriously hurt. He at once ordered his headquarters troops to help rescue civilians in Frascati, and his signals troops quickly began to repair the damage to the communications system. He found, however, that he could communicate to OKW over only one telephone, which was located in General Westphal's bedroom. Communications between the field marshal and his subordinates would be disrupted for some time. Shortly thereafter, Kesselring was handed a map taken from a downed enemy bomber. The buildings housing his headquarters and that of Richthofen had been marked exactly—a sure indication that the Italians had given away its location to the Allies.

Meanwhile, Badoglio sent a message to Eisenhower, basically asking him not to announce the Italian surrender until he was within striking distance of Rome. Badoglio's message came as a complete surprise to Ike and threw him into an uncharacteristic fit of rage. He took the dispatch to mean that the Italians wanted to postpone their defection until they were certain that the Allied attack would succeed. When they saw the meager strength of the forces which would soon be landing at Salerno, they might well not change sides at all. Eisenhower dictated a tough reply to Badoglio:

I intend to broadcast the existence of the armistice at the hour originally planned. If you or any part of your armed forces fail to cooperate as previously agreed, I will publish to the world the full record of this affair. I do not accept your message of this morning postponing the armistice. Your accredited representative has signed an agreement with me, and the sole hope of Italy is bound up in your adherence to that agreement.[3]

Eisenhower's reply did not arrive in Rome until late afternoon and was not decoded until 5:30. When they saw it, panic broke out in the Italian government. Until then, they assumed that the Allies were willing to enter into new negotiations. Eisenhower's message disspelled their last illusions. The announcement of the armistice would come in an hour, and General Roatta's preparations for the defense of Rome would not be complete for days. An emergency meeting of the Italian leadership was held in the Quirinal Palace at 6:15 P.M. Several of the generals implored the king to repudiate the negotiations, dismiss Badoglio if necessary, and disavow any agreements reached in his name. Foreign Minister Raffaele Guariglia, however, said that he did not approve of the methods used to negotiate the surrender, but at this stage, it would be absurd to disavow them. To try to do so would leave Italy in the position of facing both German and Allied hostility. Gen. Vittorio Ambrosio, the chief of Commando Supremo, agreed with the foreign minister.

The discussions continued for a few more minutes before word arrived that Eisenhower was even now personally broadcasting the text of the armistice on the radio. All sentiment for reputation now vanished, and all eyes turned to Badoglio, who refused to make the final decision. The king finally did it himself. It was no longer possible to change sides again, he declared. Rome was committed to the defection.

Once the decision was made, Badoglio rushed to Radio Rome and at 7:45 P.M. (one hour late), he read an announcement of the armistice. It was a weak message, for it offered the armed forces no definite instructions about how to behave or what attitude to assume toward the Germans.

The Germans were also taken by surprise. Roatta was conferring with Westphal and Gen. of Infantry Rudolf Toussaint at his headquarters in Monterotondo when the German embassy telephoned with the news of the armistice announcement. Roatta, shaken by the timing of the announcement, had no difficulty convincing the two German generals that he knew nothing about the armistice, which, he said, was an Allied trick. Westphal and Toussaint left at once. Roatta then issued orders to the three corps in the vicinity of the capital to man roadblocks leading into the city. German troops wishing to leave Rome were to be allowed to go; those trying to enter were to be halted, by force if necessary.

On the German side of the line, Kesselring felt personally betrayed by the Italian defection. The Italians had "committed the basest teachery . . . behind our backs," he declared, but the German forces would continue to fight for the salvation of Europe. He signaled Vieting-hoff:

> If we retain our fighting spirit and remain dead calm, I am confident that we will continue to perform the tasks entrusted to us by the Fuehrer. Italian troops will be asked to continue the fight on our side by appeals to their honor. Those who refuse are to be ruthlessly disarmed. No mercy must be shown the traitors. Long live the Fuehrer.[4]

About midnight, the situation began to worsen for the Italians. South of Rome, the 2nd Parachute Division surrounded several Italian batteries along the coast and attacked the strongpoints of the Piacenza Division. To the north, the 3rd Panzer Grenadier Division clashed with the Ariete Armored Division, and it was obvious that the capital was under a concentric German attack. By 3:45 A.M., the Germans had nearly surrounded the city, and the Via Tiburtina was the only exit out of Rome that remained open.

About 4 A.M., Roatta informed Prince Humbert that if the king, the government, and the royal family wished to escape, they had better move quickly. This they did within an hour. Before he departed, Badoglio placed Umberto Ricci, the minister of the interior, in charge of a caretaker government without bothering to inform Ricci himself.

Generals Ambrosio and Roatta fled the city shortly after 6 A.M. They were followed by Lt. Gen. Giuseppe de Stefanis and Lt. Gen. Umberto Utili, Roatta's second in command and operations officer, shortly after dawn. Before he left, Stefanis placed an astonished Lt. Gen. Giacomo

Carboni, the commander of the Italian Motorized Corps, in charge of the defenses of Rome.

THE BATTLE OF SALERNO: D-DAY

In the Tyrrhenian Sea, the nearly 600 ships of the Allied invasion convoys steamed toward Salerno, carrying tens of thousands of light-hearted men. Eisenhower's announcement at 6:30 P.M. on September 8 had caused jubilation to break out onboard the ships. All tension evaporated: the Axis had collapsed; there would be no assault landing after all. Celebrations broke out throughout the fleet. On several ships, senior commanders took to the loudspeakers to remind their troops that the Germans had not surrendered, but they had little success in dampening the mood of triumph. Many of the Anglo-American troops thought they would dock unopposed in Naples harbor. They were in exactly the wrong frame of mind for a combat assault.

The Salerno landings began at 3:20 A.M. on September 9 under the command of Gen. Mark Clark's U.S. 5th Army. North to south, the Allies landing forces consisted of three battalions of American Rangers under Col. William O. Darby, two British Commandos under Brig. Robert C. Laycock, the British X Corps under Lt. Gen. Richard McCreery, and the U.S. VI Corps under Maj. Gen. Ernest J. Dawley. The 5th Army's front was split by the Sele River. Because of the sand bars at the mouth of river, there was a potentially dangerous eight-mile gap between the beaches of the British X and U.S. VI Corps. The map on the next page shows the Allied landings as they took place on September 9.

The Salerno sector was chosen as the landing site because it had twenty miles of good beaches, direct access to inland areas, and an ideal gradient for landing craft. On the negative side, Salerno was surrounded by mountains, lay south of Naples, and was almost at the maximum range for Allies fighters (a Spitfire operating with auxiliary fuel tanks, for example, could operate for only about twenty minutes over Salerno before having to return to base). The Allies hoped to quickly capture the Montecorvino airfield, which was almost adjacent to the beaches, and bring it into operation quickly.

The Allies came ashore in the zone of Maj. Gen. Rudolf Sieckenius's 16th Panzer Division. This recently rebuilt "Stalingrad" unit was nearly

THE SALERNO LANDINGS, SEPTEMBER 8, 1943

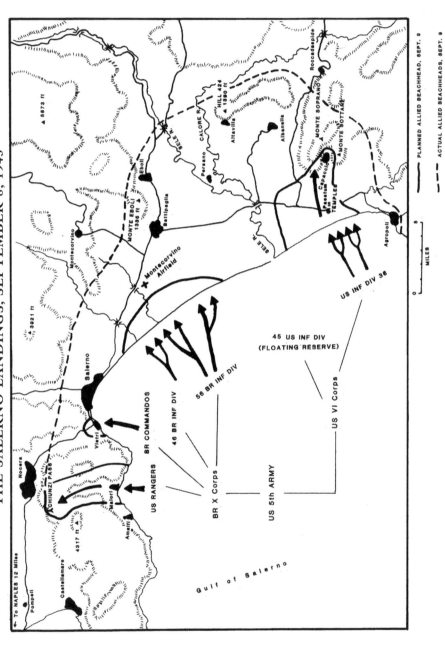

PLANNED ALLIED BEACHHEAD, SEPT. 9

ACTUAL ALLIED BEACHHEADS, SEPT. 9

US 5th ARMY

BR X Corps

US RANGERS

BR COMMANDOS

46 BR INF DIV

56 BR INF DIV

US VI Corps

45 US INF DIV
(FLOATING RESERVE)

US INF DIV 36

Gulf of Salerno

To NAPLES 12 Miles

Pompeii

Castellamare

Nocera

CHIUNZI PASS

4317 ft

Amalfi

Maiori

Vietri

Salerno

3921 ft

Montecorvino

Montecorvino
Airfield

MONTE EBOLI
1336 ft

Eboli

Battipaglia

SELE R.

SELE R.

Persano

CALORE R.

HILL 424
1390 ft

Altavilla

Albanella

MONTE SOPRANO

Capaccio

Paestum
TEMPLES

MONTE SOTTALE

Roccadaspide

Agropoli

5873 ft

MILES

0   5

fully equipped, but once again, it was the same old story: too much front to cover with too few men. The 16th Panzer had 17,000 men, more than 100 tanks, 36 assault guns, and three battalions of artillery, but it had to cover a front that was thirty miles long, so no continuous defensive system along the beaches was possible.

At first, the Allied invasion went well. The Rangers landed on schedule at 3:20 A.M. and quickly advanced six miles inland, capturing the important railroad town of Nocera and the 4,000-foot-high peaks on either side of Chiunzi Pass, which commanded the road and railroad communications between Salerno and Naples. Without this pass, it would be impossible for the Germans to mount a flanking attack against the Allied left. Meanwhile, the British Commandos took Vietri sul Mare, seized the heights dominating the Molina Defile (a second pass to Naples), and stormed the town of Salerno.

The Allied plan called for the X Corps (three divisions) to land and quickly take Naples while the U.S. VI Corps (four divisions) protected its rear and extended its right flank south to link up with Montgomery. Things here started to go wrong almost immediately. The Americans landed six miles south of Salerno at 3:30 A.M. and were quickly brought under heavy German artillery fire. There was near-panic in American ranks because the men, overconfident after Eisenhower's announcement, expected no opposition whatsoever.

Baron von Richthofen's 2nd Air Fleet launched its main attack at 4:15 A.M.—less than an hour after the first Allied soldiers jumped out of their assault vessels and raced across the beach. It attacked for more than an hour, damaging several landing craft and sinking the USS *Nauset*, a 1,270-ton tug.

In the British sector, Maj. Gen. Douglas A. H. Graham's 56th Infantry Division landed against little opposition and captured the Montecorvino airfield. As Graham attempted to advance beyond the airfield, however, a battle group of the 16th Panzer Division counterattacked. The struggle for the airfield continued all day, but neither side was able to gain a decisive advantage. By nightfall, the airfield was still a no-man's-land.

The 16th Panzer launched its first medium-scale counterattack against the U.S. 36th Infantry Division at 7 A.M. while its troops were still scattered and disorganized on the beaches. It was past noon before the panzers were forced to withdraw, but German infantry continued to defend behind stone walls and in farm buildings immediately behind the beaches. At the same time, German artillery, mortars, and even a few heavy machine guns blasted fire into several of the beaches, causing confusion and disorganization in the landing zones.

At his 10th Army Headquarters, Heinrich von Vietinghoff had a major decision to make. With the exception of Hube, Vietinghoff was arguably the best German commander in the Italian theater of operations. He was a tall, monocled East Prussian infantryman who radiated an impression of rock-like solidity, reinforced by years of experience. The son of an officer, he was born in the Rhineland garrison town of Mainz in 1887 and, after attending the cadet schools, joined the 2nd Guards Grenadier Regiment in 1906. Early to recognize the potential of the tank, he transferred to the armored branch, led the 5th Panzer Division in Poland, the XIII Corps in France, and the XXXXVI Panzer Corps in the Balkans and Russia, before being named acting commander of the 9th Army in the Rzhev salient in September 1942, after Model was wounded. Three months later, he assumed command of the 15th Army in France and Belgium, before taking charge of the 10th Army in August 1943. One American intelligence report described him as "the most capable officer on this front and the driving power behind Kesselring." Wallace called him "an exceedingly tough commander who, as the Italian campaign unfolded, would win the respect of everyone who fought him."[5]

On D-Day, Vietinghoff received no guidance from OB South, whose communications were still in shambles and which was fully occupied with its own problems in Rome. This Prussian was not a man who had trouble making decisions. As early as 8 A.M. on September 9, he concluded that another Allied landing farther north was unlikely and ordered the XIV Panzer Corps to make a "ruthless concentration of all forces at Salerno" and drive the Allies back into the sea.[6]

Unfortunately for the Germans, Hans Valentin Hube, the one-armed hero of the Sicilian campaign, was on leave that day, and the order was received by Lt. Gen. Hermann Balck. Balck had distinguished himself in Russia, but he was uncharacteristically cautious and hesitant on September 9 because of the Italian defection and the possibility of more landings. He ordered most of the 15th Panzer Grenadier Division to the Volturno River to guard against a possible Allied amphibious attack and left the Hermann Goering Division in place. He did not help Siecke-nius, who fought alone on the first day of the Salerno invasion. He inflicted heavy casualties on both the British and Americans, but by the end of the day, the Americans had advanced four miles inland and seized a large stretch of Highway 18, the main road along the coast, and estab-lished themselves along the approaches to Monte Soprano. By nightfall, Sieckenius had only about thirty-five operational panzers left.

That evening, Vietinghoff personally took charge of the battle. He ordered Traugott Herr's LXXVI Panzer Corps (the 29th Panzer Grenadier and 26th Panzer Divisions) to break contact with the British 8th Army and rush for Salerno, leaving behind only small rear guards and the ubiquitous demolition squads to slow down Montgomery. He also ordered Sieckenius to concentrate against the British while the 29th Panzer Grenadier took over the sector opposite the U.S. VI Corps. Finally, he got the 27,000 men of the 15th Panzer Grenadier and Her-mann Goering Panzer Divisions moving south toward the battlefield. He felt sure that he could concentrate against the U.S. 5th Army at Salerno and destroy it before Montgomery had a chance to intervene.

Kesselring apparently agreed. He urged OKW to give him Rom-mel's two panzer divisions, the 24th and the 1st SS, so that he could rein-force Vietinghoff, but he was turned down. Later, he said that his request "might have led to a decisive German victory if Hitler had acceded to my very modest demands."[7]

ROME FALLS TO THE GERMANS

What was happening in Rome all this time?

Throughout the night of September 8–9, Field Marshal Kesselring was conducting a brilliant propaganda and deception campaign. Under flags of truce, his troops approached Italian units, which were confused and lacking central direction, and appealed to their honor. Local truces were arranged. The war was over for Italy, the Germans told the Italian soldiers. They could go home if they wanted to. This was exactly what many of the Italians wished to hear, and many of them threw away their weapons and disappeared, some of them led by their officers. By noon, the Piacenza Division had ceased to exist, and many of the members of the Centauro Armored Division had deserted as well.

There was also some shooting between German and Italian forces. The most significant casualty was *Luftwaffe* Maj. Gen. Hermann Ramcke, the commander of the 2nd Parachute Division, who was seriously injured in an automobile crash when his driver ran into a ditch to avoid bullets from an attacking Italian fighter-bomber. Most of the Italians, however, were quickly subdued.

General Carboni tried to stur up a popular uprising against the Germans. He handed thousands of weapons over to the Communist Party and urged the political leaders and their followers to join. The Italian people, however, were disillusioned and sick of war and preferred surrender and German occupation to fighting panzers in the streets of Rome. There would be no uprising. Under the threat of an aerial and artillery bombardment from Kesselring, the Italian government capitulated at Frascati at 4:30 P.M. on September 9.

THE FATE OF THE ITALIAN ARMED FORCES

The Italian armed forces virtually ceased to exist. On September 8, the Italian Army alone had 1,700,000 men in sixty divisions, but they were poorly equipped, lacked central direction, and had low morale. Many of these soldiers did not even have shoes.

Hitler's attitude toward the Italian armed forces had been described as "contemptuous and passionately vindictive."[8] His orders, as issued by Keitel, instructed the German commanders that they could accept into their units any Italians who volunteered to serve under German command, but all others were to be taken as prisoners of war and used for forced labor. The skilled workers would go to the armaments industry; the unskilled laborers were to be sent to the Eastern Front to construct fortifications.

In France and Liguria, the Italian 4th Army was quickly overrun by four divisions of Field Marshal Gerd von Rundstedt's OB West, and about 40,000 Italian prisoners were taken prisoner and sent to Germany as labor troops.

In the Brenner Pass sector, the German 44th Infantry Division, which was made up almost exclusively of Austrians, reclaimed South

Tyrol with enthusiasm. They overran General Gloria's XXXV Corps, captured his headquarters at Bolzano on September 9, and occuped Bologna the same day.

In the zone of Army Group B, Rommel's troops obeyed Hitler's orders to the letter. All Italian troop units were surrounded, disarmed, and sent to Germany as labor battalions.

In southern Italy lay the 7th Army, which was commanded by Generale di Corpo Mario Arisio, who had led the XII Corps in Sicily. He was sympathetic to the *Wehrmacht* and was trusted and respected by the German generals. Surprised by Badoglio's armistice, Arisio felt shocked and humiliated by what he regarded as his government's betrayal of the Axis. He immediately assured the Germans of his continued full cooperation, and he and his commanders freely turned their vehicles, supplies, and installations over to the Germans. In turn, the troops were allowed to go home without being molested.

The headquarters of the Italian Army, located near Monte Rotondo, was captured via airborne assault on September 9 by Maj. Walter Gericke's II Battalion of the 6th Parachute Regiment. Although several important generals and staff officers were captured, the Germans were somewhat disappointed because General Roatta had already fled.[9]

Only Generale di Brigata Don Ferrante Gonzaga, the commander of the 222nd Coastal Defense Division, refused to order his troops to disarm. Major Alvensleben of General Hube's staff was sent to obtain his surrender, but Gonzaga tried to resist, and Alvensleben cut him down with his Schmeisser machine pistol. He commented later that Gonzaga had died "a great soldier."

Only the 209th Coastal Defense Division at Bari remained intact and joined the Germans. Parts of the 58th (Legnano), the 152nd (Piceno), and 104th (Mantova) Infantry Divisions did the same. The rest of Arisio's army—three regular and six coastal divisions, under four corps headquarters—was disarmed and sent home.

In the Balkans, the situation was potentially dangerous for Field Marshal Weichs's OB Southeast, which included his own Army Group F in Yugoslavia and Albania, Gen. of Infantry Dr. Lothar Rendulic's 2nd Panzer Army in charge of the Adriatic coastal defenses, and *Luftwaffe* Col. Gen. Alexander Loehr's Army Group E in operational command of the troops in Greece and on the Aegean islands. The Italians held most of the Balkans, including the western third of Croatia, all of Montenegro, an enlarged Albania, and two-thirds of Greece. Weichs had the simultaneous tasks of subduing the Italians, defending the coasts of the Balkans and the islands against the Allies, and containing the guerrilla movements in the interior. He had only nineteen German divisions, as opposed to twenty-nine Italian divisions (more than 600,000 men), and was definitely vulnerable at a number of points. He had only one German battalion in Albania on September 8, for example; when the Italians defected, one Allied regiment could have captured the entire country. Nevertheless, Weichs was prepared, and the Italians were not. Most of the Italians surrendered without a struggle although there was considerable fighting in the region. Tito's guerrillas thought that the Italian defection meant that an Allied invasion was imminent, so they came out into the open and soon controlled large sections of the interior. Hitler was also nervous about the prospect of an Allied invasion and conferred several times with Weichs in September and October; the field marshal did not think that an invasion was likely before spring. Tito, he said, was the most dangerous enemy, and in the end, Hitler let him have his way. Weichs marched his divisions all across the peninsula, disarming the Italians after an occasional brief battle and suppressing the partisans. The Italian Acqui Division held the island of Cephalonia until September 22, when it finally ran out of ammunition. It was nearly wiped out after it surrendered. The Italian Bergamo Division defended Spalato for nineteen days against the 8th SS Cavalry Division "Prinz Eugen," which finally slaughtered it. Many individual Italians preferred to join Tito or the Greek guerrillas in the Pindus Mountains or in the Peloponnese rather than surrender to the Germans.

Weichs mastered a difficult situation in Balkans although the British did manage to seize the key islands of Cos, Leros, and Samos in September while Weichs was busy suppressing Tito's uprising. The field marshal then turned his attention back to the islands that he had lost. He supplied Lt. Gen. Friedrich-Wilhelm Mueller, the commander of the 22nd Air Landing Division, with enough landing craft to outfit a sizable amphibious force. Because Cos was out of range of any major RAF bases, he assigned several obsolete Stuka units to support the 22nd. Mueller landed on Cos, which three miles from the Turkish mainland, on October 3, soundly defeated the British-Italian garrison, and quickly overran the island. The battle ended on October 4. Mueller had captured

1,338 British and 3,145 Italian soldiers and airmen in the process, along with forty guns, sixteen antiaircraft guns, and eleven undamaged airplanes. The 22nd lost only fifteen killed and seventy wounded in the fighting. Mueller then executed ninety Italian officers as traitors to the Axis, including the garrison commander, Col. Felice Leggio. (Mueller himself would be executed as a war criminal in Athens in 1947.)

From November 12 to 16, the 22nd Air Landing's amphibious battle group overran the island of Leros, bringing the entire Dodecanese coast back under German control. Mueller captured 3,200 British and 5,700 Italian soldiers, but this time, the operation was more difficult. The Germans lost 260 killed, 746 wounded, and 162 missing—41 percent of the invading force. Again, several Italian officers were executed after they surrendered.[10]

On the subject of the Balkans, which he hated, Adolf Hitler said, "If the British said Germany's job will be to keep the Balkans in order, we'd be busy for the next thirty years—marching in and out and back again, banding heads together and getting out again."[11] By the end of 1943, however, it was at least nominally subdued and—for the moment, at least—under German hegemony.

From the Allied point of view, the most important component of the Italian armed forces was the surface fleet, most of which was based at La Spezia. Under the terms of Badoglio's agreement with Eisenhower, it was to sail to Bizerte or Malta, where it was to surrender to the Allies.

The bulk of the fleet left La Spezia late in the afternoon of September 8, led by the battleships *Roma*, *Italia*, and *Vittorio Veneto*, without interference from the *Wehrmacht*. Admiral De Courten had convinced them that he was moving out to attack the Allied convoys heading toward Salerno. Meanwhile, the better part of the Italian cruiser and destroyer forces left Genoa and joined the fleet off the west coast of Corsica on the morning of September 9. The *Luftwaffe* had two nasty surprises waiting for them: the 3,454 pound armor-piercing, remote controlled PC-1400-X guided bomb, known as the Fritz-X, and the Hs 293 glider bomb. Both were fitted with fins and rocket boosters and carried 704 and 660 pounds of explosives, respectively. They were launched by the Do 17s of the 100th Bomber Wing, which struck with considerable effect. Led by the wing commander, Maj. Bernhard Jope, eleven Dorniers attacked the *Roma* from 20,000 feet at 2:40 P.M. Adm. Carlo

Bergamini, the fleet commander, mistook the airplanes for friendly escorts and did not take evasive action or open fire until the attack began. The ensuing explosions tore the battleship in half. The *Roma* sank almost immediately, carrying 1,254 of her 1,830 crewmen down with her; Admiral Bergamini was among the dead. The *Italia* was also severely damaged. Adm. Romeo Oliva took charge of the rest of the fleet and headed south toward Malta, where it surrendered.

Back at La Spezia, the Germans—enraged by the escape of the Italian fleet—rounded up several Italian naval captains who had scuttled their vessels after they had been unable to leave port and summarily executed them.

Elsewhere, SS Capt. Otto Skorzeny learned that Mussolini was being held prisoner at Gran Sasso, the highest peak in the Apennines, 100 miles north of Rome. On September 12, he rescued him via glider assault, much to Hitler's delight. The battle for his former empire was just beginning.

THE BATTLE OF SALERNO

While Skornezy celebrated his amazing success in his hometown of Vienna, the Battle of Salerno reached its climax in the vineyards, wheatfields, and cornfields on the coastal plain of the Gulf of Salerno.

On September 10, the second day of the battle, the 16th Panzer Division counterattacked in the Salerno sector, with the heaviest concentration against the Royal Fusiliers, who had occupied the town of Battipaglia during the night. The 16th Panzer overran the town and took nearly 1,500 prisoners. Meanwhile, the British 201st Guards Brigade continued to fight for the Montecorvino airfield and the surrounding area. Between Battipaglia and the field lay the tobacco factory, a prominent local landmark of five large buildings held by the Germans. The Guards launched several attacks on the factory, but the Germans fought back from well-hidden positions with Spandau machine guns, mortars, and 88-millimeter antiaircraft guns. A close-quarter battle developed in the factory buildings, but the British could not take them.

In contrast to the fierce fighting and negligible progress in the British sector, the U.S. VI Corps advanced rapidly against weak resistance. This was because Vietinghoff's plan for the 29th Panzer Grenadier

Division to take over the left flank during the night of September 9–10 had misfired. The recently organized 10th Army had no organic quartermaster department, and OB South's logistical operations were not functioning properly, leaving General Fries and his men without petrol; in fact, much of the 10th Army was without fuel. Vietinghoff had to take emergency measures to keep the 26th Panzer Division, which was directly in the path of the British 8th Army, from running out of gas in Calabria. Instead of coming up on the night of September 9–10 as planned, the 29th Panzer Grenadier Division came into the battle zone one unit at a time over the next three days. The entire division was not up until September 12.

This German supply disaster allowed the Americans to advance on Eboli on their left flank and push forward four miles before their vanguard was ambushed by the 29th Panzer Engineer Battalion as it attempted to ford the Calore River. On the U.S. right flank, the 36th Infantry Division advanced into the area of the Temples of Paestum— two perfect Greek temples and the decaying columns of a third, almost all that remained of the Greek city of Poseidonia—which overlooked the American beachhead. Behind the Paestum lay the two mountains which dominated the battlefield: Monte Soprano (3,556 feet) and Monte Sottane (2,079 feet). Between them lay the town of Capaccio. On the U.S. right flank, a battalion of the 142nd Regimental Combat Team occupied Monte Soprano and expanded the bridgehead while another battalion took Altavilla on the high ground near the Paestum. By the end of the day, the Germans had recaptured Altaville, and the U.S. VI Corps was still unable to close the gap between it and the British X Corps.

To the south, because his army was getting very strung out, Montgomery halted for two days. The 8th Army was still 120 miles away when the Germans launched their major counterattack three days later.

September 11, the third day of the invasion, was another day of heavy fighting in the British sector. Early in the evening, the 16th Panzer launched a combined panzer-infantry attack south of Battipaglia and pushed the 201st Guards back toward the beach. By the end of the day, the Germans had taken more than 1,500 prisoners, most of them British. The X Corps finally managed to capture the Montecorvino airfield by nightfall, thanks largely to the heavy guns of the Royal Navy, but

German infantry and artillery in the nearby hills prevented Allied airplanes from using it.

Richthofen's 2nd Air Fleet threw everything it had into the battle. Between September 9 and 11 alone, the *Luftwaffe* flew almost 550 sorties, mostly against Allied shipping in the Gulf of Salerno. Balck correctly concluded that the heavy gunfire of the enemy battleships, cruisers, and destroyers might well win the battle for the Allies, and he called on Richthofen to neutralize them. The nephew of the famed Red Baron did his best, and the 100th Bomber Wing (KG 100) had a field day. At 9 A.M. on September 11, the U.S. cruiser *Savannah* was hit by a PC-1400-X glide bomb, which killed almost everyone on the bridge, blew a hole in the ship's bottom, and opened a seam in its side, killing 197 crewmen in the process. The ship was escorted back to Malta and never saw action again. Two days later, the HMS *Uganda*, a British cruiser, was hit by a 1.4-ton glider bomb, which penetrated seven steel decks and exploded beneath the ship. The *Uganda* was flooded with 1,300 tons of water, had to be towed out of the battle zone, and eventually had to be sent to the United States for repairs. Several other ships were also damaged, including the U.S. cruiser *Philadelphia*. The British battleship *Warspite* was also knocked out and had to be towed to Malta. The *Luftwaffe* also sank four transports, a heavy cruiser, and seven landing craft, damaged several other vessels, and scored a total of eighty-five hits on Allied vessels.

By September 12, Vietinghoff's reinforcements were arriving and beginning to have an effect on the battle. By now, Balck's XIV Panzer Corps had taken charge of the northern half of the battlefield and was engaging the British X Corps with the Hermann Goering Panzer and 15th Panzer Grenadier Divisions. Kesselring had also sent Balck strong elements of the 3rd Panzer Grenadier Division now that Rome was subdued. To the south, Herr's LXXVI Panzer Corps faced the U.S. VI Corps with the 29th Panzer Grenadier and the 16th Panzer Divisions, plus most of the 26th Panzer Division. On the twelfth, Herr counterattacked and retook Altavilla and Hill 424 from the Americans, inflicting heavy casualties. In the meantime, the British 56th Infantry Division retook Battipaglia, only to be thrown out again by nightfall. The battle was nearing a stalemate.

On September 13, Vietinghoff continued to marshal his forces and planned to launch his major offensive the next day. Sometime during the morning, he finally discovered the gap between the American and British corps and jumped to the conclusion that the Allies had voluntarily split their beachhead. That could only mean one thing: they were planning an evacuation. There were other indications as well: more ships off Salerno, the use of smoke near Battipaglia, and an intercepted radio message. Neither Herr nor Balck were convinced, but Vietinghoff was certain. Sensing a decisive victory, he ordered an all-out attack for that afternoon to hasten and disrupt the Allied evacuation.

Vietinghoff had made a rare mistake; in fact, he had completely misread the situation. The Allies had no intention of evacuating the beachhead. Even so, Vietinghoff's attack almost won the battle for the Third Reich.

The main attack began at 5:15 P.M. when elements of the 29th Panzer Grenadier Division rolled down the Sele-Calore corridor. They captured Persano and overran an American infantry battalion, killing or capturing more than 500 men. They continued to push on to the junction of the Sele and Carole Rivers, only two miles from the beaches. "At this point," Clark recalled, "we were almost certainly at the mercy of Kesselring, provided he massed his strength and threw it at us relentlessly."[12] Between the Germans and the sea stood only a few American infantrymen, two 105-millimeter field artillery battalions, and a few tank destroyers. Clark's command post was only a few hundred yards behind the guns and was prepared to evacuate by PT boat on ten minutes' notice. Clerks, cooks, mechanics, drivers, and headquarters troops were put into the line as infantry. General Dawley, the U.S. VI Corps commander, was planning the evacuation of the American bridgehead.

Fries had only fifteen panzers in his strike force. The guns of the American artillery battalions were lined up, almost hub to hub, firing eight rounds a minute at the German tanks and the panzer grenadiers. They were joined by the heavy guns of the U.S. Navy. It was the concentrated fire of the big naval guns and field artillery that won the battle that day and saved the U.S. foothold on the mainland of Europe. The survivors of the German strike force withdrew at nightfall.

In the meantime, the XIV Panzer Corps brought the British X Corps under heavy attack, especially on the open plain southeast of Battipaglia. The battle lasted for three hours, but the British held their positions despite heavy losses on both sides.

That night, Mark Clark shortened his line and reinforced it with everything that was available, including 1,300 paratroopers from the 82nd Airborne Division who dropped near the coast at 1:30 A.M. Their arrival had a tremendous psychological effect on the defenders, whose morale needed a boost. On the other side of the line, Vietinghoff prepared to strike again despite the pessimistic views of both of his corps commanders. During the night, he was reinforced by a panzer grenadier regiment from Maj. Gen. Baron Smilo von Luettwitz's 26th Panzer Division. Luettwitz, incidently, was doing a brilliant job in delaying Montgomery. There was not an intact bridge and hardly an extant culvert south of Castrovillari, and the British had to work their way through thousands of mines and booby-traps. The 26th Panzer had suffered only 113 casualties (30 of them killed) and had not lost any of its weapons or heavy equipment.

The German attacks of September 14 were not nearly as dangerous as the attack of the previous day. More than 500 B-17s, B-25s, and B-26s blasted German positions and troop concentrations, and American artillery and naval fire support continued to be lavish. "Our attack this morning pushed on into stiffened resistance," Vietinghoff reported,

> but above all the advancing troops had to endure the most severe fire that had hitherto been experienced; the naval gunfire from at least sixteen to eighteen battleships, cruisers, and large destroyers lying in the roadstead. With astonishing precision and freedom of maneuver, these ships shot at every identifiable target with overwhelming effect.[13]

By the end of the day, the U.S. VI Corps alone had knocked out almost thirty German tanks. Earlier, the British 7th Armoured Division came ashore, and that afternoon, the British X and U.S. VI Corps finally linked up southeast of Battipaglia. Both Allied corps were moving inland and expanding the bridgehead when darkness descended on the battlefield.

The next day, September 15, the Germans continued to probe Allied lines, but their attacks were much weaker. The Allies continued to move forward cautiously and began to suspect that the Germans might be withdrawing. They were not; Vietinghoff was merely marshaling his forces for one more all-out attack. This effort was made on the morning of September 16, when the 26th Panzer Division struck from Battipaglia toward Salerno against the British 56th Infantry and 7th Armoured Divisions, while the 16th Panzer Division struck from Battipaglia against the U.S. 45th Infantry Division. Both attacks were overwhelmed by Allied firepower.

That afternoon, the Hermann Goering Panzer Division, supported by elements of the 3rd and 15th Panzer Grenadiers, finally attacked the British 46th Infantry Division, which had received considerable armored reinforcements. The attack was easily beaten back.

This was Vietinghoff's last throw of the dice. Late that afternoon, he received word that the advance elements of the British 8th Army had finally reached Lagonegro, fifty miles south of Paestum. Convinced now that the Salerno bridgehead could not be wiped out, he disengaged, and the U.S. 5th and British 8th Armies linked up that evening. The Battle of Salerno was over.

Hitler, Kesselring, and Vietinghoff were all moderately well satisfied with the results of the Salerno operations and the events of September 8–16. The German forces in Italy had survived the Italian defection; they had successfully extricated their forces from southern Italy; they had disarmed an army of 1,700,000 men; and they had prevented the Allies from exploiting the Italian surrender to any significant degree. They were now in a position to pivot on the mountains northwest of Salerno and create a continuous front across the Italian peninsula from the Tyrrhenian Sea to the Adriatic. They had also inflicted more casualties on the Allies than they had suffered themselves, despite Allied aerial superiority and naval supremacy. In all, German losses totaled about 3,500—about the same as the Americans, who lost 500 killed, 1,800 wounded, and 1,200 missing. The British lost another 5,500 men. "The Germans may claim with some justification to have won if not a victory at least an important success over us," General Alexander concluded on September 25.[14]

In addition, Skorzeny's rescue of Mussolini had been a propaganda victory of the highest order and had spared the Germans the necessity of establishing a military government in Italy. On September 18, Mussolini and his cronies proclaimed the Italian Social Republic (*Repubblica Sociale Italiana*, or RSI), which is commonly known as the Salo Republic, after Mussolini's residence on Lake Garda. With the rescue of Mussolini,

Hitler controlled one symbol of Italian leadership, while the Allies controlled the other in the king.

So what had the Allies gained in Italy to date? Not much. Hitler now occupied four-fifths of the peninsula, including the best agricultural regions and all of the major industrial cities. The U.S. official history recorded:

> The surrender of Italy achieved by the armistice of Cassibile was not much more than a paper capitulation, for the Allies had neither the Italian capital nor the administrative apparatus of government. What the Allies had was a symbol of sovereignty scarcely one whit more appealing to the Italian people than the discredited Duce.[15]

CHAPTER 14

Salerno to the Gustav Line

"Kesselring was a master of delaying tactics," Gen. Mark Clark wrote after the war.[1] To many historians, Field Marshal Albert Kesselring was a military genius. He was not, but he did show flashes of genius, and as commander in chief of OB South (later Southwest) and Army Group C during the Italian campaign (1943–45), he did perform, with a few lapses, at or near the genius level. This was his masterpiece.

It is ironic that as his greatest campaign began, Kesselring was on probation as a military commander. Initially, like Rommel and Jodl, Hitler did not believe that the Italian peninsula could be held without Italian help. He intended to give Rommel sole command in Italy after the forces of OB South retreated to the Pisa-Arezzo-Ancona line; Kesselring was earmarked to replace Col. Gen. Nikolaus von Falkenhorst as commander in chief in Norway.

Kesselring's strategic theory of holding as far south as possible gained credibility at Fuehrer Headquarters after he successfully disarmed the Italian Army, eliminated five Italian divisions at Rome when he had only two himself, and simultaneously checked two Allied armies at Salerno and Calabria, almost driving one of them back into the sea. Hitler still had not decided which of the strategic theories—Rommel's or Kesselring's—was correct. Kesselring made six major points: (1) a prolonged German defense in southern Italy would delay an Allied offensive against the Balkans; (2) a defensive line in the south would make the strategic bombing of the Po River Valley, Austria, and southern Germany more difficult; (3) the Bernhardt Line, which Kesselrlng wanted to defend, could be held with eleven divisions while the defense of Rommel's longer Apennine line would require an estimated thirteen to twenty divisions; (4) if the Allies breached the Apennine line, the Po Valley would be lost and the Germans would have to retreat to the Alps; (5) the possession of Rome would have immense propaganda value; and (6) holding the Bernhardt Line would make a counteroffensive against Apulia possible if Allied preparations for an invasion of the Balkans resulted in the withdrawal of Allied troops from the Italian front.[2]

Hitler gradually came over to Kesselring's way of thinking. In addition, Kesselring's constant optimism—a source of irritation to Hitler prior to the Italian defection—now began to work in his favor, especially in the face of Rommel's outspoken pessimism. On September 17, Hitler approved Kesselring's plan for a slow withdrawal to the north and indicated that it was important to hold the Bernhardt Line "for a longer period of time."[3]

The Italian boot is about 750 miles long, 85 to 120 miles wide, and is very mountainous. The Apennines, the central range, vary in height from 2,500 to more than 6,000 feet, with a series of ridges running down each side. Both of the Italian coastal plains are very narrow, averaging perhaps 20 miles wide on the west and only 10 miles on the east (Adriatic) coast. The result is few major roads and little room for armies to deploy. In short, the boot was easy to defend—except for the fact that any line in Italy could be outflanked via a seaborne attack on either side.

Beginning on September 18, Vietinghoff's 10th Army began its retreat from Salerno. He deployed the XIV Panzer Corps on the western coast and the LXXVI Panzer on the east, with a view toward eventually extending his units across the entire peninsula and forming a continuous front. The following evening, Field Marshal Rommel fell victim to a severe appendicitis attack. While he recovered, Vietinghoff was named acting commander of Army Group B, and Hube temporarily replaced him as commander of the 10th Army.

The next several days, the U.S. VI Corps advanced slowly, tied up in dozens of small delaying actions. Between Paestum and Oliveto, only twenty-five miles inland, the Germans blew up more than twenty-five bridges. Usually, the Germans also posted a few machine guns and perhaps a panzer or self-propelled gun or two to cover the crossing site. This forced the American infantry to deploy and maneuver, and they had usually suffered several casualties before the German rear guard retreated—to the next bridge—before it could be decisively engaged. The American advance continued to be very slow because of the demolitions, mountainous terrain, rain, and the Germans.

General McCreery's X British Corps on the left flank of the U.S. 5th Army was not making much progress either, although Montgomery's 8th Army came up on the Allied right (Adriatic) flank and took the major Italian airfield complex at Foggia on September 27, giving the Allied heavy bombers a base from which to attack the Romanian oilfields at Ploesti, as well as targets in southern Germany and Austria.

Kesselring had ordered Vietinghoff, and later Hube, to delay forward of the Bernhardt Line until October 15. The marshal himself was busy fortifying a line through Mignano about fifty miles north of Naples. He also planned to fortify a line north of that anchored on Cassino, if Hitler approved.

On September 28, the U.S. Rangers forced their way to the Plain of Naples. Now that the Allies had reached relatively flat terrain, the 10th Army, now again under Vietinghoff, was forced to evacuate Naples, which the King's Dragoon Guards entered on the morning of October 1. They found the facilities of both the port and city as thoroughly destroyed as was humanly possible. By orders of Kesselring, the monasteries and churches were spared, as were hospitals, museums, and historical buildings. The machinery of the Alfa Romeo plant and several other factories was dismantled and shipped north. The Allies found the warehouses and other buildings in the port area on fire, along with huge piles of burning coal. It would take the engineers three days just to put out the fires. More than 130 ships had been scuttled in the harbor, and locomotives had been run off their lines into the docks. The seventy-three electric dockside cranes had all been destroyed by dynamite. The city's water system had been polluted, the electrlcal facilities demolished, the aqueduct destroyed, and the sewer system blasted in more than fifty places. Even the spaghetti factories had been blown away, and road and railroad tunnels had been collapsed by explosions. In addition, dozens of booby traps and delayed charges had been hidden throughout the city. Some explosions took place forty-two days after the German engineers left Naples. On October 7, a bomb exploded in the central post office, killing or wounding seventy people. Four days later, another bomb went off in the barracks occupied by the U.S. 82nd Airborne Division, killing eighteen paratroopers and wounding many others. Allied engineer and salvage crews, however, worked miracles in Naples. By the end of October, they were unloading 7,000 tons a day at the port. Its average prewar capacity had been just 8,000 tons a day.

By October 2, General Clark had 100,000 men trying to advance on the Volturno. It was now winter, the rainy season in the Mediterranean. The normally dry Italian streams turned into raging torrents, and everything seemed to be turning into mud. One Allied division reported that it had only eight jeeps able to move, and the rest of its transport had sunk to the axles.[4] As the Allied advance pushed forward at almost glacial speed, Hitler's attitude continued to shift toward Kesselring's strategy. He still could not make up his mind, but on October 4, for the first time, he ordered Rommel to send reinforcements to Kesselring in the form of two infantry divisions and several artillery units.

Meanwhile, General Hube returned to the Eastern Front, where he was slated to assume command of the 1st Panzer Army. Lt. Gen. Hermann Balck replaced him as commander of the XIV Panzer Corps, but after less than a week in command, his scout plane piled up while landing and almost killed the general, who suffered several broken bones. Hube was quickly recalled to Italy, where he resumed command of the XIV Panzer for about two weeks. Senger assumed permanent command of the corps on October 23. Balck received his promotion to general of panzer troops in the hospital eight days later. He returned to duty on November 15 as commander of the XXXXVIII Panzer Corps on the Russian Front.

On October 7, the Allied vanguards reached the Volturno, twenty miles north of Naples and twenty miles south of the Bernhardt Line. Normally, this river is 6 feet deep and 250 to 300 feet wide. Now it was flooded by the winter rains and was 1 to 6 feet above its banks. German resistance was stiff, and it was October 19 before the Allies had complete control of the Volturno Line. The Germans then merely continued their retreat to the north toward the Bernhardt Line. Both the Allied military leaders and the Badoglio government, which declared war on Germany on October 13, thought the liberation of Rome was only a matter of time. They had no idea of the nasty surprise Kesselring had prepared for them a few miles to the north.

The Bernhardt Line, twenty miles behind the Volturno, extended ninety miles from the mouth of the Garigliano River on the west coast of Italy to the Sangro on the east. It was actually three lines: the Barbara, Bernhardt, and Gustav. The first, the Barbara, was a delaying position only. Ten miles behind it lay the main Bernhardt Line, which was much stronger. It ran from the mouth of the Garigliano River to the Matese Mountains in the interior and then along the Sangro River to the Adriatic. Finally, there was the Gustav Line, the most intensively fortified of the three and the one Kesselring intended to hold no matter what. Along the Garigliano River, the Gustav and Bernhardt were the same. Sometimes this part of the fortifications was called the Bernhardt-Gustav Line. Farther inland, the two diverged. The Gustav bent twelve miles to the rear and was anchored on the natural fortress of Monte Cassino. It continued east until it reached the Adriatic, some twenty miles northwest of the Sangro. Collectively, the Allies referred to all three lines as the Winter Line. The map on the next page shows Kesselring's retreat to this strong defensive position.

From Naples, only two main roads led to Rome. One was the famous Appian Way (Highway 7), which ran along the coast through the Aurunci Mountains and the Pontine Marsh, which had been drained by Mussolini and was now open meadow. This route was easy to defend, and the Germans made it virtually impassable. The other road, Highway 6, was about thirty-five miles inland. It had been built by the Romans as Via Casilina about 500 B.C. It passed Cassino and the Rapido River and then led into the Liri River Valley, the gateway to Rome. If the Allies could get past Monte Cassino, the road to Rome (eighty miles to the northwest) would be clear. Unfortunately, to get there, the Allies would have to overcome the Barbara Line; the Mignano Gap, a narrow corridor between the mountains behind the Barbara; the Bernhardt Line; Cassino; and the Rapido River.

Maj. Gen. Hans Bessell was in charge of the construction of the fortifications. He had been commissioned in the 11th Engineer Battalion in 1914 and had spent most of his life in the engineers. To build the lines, Bessell employed German Army construction battalions, divisional combat engineer battalions, the workers of the Organization Todt, and

TO THE GUSTAV LINE

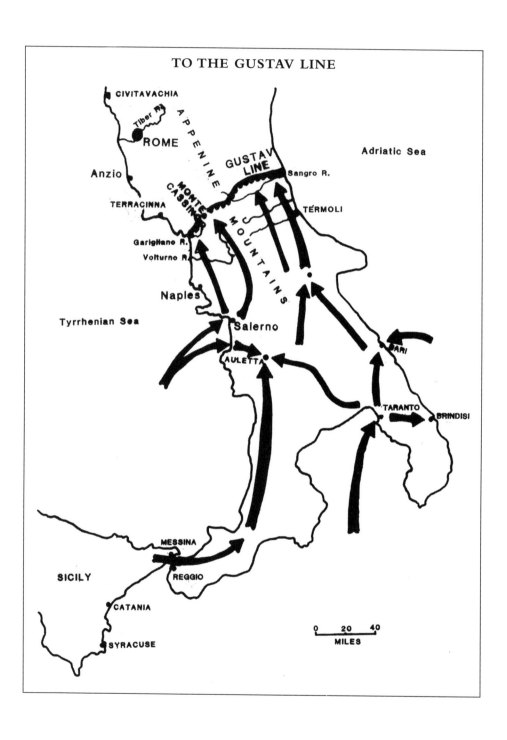

CIVITAVACHIA

Tiber R.

ROME

APPENINE

GUSTAV LINE

Adriatic Sea

Anzio

Sangro R.

TERRACINNA

MONTE CASSINO

TÉRMOLI

Garigliano R.

MOUNTAINS

Volturno R.

Naples

Tyrrhenian Sea

Salerno

AULETTA

BARI

TARANTO

BRINDISI

MESSINA

REGGIO

SICILY

CATANIA

SYRACUSE

0   20   40
MILES

thousands of Italian civilians. Kesselring paid them well and gave them bonuses in the form of food and tobacco, both of which were scarce in Italy in late 1943. As a result, they worked hard and did their jobs well. The lines included gun positions, strongpoints, barbed-wire entanglements, minefields, booby traps, machine-gun emplacements with interlocking fields of fire, dug-in tanks, and pillboxes, some of which featured five-inch-thick armor.

Bessell's minefields were not extensive; only about 75,000 mines were laid. However, they included some very deadly mines. One, the S-mine, was known to the Allies as the "Bouncing Betty." After it was stepped on, this mine would jump several feet in the air before it exploded, a feature which greatly increased its casualty radius. Another mine used extensively was the *Schu* mine, which was in a case made almost entirely of wood. It did not register on standard mine detectors and was designed to blow off a foot.

It took the Allies more than two weeks to push through the Barbara and advance fifteen to twenty miles north of the Volturno along a forty-mile front. The U.S. 5th Army reached the main German positions in early November. Despite Vietinghoff's skillful withdrawal, Kesselring expressed disapproval with what he considered the quick fall of the Barbara Line, and on November 5, he questioned the 10th Army commander's conduct of the operation. The tough Prussian quickly took umbrage and went on sick leave that same day. Kesselring took charge of the 10th Army for two days until Gen. of Panzer Troops Joachim Lemelsen, the commander of the XXXXVII Panzer Corps, could arrive from Russia to assume acting command. Kesselring apparently realized later that he had made a mistake in his dealings with Vietinghoff. On December 28, when Vietinghoff returned to Italy, Kesselring treated him as if nothing had happened.

As Kesselring anticipated, the Allies made their main attempt to pierce his line through the Highway 6–Mignano Gap corridor. The Mignano Gap was a winding, six-mile passage between steep mountains that would have to be taken one by one. The American advance was hampered not only by the mountainous terrain, but also by the rocky nature of the ground. Exploding mortar and artillery shells would send rock fragments flying in all directions. These fragments were every bit as dangerous as shrapnel and greatly increased Allied casualties.

The Americans countered the defenses by driving flocks of Italian sheep and goats in front of them to set off mines, especially the unde- tectable *Schu* mines. They answered artillery with artillery. In this area, the Allies had tremendous superiority. In one two-week period, the U.S. 36th Infantry Division alone fired 95,000 shells at German lines. The 10th Army's positions, however, were too well sited and too well pro- tected, and the German positions were still intact when the Allies attacked. On the Allied left, the British 56th Infantry Division fought for eight days, trying to take Monte Camino from the 15th Panzer Grenadier Division. It failed. The U.S. 3rd Infantry Division tried for ten days to take Monte la Difensa, but it was beaten back every time and suffered heavy losses. The terrain here was so steep that it took about six hours to get a wounded man down the mountain. When, after tremen- dous effort, the Allies did succeed in capturing a mountain, the Germans simply fell back to the next mountain. Finally, on November 15, General Clark was forced to acknowledge that his army was on the verge of exhaustion and called a halt to the offensive for two weeks.

Back at Fuehrer Headquarters, Hitler finally signed the directive naming Kesselring German commander in chief in Italy on November 6. Army Group B was discontinued as an active command on November 21. Its troop units and the defense of northern Italy were handed over to the newly formed 14th Army, which had been activated three days before under the command of Col. Gen. Eberhard von Mackensen.

On the other side of the Apennines, the British 8th Army began its offensive on the Adriatic side of the boot on November 20. It forced the Sangro River and smashed the inexperienced 65th Infantry Division, but the river flooded and washed out their bridges before they could advance very far. Montgomery resumed his offensive on November 27, supported by more than 4,000 airplanes. Kesselring had also sent another division, Lt. Gen. Carl-Hans Lungershausen's 90th Panzer Grenadier, just up from Sardinia, to the threatened sector, along with part of the 16th Panzer. The relatively poor 65th Infantry gave way altogether after its capable commander, Maj. Gen. Gustav Heistermann von Ziehlberg, was seriously wounded on December 1, and General Westphal recorded that "to all intents and purposes [it] no longer existed."[5] While Heistermann's arm was being amputated in a nearby hospital, the 90th Panzer Grenadier picked up the slack, and the British advance was very slow indeed. It gained fewer than fifteen miles before it stalled outside the town of Ortona on the Adriatic coast. No one was satisfied with the performance of Lungershausen, who had demonstrated signs of incompetency both during the approach march and during the battle. He was replaced by Col. Ernst-Guenther Baade on December 20. Baade defended Ortona quite tenaciously. The 1st Canadian Infantry Division finally took it on December 28, after a seven-day battle.

Meanwhile, on the western side of the Apennines, General Clark waited for Montgomery to force Lemelsen to commit his reserves; then he resumed his offensive on December 1. Three hundred forty-six Allied guns fired 22,000 artillery shells in one hour. In the first forty-eight hours of the offensive, the 925 guns firing in support of the U.S. II Corps fired almost 75,000 shells on German positions, and Allied tactical air units flew 900 bombing sorties against the Germans. Still the resistance was fierce. The British 56th Infantry Division finally stormed Monte Camino after five days of heavy fighting, virtually wiping out the 15th Panzer Reconnaissance Battalion in the process. The 1st Special Service Force, a mixed American-Canadian unit, lost 511 of its 1,800 men during this battle.

Following the fall of Monte Camino, the 142nd Regimental Combat Team of the U.S. 36th Infantry Division overran Monte Maggiore with surprising ease. Allied troops now held both sides of the entrance to the Mignano Gap, but the Germans still did not abandon the nearby peaks, and the battle continued. A few days earlier, after conferring with Badoglio, General Alexander had accepted the 1st Italian Motorized Group (5,500 men) and assigned it to the U.S. 5th Army. This was the first pro-Allied Italian unit committed to combat, so Clark gave it what he thought was an easy assignment: clearing Monte Lungo of Germans. At the same time, U.S. Maj. Gen. Fred L. Walker's 36th Infantry Division, with Ranger battalions attached, was to take Monte Sammucro and sweep through the town of San Pietro on the valley floor. Nobody had any way of knowing that the mountain and town were defended by Walter Fries's firmly entrenched 29th Panzer Grenadier Division or that the one-armed, one-legged general had received a personal order from Adolf Hitler that there were to be no withdrawals.

The battle began with another massive artillery bombardment. Then the Italians, dressed with long feathers in their hatbands, advanced in close formation, two battalions abreast. They were slaughtered and routed by noon.

The Americans continued the battle, which lasted for more than a week. One U.S. regiment lost 21 percent of its men, another almost half. By mid-afternoon on December 16, the Texans cleared Monte Lungo, and the Americans held both sides of San Pietro. The Germans abandoned the town that night and fell back about two miles. The U.S. 5th Army continued to push slowly forward from one mountain to another across rocky slopes and through the deep Italian mud. Finally, on January 15, 1944, they took an isolated height named Monte Trocchio, the last height before Cassino. It had taken eight divisions six weeks to advance seven miles at a cost of 16,000 casualties. More hard fighting lay ahead in 1944.

APPENDIX A

Comparative Ranks

U.S. Army	German Army and Luftwaffe
	Reichsmarschall (Luftwaffe only)[a]
General of the Army	Field Marshal (Generalfeldmarschall)
General	Colonel General (Generaloberst)
Lieutenant General	General of (Infantry, Panzer Troops, etc.)
Major General	Lieutenant General (Generalleutnant)
Brigadier General	Major General (Generalmajor)
Colonel	Colonel (Oberst)
Lieutenant Colonel	Lieutenant Colonel (Oberstleutnant)
Major	Major (Major)
Captain	Captain (Hauptmann)
First Lieutenant	First Lieutenant (Oberleutnant)
Second Lieutenant	Second Lieutenant (Leutnant)
	Senior Officer Cadet or Ensign (Faehnrich)
Officer Candidate	Officer-Cadet (Fahnenjunker)
Master Sergeant	Sergeant Major (Stabsfeldwebel)
First Sergeant	
Technical Sergeant	Technical Sergeant (Oberfeldwebel)
Staff Sergeant	Staff Sergeant (Feldwebel)
Sergeant	Sergeant (Unterfeldwebel)
Corporal	Corporal (Unteroffizier)
	Lance Corporal (Gefreiter)
Private First Class	Private First Class (Obersoldat)
Private	Private (Soldat, Grenadier, Jaeger, etc.)

Note:
a. Held only by Hermann Goering, July 19, 1940 to April 23, 1945.

U.S. Army	Waffen-SS
General of the Army	Reichsfuehrer-SS
General	SS Colonel General (SS-Oberstgruppenfuehrer)
Lieutenant General	SS General (SS-Obergruppenfuehrer)
Major General	SS Lieutenant General (SS-Gruppenfuehrer)
Brigadier General	SS Major General (SS-Brigadefuehrer)
none	SS Oberfuehrer (SS-Oberfuehrer)
Colonel	SS Colonel (SS-Standartenfuehrer)
Lieutenant Colonel	SS Lieutenant Colonel (SS-Obersturmbannfuehrer)
Major	SS Major (SS-Sturmbannfuehrer)
Captain	SS Captain (SS-Hauptsturmfuehrer)
First Lieutenant	SS First Lieutenant (SS-Obersturmfuehrer)
Second Lieutenant	SS Second Lieutenant (SS-Untersturmfuehrer)
Officer Candidate	SS Officer-Cadet (SS Fahnenjunker)
Master Sergeant	SS Sergeant Major (SS-Sturmscharfuehrer)
First Sergeant	SS First Sergeant (SS-Hauptscharfuehrer)
Technical Sergeant	SS Technical Sergeant (SS-Oberscharfuehrer)
Staff Sergeant	SS Staff Sergeant (SS-Scharfuehrer)
Sergeant	SS Sergeant (SS-Unterscharfuehrer)
Corporal	SS Corporal (SS-Rottenfuehrer)
Private First Class	SS Private First Class (SS Sturmann)
Private	SS Private (SS-Mann)
	SS Aspirant (SS-Anwaerter)

German Army/Luftwaffe	German Navy (Officer Ranks Only)
Reichsmarschall (Luftwaffe only)	Grand Admiral (Grossadmiral)
Field Marshal (Generalfeldmarschall)	———
Colonel General (Generaloberst)	General Admiral (Generaladmiral)
General (General der ...)	Admiral (Admiral)
Lieutenant General (Generalleutnant)	Vice Admiral (Vizeadmiral)
Major General (Generalmajor)	Rear Admiral (Konteradmiral)
Colonel (Oberst)	Captain (Kapitaen zur See)
Lieutenant Colonel (Oberstleutnant)	Commander (Fregattenkapitaen)
Major (Major)	Lieutenant Commander (Korventtenkapitaen)
Captain (Hauptmann)	Lieutenant (Kapitaenleutnant)
First Lieutenant (Oberleutnant)	Leutnant[b]
Second Lieutenant (Leutnant)	Leutnant zur See[c]
Officer-Cadet (Fahnenjunker)	Seekadett

Notes:
  b. Equivalent to lieutenant (j.g.) in U.S. Navy.
  c. Equivalent to ensign in the U.S. Navy.

German Staff Positions

Chief of Staff (Not present below the corps level)

Ia   Chief of Operations

Ib   Quartermaster (Chief Supply Officer)

Ic   Staff Officer, Intelligence (subordinate to Ia)

Id   Director of Training (Not present below army level)

IIa   Chief Personnel Officer (Adjutant)

IIb   Second Personnel Officer (subordinate to IIa)

III   Chief Judge Advocate (subordinate to IIa)

IVa   Chief Administrative Officer (subordinate to Ib)

IVb   Chief Medical Officer (subordinate to Ib)

IVc   Chief Veterinary Officer (subordinate to Ib)

IVd   Chaplain (subordinate to IIa)

V   Motor Transport Officer (subordinate to Ib)

National Socialist Guidance Officer (added in 1944)

Special Staff Officers (Chief of Artillery, Chief of Projectors [Rocket Launchers], Chief Signal Officer, etc.)

Note: The Ia was referred to as the Generalstabsoffizier 1 (1st General Staff Officer, or GSO 1); the Ib was the Generalstabsoffizier 2; the Ic was the Generalstabsoffizier 3; and the Id was the Generalstabsoffizier 4.

APPENDIX C

German Units, Ranks, and Strengths

Unit	Rank of Commander[a]	Strength
Army Group	Field Marshal	2 or more armies
Army	Colonel General	2 or more corps
Army Detachment	General	1 or more corps plus independent divisions
Corps	General	2 or more divisions
Division	Lieutenant General/ Major General	10,000– 18,000 men[b] 200-350 tanks (if panzer)
Brigade[c]	Major General/ Colonel	2 or more regiments
Regiment	Colonel	2–7 battalions
Battalion	Lieutenant Colonel/ Major/Captain	2 or more companies (approximately 500 men per infantry battalion; usually 50–80 tanks per panzer battalion)
Company[d]	Captain/Lieutenant	3–5 platoons
Platoon	Lieutenant/ Sergeant Major	Infantry: 30–40 men Panzer: 4 or 5 tanks
Section	Warrant Officer/ Sergeant Major	2 squads (more or less)
Squad	Sergeant	Infantry: 7–10 men Armor: 1 tank

Notes:

a. Frequently, units were commanded by lower-ranking men as the war went on.

b. As the war progressed, the number of men and tanks in most units declined accordingly. SS units usually had more men and tanks than army units.

c. Brigade Headquarters were rarely used in the German Army after 1942.

d. Called batteries in the artillery (4 or 5 guns per battery).

Characteristics of Select German and Allied Tanks

Model	Weight (in tons)	Speed (mph)	Range (miles)	Main Armament	Crew
BRITISH					
Mark IV "Churchill"	43.1	15	120	16-pounder	5
Mark VI "Crusader"	22.1	27	200	12-pounder	5
Mark VIII Cromwell	30.8	38	174	175mm	5
AMERICAN[a]					
M3A1 "Stuart"[b]	14.3	36	60	137mm	4
M4A3 "Sherman"	37.1	30	120	176mm	5
GERMAN					
PzKw II	9.3	25	118	120mm	3
PzKw III	24.5	25	160	150mm	5
PzKw IV	19.7	26	125	175mm	5
PzKw V "Panther"	49.3	25	125	175mm	5
PzKw VI "Tiger"	62.0	23	73	188mm	5
RUSSIAN					
T34/Model 76	29.7	32	250	176mm	4
T34/Model 85	34.4	32	250	185mm	5
KV 1	52	25	208	176.2mm	5
JSII "Joseph Stalin"	45.5	23	150	122mm	4

Notes:

a. Characteristics of each tank varied somewhat from model to model.

b. All American tanks were also in the British inventory. The British Shermans were sometimes outfitted with a heavier main battle gun. These Shermans were called "Fireflies."

Luftwaffe Aviation Units, Strengths, and Ranks

Unit	Composition	Rank of Commander
OKL	All Luftwaffe Units	Reichsmarschall
Air Fleet	Air Corps and Air and Flak Division	General to Field Marshal
Air Corps	Air and Flak Divisions plus various miscellaneous units	Major General to General
Air Division	2 or more wings	Colonel to Major General
Wings	2 or more groups	Major to Colonel (Rarely Major General)
Group	2 or more squadrons 30 to 36 aircraft	Major to Lieutenant Colonel
Squadrons	2 or more sections 9 to 12 aircraft	Lieutenant to Captain
Section	3 or 4 aircraft	Lieutenant

NOTES

CHAPTER 1: NAZI GERMANY AND THE WEHRMACHT, 1933–42

1. Despite being cleared of these false charges, Werner von Fritsch's career was over just the same. Named honorary colonel of the 12th Artillery, he accompanied his regiment to the field when Germany invaded Poland. On September 22, 1939, he committed suicide by deliberately exposing himself to Polish machine-gun fire. Ironically, he is buried in the same cemetery as Heydrich, although Heydrich's headstone has since been removed.

2. Wilhelm Keitel was born on the family farm in Hanover in 1892. He wanted to be a farmer, but the farm was too small to be divided, so Keitel joined the army as a *Fahnenjunker* in the artillery in 1901. He served in artillery and in General Staff positions throughout his career and was chief of the organizational branch of the army when Hitler came to power. He was chief of the armed forces office of the war department under Blomberg. He was hanged as a war criminal at Nuremberg in 1946. Although he was universally considered a blockhead, Keitel did have a talent for organization. Even his personal enemies, such as Field Marshal Erich von Manstein, had nothing but praise for Keitel's work in the organizational branch.

3. Jodl, who was born in Bavaria in 1890, was an artillery officer. He was chief of operations of OKW until October 1, 1938, when he assumed command of *Arko 44* (the 44th Artillery Command) in Vienna. He returned to OKW when the war began and was again chief of operations from September 1, 1939, to May 9, 1945, when the western Allies arrested Keitel. He was commander of OKW from then until May 23, when it was dissolved and he was arrested. Like Keitel, he was hanged at Nuremberg on October 16, 1946.

4. Walter von Brauchitsch was born into a prominent Pomeranian military family in 1881. (Pomerania was considered the most of Prussian of the Prussian provinces.) He was the son of Gen. of Cavalry Bernhard von Brauchitsch, and his older brother Adolf (1876–1935) was a major general when he retired in 1929. Walter was educated in cadet schools, and like so many senior officers, including Keitel, Jodl, Ludwig Beck, and Franz Halder, he was an artilleryman.

5. Viktor von Schwedler (1885–1954) was also a product of the German cadet schools. He had been chief of personnel since 1933. When *Wehrkreis IV* was divided into its territorial and command components, Schwelder went to the field as commander of the IV Corps. He led it until October 18, 1942, when he was relieved of his command for criticizing Frederick Paulus's conduct of the Battle of Stalingrad. When he was proved right, he was taken out of retirement, and he again assumed command of *Wehrkries IV* on March 1, 1943. He held this post until January 31, 1945, when he was again placed in Fuehrer Reserve. As a result, he was able to escape Soviet captivity.

6. Bodewin Keitel (1888–1953) was born on the family farm in Hanover and joined the army as an officer-cadet in 1909. He served as a personnel officer until Septem-

ber 1942, when Hitler fired him in the same fit of rage in which he fired Franz Halder as chief of the General Staff and Field Marshal Wilhelm List as commander of Army Group A. Six months later, after Hitler cooled down, Bodewin was given command of *Wehrkreis XX* in West Prussia and Poland. He held this post until the Soviets overran the area in early 1945. A retired general of artillery, he resided in Goettingen, Lower Saxony, West Germany, after the war.

7. Adolf Kuntzen (1889–1969) had served in the HPA since 1929. He was transferred to Cottbus (about seventy-five miles southeast of Berlin) and was "kicked upstairs" as commander of the 3rd Light (later 8th Panzer) Division, which he led in Poland and France. He was promoted to major general on March 1, 1938, lieutenant general on April 1, 1940, and general of panzer troops on April 1, 1941. He commanded the LVII Corps in Russia (1941) and LXXXI Corps in France until September 4, 1944, when he was sacked for poor performance during the retreat to Germany. The charges seem to have been fully justified, and he was never reemployed.

   East Prussian Hans Behlendorff (1889–1961) was promoted to the leadership of the 31st Artillery Command (*Arko 31*) in Braunschweig. He rose to the rank general of artillery during World War II and commanded the 34th Infantry Division in Russia and LXXXIV Corps in France. He was placed in Fuehrer Reserve in the spring of 1943 and retired in late 1944. Wolf Keilig, *Die Generale des Heeres: Truppenoffiziere, Sanitaetsoffiziere im Generalstrang, Waffenoffiziere im Generalstrang, Offiziere d. Kraftfahrparktruppe im Generalstrang, Ingenieur-Offiziere im Generalstrang, Wehrmachtsrichter im Generalstrang, Verwaltungsoffiziere im Generalstrang, Veterinaeroffiziere im Generalstrang* (Friedberg, Germany: Podzun-Pallas-Verlag, 1983), 193; Dermot Bradley et al., *Die Generale des Heeres, 1921–1945: Die Militaerischen Werdegaenge der Generale, sowie der Aerzte, Veterinaere, Intendanten, Richter und Ministerialbeamten im Generalsrang* (Osnabrueck, Germany: Biblio, 1993–2006), 7:319–20.

8. Oswald Lutz was briefly recalled to active duty in 1941 to head a special transportation staff headquartered in Frankfurt am Oder, but he never again held an important position. He retired again in the summer of 1942 and died in Munich on February 26, 1944, at the age of sixty-seven.

9. General Beck was born in the Rhineland in 1880. He was chief of the General Staff from 1933 to 1938 and was discharged with an honorary promotion to colonel general. He briefly commanded the 1st Army in late 1938. He was deeply involved in the anti-Hitler conspiracy and committed suicide on July 20, 1944, after the Stauffenberg assassination attempt failed.

   Wilhelm Adam (1877–1949) was known as the "Father of the Mountain Branch." He had been chief of the General Staff from 1930 to 1933 and later commanded *Wehrkreis VII*, the Armed Forces Academy, and (briefly) Army Group 2. Like Beck, he was retired with an honorary promotion to colonel general.

10. Matthew Cooper, *The German Air Force, 1933–1945: An Anatomy of Failure* (New York: Jane's, 1981), 222.

11. Franz Halder (1884–1972) was a Bavarian artillery officer. He directed Artillery Command VII (1933–35) and the 7th Infantry Division in Munich (1935–36) before returning to the General Staff in Berlin in 1936. He became deputy chief of the General Staff in 1938 and chief of the General Staff late that year. Relieved by Hitler on September 24, 1942, his involvement in the anti-Hitler plotting of 1938 and 1939 was later discovered by the Gestapo, and he ended the war in a concentration camp.

12. Franz Halder, *The Halder War Diary, 1939-1942*, Charles Burdick and Hans-Adolf Jacobsen, eds. (Novato, CA: Presidio Press, 1988), entry for January 5, 1942.

13. Burkhart Mueller-Hillebrand, *Das Heer, 1933–1945: Entwicklung des organisatorischen Aufbaues* (Darmstadt, Germany: E. S. Mittler und Sohn, 1954–69), 3:Table 38.

14. Albert Seaton, *The German Army, 1933-1945* (New York: New American Library, 1982), 90.

15. Joachim Kramarz, *Stauffenberg: The Architect of the Famous July 20th Conspiracy to Assassinate Hitler* (New York: Macmillan, 1967), 95.

16. Also see Paul Carell, *Hitler Moves East, 1941–1943* (Boston: Little, Brown, 1965). Paul Carell (1911–97) was the pseudonym for Paul Karl Schmidt, who was press secretary for the Foreign Ministry from 1940 to 1945.

17. Alan S. Milward, *The German Economy at War* (London: University of London, Athlone Press, 1965), 17.

18. Juergen Thorwald, *The Illusion: Soviet Soldiers in Hitler's Armies*, Richard and Clara Winston, trans. (New York: Harcourt Brace Jovanovich, 1975), xiv–xv.

19. Kramarz, *Stauffenberg*, 98.

20. Earl F. Ziemke, *Stalingrad to Berlin: The German Defeat in the East* (Washington, DC: Office of the Chief of Military History, U.S. Army, 1968), 34.

21. Earl F. Ziemke and Magna E. Bauer, *Moscow to Stalingrad: Decision in the East* (Washington, DC: Center of Military History, United States Army, 1975), 283–303; *Kriegstagebuch des Oberkommando der Wehrmacht* (Frankfurt am Main, Germany: Bernard & Graefe, 1961–65), entry for 28 June 1942.

22. Hermann Plocher, "The German Air Force Versus Russia, 1943," manuscript on file at Maxwell Air Force Base, Alabama; R. J. Overy, *The Air War, 1939–1945* (New York: Stein and Day, 1980), 62.

23. As a lieutenant during World War I, Ernst Udet was part of Baron Manfred von Richthofen's "Flying Circus," whose last commander was his close personal friend, Hermann Goering. Udet ended the Great War with sixty-two kills, the most of any ace who survived the war. A high-school dropout with no General Staff or advanced industrial training, he was completely unqualified to head the *Luftwaffe's* most important technical office.

24. Cooper, *German Air Force*, 245.

25. Werner Moelders had been killed in an air accident near Breslau on November 22, 1941. He was returning to the Eastern Front after attending the funeral of Ernst Udet.

26. Adolf Galland, *The First and the Last: The Rise and Fall of the German Fighter Forces, 1938–1945* (New York: Holt, 1954), 87–88.

27. Dana V. Sadarananda, *Beyond Stalingrad: Manstein and the Operations of Army Group Don (New York: Praeger, 1990),* 7.

28. Manstein was the eleventh child of Gen. of Artillery Eduard von Lewinski (1829–1906) and his wife, but because his wife's sister was childless, Lewinski allowed his sister-in-law, Hedwig von Manstein (nee von Sperling), the daughter of Gen. Oskar von Sperling, to adopt him. Erich's stepfather was Gen. of Infantry Georg von Manstein. One of his brothers, Maj. Gen. Alfred von Lewinski, was killed in action in 1914. Another, August von Lewinski (1866–1957), retired as a major general in 1921. One of his uncles was Field Marshal Paul von Hindenburg, the victor of Tannenberg, who later served as president of Germany until his death in 1934.

Born to be a general, Erich von Manstein first saw the light of day in Berlin on November 24, 1885. He was educated in the cadet school system, was a member of the corps of pages to Kaiser Wilhelm II, graduated from Gross Lichterfelde (Germany's West Point), and entered the Imperial Army as a *Faehnrich* (senior officer cadet) in 1906. He was commissioned second lieutenant in the elite 3rd Guards Regiment of Foot on January 27, 1907. He entered the War Academy in 1913 to undergo General Staff training but did not complete the course because World War I began in August 1914. Manstein was nevertheless admitted to the elite General Staff. He went to the field as adjutant of the 2nd Guards Reserve Regiment and fought in Belgium and on the Eastern Front, where he was seriously wounded in November. When he was able to return to active duty eight months later, he was assigned to the staff of an army group and served in Poland and Serbia. He was promoted to captain in 1915 and became adjutant of the 12th Army and operations officer of the 4th Cavalry Division in Courland (1917–18), and he ended the war as Ia (chief of operations) of the 213th Reserve Assault Division on the Western Front. In 1920, he married Jutta von Loesch, who gave him two sons and a daughter. (His oldest son became an infantry officer and was killed in action on the Eastern Front in the fall of 1942.)

By the time Hitler came to power in 1933, Manstein was a lieutenant colonel commanding the *jaeger* battalion of the 4th Infantry Regiment at Kolberg. Later, he was chief of staff of Wehrkreis III in Berlin (1934–35), chief of the operations branch of the General Staff of the army (1935–36), deputy chief of the General Staff (1936–38), and commander of the 18th Infantry Division at Liegnitz (1938–39). He was chief of staff to Field Marshal Gerd von Rundstedt's Army Group South (later A) in the Polish campaign and in the preparation for the invasion of France (1939–40), was commander of the XXXVIII Corps in France (1940–41), commanded the LVI Panzer Corps in Russia (1941), and became commander of the 11th Army on the Eastern Front on September 1941, when Col. Gen. Ritter Eugen von Scholbert was killed in action. Among other things, Manstein originated the plan that conquered France (1940), the Crimea (1941), and the Soviet naval fortress of Sevastopol (1942). A tactical and strategic genius, he was promoted to field marshal on July 1, 1942. He was considered impressive even by the German generals, a group not exactly noted for its lack of arrogance. He was even respected by Adolf Hitler, who also feared him.

29. Friedrich Kirchner (1885–1960) was a Saxon. He had previously commanded the 1st Rifle Brigade (1938–39) and the 1st Panzer Division (1939–41). He led the LVII Panzer Corps from November 1941 until the end of the war. He managed to surrender to the western Allies.

30. The 11th Panzer Regiment was part of Maj. Gen. Erhard Raus's 6th Panzer Division. Raus was promoted to lieutenant general on January 1, 1943.

CHAPTER 2: MANSTEIN RESTORES THE SOUTHERN FLANK

1. Hans von Salmuth (born 1888) was promoted to colonel general on January 1, 1943. He had previously commanded the XXX Corps (1941), 17th Army (1942), and 4th Army (1942), and he had commanded the 2nd Army since July 15, 1942. Hitler, who was looking for scapegoats, would relieve him of his command on February 4, 1943, for failing to check Stalin's offensive. This earned the Nazis Salmuth's

undying hatred. Later, in June 1943, he was recalled to active duty and was named acting commander of the 4th Army and, in August 1943, became commander of the 15th Army in France and Belgium. Most German military experts thought that the Allied D-Day invasion would land in his sector, but they attacked the 7th Army in Normandy instead. Salmuth was sacked again on August 25, 1944, after the Gestapo learned that he had known about the Stauffenberg plot to overthrow Hitler, but had not done anything to warn the Nazis. He was convicted as a war criminal in 1948 for assisting *Einsatzgruppe D* in murdering Jews and was sentenced to twenty years' imprisonment, but he was released in 1953. He died during the night of December 31, 1961–January 1, 1962.

2. Sadarananda, *Beyond Stalingrad*, 32–33.
3. Balck was promoted to major general, effective January 1, 1943.
4. Officially, at this time, these divisions were designated SS Panzer Grenadier Division "Leibstandarte Adolf Hitler," SS Panzer Grenadier Division "Das Reich," and SS Panzer Grenadier Division "Totenkopf." The SS divisions did not officially receive their numerical designations until October 22, 1943—the same day all three divisions, as well as the SS Panzer Grenadier Division "Viking," were upgraded to panzer divisions. The numerical designations are nevertheless used here to avoid confusion.
5. Paul Carell, *Scorched Earth: The Russian-German War, 1943–1944* (Boston: Little, Brown, 1970), 130. The Annus Carell referred to was probably Gottfried Annuss, who was a lieutenant colonel and Ia of the 114th Jaeger Division in late 1944. Horst Scheibert, *Die Traeger des deutschen Kreuzes in Gold: Das Heer* (Friedberg, Germany: Podzun-Pallas-Verlag, 1983), 22.
6. The son of Field Marshal August von Mackensen (1849–1945), Eberhart was born in Bromberg, Posen province (now Bydgoszcz, Poland), in 1889. He joined the army as a *Fahnenjunker* (officer-cadet) in the 1st Hussar Regiment in 1908. He fought in World War I and was wounded in 1915, and he served in the *Reichsheer* and became commander of the 1st Cavalry Brigade in 1937. Later, he was chief of staff of the 14th (later 12th) Army (1939–42) and commanded the III Panzer Corps (January–December 1942). He was promoted to colonel general in July 1943 but was less than successful as commander of the 14th Army in Italy (1943–44). Relieved of his command by Field Marshal Kesselring on July 6, he was never reemployed. He was sentenced to death as a war criminal in 1947, but his sentence was commuted, and he was released in 1952. He died in Alt-Muehlendorf, near Nortorf, Schleswig-Holstein, in 1969. Keilig, *Die Generale des Heeres*, 214.
7. Sadarananda, *Beyond Stalingrad*, 93–94.
8. Hubert Lanz (1896–1982) had previously commanded the 1st Mountain Division (late 1940–43). He commanded the XXII Mountain Corps in the Balkans until the end of the war. Captured by the Americans in 1945, he was sentenced to twelve years' imprisonment as a "Southeastern" general in 1947 but was pardoned in January 1951.
9. Corps Cramer was commanded by Lt. Gen. (later Gen. of Panzer Troops) Hans Cramer (1896–1968), who was later the last commander of the Afrika Korps. He had previously commanded the XXXXVIII Panzer Corps (November 20–26, 1942), but he was not highly rated as a corps commander on the Eastern Front. His former colleagues in North Africa, however, thought more of him.

10. Sadarananda, *Beyond Stalingrad*, 101–2, 134. These exclude twenty tanks from the 27th Panzer Division which Army Group B had posted to its own headquarters. The 27th Panzer, which never exceeded regimental strength by much, was, in fact, scattered all over the map by the army group. At one point, it was broken into seven different battle groups, each fighting in a different location.

11. Hermann Plocher, "The German Air Force Versus Russia, 1942," manuscript on file at Maxwell Air Force Base, Alabama. See also Erich von Manstein, *Lost Victories* (Chicago: Regnery, 1958).

12. Sadarananda, *Beyond Stalingrad*, 88.

13. Ibid., 134.

14. Born in 1880, Hausser was the son of a Prussian officer and was himself a product of Gross Lichterfelde, Imperial Germany's equivalent of West Point, graduating in the same class was Guenther von Kluge. He was commissioned in 1899 and had had a long and distinguished career as a General Staff officer, retiring from the *Reichswehr* as a major general (with an honorary promotion to lieutenant general) in 1932. He joined the SS as a colonel in 1934, serving as commandant of the SS Officer Training School at Brunswick and as chief training officer for the *SS-Verfuegungstruppe* (SS-VT), the embryo of the Waffen-SS. Within a short period of time, he was named Inspector of SS Officer Schools and was a brigadier general by mid-1936. Intelligent and broad-minded in the areas of training and tactics, it was Hausser who saw to it that the SS-VT troops were the first to wear camouflaged uniforms in the field, despite the fact that the army troops laughed at them and called them "tree frogs." (These SS uniforms were very much like the present-day U.S. Army fatigues.) Hausser later commanded the first Waffen-SS combat division, the SS-VT, and led it with distinction in the French campaign. When it was broken up to form new SS divisions, Hausser took command of the "Das Reich" (later 2nd SS Panzer) Division. He took charge of the newly created SS Panzer Corps (1st and 2nd SS Panzer Grenadier Divisions) in May 1942. He was not the kind of officer to sacrifice his men to a senseless order, even if it came from Hitler.

15. Paul Carell, *Scorched Earth*, 196. See also Paul Carell, *Verbrannte Erde: Schlacht zwischen Wolga und Weichsel* (Berlin, Germany: Ullstein, 1966); and Samuel W. Mitcham Jr. and Gene Mueller, *Hitler's Commanders* (Lanham, MD: Scarborough House, 1992).

16. Sadarananda, *Beyond Stalingrad*, 88.

17. Alexander Stahlberg, *Bounden Duty: The Memoirs of a German Officer, 1932–45*, Patricia Crampton, trans. (Washington, DC: Brassey's, 1990), 270.

18. Ibid., 270–71.

19. Ibid., 275.

20. As of February 3, 1943. Georg Tessin, *Verbaende und Truppen der deutschen Wehrmacht und Waffen-SS im Zweiten Weltkrieg* (Osnabrueck, Germany: Biblio-Verlag, 1973–81), 2:7.

21. Carell, *Scorched Earth*, 214.

22. Manstein, *Lost Victories*, 433–34.

23. Sadarananda, *Beyond Stalingrad*, 145–46.

CHAPTER 3: THE DEFEAT OF THE GERMAN NAVY

1. Tonnage tabulated from Juergen Rohwer, *Axis Submarine Successes, 1939–1945* (Annapolis, MD: Naval Institute Press, 1983), 265–66.

2. Edwin P. Hoyt, *U-Boat Wars* (New York: Arbor House, 1984), 160.
3. Hinsch (1914–67) sank four ships and a British submarine during World War II. Erich Topp (1914–2005) sank thirty-five ships (197,460 gross registered tons) and the U.S. destroyer *Reuben James*. He later became a West German admiral and an architect in Remagen. His daughter married an American, and he visited Texas at Christmas for years.
4. Wolfgang Frank, *The Sea Wolves: The Story of German U-Boats at War* R. O. B. Long, trans. (New York: Rinehart, 1955), 125–26.
5. Ibid., 130.
6. A. E. Sokol, "German Attacks on the Murmansk Run," *Proceedings* 88 (December 1952): 1,328; Plocher, "The German Air Force versus Russia, 1942."
7. Sokol, "German Attacks on the Murmansk Run," 1,329.
8. Cajus Bekker, *The Luftwaffe War Diaries* (Garden City, NY: Doubleday, 1968), 391–93; Cyril March, ed., *The Rise and Fall of the German Air Force, 1933–1945* (London: Her Majesty's Stationery Office, 1948), 114.

   Hans-Juergen Stumpff (1889–1968) was born in Kolberg, East Prussia (now Kolobrzeg, Poland), and joined the army as an infantry officer-cadet in 1907. He joined the then-secret *Luftwaffe* in 1933, was its chief of personnel (1933–37) and chief of the General Staff (1937–early 1939). After a year as chief of Air Defense in the Air Ministry, he led 1st Air Fleet (1940) and 5th Air Fleet (May 10, 1940–November 6, 1943). Later, he was commander in chief of Air Fleet Reich (1944–45) and commander in chief of the *Luftwaffe* (May 8–23, 1945). He was tried as a war criminal for failing to protect downed Allied airmen from German civilians but was acquitted. He was released in October 1947 and settled in Frankfurt am Main.
9. March, *Rise and Fall of the German Air Force*, 114; Bekker, *Luftwaffe War Diaries*, 398; Carell, *Hitler Moves East*, 466–67.
10. Otto Schniewind (1887–1964) was born in Saarlouis, joined the navy as a senior officer-cadet in 1908, and was a torpedo boat commander during World War I. He spent most of the 1920s in the torpedo boat branch, commanded the cruiser *Koeln* (1934–37), and held a variety of senior posts at OKM. He became fleet commander on June 12, 1941, and held the post until July 30, 1944, when he was relieved by Grand Admiral Doenitz. He was promoted to *Generaladmiral* on March 1, 1944. Schniewind was tried at Nuremberg for war crimes, but was acquitted and released in October 1948. He died at Linz am Rhine.
11. Sokol, "German Attacks on the Murmansk Run," 1,336.
12. Cajus Bekker, *Hitler's Naval War*, Frank Ziegler, trans. and ed. (Garden City, NY: Doubleday, 1974), 279.
13. Bekker, *Luftwaffe War Diaries*, 398.
14. Ibid., 115; Carell, *Hitler Moves East*, 467.
15. Sokol, "German Attacks on the Murmansk Run," 1,336–37.
16. Ibid., 1,337.
17. Oskar Kummetz was born in the Neidenburg district of East Prussia (now Nidzica, Poland) in 1891. He joined the Imperial Navy as a senior officer-cadet in 1911 and served on battleships until 1916, when he transferred to the torpedo boat branch. He remained associated with coastal defense units for most of the rest of his career and was inspector of torpedo affairs from 1939 until the summer of 1942, when he

became commander of cruisers. He ended the war as commander in chief of Naval Group Baltic. Promoted to admiral on March 1, 1943, and to *Generaladmiral* in September 1944, he was a POW from 1945 to 1946. He died at Neustadt an der Weinstrasse, Rhineland-Palatinate, in late 1980.

18. Bekker, *Hitler's Naval War*, 283.
19. Pro-Nazi Theodor Krancke (1893–1973) had commanded the heavy cruiser ("pocket battleship") *Admiral Scheer* (1939–41), which he led on a highly successful raiding cruise in the Atlantic and Indian Oceans, during which he sank or captured seventeen Allied ships. He was later commander in chief of Naval Group West (1944–45) and Naval Group Norway (1945), where he was less successful.
20. Bekker, *Hitler's Naval War*, 290–94.
21. Shortly before Hitler committed suicide on April 30, 1945, he named Grand Admiral Doenitz President of the Reich and Supreme Commander of the *Wehrmacht*. Doenitz promoted Friedeburg to the rank of *Generaladmiral* and named him commander in chief of the navy on May 1. After leading the German surrender delegation to Field Marshal Montgomery, Friedeburg committed suicide on May 23, 1945. He had been born in Strassburg, Alsace, in 1895 and served on heavy cruisers and battleships until 1917, when he first served in the U-boats.
22. For the personnel records of all of the admirals involved in the Doenitz controversy, see volumes 1, 2, and 3 of Hans H. Hildebrand and Ernst Henriot, *Deutschlands Admirale, 1849–1945: Die Militaerischen Werdegaenge der See-, Ingenieur-, Sanitaets-, Waffen- und Verwaltungsoffiziere im Admiralsrang*, 4 vols. (Osnabrueck, Germany: Biblio, 1988–96).
23. Frank, *Sea Wolves*, 144–45; Rohwer, *Axis Submarine Successes*, 263–66. Karl–Friedrich Merten (1905–93) sank twenty-seven ships (170,151 gross registered tons) during World War II and was promoted to *Kapitaen zur See* in 1945. He commanded the 26th U-Boat Flotilla at Pillau (1943) and the 24th U-Boat Flotilla at Memel (1943–45). The latter was a training command. Immediately after the war, he helped run a ship-salvaging business on the Rhine. He worked in the West German shipping industry thereafter.
24. Frank, *Sea Wolves*, 144–45; Rohwer, *Axis Submarine Successes*, 263–66. Carl Emmermann (1915–90) sank twenty-six ships (152,080 gross registered tons) during World War II. He ended the war as a lieutenant commander (*Korvettenkapitaen*) and was commander of the 31st U-Boat Flotilla at Hamburg.

    Wolfgang Lueth was the number two U-boat ace of World War II, sinking forty-six ships (225,204 gross registered tons), as well as a French submarine. A strong Nazi, he was born in Riga, Latvia, in 1913, but his family was expelled to Germany after the war. Lueth studied law for three semesters but joined the navy in 1933. He sailed around the world on the light cruiser *Karlsruhe* but transferred to the submarines in 1937 and fought in the Spanish Civil War. He was given command of his own U-boat in late 1939. After a 205-day cruise (the second longest of the war), he became commander of the 22nd U-Boat Flotilla (a training command) and assumed command of Naval School Flemsburg-Muerwik in September 1944. Promoted to captain on September 1, 1944, he was shot by one of his own sentries on May 13, 1945, after he failed to answer the sentry's challenge. The weather was bad that night, and some historians have speculated that Lueth did answer the challenge, but his response was drowned out by the wind. The guard was tried and acquitted of any wrongdoing. Lueth received the last state funeral in the history of Nazi Germany.
25. Frank, *Sea Wolves*, 158–62.

CHAPTER 4: TUNISGRAD

1. Lloyd R. Fredendall (1883–1963) was simultaneously commander of the U.S. II Corps, a post he had held since 1941. Charles W. Ryder (1892–1960) was commander of the U.S. 34th Infantry Division. Later, he commanded the U.S. IX Corps in the Pacific (1944-48). Gen. George S. Patton Jr. (1885–1945) was the former commander of the U.S. 2nd Armored Division (1940–42).

2. Paul Carell, *The Foxes of the Desert*, Mervyn Savill, trans. (New York: Dutton, 1961), 310. Lungershausen was the commander of the 164th Light Afrika Division.

3. Ibid., 317.

4. Friedrich Ruge, *Der Seekrieg, 1939–1945* (Stuttgart, Germany: K. F. Koehler, 1954), 328.

5. Walter Nehring (1892–1983) was an armored pioneer and one of the founders of the *blitzkrieg*. He had commanded the 5th Panzer Regiment (1937–39), served as Guderian's chief of staff (1939–late 1940), and commanded the 18th Panzer Division in Russia (1941–42) and the Afrika Korps (1942). During World War I, he began training as an aerial observer. A week later, his airplane crashed, and he suffered a broken jaw. By the time he recovered, his ardor for flying had cooled, and he returned to the infantry.

6. This battery was part of the 20th Flak Division, which was just arriving in North Africa.

7. Baron von Broich (1896–1974) was an Alsacian who had spent his entire career in the cavalry. During World War II, he commanded the 6th, 21st, and 22nd Cavalry Regiments and the 1st Cavalry Brigade. The 1st Cavalry was converted into the 24th Panzer Grenadier Brigade in December 1941, which explains how Broich ended up in the armored branch. He was promoted to major general on January 1, 1943, and led the 10th Panzer Division from February 5, 1943, until it surrendered on May 12, 1943, despite being wounded and having to walk with a cane. His Ia was Col. Count Claus von Stauffenberg.

8. George F. Howe, *Northwest Africa: Seizing the Initiative in the West* (Washington, DC: Office of the Chief of Military History, Dept. of the Army, 1957), 280–83.

9. Joseph Goebbels, *The Goebbels Diaries*, Louis P. Lochner, trans. and ed (London: H. Hamilton, 1948).

10. Albert Kesselring, *Kesselring: A Soldier's Record*, Lynton Hudson, trans. (New York: Morrow, 1954), 169.

11. Gustav Fehn was born in Nuremberg, Franconia, in 1892 and joined the army as an infantry *Fahnenjunker* in 1911. During World War II, he commanded the 33rd Infantry Regiment (1939–40), 4th Rifle Brigade (1940), 5th Panzer Division (1940–42), and, briefly, the XXXX Panzer Corps (1942). He led the Afrika Korps until January 15, 1943, when he was seriously wounded. When he returned to active duty six months later, he was named acting commander of the XXVI Panzer Corps, which he led in the siege of Leningrad. He was then sent to the Balkans, where he commanded the XXI Mountain and XV Mountain Corps. He was murdered by Yugoslav partisans on June 5, 1945, a month after the end of the war.

12. Carell, *Foxes*, 313–14.

13. Hans-Juergen Theodor "Dieter" von Arnim was born at Ernsdorf, Silesia, in 1889. From the moment of his birth, he was destined for a military career, for his ancient Prussian family had produced officers for its fatherland since its first documented appearance in 1388. Arnim's father, Hans, retired as a major general, and his grandfather ended up as a lieutenant general. More than a dozen members of the various branches of his family served in World War II, including four generals.

Juergen entered the Royal Prussian Army as a *Fahnenjunker* in 1907, three days before his eighteenth birthday. He was commissioned in the elite 4th Prussian Foot Guards Regiment and followed a fairly standard career pattern for a young Prussian general-in-training. He fought on both the Eastern and Western Fronts, serving as a company commander, acting battalion commander, and regimental adjutant. Selected for the *Reichswehr* as a matter of course, he did his clandestine General Staff training in Berlin in the 1920s and was named commander of the 52nd Infantry Division when the war broke out. Strangely enough, the division as a whole was not engaged in the fighting in Poland (1939) or in France (1940). Despite this fact, Arnim was given command of the 17th Panzer Division in Munich in the fall of 1940, even though he had no previous training in or connection with the armored branch. His promotion can be explained only by his general competence and by the fact that he had friends in Berlin.

Arnim first saw action as panzer commander in Russia on June 22, 1941, but was seriously wounded on June 27 and hastily evacuated back to a military hospital in Poland. He returned to Russia and resumed command on September 17, replacing the acting commander, Maj. Gen. Ritter von Thoma.

14. Charles Whiting, *Kasserine: First Blood* (New York: Stein and Day, 1984), 116.
15. Dwight D. Eisenhower, *Crusade in Europe* (Garden City, NY: Doubleday, 1949), 124.
16. I. S. O. Playfair and C. J. C. Molony, *The Mediterranean and the Middle East*, vol. 4, *The Destruction of the Axis Forces in Africa* (London: H. M. Stationery Office, 1966), 274.
17. Chester Wilmot, *The Struggle for Europe* (New York: Harper, 1952), 123.
18. Albert C. Wedemeyer, *Wedemeyer Reports!* (New York: Holt, 1958), 95.
19. Georg Thomas nevertheless ended up in a concentration camp because his earlier role in anti-Hitler plots was uncovered by the Gestapo in 1944. His health was shattered, and he died in late 1946 at the age of fifty-six.
20. William B. Breuer, *Drop Zone Sicily: Allied Airborne Strike, July 1943* (Novato, CA: Presidio, 1983), xiv.
21. Giovanni Messe (1883–1968) had previously commanded Italian forces in Russia. Highly competent, he was promoted to marshal of Italy and became chief of the General Staff of the Royalist Italian forces operating against the Germans. He retired in 1947.
22. B. H. Liddell Hart, *History of the Second World War* (New York: Putnam, 1971), 2:402.
23. Martin Blumenson, *Kasserine Pass* (Boston: Houghton Mifflin, 1967), 177.
24. Whiting, *Kasserine*, 202.
25. Somewhat surprisingly, Hans-Georg Hildebrandt (1896–1967) was promoted to major general on March 1, 1943. He was replaced as divisional commander fifteen days later by Maj. Gen. Heinrich-Hermann von Huelsen (1895–1982), who surrendered the elite 21st Panzer Division to the British on May 13, 1943. Like Hildebrandt and Broich, Huelsen had spent most of his career in the cavalry. Hildebrandt later commanded the 715th Infantry Division and the Italian 3rd Infantry Division in Italy.
26. Blumenson, *Kasserine Pass*, 236.
27. Whiting, *Kasserine*, 212.
28. Playfair and Molony, *The Destruction of the Axis Forces in Africa*, Map 29, ff. 286.
29. Westphal (1902–82) had previously been Rommel's Ia and chief of staff. He ended the war as a general of cavalry and chief of staff of OB West. He was very proud of

the fact that he had briefly served as acting commander of the 164th Light Afrika Division in December 1942.

30. Liddell Hart, *Second World War*, 411.

31. Manteuffel later commanded the 7th Panzer Division and the Grossdeutschland Panzer Grenadier Division in Russia, the 5th Panzer Army in the Battle of the Bulge, and the 3rd Panzer Army on the Eastern Front.

32. Blumenson, *Kasserine Pass*, 299.

33. Erwin Rommel, *The Rommel Papers*, B. H. Liddell Hart, ed. (New York: Harcourt, Brace, 1953), 415.

34. Howe, *Northwest Africa*, 510; Liddell Hart, *Second World War*, 2:412.

35. Playfair and Molony, *The Destruction of the Axis Forces in Africa*, 359.

36. Trevor J. Constable and Raymond F. Toliver, *Horrido! Fighter Aces of the Luftwaffe* (New York: Macmillan, 1968), 227.

37. Cooper, *German Air Force*, 216–17.

38. Count Theodor von Sponeck (1896–1982) had previously served as Ia of the XV Motorized (later Panzer) Corps (1938–40) and commander of the 11th Rifle Brigade in Russia (1940–early 1942). He was unemployed from January to November 1, 1942, when he assumed command of the 90th Light. This period of unemployment was apparently because of the fact that his older cousin, Lt. Gen. Hans von Sponeck, the commander of the XXXXII Corps in the Crimea, had run afoul of Hitler, who personally ordered him thrown into prison. Hans was executed without trial on July 23, 1944. When the African Front collapsed, Theodor made no attempt to escape back into Nazi Germany, as did several of his peers. He spent most of the rest of the war in a POW camp in Dermott, Arkansas.

39. Fritz Krause (1895–1975) had commanded Rommel's artillery since late 1941. He was the Higher Artillery Commander in Afrika until he assumed command of the 334th. He had briefly served as acting commander of the 164th Light Afrika Division (January 16–March 13, 1943). He was captured near Bizerte on May 9 and was a POW until June 1947. He had entered the service in 1913.

    Friedrich Weber (1892–1974) later commanded the 298th and 131st Infantry Divisions, as well as Division Warsaw. He was relieved of his command on January 25, 1945, for complicity in the unauthorized evacuation of the Polish capital and was lucky he was not shot or imprisoned by the Nazis. He had joined the Imperial Army as a *Fahnenjunker* in the Bavarian 2nd Foot Artillery Regiment when World War I began and was promoted to lieutenant general in 1944.

40. Playfair and Molony, *The Destruction of the Axis Forces in Africa*, 460.

41. Baron Kurt von Liebenstein (1899–1975) had previously been chief of staff of Col. Gen. Heinz Guderian's 2nd Panzer Army and commander of the 6th Panzer Regiment on the Eastern Front. After the war, he became commander the V Military District (a corps-level command) in the West German Army.

42. Blumenson, *Kasserine Pass*, 311.

43. Seaton, *German Army*, 198.

CHAPTER 5: THE BOMBING INTENSIFIES

1. Adolphe Goutard, *The Battle of France, 1940*, A. R. P. Burgess, trans. (New York: I. Washburn, 1959), 39.

2. Ibid.

3. Richard Suchenwirth, "Command and Leadership in the German Air Force," United States Air Force Historical Studies Number 174 (1969).

4. Cooper, *German Air Force*, 261.

5. Richard Suchenwirth, "Historical Turning Points in the German Air Force War Effort," United States Air Force Historical Studies Number 189 (1969).

6. Hereafter referred to as U.S. Air Force. Although it did not become an independent service until 1947, I will refer to it as the United States Air Force for the sake of clarity and convenience.

7. Noble Frankland, *Bomber Offensive: The Devastation of Europe* (New York: Ballantine Books, 1970), 59; Walter A. Musciano, *Messerschmitt Aces* (New York: Arco, 1982), 57.

8. Earl R. Beck, *Under the Bombs: The German Home Front, 1942–1945* (Lexington, KY: University Press of Kentucky, 1986), 46.

9. *True to Type: A Selection from Letters and Diaries of German Soldiers and Civilians, Collected on the Soviet German Front* (New York: Hutchinson & Co., 1945), 132.

10. Frankland, *Bomber Offensive*, 59–60.

11. Beck, *Under the Bombs*, 48.

12. David Irving, *The Rise and Fall of the Luftwaffe: The Life of Luftwaffe Marshal Erhard Milch* (London: Weidenfeld & Nicolson, 1973), 207–8, 273; Frankland, *Bomber Offensive*, 61.

13. Kit C. Carter and Robert Mueller, comp., *The Army Air Forces in World War II: Combat Chronology, 1941–1945* (Maxwell, AL: Albert F. Simpson Historical Research Center, Air University, 1975), 116–23.

14. Irving, *Rise and Fall of the Luftwaffe*, 215.

15. Sybil Bannister, *I Lived under Hitler: An English Woman's Story* (London: Rockliff, 1957), 145–54.

16. Irving, *Rise and Fall of the Luftwaffe*, 215–16; Beck, *Under the Bombs*, 61–62.

17. Goebbels, *Diaries*, May 25, 1943.

18. Toliver and Constable, *Horrido!*, 155–56.

19. Beck, *Under the Bombs*, 68–70.

20. Irving, *Rise and Fall of the Luftwaffe*, 230.

21. Albert Speer, *Inside the Third Reich: Memoirs*, Richard and Clara Winston, trans. (New York: Macmillan, 1970), 281.

22. Hans-Georg von Studnitz, *While Berlin Burns: The Diary of Hans-Georg von Studnitz, 1943–1945* (Englewood Cliffs, NJ: Prentice-Hall, 1964), 93.

23. Galland, *First and the Last*, 174.

24. Frankland, *Bomber Offensive*, 72–74.

25. Marie Vassiltchikov, *Berlin Diaries, 1940–1945* (New York: Knopf, 1985), December 22, 1943.

26. Hubert Weise (1884–1950) was commander of Luftwaffe Command Center, the air defense region which included northern Germany and Denmark (1940–44). Held partially responsible for the Hamburg debacle, he was placed in Fuehrer Reserve in early 1944. He returned to active duty in March 1944 as chief of the Flak Technical Office. Previously, he commanded the I Flak Corps (1939–41).

27. Galland, *First and the Last*, 174.

28. Leonard Mosley, *The Reich Marshal: A Biography of Hermann Goering* (Garden City, NY: Doubleday, 1974), 368–69.

CHAPTER 6: THE STATE OF THE WEHRMACHT, SPRING 1943

1. Albert Seaton, *The Russo-German War, 1941–45* (New York: Praeger, 1971), 352.
2. *Kriegstagebuch des Oberkommando des Wehrmacht*, entry for January 23, 1943. These figures do not include assault guns.
3. Geoffrey Jukes, *Kursk: The Clash of Armour* (New York: Ballantine Books, 1968), 25.
4. Seaton, *Russo-German War*, 200.
5. Juergen E. Foerster, "The Dynamics of Volkegemeinschaft: The Effectiveness of German Military Establishment in the Second World War," in Alan R. Millet and Williamson Murray, eds., *Military Effectiveness*, vol. 3, *The Second World War* (Boston: Unwin Hyman, 1988), 190.
6. Mueller-Hillebrand, *Das Heer*, 3: Tables 48–50.
7. Matthew Cooper, *The German Army, 1933–1945: Its Political and Military Failure* (New York: Stein and Day, 1978), 453.
8. Foerster, "Dynamics of Volkegemeinschaft," 207–8.
9. Kramarz, *Stauffenberg*, 92.
10. Wegner, Bernd. "The 'Aristocracy of National Socialism': The Role of the SS in National Socialist Germany," in H. W. Koch, ed., *Aspects of the Third Reich* (New York: St. Martin's Press, 1985), 222.
11. Ibid., 440.
12. Albert Speer, *Infiltration: How Heinrich Himmler Schemed to Build an SS Industrial Empire*, Joachim Neugroschel, trans. (New York: Macmillan, 1981).
13. Kramarz, *Stauffenberg*, 92.

CHAPTER 7: HITLER'S SUMMER OFFENSIVE

1. Carell, *Scorched Earth*, 295–304. Paul Laux was born in Weimar, Thuringia, in 1887 and joined the army as an infantry *Fahnenjunker* in 1908. A major when Hitler came to power in 1933, he rose to the rank of general of infantry in 1942. Before that, he commanded the 24th Infantry Regiment (1935–37), 10th Infantry Command (1938–39), 126th Infantry Division (1940–42), II Corps (1942–44), and 16th Army (July–September 1944). General Laux was killed near Riga on September 3, 1944, when the reconnaissance airplane he was in was shot down.
2. Carell, *Scorched Earth*, 313.
3. Heinz Guderian, *Panzer Leader*, Constantine Fitzgibbon, trans. (New York: Dutton, 1952), 246–47.
4. Martin Caidin, *The Tigers Are Burning* (New York: Hawthorn Books, 1974), 79.
5. Ibid., 118.
6. Adolf Heusinger was born in Holzminden, Lower Saxony, in 1896 and joined the army as a *Fahnenjunker* in 1915. He was so seriously wounded at Verdun that December that he could not return to active duty for more than a year. He was wounded twice in Flanders in 1917 and was captured by the British in July. Released after the armistice, he served in the infantry until 1926, when he began his secret General Staff training. Thereafter, he alternated between infantry and General Staff assignments, and in 1935, he became Ia of the 11th Infantry Division in Allenstein, East Prussia. He was assigned to the operations staff at OKH in 1937 and became chief of operations in October 1940. He was named deputy chief of the General Staff in June 1944 while retaining his previous position. Promoted to colonel (1940), major general (1941), and lieutenant general (January 1, 1943), he

was arrested by the Gestapo on July 22, 1944, for suspected involvement in the July 20 attempt to overthrow Adolf Hitler—despite the fact that Heusinger was in the room with the dictator when the bomb went off and was painfully wounded. (He was, in fact, speaking at the time.) He was released in October and never reemployed. Heusinger later became a full general in the West German Army, retired in 1964, and died in Cologne in 1982. Until the day he died, Heusinger was convinced that the chief of the General Staff, Kurt Zeitzler, knew about the assassination attempt of July 20, 1944, before it took place. He never forgave Zeitzler for leaving him in the room with the bomb. Zeitzler himself was nowhere near the place when the bomb exploded.

7. Otto von Knobelsdorff (1886–1966) was a Gross-Lichterfeld graduate who joined the army in 1905. He distinguished himself during World War I as a company commander and a General Staff officer. A major general in 1939, he became a general of panzer troops in 1942. In the process, he served as commander of the 102nd Infantry Regiment (1935–39), chief of staff of the XXXIII Corps Command (1939), and commander of the 19th Infantry (later 19th Panzer) Division (1940–early 1942), X Corps (1942), II Corps (1942), and XXIV Panzer Corps (1942). He had led the XXXXVIII Panzer Corps since December 4, 1943. Later in the war, he commanded the XXXX Panzer Corps in Russia (1944) and the 1st Army on the Western Front. He was relieved of his command on November 30, 1944, for losing ground and for opposing Hitler's Ardennes offensive. He was never reemployed.

8. Luftwaffe Command East was redesignated 6th Air Fleet on May 11, 1943. Dessloch succeeded Richthofen as commander of the 4th Air Fleet on June 12, 1943.

9. Hermann Hoth was born in Neurppin, north Brandenburg, in 1885. A product of the cadet schools, he joined the 72nd Infantry Regiment as a *Faehnrich* in 1904. By 1932, he was commander of the 17th Infantry Regiment. Later, he became Infantry Leader III (1934) and then commander of the 18th Infantry Division (1935), XV Motorized (later Panzer) Corps (1939–40), 3rd Panzer Group (1940–41), and 17th Army (October 5, 1941). He assumed command of the 4th Panzer Army on June 1, 1942.

10. Caidin, *Tigers Are Burning*, 224.

11. Dietrich von Saucken (1892–1980) was a very brave officer and one of the twenty-seven holders of the Knights Cross with Oak Leaves, Swords, and Diamonds. He had previously commanded the 2nd Cavalry Regiment (1937–40), 4th Rifle Brigade (1940–41), and School for Mobile Troops (1942–43), and he had been acting commander of the 4th Panzer Division for almost a week at the end of 1941. On May 31, 1943, he began his second tour as commander of the 4th Panzer. Later, he led the XXXIX Panzer Corps (1944), Grossdeutschland Panzer Corps (1944–45), and 2nd Army in his native East Prussia. He surrendered to the Russians in May 1945 and spent ten years in Soviet prison camps.

12. Jukes, *Kursk*, 91.

13. August Schmidt (1893–1972) was a Bavarian infantryman. He fought in World War I, served in the *Reichsheer*, and commanded the 20th Infantry Regiment (1939–40) and 21st Infantry Regiment (1940–41) before assuming command of the 10th Motorized Infantry (later Panzer Grenadier) Division on April 25, 1942. He was captured in Romania in September 1944 and remained in Soviet POW camps until October 1955.

14. Rudolf Schmidt retired to Krefeld, North Rhine-Westphalia, where he died on April 7, 1957.

15. Musciano, *Messerschmitt Aces*, 53; Plocher, "The German Air Force Versus Russia, 1943."

16. Mikhail Katukov (1900–76) later became a marshal of the Soviet Union and inspector general of the army in the 1960s.

17. Pat McTaggart, "War's Greatest Tank Duel," *World War II* (June 1993): 34.

18. Keilig, *Die Generale des Heeres*, 164.

19. Hans-Ulrich Rudel, the son of a Lutheran minister, was born in Silesia in 1911. He became the most successful dive-bomber pilot in history. During the campaign in the East, he flew 2,530 combat missions and destroyed 519 tanks, 800 other vehicles, 150 artillery pieces and self-propelled guns, a destroyer, 2 cruisers, the battleship *Marat*, four armored trains, and 70 landing craft. He also shot down 9 enemy aircraft. He was shot down or forced to make emergency landings thirty-two times and was wounded five times. The last time he lost a leg, but he continued flying. Stalin himself placed a 100,000-ruble bounty on Rudel's head, but it was never collected. Rudel was promoted from lieutenant in 1941 to colonel in 1945 and was the only man awarded the Knights Cross with Golden Oak Leaves, Swords, and Diamonds. He died in Rosenheim, Bavaria, in 1982.

20. Caidin, *Tigers Are Burning*, 225.

21. McTaggart, "Tank Duel," 35.

22. Ibid., 36.

23. Ibid.

24. Jukes, *Kursk*, 103.

25. Mueller-Hillebrand, *Das Heer*, 3:Table 55.

CHAPTER 8: THE RETREAT BEGINS IN THE EAST

1. Peter Young, ed., *The Marshal Cavendish Illustrated Encyclopedia of World War II: An Objective, Chronological, and Comprehensive History of the Second World War* (New York: Marshall Cavendish, 1981), 5:1,197–98.

2. Plocher, "The German Air Force versus Russia, 1942."

3. Ibid.

4. Ibid.

5. Jukes, *Kursk*, 110.

6. Ibid., 114–15.

7. Ziemke, *Stalingrad to Berlin*, 139.

8. Young, *Encyclopedia of World War II*, 5:1,200.

9. Omar Bartov, *The Eastern Front, 1941–45: German Troops and the Barbarisation of Warfare* (New York: St. Martin's Press, 1986), 140–41.

10. Ziemke, *Stalingrad to Berlin*, 151.

11. Jukes, *Kursk*, 115.

12. Ziemke, *Stalingrad to Berlin*, 151.

13. Caidin, *Tigers Are Burning*, 248.

14. Otto Woehler was born in Grossburgwedel, Lower Saxony, in 1984. He joined the Imperial Army as an infantry officer-cadet in 1913, fought in World War I, served in the *Reichswehr*, and was Ia of the 14th Army in the Polish campaign. He became chief of staff of the XVII Corps (1939), 11th Army (1940), and Army Group Center

(1942–43). He was named commanding officer of the I Corps on April 1, 1943, and was promoted rapidly from major to lieutenant colonel (1935), colonel (1938), major general (1942), lieutenant general (1942), and general of infantry (1943). He later commanded Army Group South from December 28, 1944, to March 25, 1945, when Hitler sacked him. He retired to the town of his birth, where he died in 1987.

15. Paul John von Ruhland, *As the World Churns* (New York: Vantage Press, 1986), 92.

16. *True to Type*, 18.

17. Ibid., 119.

18. Ruhland, *As the World Churns*, 120.

19. Johannes Steinhoff et al., *Voices from the Third Reich: An Oral History* (Washington, DC: Regnery Gateway, 1989), 277–78. Greffrath now lives in Berlin.

20. Seaton, *German Army*, 212.

21. Maximilian Fretter-Pico, *Missbrauchte Infanterie: Deutsche Infanteriedivisionen im osteuropaeischen Grossraum 1941 bis 1944: Erlebnisskizzen, Erfahrungen und Erkenntnisse* (Frankfurt am Main, Germany: Verlag fuer Wehrwesen Bernard & Graefe, 1957), 121.

CHAPTER 9: DECAY AND DISARRAY IN THE MEDITERRANEAN

1. Elizabeth Wiskemann, *The Rome-Berlin Axis: A History of the Relations between Hitler and Mussolini* (New York: Oxford University Press, 1949), 1.

2. Henri Nogueres, *Munich: Peace for Our Time*, Patrick O'Brian, trans. (New York: McGraw-Hill, 1965), 152n.

3. Trumbull Higgins, *Soft Underbelly: The Anglo-American Controversy over the Italian Campaign, 1939–1945* (New York: Macmillan, 1968), 1.

4. D. J. Goodspeed, *The German Wars, 1914–1945* (New York: Bonanza Books, 1977), 17.

5. Heinrich von Vietinghoff, "Overall Situation in the Mediterranean," Foreign Military Studies MS # D-116.

6. Wiskemann, *Rome-Berlin Axis*, 296; Albert N. Garland and Howard McGaw Smyth, *Sicily and the Surrender of Italy* (Washington, DC: Office of the Chief of Military History, Department of the Army, 1965), 38.

7. Siegfried Westphal, *The German Army in the West* (London: Cassell, 1951), 139.

8. Burkhart Mueller-Hillebrand, *Germany and Its Allies: A Record of Axis Collaboration Problems* (Frederick, MD: University Publications of America, 1980), 118.

9. Garland and Smyth, *Sicily and the Surrender of Italy*, 37.

10. Pietro Badoglio, *Italy in the Second World War: Memories and Documents*, Muriel Currey, trans. (Westport, CT: Greenwood Press, 1976), 48.

11. Wiskemann, *Rome-Berlin Axis*, 277.

12. Badoglio, *Italy in the Second World War*, 32.

13. For the full story of Operation Mincemeat, see Ewen Montgau, *The Man Who Never Was* (Philadelphia: Lippincott, 1954).

14. "Fuehrer Conferences on Naval Affairs, 1943," in H. G. Thursfield, ed., *Brassey's Naval Annual, 1948* (London: Clowes and Sons, 1948), 327.

15. G. W. L. Nicholson, *The Official History of the Canadian Army in the Second World War*, vol. 2, *The Canadians in Italy* (Ottawa: Queen's Printer, 1966), 61–62.

16. Ibid., 58.

17. Kesselring, *Soldier's Record*, 193.

18. Hugh Pond, *Sicily* (London: W. Kimber, 1962), 11.

19. Ibid., 27.

20. Nicholson, *Canadians in Italy*, 57.

21. Westphal, *German Army in the West*, 139.

22. For details of the measures Roatta took to improve the defenses of Sicily, see Samuel W. Mitcham Jr. and Friedrich von Stauffenberg, *The Battle of Sicily: How the Allies Lost Their Chance for Total Victory* (Mechanicsburg, PA: Stackpole Books, 2007).

23. Magna E. Bauer, "Axis Tactical Operations in Sicily," MS # R-138 to MS # R-141. (U.S. Army War College, n.d.)

24. Fridolin von Senger und Etterlin, "Liaison Activities with the Italian 6th Army," Foreign Military Studies MS # C-095.

25. Fridolin von Senger und Etterlin, "War Diary of the Italian Campaign: Sardinia and Corsica," Foreign Military Studies MS # C-095a.

26. Ibid.

27. Senger, "Liaison Activities with the Italian 6th Army."

28. March, *Rise and Fall of the German Air Force*, 258.

29. Johannes Steinhoff, *The Straits of Messina: Diary of a Fighter Commander*, Peter and Betty Ross, trans. (London: Deutsch, 1971), 132–33.

CHAPTER 10: THE ALLIED INVASION OF SOUTHERN EUROPE

1. Hart, *Second World War*, 2:439.

2. Wedemeyer, *Wedemeyer Reports*, 168–69.

3. Samuel Eliot Morison, *History of United States Naval Operations in World War II*, vol. 9, *Sicily-Salerno-Anzio* (Boston: Little, Brown, 1962).

4. Wedemeyer, *Wedemeyer Reports*, 189.

5. Ibid., 235, 241.

6. Carlo D'Este, *Bitter Victory: The Battle for Sicily* (New York: E. P. Dutton, 1988), 289.

7. Pond, *Sicily*, 108.

8. Bauer, "Axis Tactical Operations in Sicily," MS # R-139.

9. Liddell Hart, *Second World War*, 2:442.

10. Nicholson, *Canadians in Italy*, 82–83.

11. Kesselring, *Soldier's Record*, 196.

12. Nigel Hamilton, *Master of the Battlefield: Monty's War Years, 1942–1944* (New York: McGraw-Hill, 1983), 303.

13. Pond, *Sicily*, 115.

14. Francis de Guingand, *Operation Victory* (London: Hodder and Stoughton, 1947), 298–99.

15. Pond, *Sicily*, 142.

16. Guingand, *Operation Victory*, 298–99.

17. Ibid., 299.

18. Pond, *Sicily*, 132.

19. Nicholson, *Canadians in Italy*, 116 (citing OKW SITREP, 13 July 1943).

20. Albert Seaton, *The Fall of Fortress Europe, 1943–1945* (New York: Holmes & Meier Publishers, 1981), 77.

CHAPTER 11: THE FALL OF FASCISM AND THE LOSS OF SICILY

1. Albert Kesselring, "Special Reports on the Events in Italy between 25 July and 8 September 1943," Foreign Military Studies MS # C-013.
2. Westphal, *German Army in the West*, 137.
3. Melton S. Davis, *Who Defends Rome? The Forty-Five Days, July 25–September 8, 1943* (New York: Dial Press, 1972), 133. Grandi was born in Bologna province in 1895. He became a lawyer and an early Fascist and joined the Blackshirts at the age of twenty-five. A Fascist member of the Chamber of Deputies in 1921, he took part in the march on Rome in 1922. Over the next twenty years, he served Mussolini as undersecretary in the interior ministry, minister of foreign affairs (1929–32), ambassador to London, and minister of justice (1939–41). He opposed the alliance with the Germans and the Italian entry to World War II. After being double-crossed by the king, Grandi had the good sense to flee to Spain—unlike Ciano, who was later captured by Mussolini's confederates, tried, and then executed. Grandi later lived in Portugal and Brazil before returning to Italy in the 1960s after postwar passions had cooled down. He died in Bologna in 1988.
4. Badoglio, *Italy in the Second World War*, 46.
5. Irving, *Hitler's War* (New York: Viking Press, 1977), 2:597.
6. John Strawson, *Hitler's Battles for Europe* (New York: Scribner, 1971), 178.
7. Kesselring, "Special Reports on the Events in Italy Between 25 July and 8 September 1943."
8. Garland and Smyth, *Sicily and the Surrender of Italy*, 273.
9. Irving, *Hitler's War*, 2:600.
10. Ibid., 600–601.
11. See Mitcham and Stauffenberg, *Battle of Sicily*, for the details of these battles.
12. The arrival of the 2nd Parachute Division in the Rome area surprised OB South as much as it did the Italians. Hitler had not seen fit to inform Kesselring that it was coming.
13. Higgins, *Soft Underbelly*, 94.
14. Galland and Smyth, *Sicily and the Surrender of Italy*, 297.
15. Davis, *Who Defends Rome?*, 230.
16. Winston S. Churchill, *Closing the Ring* (Boston: Houghton Mifflin, 1951), 102. Anthony Eden (1897–1977) served three terms as foreign secretary in the 1935–55 period, as well as a tour as secretary of state for war (1940). He became deputy prime minister in 1951 and succeeded Churchill as prime minister in 1955. He served until early 1957.
17. C. J. C. Molony et al., *The Mediterranean and Middle East*, vol. 5, *The Campaign in Sicily and the Campaign in Italy* (London: H.M. Stationery Office, 1973), 168.
18. Heinrich von Vietinghoff, "Die Kaempfe der 10. Armee in Sued- und Mittelitalien," in Siegfried Westphal et al., "Feldzug in Italien," Foreign Military Studies MS # T-1a.
19. Garland and Smyth, *Sicily and the Surrender of Italy*, 417; Robert Wallace and the Editors of Time-Life Books, *The Italian Campaign* (Alexandria, VA: Time-Life Books, 1978), 33; Breuer, *Drop Zone Sicily*, 201.
20. Bauer, "Axis Tactical Operations in Sicily," MS # R-139.

CHAPTER 12: CRACKING THE FLOODGATES: THE RUSSIAN FRONT FROM 1943 TO EARLY 1944

1. Kramarz, *Stauffenberg*, 152.
2. Kurt Zeitzler, "Men and Space in War: A German Problem in World War II," *Military Review* 42 (April 1962): 87–88.
3. Ibid., 88–89.
4. Ibid., 89.
5. Ibid., 90–91.
6. Jukes, *Kursk*, 41.
7. Foerster, "Dynamics of Volkegemeinschaft," 211.
8. French L. MacLean, "German General Officer Casualties in World War II: Lessons for Future War," *Military Review* 70 (April 1990): 46.
9. Foerster, "Dynamics of Volkegemeinschaft," 208.
10. Ibid.
11. Siegfried Knappe, *At What Cost!* Manuscript in possession of the author. A modified version of this book was later published as *Soldat: Reflections of a German Soldier, 1936–1949* (New York: Orion Books, 1992).
12. Young, *Encyclopedia of World War II*, 5:120.
13. Ziemke, *Stalingrad to Berlin*, 207.
14. After the war, Hermann Hoth was convicted as a minor war criminal in late 1948 and sentenced to fifteen years in prison at Landsberg, where Hitler was imprisoned in 1924. He was released in 1954 and died in Goslar am Harz on January 25, 1971, at age eighty-five.
15. The 18th Artillery Division was a mobile division created from remnants of the 18th Panzer Division.
16. Like Kleist, Manstein was never reemployed. He was captured by the British at the end of the war and tried as a war criminal by a British military court in Hamburg in late 1949 after four years of imprisonment. He was acquitted of two indictments concerning the massacre of Jews but was convicted of neglecting to protect civilian life and sentenced to eighteen years' imprisonment. He may have been guilty of war crimes, but his trial was unfair; the prosecution was allowed to alter the charges after the defense (which was forced to present its case first) had rested. Many Allied observers were outraged by this unfair behavior, including the famous British military historian B. H. Liddell Hart. As a result of pressure applied by Hart and like-minded people, Manstein was released in May 1953. He later worked as an advisor to the West German government and wrote his memoirs, *Lost Victories*. He died at Irschenhausen, Bavaria on June 12, 1973, at the age of eighty-five.

    Ewald von Kleist retired to Weidebrueck, Silesia, but he fled when the Russians invaded Silesia in early 1945. He was apparently captured by the U.S. 26th Infantry Division on April 25, 1945, although at least one source says he was captured by the British. In any case, he was turned over to the Yugoslavs, who conducted an extremely questionable trial and sentenced him to fifteen years' imprisonment as a war criminal in 1946. He was handed over to the Soviets in 1948. He was not permitted to correspond with his family until March 1954, when he was allowed to write and receive one postcard per month. He died on October 15, 1954, as the only one of Hitler's marshals to die in Soviet captivity. He had at least eleven grandchildren but never saw one of them. He was buried in an unmarked grave.

17. Karl Adolf Hollidt settled in Westphalia. From February 20 to April 17, 1945, he served as military advisor to the Gauleiter of Rhineland-Westphalia. He was tried at Nuremberg and sentenced to five years' imprisonment at Landsberg. Released just before Christmas 1949, he died at Siegen, Westphalia, in 1985 at age ninety-four.

18. Erwin Jaenecke was arrested by the Soviets in June 1945, tried, and sentenced to twenty-five years' imprisonment. He was released in October 1955 in a general amnesty engineered by West German Chancellor Konrad Adenauer. Jaenecke settled in Cologne. He died in 1960 at the age of seventy.

19. Ernst von Leyser was born in Steglitz, a borough of Berlin, in 1889. He was educated in the cadet schools and joined the Imperial Army as a lieutenant in the 5th Guards Regiment in 1909. He fought in World War I, serving progressively as a platoon leader, battalion adjutant, company commander, regimental adjutant, and battalion commander. Discharged as a captain at the end of 1920, he joined the police but returned to active duty as a lieutenant colonel in 1935. During World War II, he commanded the 6th Replacement Regiment (1939), 169th Infantry Regiment (1939–41), 269th Infantry Division (April 1941–September 1942), XXVI Corps (October 1, 1942–October 1943), XV Mountain Corps (November 1943–July 1944), and XXI Mountain Corps (August 1, 1944–end). The last two assignments were in the Balkans. He surrendered to the Americans. Tried as a war criminal in Yugoslavia, he was sentenced to ten years' imprisonment in 1947, but he was released in 1951. He settled in Garstedt, where he died in 1962.

20. Ziemke, *Stalingrad to Berlin*, 257–58.

21. Georg von Kuechler was never reemployed. He was tried at Nuremberg as a minor war criminal and sentenced to twenty years' imprisonment in 1948 for his treatment of partisans in Russia. He was released in February 1955 and retired to a village in the Garmisch-Partenkirchen area. He died on May 25, 1968, five days short of his seventy-eighth birthday.

22. Johannes Friessner was born in Chemnitz, Saxony, in 1892 and joined the army as a *Fahnenjunker* in the infantry in 1911. He fought in World War I, became a General Staff trainee in 1916, served in the *Reichswehr*, and was a colonel and chief of staff to the Inspector of War Schools when World War II began. He served on the staff of the Home Army until May 1, 1942, when he became commander of the 102nd Infantry Division on the Russian Front. He assumed command of the XXIII Corps on January 19, 1943, and was promoted to general of infantry on April 1, 1943.

CHAPTER 13: THE ITALIAN DEFECTION AND THE BATTLE OF SALERNO

1. Senger, "Liaison Activities with the Italian 6th Army," MS # C-095.

2. The headquarters of Army Group B included some of Rommel's staff members from North Africa and former members of Field Marshal Baron von Weichs's staff of Army Group B, which had recently been recalled from Russia.

3. Garland and Smyth, *Sicily and the Surrender of Italy*, 505–7.

4. Martin Blumenson, *Salerno to Cassino* (Washington, DC: Office of the Chief of Military History, U.S. Army, 1969), 69.

5. Wallace, *Italian Campaign*, 51.

6. Irving, *Hitler's War*, 584.

7. Kesselring, *Soldier's Record*, 225.

8. Garland and Smyth, *Sicily and the Surrender of Italy*, 534.
9. Rudolf Boehmler and Werner Haupt, *Fallschirmjaeger, 1939–1945: Weg und Schicksal einer Truppe* (Friedberg, Germany: Podzun-Pallas-Verlag, 1979), 163.
10. See Peter C. Smith and Edwin Walker, *War in the Aegean* (London: Kimber, 1974; reprint ed., Stackpole Books, 2008), and Friedrich-August von Metzsch, *Die Geschichte der 22. Infanterie-Division, 1939–1945* (Kiel, Germany: H. H. Podzun, 1952), for the story of the eastern Aegean campaign.

   Friedrich-Wilhelm Mueller was born in Mannheim, Baden, in 1897 and joined the army as a war volunteer in 1914. He earned a reserve commission the following year at the age of eighteen. He was not selected for the *Reichswehr*, so he joined the police and returned to the army as a major in 1935. He commanded the III Battalion of the 105th Infantry Regiment (1935–40) at Zweibruecken, on the Saar-Mosel, and in the French campaign, and the regiment itself on occupation duty and on the Russian Front (1940–42). He assumed command of the 22nd Air Landing Division and led it in the Crimea and on Crete and distinguished himself at Sevastopol and on Cos. He became Fortress Commander Crete on July 1, 1944 (the day he was promoted to general of infantry), and he later commanded the XXXIV Corps in Yugoslavia (1944), the LXVIII Corps in Serbia and Hungary (late 1944–1945), and the 4th Army in East Prussia (January 29–April 27, 1945). This army was dissolved three days before Hitler committed suicide, and its staff was used to form the 21st Army. Mueller was without a command and apparently without an assignment at the end of the war. He was extradited to Greece after the war and shot in Athens on May 20, 1947.
11. Irving, *Hitler's War*, 584.
12. Wallace, *Italian Campaign*, 61.
13. David Mason, *Salerno: A Foothold in Europe* (New York: Ballantine Books, 1972), 125.
14. Blumenson, *Salerno to Cassino*, 143.
15. Garland and Smyth, *Sicily and the Surrender of Italy*, 539.

CHAPTER 14: SALERNO TO THE GUSTAV LINE

1. Mason, *Salerno*, 139, citing Mark Clark.
2. Ralph S. Mavrogordato, "Hitler's Decision on the Defense of Italy," in Kent Roberts Greenfield, ed., *Command Decisions* (New York: Harcourt, Brace, 1959), 318.
3. Ibid., 319.
4. Mason, *Salerno*, 151.
5. Westphal et al, "Feldzug in Italien," Foreign Military Studies MS # T-1a.
6. Heistermann von Ziehlberg (born 1898) later recovered and commanded the 28th Jaeger Division on the Eastern Front from April 28 to November 19, 1944, when he was arrested after his involvement in the anti-Hitler plot of July 20 was uncovered. He was shot at Spandau on Hitler's personal orders on February 2, 1945. He was promoted to lieutenant general on June 1, 1944. Baade was promoted to major general on February 1, 1944, and to lieutenant general on August 1, 1944.

BIBLIOGRAPHY

Absolon, Rudolf, comp. *Rangliste der Generale der deutschen Luftwaffe Nach dem Stand vom 20. April 1945: mit einer Stellenbesetzung der Kommandobehoerden der Luftwaffe vom 1. Maerz 1945, Dienstalterslisten der Sanitaetsoffiziere usw. im Generalsrang sowie Kurziographien ueber den Reichsmarschall und die Generalfeldmarschaelle*. Friederberg, Germany: Podzun-Pallas-Verlag, 1984.

Accoce, Pierre, and Pierre Quet. *A Man Called Lucy, 1939–1945*. New York: Coward-McCann, 1967.

Addington, Larry. *The Blitzkrieg Era and the German General Staff, 1865–1941*. New Brunswick, NJ: Rutgers University Press, 1971.

Air University Archives.

Air University Files SRGG 1106 (c).

Allmayer-Beck, Johann Christop von. *Die Geschichte der 21. (ostpr./westpr.) Infanterie-Division*. Munich, Germany: Schild, 1990.

Assmann, Karl. "Hitler and the German Officer Corps." *Proceedings* 82 (May 1956): 508–20.

Badoglio, Pietro. *Italy in the Second World War: Memories and Documents*. Muriel Currey, trans. Westport, CT: Greenwood Press, 1976.

Balck, Hermann and F. W. von Mellenthin, "Generals Balck and von Mellenthin on Tactics: Implications for NATO Military Doctrine, Dec. 19, 1980." United States Army Command and General Staff College Publication *M-313-5*. 1981.

Baldwin, Hanson W. *Battles Won and Lost: Great Campaigns of World War II*. New York: Harper & Row, 1966.

Bannister, Sybil. *I Lived under Hitler: An English Woman's Story*. London: Rockliff, 1957.

Barnett, Correlli, ed. *Hitler's Generals*. New York: Grove Weidenfeld, 1989.

Bartov, Omar. *The Eastern Front, 1941–45: German Troops and the Barbarisation of Warfare*. New York: St. Martin's Press, 1986.

Bauer, Magna E. "Axis Tactical Operations in Sicily." MS # R-138 To MS # R-141. U.S. Army War College. N.d.

Baumann, Hans. *Die 35 Infanterie Division im Zweiten Weltkrieg 1939–1945.* Karslruhe, Germany: Verglag G. Braun, 1964.

Baumbach, Werner. *The Life and Death of the Luftwaffe.* New York: Coward-McCann, 1960.

Beck, Earl R. *Under the Bombs: The German Home Front, 1942–1945.* Lexington, KY: University Press of Kentucky, 1986.

Bekker, Cajus. *Hitler's Naval War.* Frank Ziegler, trans. and ed. Garden City, NY: Doubleday, 1974.

———. *The Luftwaffe War Diaries.* Garden City, NY: Doubleday, 1968.

Blumenson, Martin. *Kasserine Pass.* Boston: Houghton Mifflin, 1967.

———. *Salerno to Cassino.* Washington, DC: Office of the Chief of Military History, U.S. Army, 1969.

Boehmler, Rudolf, and Werner Haupt. *Fallschirmjaeger, 1939–1945: Weg und Schicksasl einer Truppe.* Friedberg, Germany: Podzun-Pallas-Verlag, 1979.

Boucsein, Heinrich. *Halten oder Sterben: Die hessisch-thueringische 129. Infanterie-Division in Russlandfeldzug und Ostpreussen, 1941–1945.* Potsdam, Germany: Kurt Vowinckel Verlag, 1999.

Braake, Guenther. *Bildchronik der 126. rheinisch-westfaelischen 126. Infanterie-Division.* Friedberg, Germany: Podzun-Pallas-Verlag, 1985.

Bradley, Dermot, et al. *Die Generale des Heeres, 1921–1945: Die Militaerischen Werdegaenge der Generale, sowie der Aerzte, Veterinaere, Intendanten, Richter und Ministerialbeamten im Generalsrang.* 7 vols. Osnabrueck, Germany: Biblio, 1993–2006.

Brehm, Werner. *Mein Kriegstagebuch, 1939–1945: Mit der 7. Panzer-Division 5 Jahre in West und Ost.* Self-published, 1953.

Breuer, William B. *Drop Zone Sicily: Allied Airborne Strike, July 1943.* Novato, CA: Presidio, 1983.

———. *Death of a Nazi Army: The Falaise Pocket.* New York: Stein and Day, 1985.

Brown, Dale M., and the Editors of Time-Life Books. *The Luftwaffe.* Alexandria, VA: Time-Life Books, 1982.

Buchner, Alex. *Ostfront, 1944: The German Defensive Battles on the Russian Front.* David Johnston, trans. West Chester, PA: Schiffer, 1991.

Burchardt, Lothar. "The Impact of the War Economy on the Civilian Population of Germany during the First and Second World Wars," in Wilhelm Deist, ed. *The German Military in the Age of Total War.* Dover, NH: Berg Publishers, 1985.

Caidin, Martin. *The Tigers Are Burning.* New York: Hawthorn Books, 1974.

Carell, Paul. *The Foxes of the Desert.* Mervyn Savill, trans. New York: Dutton, 1961.

———. *Hitler Moves East, 1941–1943.* Boston: Little, Brown, 1965.

———. *Invasion—They're Coming.* New York: Dutton, 1963.

———. *Scorched Earth: The Russian-German War.* Boston: Little, Brown, 1970.

———. *Verbrannte Erde: Schlacht zwischen Wolga und Weichsel.* Berlin, Germany: Ullstein, 1966.

Carlson, Verner R. "Portrait of a German General Staff Officer." *Military Review* 70, No. 4 (April 1990): 69–81.

Carter, Kit C., and Robert Mueller, comp. *The Army Air Forces in World War II: A Combat Chronology, 1941–1945.* Maxwell, AL: Albert F. Simpson Historical Research Center, Air University, 1975.

Chant, Christopher, et al. *The Marshall Cavendish Illustrated History of World War II*. 25 vols. New York: Times Books, 1979.

Chant, Christopher, et al. *Hitler's Generals and Their Battles*. London: Salamander Books, 1977.

Charman, Terry C. *The German Home Front, 1939–45*. New York: Philosophical Library, 1989.

Churchill, Winston S. *Closing the Ring*. Boston: Houghton Mifflin, 1951

Ciano, Galeazzo. *The Ciano Diaries, 1939–1943*. Hugh Gibson, ed. Garden City, NY: Doubleday, 1946.

Clark, Alan. *Barbarossa: The Russian-German Conflict, 1941–45*. New York: W. Morrow, 1965.

Constable, Trevor J., and Raymond F. Toliver. *Horrido! Fighter Aces of the Luftwaffe*. New York: Macmillan, 1968.

Conze, Werner. *Die Geschichte der 291. Infanterie-Division, 1940–1945*. Bad Nauheim, Germany: Podzun, 1953.

Cooksley, Peter G. *Flying Bomb: The Story of Hitler's V-Weapons in World War II*. New York: Scribner, 1979.

Cooper, Matthew. *The German Air Force, 1933–1945: An Anatomy of Failure*. New York: Jane's, 1981.

———. *The German Army, 1933–1945: Its Political and Military Failure*. New York: Stein and Day, 1978.

Cooper, Matthew, and James Lucas. *Panzer: The Armoured Force of the Third Reich*. London: Macdonald and Jane's, 1976.

Craig, William. *Politics of the Prussian Army, 1640–1945*. New York: Oxford University Press, 1956.

Dallin, Alexander. *German Rule in Russia, 1941–1945: A Study of Occupation Policies*. New York: St. Martin's Press, 1957.

Davis, Melton S. *Who Defends Rome? The Forty-Five Days, July 25–September 8, 1943*. New York: Dial Press, 1972.

De Guingand, Francis. *Operation Victory*. New York: C. Scribner's Sons, 1947.

Deist, Wilhelm, ed. *The German Military in the Age of Total War*. Dover, NH: Berg Publishers, 1985.

Deist, Wilhelm. *The Wehrmacht and German Rearmament*. Buffalo, NY: University of Toronto Press, 1981.

Denzel, Egon. *Die Luftwaffen-Felddivision, 1942–1945, sowie die Sonderverbaende der Luftwaffe im Kriege 1939–45*. Neckargemuend, Germany: K. Vowinckel, 1963.

D'Este, Carlo. *Bitter Victory: The Battle for Sicily*. New York: E. P. Dutton, 1988.

Detlev von Plato, Anton. *Die Geschichte der 5. Panzer-Division, 1939–1945*. Regensburg, Germany: Walhalla und Praetoria Verlag KG Geog Zwickenpflug, 1978.

Dieckhoff, Gerhard. *3. Infanterie-Division, 3. Infanterie-Division (mot.), 3. Panzergrenadier-Division*. Cuxhaven, Germany: G. Dieckhoff, 1960.

DiNardo, Richard L. *Mechanized Juggernaut or Military Anachronism? Horses and the German Army of World War II*. Westport, CT: Praeger, 1991.

Doenitz, Karl. *Memoirs: Ten Years and Twenty Days*. London: Weidenfeld and Nicolson, 1959.

Dupuy, Trevor N. *A Genius for War: The German Army and General Staff, 1807–1945*. Englewood Cliffs, NJ: Prentice-Hall, 1977.

Dupuy, Trevor N., and Paul Martell. *Great Battles on the Eastern Front: The Soviet-German War, 1941–1945.* Indianapolis, IN: Bobbs-Merrill, 1982.

Elstob, Peter. *Battle of the Reichswald.* New York: Ballantine Books, 1970.

Edwards, Roger. *German Airborne Troops, 1939–45.* Garden City, NY: Doubleday, 1974.

———. *Panzer: A Revolution in Warfare, 1939–1945.* London: Arms and Armour, 1989.

Eisenhower, Dwight D. *Crusade in Europe.* Garden City, NY: Doubleday, 1949.

Finnegan, Jack. "A Man Called Lucy." *World War II* 3, No. 5 (January 1989): 12–16.

Fisher, Ernest F., Jr. *Cassino to the Alps.* Washington, DC: Office of the Chief of Military History, U.S. Department of the Army, 1977.

Foerster, Juergen E. "The Dynamics of Volkegemeinschaft: The Effectiveness of German Military Establishment in the Second World War," in Alan R. Millet and Williamson Murray, eds. *Military Effectiveness*, vol. 3, *The Second World War.* Boston: Unwin Hyman, 1988.

Frank, Wolfgang. *The Sea Wolves: The Story of German U-Boats at War.* R. O. B. Long, trans. New York: Rinehart, 1955.

Frankland, Noble. *Bomber Offensive: The Devastation of Europe.* New York: Ballantine Books, 1970.

Fraser, David. *Knight's Cross: A Life of Field Marshal Erwin Rommel.* New York: Harper-Collins, 1993.

Fretter-Pico, Maximilian. *Missbrauchte Infanterie: Deutsche Infanteriedivisionen im osteuropaeischen Grossraum 1941 bis 1944: Erlebnisskizzen, Erfahrungen und Erkenntnisse.* Frankfurt am Main, Germany: Verlag feur Wehrwesen Bernard & Graefe, 1957.

Frischauer, Willi. *The Rise and Fall of Hermann Goering.* Boston: Houghton Mifflin, 1951.

Fuller, J. F. C. *The Second World War, 1939–1945: A Strategical and Tactical History.* New York: Duell, Sloan and Pearce, 1949.

Galland, Adolf. *The First and the Last: The Rise and Fall of the German Fighter Forces, 1938–1945.* New York: Holt, 1954.

Garland, Albert N., and Howard McGaw Smyth. *Sicily and the Surrender of Italy.* Washington, DC: Office of the Chief of Military History, Department of the Army, 1965.

Goebbels, Joseph. *The Goebbels Diaries.* Louis P. Lochner, ed. and trans. London: H. Hamilton, 1948.

Goerlitz, Walter. *The German General Staff, 1657–1945: Its History and Structure.* New York: Praeger, 1953.

———. *Walter Model: Strategie der Defensives.* 2nd ed. Wiesbaden, Germany: Limes-Verlag, 1975.

Goodspeed, D. J. *The German Wars, 1914–1945.* New York: Bonanza Books, 1977.

Goralski, Robert. *World War II Almanac, 1931–1945: A Political and Military Record.* New York: Putnam, 1981.

Graber, Gerry. *Stauffenberg.* New York: Ballantine Books, 1973.

Graser, Gerhard. *Zwischen Kattegat und Kaukasus: Weg und Kaempfe der 198. Infanterie-Division, 1939–1945.* Tuebingen, Germany: Self-published, 1961.

Greenfield, Kent Roberts, ed. *Command Decisions.* New York: Harcourt, Brace, 1959.

Grossmann, Horst. *Geschichte der rheinisch-westfaelischen 6. Infanterie-Division, 1939–1945.* Bad Nauheim, Germany: H. H. Podzun, 1958.

Grube, Rudolf. *Unternehmen Erinnerung: Eine Chronik ueber den Weg und den Einsatz des Grenadier-Regiment 317 in der 211. Infanterie-Division, 1935–1945.* Bielefeld, Germany: Verlag Gieseking, 1961.

Grunberger, Richard. *The 12-Year Reich: A Social History of Nazi Germany, 1933–1945.* New York: Holt, Rinehart and Winston, 1971.

Guderian, Heinz. *Panzer Leader.* Constantine Fitzgibbon, trans. New York: Dutton, 1952.

Halder, Franz. *The Halder War Diary, 1939-1942.* Charles Burdick and Hans-Adolf Jacobsen, eds. Novato, CA: Presidio Press, 1988.

Hamilton, Nigel. *Master of the Battlefield: Monty's War Years, 1942–1944.* New York: McGraw-Hill, 1983.

Hastings, Max. *Das Reich: Resistance and March of the 2nd SS Panzer Division through France, June 1944.* London: M. Joseph, 1981.

Haupt, Werner. *Das Buch der Panzertruppe, 1916–1945.* Friedberg, Germany: Podzun-Pallas, 1989.

———. *Heeresgruppe Nord, 1941–1945.* Bad Nauheim, Germany: Podzun, 1966.

———. *A History of the Panzer Troops, 1916–1945.* Edward Force, trans. Atglen, PA: Schiffer, 1990.

———. *Der springende Reiter: 1. Kavallerie-Division-24. Panzer-Division im Bild.* Neckargemuend, Germany: Vowinckel, 1962.

Hermann, Carl Hans. *68 Kriegsmonate: Der Weg der 9. Panzerdivision durch zweiten Weltkrieg.* Vienna, Austria: Kameradschaft der Schnell Division des ehemaligen Oesterreichischen Bundesheeres, 1975.

———. *Die 9. Panzerdivision, 1939–1945: Bewaffnung, Einsaetze, Maenner.* Friedberg, Germany: Podzun-Pallas-Verlag, 1976.

Higgins, Trumbull. *Soft Underbelly: The Anglo-American Controversy over the Italian Campaign.* New York: Macmillan, 1968.

Hildebrand, Hans H. and Ernst Henriot. *Deutschlands Admirale, 1849–1945: Die Militaerischen Werdegaenge der See-, Ingenieur-, Sanitaets-, Waffen- und Verwaltungsoffiziere im Admiralsrang.* 4 vols. Osnabrueck, Germany: Biblio, 1988–96.

Hildebrand, Karl-Friedrich. *Die Generale der deutschen Luftwaffe, 1935–1945: Die Militaerischen Werdegaenge der Flieger-, Flakartillerie-, Fallschirmjaeger-, Luftnachrichten- und Ingenieur-Offiziere einschliesslich der Aerzte, Richter, Intendanten und Ministerialbeamten im Generalsrang: mit einer Einfuehrung in die Entwicklung und Organisation der Luftwaffe.* 3 vols. Osnabrueck, Germany: Biblio, 1990–92.

Hoehne, Heinz. *Canaris.* J. Maxwell Brownjohn, trans. Garden City, NY: Doubleday, 1979.

———. *The Order of the Death's Head: The Story of Hitler's S.S.* Richard Berry, trans. New York: Coward-McCann, 1970.

Hoffmann, Dieter. *Die Magdeburger Division: Zur Geschichte der 13. Infanterie- und 13. Panzer-Division, 1935–1945.* Hamburg, Germany: Mittler, 2001.

Howe, George F. *Northwest Africa: Seizing the Initiative in the West.* Washington, DC: Office of the Chief of Military History, Dept. of the Army, 1957.

Hoyt, Edwin P. *U-Boat Wars.* New York: Arbor House, 1984.

International Military Tribunal. *Trial of the Major War Criminals before the International Military Tribunal, Nuremburg, 14 November 1945–1 October 1946.* 42 vols. Nuremberg, Germany: n.p., 1947–49.

Irving, David. *Hitler's War.* New York: Viking Press, 1977.

———. *The Rise and Fall of the Luftwaffe: The Life of Field Marshal Erhard Milch.* London: Weidenfeld & Nicolson, 1973.

Jackson, W. G. F. *The Battle for North Africa, 1940–43.* New York: Mason/Charter, 1975.

Jacobsen, Hans-Adolf, and J. Rohwer. *Decisive Battles of World War II: The German View.* Edward Fitzgerald, trans. New York: Putnam, 1965.

Jenner, Martin. *Die 216/272. niedersaechsische Infanterie-Division, 1939–1945.* Bad Nauheim, Germany: Podzun, 1964.

Kamenetsky, Ihor. *Hitler's Occupation of Ukraine, 1941–1944: A Study of Totalitarian Imperialism.* Milwaukee: Marquette University Press, 1956.

Kameradschaftsbund der 8. Jaeger-Division. *Die Geschichte der 8. (Oberschlesisch-sudetendeutschen) Infanterie-Jaeger-Division.* N.p.: Kameradschaftsbund der 8. Jaeger-Division, 1979.

Kameradschaftsbund der 16. Panzer- und Infanterie-Division. *Bildband der 16. Panzer-Division.* N.p.: Kameradschaftsbund der 16. Panzer- und Infanterie-Division, 1956.

Kameradschaftsdienst der 35. Infanterie-Division. *Die 35. Infanterie-Division, 1935-1945, Deutsche Infanterie-Divisionen im Bild.* N.p.: Kameradschaftsdienst der 35. Infanterie-Division, 1980.

Kardorff, Ursula von. *Diary of a Nightmare: Berlin, 1942–1945.* Ewan Butler, trans. New York: John Day Co., 1965.

Keegan, John. *Waffen SS: The Asphalt Soldiers.* New York: Ballantine Books, 1970.

Keilig, Wolf. *Die Generale des Heeres: Truppenoffiziere, Sanitaetsoffiziere im Generalstrang, Waffenoffiziere im Generalstrang, Offiziere d. Kraftfahrparktruppe im Generalstrang, Ingenieur-Offiziere im Generalstrang, Wehrmachtsrichter im Generalstrang, Verwaltungsoffiziere im Generalstrang, Veterinaeroffiziere im Generalstrang.* Friedberg, Germany: Podzun-Pallas-Verlag, 1983.

Keitel, Wilhelm. *In the Service of the Reich.* Walter Goerlitz, ed. New York: Stein and Day, 1979.

Kesselring, Albert. *Kesselring: A Soldier's Record.* New York: Morrow, 1954.

———. "Special Reports on the Events in Italy between 25 July and 8 September 1943." Foreign Military Studies MS # C-013. 1947.

Kissel, Hans. *Vom Dnjepr zum Dnjestr: Rueckzugskaempfe d. Grenadierregiments 683.* Freiburg, Germany: Rombach, 1970.

Klatt, Paul. *Die 3. Gebirgs-Division, 1939–1945.* Bad Nauheim, Germany: Hans-Henning Podzun Verlag, 1958.

Knappe, Siegfried. *At What Cost!* Manuscript in possession of the author.

———. *Soldat: Reflections of a German Soldier, 1936–1949.* New York: Orion Books, 1992.

Knobelsdorf, Otto von. *Geschichte der niedersaechsischen 19. Panzer-Division.* Bad Nauheim, Germany: Verlag Hans-Henning, 1958.

Koch, Horst-Adalbert. *Die Geschichte der deutschen Flakartillerie, 1935–1945.* Bad Nauheim, Germany: Podzun, 1965.

Kraeutler, Matthias, and Karl Springenschmid. *Es war ein Edelweiss: Schicksal und Weg der 2. Gebirgs-Division.* Graz, Austria: L. Stocker, 1962.

Kramarz, Joachim. *Stauffenberg: The Architect of the Famous July 20th Conspiracy to Assassinate Hitler.* New York: Macmillan, 1967.

Krancke, Theodor, and H. J. Brennecke. *Pocket Battleship: The Story of Admiral Scheer.* New York: Berkley, 1958.

Kriegstagebuch des Oberkommando der Wehrmacht. 4 vols. Frankfurt am Main, Germany: Bernard & Graefe, 1961–65.

Kurowski, Frank. *Panzer Aces.* David Johnston, trans. New York: Ballantine Books, 2002.

Kursietis, Andris J. *The Wehrmacht at War, 1939–1945: The Units and Commanders of the German Ground Forces during World War II.* Soesterberg, The Netherlands: Aspekt, 1999.

Kuznetsov, Anatoli A. *Babi Yar.* David Floyd, trans. New York: Farrar, Straus and Giroux, 1970.

Lamey, Hubert. *Der Weg der 118. Jaeger-Division.* Augsburg-Hochzoll, Germany: n.p., 1954.

Law, Richard D., and Craig W. H. Luther. *Rommel: A Narrative and Pictorial History.* San Jose, CA: R. J. Bender, 1980.

Lehmann, Rudolf. *The Leibstandarte.* Nick Olcott, trans. 4 vols. Winnipeg, Canada: J. J. Fedorowicz, 1987–98

Liddell Hart, B. H. *History of the Second World War.* 2 vols. New York: Putnam, 1971.

Linklater, Eric. *The Campaign in Italy.* London: H. M. Stationery Office, 1951.

Loeser, Jochen. *Bittere Pflicht: Kampf und Untergang der 76. Berlin-Brandenburgischen Infanterie-Division.* Osnabrueck, Germany: Biblio Verlag, 1986.

Logusz, Michael O. *Galicia Division: The Waffen-SS 14th Grenadier Division, 1943–1945.* Atglen, PA: Schiffer, 1997.

Lohse, Gerhard. *Geschichte der rheinisch-westfaelischen 126. Infanterie-Division.* Bad Nauheim, Germany: Podzun, 1957.

Lucas, James. *Alpine Elite: German Mountain Troops in World War II.* New York: Jane's, 1980.
———. *Germany's Elite Panzer Force: Grossdeutschland.* London: Macdonald and Jane's, 1978.
———. *Hitler's Enforcers.* London: Arms and Armour, 1996.

Luck, Hans von. *Panzer Commander: The Memoirs of Colonel Hans von Luck.* New York: Praeger, 1989.

Macksey, Kenneth. *Kesselring: The Making of the Luftwaffe.* London: Batsford, 1978.

MacLean, French L. "German General Officer Casualties in World War II: Lessons for Future War." *Military Review* 70 (April 1990): 45–56.

Maier, Klaus A. "Total War and German Air Force Doctrine Before the Second World War" in Wilhelm Deist, ed. *The German Military in the Age of Total War.* Dover, NH: Berg Publishers, 1985.

Manstein, Erich von. *Lost Victories.* Chicago: Regnery, 1958.

Manvell, Roger, and Heinrich Fraenkel. *Goering.* New York: Simon and Schuster, 1962.

March, Cyril, ed. *The Rise and Fall of the German Air Force, 1933–1945.* London: Her Majesty's Stationery Office, 1948.

Mason, David. *Salerno: A Foothold in Europe.* New York: Ballantine Books, 1972.

Mavrogordato, Ralph S. "Hitler's Decision on the Defense of Italy," in Kent Roberts Greenfield, ed. *Command Decisions.* New York: Harcourt, Brace, 1959.

Mehner, Kurt, ed. *Die Geheimen Tagesberichte der deutschen Wehrmachtfuehrung im Zweiten Weltkrieg, 1939–1945.* 12 vols. Osnabrueck, Germany: Biblio Verlag, 1984–95.

Mellenthin, F. W. von. *German Generals of World War II.* Norman, OK: University of Oklahoma Press, 1977.
———. *Panzer Battles: A Study of the Employment of Armor in the Second World War.* Norman, OK: University of Oklahoma Press, 1956.

Metzsch, Friedrich-August. *Die Geschichte der 22. Infanterie-Division, 1939–1945.* Kiel, Germany: H. H. Podzun, 1952.

Military Intelligence Division, U.S. War Department. "The German Replacement Army (Ersatzheer)." 1945. On file at the U.S. Army War College, Carlisle Barracks, Pennsylvania.

Milward, Alan S. *The German Economy at War.* London: University of London, Athlone Press, 1965.

Mitcham, Samuel W. *German Order of Battle.* 3 vols. Mechanicsburg, PA: Stackpole Books, 2007.

———. *Panzer Legions: A Guide to the German Army Tank Divisions of World War II and Their Commanders.* Westport, CT: Praeger, 2001.

———. *Rommel's Desert Commanders: The Men Who Served the Desert Fox, North Africa, 1941–1942.* Westport, CT: Praeger, 2007.

Mitcham, Samuel W., and Gene Mueller. *Hitler's Commanders.* Lanham, MD: Scarborough House, 1992.

Mitcham, Samuel W., and Friedrich von Stauffenberg. *The Battle of Sicily: How the Allies Lost Their Chance for Total Victory.* Mechanicsburg, PA: Stackpole Books, 2007.

Moll, Otto E. *Die deutschen Generalfeldmarshaelle, 1939–1945.* Rastatt, Germany: E. Pabel, 1961.

Montgau, Ewen. *The Man Who Never Was.* Philadelphia: Lippincott, 1954.

Montgomery, Bernard Law, The Viscount of Alamein. *Normandy to the Baltic.* Boston: Houghton Mifflin, 1948.

Morison, Samuel Eliot. *History of the United States Naval Operations in World War II.* Vol. 9: *Sicily-Salerno-Anzio.* Boston: Little, Brown, 1962.

Musciano, Walter A. *Messerschmitt Aces.* New York: Arco, 1982.

Mueller-Hillebrand, Burkhart. *Germany and Its Allies: A Record of Axis Collaboration Problems.* Frederick, MD: University Publications of America, 1980.

———. *Das Heer: 1933–1945: Entwicklung des organisatorischen Aufbaues.* 3 vols. Darmstadt, Germany: E. S. Mittler und Sohn, 1954–69.

Munoz, Antonio J. *Forgotten Legions: Obscure Combat Formations of the Waffen-SS.* Boulder, CO: Paladin Press, 1991.

Munzel, Oskar. *Die deutschen gepanzerten Truppen bis 1945.* Herford, Germany: Maximilian-Verlag, 1965.

Murray, Williamson. *Strategy for Defeat: The Luftwaffe, 1933–1945.* Maxwell Air Force Base, AL: Air University Press, 1983.

Nicholson, G. W. L. *The Canadians in Italy, 1943–1945.* Ottawa, Canada: Queen's Printer, 1966.

Nogueres, Henri. *Munich: Peace for Our Time.* Patrick O'Brian, trans. New York: McGraw-Hill, 1965.

Overy, R. J. *The Air War, 1939–1945.* New York: Stein and Day, 1980.

Packard, Reynolds. *Balcony Empire.* New York: Oxford University Press, 1942.

Paul, Wolfgang. *Geschichte der 18. Panzer-Division, 1940–1943.* Rinteln, Germany: H. Thiemann, 1975.

———. *Die Truppengeschichte der 18. Panzer-Division, 1940–1943 (mit 18. Artillerie-Division, 1943–44 und Heeres-Artillerie Brigade 88, 1944–1945.* N.p.: n.p., 1988.

Perrett, Bryan. *Knights of the Black Cross: The Panzerwaffe and Its Leaders.* New York: St. Martin's Press, 1986.

Pesch, Franz, et al. *Die 72. Infanterie-Division, 1939–1945.* Bad Nauheim, Germany: Podzun-Pallas-Verlag, 1982.

Pfannes, Charles E., and Victor A. Salamone. *The Great Admirals of World War II.* New York: Zebra Books, 1983.

Pitt, Barrie, and the Editors of Time-Life Books. *The Battle of the Atlantic.* Alexandria, VA: Time-Life Books, 1977.

Plocher, Hermann. "The German Air Force Versus Russia, 1941. United States Air Force Historical Studies Number 153. United States Air Force Historical Division, Aerospace Studies Institute, Maxwell Air Force Base, Alabama: 1965. On file in the Air University archives.

Plocher, Hermann. "The German Air Force Versus Russia, 1942. United States Air Force Historical Studies Number 154. United States Air Force Historical Division, Aerospace Studies Institute, Maxwell Air Force Base, Alabama: 1965. On file in the Air University archives.

Plocher, Hermann. "The German Air Force Versus Russia, 1943. United States Air Force Historical Studies Number 155. United States Air Force Historical Division, Aerospace Studies Institute, Maxwell Air Force Base, Alabama: 1965. On file in the Air University archives.

Pond, Hugh. *Sicily*. London: W. Kimber, 1962.

Porten, Edward P. von der. *The German Navy in World War II*. New York: T. Y. Crowell, 1969.

Preradovich, Nikolaus von. *Die Generale der Waffen-SS*. Berg am See, Germany: Vowinckel-Verlag, 1985.

Quarrie, Bruce. *Panzer-Grenadier-Division "Grossdeutschland"*. London: Osprey, 1977.

Raeder, Erich. *My Life*. Henry W. Drexel, trans. Annapolis, MD: United States Naval Institute, 1960.

Rebentisch, Ernst. *Zum Kaukasus und zu den Tauern: Die Geschichte der 23. Panzer-Division, 1941–1945*. Esslingen, Germany: Self-published, 1963.

Reck-Malleczewen, Friedrich. *Diary of a Man in Despair*. New York: Macmillan, 1970.

Rendulic, Lothar. *Gekaempft, Gesiegt, Geschlagen*. Wels, Germany: Welsermuehl, 1952.

Riebenstahl, Horst. *The 1st Panzer Division: A Pictorial History, 1935–1945*. Edward Force, trans. West Chester, PA: Schiffer, 1990.

Ritgen, Helmut. *The 6th Panzer Division, 1937–45*. London: Osprey, 1982.

Rohwer, Juergen. *Axis Submarine Successes, 1939–1945*. Annapolis, MD: Naval Institute Press, 1983.

Rommel, Erwin. *The Rommel Papers*. B. H. Liddell Hart, ed. New York: Harcourt, Brace, 1953.

Rudel, Hans Ulrich. *Stuka Pilot*. New York: Ballantine Books, 1958.

Ruge, Friedrich. *Der Seekrieg, 1939–1945*. Stuttgart, Germany: K. F. Koehler, 1954.

Ruhland, Paul John von. *As the World Churns*. New York: Vantage Press, 1986.

Sadarananda, Dana V. *Beyond Stalingrad: Manstein and the Operations of Army Group Don*. New York: Praeger, 1990.

Sajer, Guy. *The Forgotten Soldier*. Lily Emmet Sajer, trans. New York: Harper & Row, 1965.

Salisbury, Harrison E. *The 900 Days: The Siege of Leningrad*. New York: Harper & Row, 1969.

Scheibert, Horst. *Die Traeger des deutschen Kreuzes in Gold: Das Heer*. Friedberg, Germany: Podzun-Pallas-Verlag, 1983.

Scheiderbauer, Armin. *Adventures in My Youth: A German Soldier on the Eastern Front, 1941–1945*. C. F. Colton, trans. Solihull, England: Helion, 2003.

Schick, Albert. *Die Geschichte der 10. Panzer-Division, 1939–1943*. Cologne, Germany: Trad. Gem. der ehem. 10. Pz.Div., 1993.

Schmidt, August. *Geschichte der 10. Division, 10. Infanterie-Division (mot.), 10. Panzer-grenadier- Division, 1935–1945*. Bad Nauheim, Germany: Podzun, 1963.

Schmitz, Peter, et al. *Die deutschen Divisionen, 1939–1945: Heer, Landgeschuetzte Kriegsmarine, Luftwaffe, Waffen-SS.* 4 vols. Osnabrueck, Germany: Biblio, 1993–2000.

Seaton, Albert. *The Fall of Fortress Europe, 1943–1945.* New York: Holmes & Meier Publishers, 1981.

———. *The German Army, 1933–1945.* New York: New American Library, 1982.

———. *The Russo-German War, 1941–45.* New York: Praeger, 1971.

Seemen, Gerhard von. *Die Ritterkreuztraeger, 1939–1945.* Friedberg, Germany: Podzun-Verlag, 1976.

Senger und Etterlin, Frido von. "Liaison Activities with the Italian 6th Army." Foreign Military Studies MS # C-095. 1947.

———. *Neither Fear nor Hope: The Wartime Career of General Frido von Senger und Etterlin, Defender of Cassino.* George Malcolm, trans. New York: E. P. Dutton, 1964.

———. "War Diary of the Italian Campaign: Sardinia and Corsica." Foreign Military Studies MS # C-095a. 1947.

———. "War Diary of the Italian Campaign: Cassino." Foreign Military Studies MS # C-095b. 1947.

Senger und Etterlin, Dr. F. M. von. *Die 24. Panzer-Division, vormals 1. Kavallerie-Division, 1939–1945.* Neckargemuend, Germany: K. Vowinckel, 1962.

Shaw, John, and the editors of Time-Life Books. *Red Army Resurgent.* Alexandria, VA: Time-Life Books, 1979.

Shirer, William L. *The Rise and Fall of the Third Reich: A History of Nazi Germany.* New York: Simon and Schuster, 1960.

Snyder, Louis L. *Encyclopedia of the Third Reich.* New York: McGraw-Hill, 1976.

Sokol, A. E. "German Attacks on the Murmansk Run." *Proceedings* 88 (December 1952): 1,326–41.

Spaeter, Helmuth. *Panzerkorps Grossdeutschland.* Friedberg, Germany: Podzun-Pallas-Verlag, 1984.

Speer, Albert. *Inside the Third Reich: Memoirs.* New York: Macmillan, 1970.

Stahlberg, Alexander. *Bounden Duty: The Memoirs of a German Officer, 1932–45.* Patricia Crampton, trans. Washington, DC: Brassey's, 1990.

Stauffenberg, Friedrich von. "Panzer Commanders of the Western Front." Unpublished manuscript in the possession of the author.

———. "Papers." Unpublished papers in the possession of the author.

Stein, George. *Waffen-SS: Hitler's Elite Guard at War, 1939–1945.* Ithaca, NY: Cornell University Press, 1966.

Steinhoff, Johannes. *The Straits of Messina: Diary of a Fighter Commander.* London: Deutsch, 1971.

Steinhoff, Johannes, et al. *Voices from the Third Reich: An Oral History.* Washington, DC: Regnery Gateway, 1989.

Stoves, Rolf O. G. *Die Gepanzerten und Motorisierten deutschen Grossverbaende: Divisionen und selbstaendige Brigaden 1935–1945.* Friedberg, Germany: Podzun-Pallas-Verlag, 1986.

———. *Die 1. Panzerdivision, 1935–1945.* Dorheim, Germany: Podzun-Verlag, 1976.

Studnitz, Hans-Georg von. *While Berlin Burns: The Diary of Hans-Georg von Studnitz.* Englewood Cliffs, NJ: Prentice-Hall, 1964.

Suchenwirth, Richard. "Command and Leadership in the German Air Force." United States Air Force Historical Studies Number 174. Aerospace Studies Institute. 1969.

————. "The Development of the German Air Force." United States Air Force Historical Studies Number 160. Harry R. Fletcher, ed. Aerospace Studies Institute. 1968.

————. "Historical Turning Points in the German Air Force War Effort." United States Air Force Historical Studies Number 189. Aerospace Studies Institute. 1969.

Sydnor, Charles W. *Soldiers of Destruction: The SS Death's Head Division, 1933–1945.* Princeton, NJ: Princeton University Press, 1977.

Tessin, Georg. *Verbaende und Truppen der deutschen Wehrmacht und Waffen-SS im Zweiten Weltkrieg, 1939-1945.* 16 vols. Osnabrueck, Germany: Biblio-Verlag, 1973–81.

Thomas, Franz. *Die Eichenlaubtraeger, 1940–1945.* 2 vols. Osnabrueck, Germany: Biblio, 1997–98.

Thumm, Helmut. *Der Weg der 5. Infanterie-und-Jaeger Division, 1921–1945.* Friedberg, Germany: Podzun-Pallas-Verlag, 1976.

Thursfield, H. G., ed. "Fuehrer Conferences on Naval Affairs, 1943" in *Brassey's Naval Annual, 1948.* London: Clowes and Sons, 1948.

Toland, John. *Adolf Hitler.* Garden City, NY: Doubleday, 1976.

True to Type: A Selection from Letters and Diaries of German Soldiers and Civilians Collected on the Soviet German Front. New York: Hutchinson & Co., 1945.

United Kingdom C.S.D.I.C. G.G. Interrogation Reports.

United States Chief Counsel for the Prosecution of Axis Criminality. *Nazi Conspiracy and Aggression.* 8 vols. Washington, DC: U.S. Government Printing Office, 1946.

United States Department of the Army. Pamphlet 20-260. "The German Campaign in the Balkans (Spring, 1941)." 1953.

————. Pamphlet 20-261a. "The German Campaign in Russia-Planning and Operations (1940–42)." 1955.

United States Military Intelligence Service. "Order of Battle of the German Army, 1942." 1942.

————. "Order of Battle of the German Army, 1943." 1943.

————. "Order of Battle of the German Army, 1944." 1944.

————. "Order of Battle of the German Army, 1945." 1945.

United States War Department. Technical Manual TM-E 30-451, "Handbook on German Military Forces." 1945.

Vassiltchikov, Marie. *The Berlin Diaries, 1940–1945.* New York: Knopf, 1985.

Vietinghoff, Heinrich von. "Die Kaempfe der 10. Armee in Sued- und Mittelitalien," in Westphal et al., "Feldzug in Italien." Foreign Military Studies MS # T-1a. 1947.

————. "Overall Situation in the Mediterranean." Foreign Military Studies MS # D-116. 1947.

Wallace, Robert, and the Editors of Time-Life Books. *The Italian Campaign.* Alexandria, VA: Time-Life Books, 1978.

Warlimont, Walter. *Inside Hitler's Headquarters, 1939–45.* R. H. Barry, trans. Novato, CA: Presidio, 1964.

Webster, Charles, and Noble Frankland. *The Strategic Air Offensive Against Germany, 1939–1945.* 4 vols. London: H. M. Stationery Office, 1961.

Wedemeyer, Albert C. *Wedemeyer Reports!* New York: Holt, 1958.

Weizsaecker, Ernst von. *Memoirs.* Chicago: Regnery, 1941.

Werbaneth, James P. "Helpful Conduct by the Enemy." *World War II* 7, no. 1 (May 1992): 22–28.

Werthen, Wolfgang. *Geschichte der 16. Panzer-Division, 1939–1945*. Bad Nauheim, Germany: H. H. Podzun, 1958.

Westphal, Siegfried. *The German Army in the West*. London: Cassell, 1951.

Westphal, Siegfried, et al. "Feldzug in Italien." Foreign Military Studies MS # T-1a. 1947. A copy of this manuscript is available at the library of the U.S. Army War College, Carlisle Barracks, Pennsylvania.

Wheeler-Bennett, John W. *The Nemesis of Power: The German Army in Politics, 1918–1945*. 2nd ed. New York: St. Martin's Press, 1964.

Whiting, Charles. *Hunters from the Sky: The German Parachute Corps, 1940–1945*. New York: Stein and Day, 1974.

Williamson, Gordon. *Infantry Aces of the Reich*. London: Arms and Armour, 1991.

Wilmot, Chester. *The Struggle for Europe*. New York: Harper, 1952.

Windrow, Martin. *The Panzer Divisions*. Reading, England: Osprey Publishing, 1973.

Wiskemann, Elizabeth. *The Rome-Berlin Axis: A History of the Relations between Hitler and Mussolini*. New York: Oxford University Press, 1949.

Wistrich, Robert. *Who's Who in Nazi Germany*. New York: Macmillan, 1982.

Wood, Tony, and Bill Gunston. *Hitler's Luftwaffe: A Pictorial History and Technical Encyclopedia of Hitler's Air Power in World War II*. London: Salamander Books, 1977.

Young, Desmond. *Rommel*. London: Collins, 1950.

Young, Peter, ed. *The Marshall Cavendish Illustrated Encyclopedia of World War Two: An Objective, Chronological, and Comprehensive History of the Second World War*. 20 vols. New York: Marshall Cavendish, 1981.

Zeitzler, Kurt. "Men and Space in War: A German Problem in World War II." *Military Review* 42 (April 1962).

Ziemke, Earl F. "The German Northern Theater of Operations, 1940–1945." United States Department of the Army Pamphlet #20-271. 1959.

Ziemke, Earl F. *Stalingrad to Berlin: The German Defeat in the East*. Washington, DC: Office of the Chief of Military History, U.S. Army, 1968.

Ziemke, Earl F., and Magna E. Bauer. *Moscow to Stalingrad: Decision in the East*. Washington, DC: Center of Military History, United States Army, 1975.

INTERNET SOURCES

www.diedeutschewehrmacht.de

www.feldgrau.com

www.forum.axishistory.com

www.gebirgsjaeger.4mg.com

www.lexikon.com

www.das-ritterkreuz.de

www.ritterkreuztraeger-1939-45.de

spearhead1944.com/toe1.htm

50-infanterie-division.de

INDEX

Page numbers in italics indicate illustrations